A glorious Angel appeared to me on
October 7, 2011, at 2:00 p.m. in the recovery room,
Saint Joseph's Hospital, Syracuse, New York.

October 7 is the Feast of Our Lady of the Holy Rosary

The Angel appeared to me with a dire message.

The Angel said, "Tell them it is almost time."

The message is for all Humanity!

Cover painted by Rose Mary Luke

Your purchase of this book will secure a generous donation to charity!

My Prayer for Peace in the World

Dear **God**, **You** are our Heavenly **Father** who watches over **Your** children with enormous love for all the people of the world. **You** are the **Creator** of all humankind. **You** have created Humanity in your own image. **You** know the Soul of each person intimately. Centuries ago, **Your** chosen people walked the earth with **Your Son Jesus Christ**, and they listened to **His** loving voice. Today, in the world, **Your** people have become very discouraged. **Your** children suffer because they have strayed from the safety of **Your** most gracious and divine mercy. **Your** people continue to commit grievous sins against Your **Sacred Heart** without remorse. Forgive them, dear **Lord**, because they do not realize they have grown weak without your protection. Many people have lost their way entirely. **Your** children are in great need of **Your** love and mercy. Dear **God**, the world is in urgent need of **Your** love and mercy. Greatness begins with goodness; the world needs more people that will lead us with righteousness, integrity, and dignity. Grant us strong leaders who will not hesitate to invoke **Your** precious name. Teach **Your** people how to love one another again as **You**, my **God**, have loved us. Help us to forgive one another as **You**, my **God**, have often forgiven us; and with **Your** love, **Your** people will have peace in the world. **Your** children must trust in **Your** mercy. I plead to **You**, my **God**, for forgiveness for all the injustices in this world because souls await Your mercy. In **Jesus's** name. Amen.

Jesus said, "I am the bread of life" He who comes to Me will not hunger, and he who believes in Me, will never thirst" (John 6:35).

With All My Love to Almighty God!

I dedicate this book with all my love to **Almighty God**, who is our **Father** in Heaven, thank you for the gift of my Faith. I so desire to acknowledge here how much I love **You** for granting me the Grace to be aware of **Your** presence when I was a young child. Grant me the Grace to do only what is pleasing to **You**.

Thank **You** for the Grace **You** lovingly bestowed on me all through my life.

I will always be mindful of **Your** presence every minute of the day.

Thank **You** for the Grace that allowed me to witness **Your** Angel and receive **Your** message.

I am overwhelmed with the knowledge of **Your** enduring love, patience, and mercy that await all **Your** children who believe in **You**.

Your children need only to ask for **Your** assistance and trust in **Your** infinite mercy.

Your enormous love for me has sustained me through my entire life.

I know **You** are constantly watching over me as well as all **Your** children. I remain always humble before **You**. Dear **God**, thank **You** for entrusting me with **Your** message that was conveyed to me by **Your** Angel. I pray that for the rest of my life, I will prove to be worthy in **Your** loving mercy.

I also wish to acknowledge here the following dedications:

To our Most Holy and loving Blessed Virgin Mary who is our Mother in Heaven, I love you. My Heavenly Mother has sweetly watched over me my entire life.

Without you, my dear Mother, by my side, I would not be the person I am today. I always believed you would be there waiting for me to run to you for help. There by your side, Blessed Mother, I would find contentment, love, and peace.

To my Holy Mother the Catholic Church. As a child, you nurtured my faith in order that I would be aware of **God's** tremendous love for everyone. My faith is an enormous blessing bestowed on me from **Almighty God**.

Thank **You**, my **Lord,** for the strong foundation that I received because of the teachings of my beloved Catholic Church. This powerful strength would remain with me and would sustain my lifelong devotion. I realized when I was a small child, the Catholic Church was and would always be the source of my strength, my rock. This unshakable rock is what I would build upon, that would sustain me through many difficult **times** my entire life.

To my dear Guardian Angel, who has faithfully stood by my side, thank you for never giving up on me. I always believed you were beside me, patiently waiting for me to listen to you.

Thank you for teaching me how to listen to my inner voice that I always believed was the **Holy Spirit,** guiding me on my way to **God**.

To the Magnificent Angel, the messenger sent by the **Holy Spirit**, who appeared to me on October 7, 2011, I will forever cherish the memory of your magnificent visit.

How do I express to you what I am truly feeling in mere words? Only **God** knows what is within my heart. I pray, with my whole heart and soul, that I will be worthy of completing my mission where as you said, "**Tell them it is almost time**." I can only pray, through the intercession of the **Holy Spirit**, the words you have encouraged me to write will make a difference in this world, if only to one person. If the words I have written change the heart of one person and save his or her Soul for **God**, then I have accomplished what **God** desired me to do.

To all the people throughout my life who were instrumental in guiding me with my spiritual growth, thank you.

I wish to acknowledge a special thank-you to the Sisters of Saint Francis and especially to Sister Raphael for introducing me to their extraordinary Franciscan spirituality that is the cornerstone of the life of Saint Francis. This awareness enriched my journey to **God**.

I will always cherish your friendship.

To my third-grade teacher who was a Sister of Saint Joseph and now is in Heaven. In 1953, this holy and pious Catholic Nun so wisely and lovingly taught me in a special way that the Blessed Mother is and always will be my spiritual mother. Through the intersession of the Blessed Virgin Mary, Mother of **God**, I will never be alone, and I will never forget.

To my family and especially to my husband, who over the past fifty-two years is my source of inspiration, especially while I persevered to write everything the Angel encouraged me to write.

To the children all over the world, dear **God**, I pray, protect them from the evils of this world.

Let every child on the face of the world hear **God's** Word and know **God** is watching those whom **God** has entrusted to their care. Without our precious children, there will be no love left in the world!

To my dear friends in **Christ** and especially to Mr. Alfred Barbagallo, who is the benefactor of this book. Thank you for your continued love and support. Our strength comes from **Almighty God**. It is **God's** grace that allows us to overcome adversity, and together, we will win the battle over evil.

Dear **God**, I humbly ask **You** to bless the words I have written in this book. With my whole heart, I pray that **You** are pleased with the completion of the mission **You** have entrusted to me. Only **You**, **Almighty God**, would command an Angel to instruct me to convey the issues discussed in this book. It was the profound words, my **God**, that **You** brought forth through **Your** Angel, in order to reveal the message to everyone. I pray that these six words, "**Tell them it is almost time**," will come to mean so much too so many people. In **Jesus's** name, I pray. Amen.

Contents

Preface 15
Introduction 17
Chapter 1:   I Will Begin Here 27
Chapter 2:   God Is Trying to Get Our Attention......................40
Chapter 3:   What Was I Thinking the Moment I Saw the Angel?...54
Chapter 4:   What Took Place in the Recovery Room? 60
Chapter 5:   The Awakening 69
Chapter 6:   Angels Are the Guardians of the World 74
Chapter 7:   Recognizing Evil Has a Very Bad Behavior 84
Chapter 8:   Abortion: When Will Humanity Stop It? 91
Chapter 9:   Confusion Is Denial over Sin in the Modern World 105
Chapter 10: Our Indigent Attitudes toward Almighty God........117
Chapter 11: What Is Perfection? 128
Chapter 12: Dreams about Angels and Meditation on God's Magnificent Realm 136
Chapter 13: Angels Are Messengers Sent by the Holy Spirit........146
Chapter 14: How to Recognize the Angels Are Here with You ...156
Chapter 15: There Is No Escape from the Images of Evil 164
Chapter 16: The Angel and Your Faith in Almighty God 170
Chapter 17: The Message...176
Chapter 18: The Power of Prayer 190
Chapter 19: Living a Life without God Is No Life 211
Chapter 20: Our Faith and God's Immense Love for Everyone ...227
Chapter 21: Gifts from God Comprise Great Responsibility......242
Chapter 22: Excuses for Sin in the World Lord, Forgive Us!.......248

Chapter 23: The Dawn of a New Day 265
Chapter 24: Coping with Pain and Suffering 277
Chapter 25: "I See an Angel" 285
Chapter 26: The Angel Said, "Tell Them It Is Almost Time" 293
Chapter 27: The Angel Was Already There Waiting for
           Me to Wake Up 302
Chapter 28: There Is No Future without the Protection
           of Almighty God 321
Chapter 29: Jesus Is the Light of the World! 328
Chapter 30: I Will Endeavor to Describe to You the
           Glorious Angel in Detail 333
Chapter 31: I Miss Seeing the Angel, but I Sense Her Presence... 339
Chapter 32: What Is Truth? 345
Chapter 33: Come, Holy Spirit, Enter My Life That I
           May Do Only Your Will Now and Always 351
Summary 363
Noteworthy Observations 371
Footnote 373
Here Are a Few Suggestions for Further Research 375
What Does the Bible Say about Abortion? 377
Notes 379

Preface

On my arrival home from the hospital, I began to reflect on the amazing event that occurred only two days before. In the quiet of my mind, I could recall every detail that took place in what probably were only a few brief moments in **time.** While I was recuperating, I began writing what I thought would be personal reflections regarding my visit with the Angel. I was astonished to see the words fill so many pages. It never occurred to me to write a book. I did not consider myself a professional writer. My writing over the years consisted only of private writing for my own enjoyment and spiritual meditation. This **time** as I continued to write, it became clearer to me, it was of vital importance, to convey to others all the details of my astonishing visit with the Angel. Most importantly, because the Angel said, "**Tell them,**" I needed to convey the importance of the message to everyone I meet. After a few months, I began to feel I was not reaching enough people. My heart ached because I needed to find a way to spread the message to more people than I could merely by chance. The severity of the message conveyed to me by the Angel was, yes, dire. It was overwhelmingly evident to me the content of the message was painfully significant. The words the Angel spoke, "**Tell them it is almost time**," was agonizing for me to hear. I felt myself sink to the brink of **God's** disappointment in our failures to recognize the truth. Only six words were contained in the Angel's message, but the implication of these few words meant monumental circumstances that **God's** people must not ignore. It was essential for me to convey this message repeatedly! I was gravely concerned because what I needed to achieve would not be easy. I needed a way to assure everyone possible would receive the message that the Angel directed me to share with all Humanity. This is when I seriously began writing this book.

I pray constantly to **Almighty God He** will reveal to me how to complete what began with the message from the Angel. I can still hear the Angel speaking to me, **"Tell them it is almost time."** Six words forever etched in my mind.

There is no doubt my visit with the Angel is a cherished gift from **God**. I no longer question **God's** design for the purpose of my life. This was Grace that **God** bestowed on me in order for me to see the Angel and hear the words **God** desired me to deliver to all who would listen.

The Holy Angel is by my side every minute to inspire me to continue the mission entrusted to me by the **Holy Spirit**. I must persevere, for the love of **God**, in writing this book.

> Dear **God**, I pray, in the deepest part of my very Soul, that with the completion of this book, countless souls will be saved!

Introduction

Witnessing **God's** glorious Angel was the most amazing moment of my life. Undoubtedly, there would be no way to prepare for such an experience. I could never imagine that I would have a visit with a heavenly Angel. Ultimately, seeing this magnificent Angel with my own eyes was certainly an awe-inspiring event that left me astounded. What an honor this was for me to be in the presence of the glorious perfection of a heavenly Angel. **God** in **His** loving mercy is so good to all **His** children. **God** desires all **His** children to remember that there is nothing more important to **Him** than our happiness.

Following my glorious visit with the Angel, it was very difficult for me to settle in again with my everyday routine. During my recovery from surgery, I felt I could not concentrate on anything else except the Angel and the message conveyed to me. Throughout the day, my thoughts were of the magnificent encounter with the Angel and my responsibility that would follow me now throughout the rest of my life. I was anxious to write down all the details, regarding my amazing visit with the Angel. In the past, it was customary for me to put in writing my feelings, regarding many thoughts related to **God**. I always believed this was extremely important for me to write down all the details regarding how I felt about a particular spiritual experience. I frequently wrote about those experiences that were always presented to me in a uniquely and holy way. I considered these unusual situations and experiences to be of great significance for me personally. In either a dream or other spiritual encounters, these awesome **times** were always exceptional spiritually. I knew these experiences were very important to my personal spiritual growth. I realized while writing down my thoughts and feelings, I would recapture what took place. This peaceful process would help me discern the possible meaning of a particular experience. This practice always gave my heart a chance to express what I was really feeling at the **time**. I believe writing my thoughts related to **God** is a form of prayer. Therefore, I enjoyed putting my feelings down on paper because while I was writing, I felt closer to **God**.

This **time** when I began writing, all I could think about was the Angel and her unique appearance to me. At first, it never occurred to me to write about anything other than the Angel and the profound message conveyed to me. However, the more that I thought about each situation the Angel presented to me, I understood the connection with each word I typed. It became clear that I was writing about issues that were in many ways tightly linked together like a web. I realized all the issues I needed to write about, are in direct association of my thoughts, linked to the message the Angel conveyed to me. I started seeing a distinct pattern forming that I myself was not aware of when I began. You may find that as you read this book, you may suddenly realize that many of your own thoughts and concerns may begin to surface. These issues may spark new and even some old feelings that will bring about a renewed awareness of consciousness. I noticed myself, as the words formed in my own mind, some of the various topics I will discuss I also needed to revisit. I discovered while reviewing some old issues that seriously concerned me, writing about them, provided me an opportunity to examine these issues again for possible solutions.

When I began seriously writing about the significant implications of the message, I was at first uncomfortable. I was reluctant to face the depressing issues that all of us face daily. Certainly, it is natural for me to feel overwhelmed with all the momentous problems the world is constantly confronted. All at once, I realized the amazing truth that was in front of me from the very beginning. **Almighty God** is communicating to the world, **"I love you."** Imagine just three words that are cherished and revered by millions of people all over the world and seldom is the meaning misunderstood.

A wonderful reassurance came over me regarding various issues because in my heart, I always believed **God** is still in charge! As I typed, I noticed many of these topics discussed are in a thought-provoking format. I discovered while I continued to type, this book was also in many ways a form of a retreat. What I did not realize, this retreat while meant for you the reader, the Angel intended it for me too. I became aware of a window of perception I never knew existed. Immediately, I understood the reason the Angel prompted me to write in this style. Day after day, the choice of the issues I would write were not my decisions alone. As I continued typing, I was aware I had very little control over what I would write regarding the various issues I will discuss. You see, it was not long, before this was apparent to me, the Angel would decide what was pertinent for me to write. Often, the Angel would encourage me to write through the night. I also recognized there were **times** I needed to type as fast as possible. The words appeared as in a blueprint placed on my mind that was coming to me virtually faster than I could type. I had to pay close attention to the thoughts and suggestions that continued to form in my mind. There was no doubt the Angel was silently instructing me to write what was imperative to say repeatedly. While I continued to write, I was aware the Angel never left my side. What was important to me was to get the thoughts on paper as soon as I could. I did not want to waste precious **time** unnecessarily. I was very concerned about the word **time** and initially thought I needed hasten the writing of this book.

Previously, I mentioned, when I began typing, I wanted solely to write for my own personal meditation, as I did many **times** before. This **time**, I was eager to write every single detail I could about the Angel in order to reexperience in my memory what transpired during that fascinating and holy day. However, from the beginning, with every word I typed, the words became obvious: the Angel, who appeared to me, would be responsible now for the subject matter I would convey within these pages of the book. I did not understand at first why the Angel wanted me to repeat various issues. I soon realized the reason for this was the significance of these particular areas.

Some**times**, we need to read things more than once before we can fully understand!

As my writing moved forward, it was a few months before I actually recognized writing this book would be a secure way to reach a multitude of people with the Angel's message. **"Tell them it is almost time."** It was clear writing this book was my mission, and I am so grateful. The **Holy Spirit** sent the Angel to me so I would know what to discuss and why each topic would be relevant to the message. Daily, I am fully conscious of the presence of the Angel who is directing me every step of the way. I cannot see the Angel presently; nevertheless, I know the Angel is there beside me. I can sense the loving presence of the Angel watching over me, inspiring me to persevere in my loving task.

I deeply desire to follow **God's** Commandments and to embrace these words: **"Thy will be done" (Matthew 6:10)**. Each day, my thoughts of **God** and **His** Angels strengthen my resolve. When I meditate on **God's** immense love for us, the cares of this world simply fade away. I am so thankful during this quiet **time** to reveal my inner thoughts to **God**. During this special **time**, when I am professing my love for **God**, I could burst with love for **Him**. My heart breaks to know there are still people in the world who will not accept **God's** love. Dear **God**, I pray someday these unbelievers may choose to love you. How truly lost these people would feel if they faced the truth about themselves. They have made a decision that their own self-importance has taken the place of the love for **God**. Evil has persuaded them, they are wise to feel so important. Therefore, there is no place in their world for **God**. I fear they will be the last to see the truth. **God** offers **His** pure alliance with each individual Soul. In place is our free will to accept this holy alliance with **God** or not. **God** gave us free will to choose; therefore, **He** will not interfere with our choices.

Contained throughout these chapters are some reflections of my own thoughts and feelings relative to the Angel who appeared to me on October 7, 2011. I wholeheartedly want you to know the Angel continues to inspire and direct me to reflect by writing about these complicated issues. Christians everywhere, in prayer, must discern what possible solutions we can uncover together. As I write, the Angel continues to prompt me to convey to you everything I have experienced. I continue to have little or no control over the subjects and viewpoints that **Holy Spirit** places in my mind to write. I am still astonished to see the words flow from my mind without hesitation and on to the computer screen with little effort on my part. However, what is clearer to me now, all these topics are relevant to why the Angel appeared to me. If you study the message, you will see, as I did, how complex six words can become. All the various areas of concerns and, yes, even fears do pertain to countless difficult and important problems the world faces today. I have certainly felt extremely worried about these serious and destructive issues for some **time** now. I am not alone in my anxiety because there are a great many people who share these same concerns. Proof we cannot fix anything by ourselves is the why we continue to see serious problems in the world, continue without resolution. **God's** children are living in dangerous **times**. Too many people think the world will continue no matter what they do personally. I assure you this is not true. What the world needs is for everyone to be accountable. Humanity is in dire need of **God's** love, friendship, and—most of all—**His** mercy. Without **God's** help, the world cannot continue in the harmony **God** desires for all **His** people.

After my visit with the Angel, I felt a tremendous new awakening within me, you might say; I had my eyes opened to the truth. Therefore, it was important to connect myself with others with similar cares and concerns who love **God**. The appearance of the Angel sparked a renewed sense of purpose in my life. In the deepest part of my Soul, there is a strong awareness of the truth and an even deeper concern for the issues because **God's** people need to find solutions soon. **God** sent **His** Angel to remind Humanity we all need to be more resolved in our convictions. There is no doubt **God** is not proud of our bad choices. **God's** people need to put an end to what they are doing wrong and make a sincere effort to make positive changes in their life. Whatever circumstance in your life that is keeping you from the love and mercy of **God**, you need urgently to correct. **God** is waiting for you to show **Him** you care enough to improve your life because **He** desires you to enter the **Kingdom** of **Heaven**. I am a Great-Grandmother, and I realize how imperative this unrest in the world is because we must be responsible enough to leave a brighter future for all our children and their future generations. Our children have a **God**-given right to have a happy and bright future, without the fear of hatred and war looming all around them. I love to imagine how wonderful it would be to live in a world of harmony and peace. Imagine **God's** children all over the world loving our merciful **God** and loving their fellow man in peace. I like to envision a world where all thoughts of war and people hurting one another no longer exist. This sounds like an impossible and monumental task but, at the same **time**, a most wonderful prayer. **God's** children must all remain steadfast and vigilant in their Faith that teaches Christians nothing is impossible to accomplish even when it seems impossible if we have **Almighty God** by our side. I pray most people do believe nothing is impossible for **Almighty God**. I may not see this harmony happen in my life**time**; however, this can happen if enough people truly wanted a peaceful world under the direction of **Almighty God**.

    I have heard this said so many **times**, "Evil only continues to flourish when good people stand by and do nothing." It is the love and commitment to one another that can begin to grow if more people would tell **God** they love **Him** and really mean it. When I was very young, I remember hearing on the television something I will never forget. This broadcast said, "If everyone would only light one candle, what a brighter world this would be." The meaning of this wonderful phrase was love and peace begins with one person and spreads to others in this same spirit of goodness. It is still possible for peace in the world to blossom despite what others may think. However, Humanity no longer has the luxury of **time** to waste. Everyone must take action right now, today, against all and everything that is separating you from the love and mercy of **God**.

> Come **Holy Spirit** enter my heart, and my mind with
> **Your** love, that I may help others to see the truth!

Dear **God**, may only **Your** will be done! Humanity must come together and trust in **Your** infinite love and mercy. I pray that Your people will not hesitate to ask for **Your** forgiveness. Christians must all stand together for what they know is right. All Christians should ask **God, "Forgive us, God, for what we have done and for what we have failed to do"** (**Matthew 6:12**). **God** knows **His** children are not perfect.

I want to challenge everyone who reads this book to do something, anything, to change one negative thing in your life for the love of **Almighty God**. I cannot express to you enough how important it is to have absolute family unity return to your homes. Our youth is in great danger beyond what you may think is only immaturity. Our little darlings are in great need of our protection because they are under the threat from the evil minds of others. Good people can no longer be silent. Good people cannot continue to wait for someone else to do it for them. Everyone must take action now because there is nothing else in the world more important than the salvation of all our Souls.

Description from my personal Catholic Bible of this most important term:

Description of the Term "Soul"

Soul is the primary principal of life. In plants, it is a vegetative life principal and, in animals, a sensitive life principal. However, the far superior human Soul is rational, spiritual, and immortal. Soul and body in man are so united in a single nature and person that the Soul is said to be the substantial form of the body; it is the life principal, which makes the body what it is essentially; a human body. Every individual Soul is created directly by God and is infused at the instant of conception.

The truth is we are running out of **time** because we have all greatly offended **Almighty God**. If you search your heart, you will know I am right. There is no one who could possibly comprehend what **God** is thinking at this very minute. Assuredly, **God** is now watching **His** people make perfect fools of themselves. **God** must be asking, "What are my beloved people doing? Why are there so many of my cherished people in denial? Why do my children no longer care they are not following my Commandments? Why have so many of my people found it so easy to forget the truth?" Without realizing this, people have withdrawn themselves too far from the safety of **God**. **God's** children have placed themselves in a very dangerous position where their very Souls are in danger of complete and utter destruction. All **God's** people have to be constantly on guard because your Soul trapped by evil will find itself imprisoned in the darkness of your sins. If this condition continues without resolution, the Soul will become like a black hole and can be lost without **God's** forgiveness. Scripture tells us that, **"God removes the Holy Spirit from you." (Psalm 5711)**. **God** does not dwell in the darkness of Sin. **God** resides in the light of hope, love, and mercy. **God** is urgently trying to get our attention, and **His** people are not listening. This one single thought should be the most frightening thought for anyone. Each person needs to ask himself or herself, "What is the meaning and purpose of my life?" To think your Soul could be lost forever never seeing again the face of **God**. What face will the Soul encounter? I truly believe in my heart if you really believed and understood fully the meaning of this truth, this certainty alone would be enormous enough to bring about a great change in your life. If you do not wish to believe this, then what do you believe? To whom are you listening? Who would deliberately walk through a dark door of evil on purpose? If you truly knew and believed this would be the end of your Soul forever, would this truth be enough for you to run as fast as you could toward the loving arms of **Almighty God**?

This is becoming so obvious to me why **God's** Angels are ready and waiting for **God's** command to appear. Oh yes, I believe strongly soon other people may experience **God's** special gift of seeing the Angels. All you have to do is open your eyes and heart to the truth.

I am aware there are countless people who have already encountered all kinds of spiritual awareness. Somewhere in the world, at this very moment, someone will experience privately the full measure of **God's** love. How magnificent, **God** in **His** goodness and mercy would allow these magnificent experiences to happen in the first place. Why are these experiences happening more now? **God** knows **His** children desperately need **His** presence in the world. **God** continually uses different opportunities to make Humanity aware **He** is with us. **God's** people are not alone! When the terrible tragedy of 9/11 happened, people filled the churches, and stores ran out of supplies for the American flag. What has changed since then? Why were those things so important then but not now? What needs to happen to wake up Humanity to finally see the truth? What will **God** decide to do that will finally get our undivided attention? What bolt of lightning would be grand enough to sustain the world's attention? Everyone must begin listening to what **God** is trying to tell you. **God** is communicating with us through **His** Angels to warn us a great change is indeed coming. However, this change may not be what people presume will happen. **God's** people alone hold the keys for any positive change to occur. The decisions Humanity makes now will determine what will transpire in the future. **Time** is of the essence. **Time** is precious. **God** allowed humankind **time** to discover the great potential **He** desired for all **His** people. What have **God's** children done with that precious **time**?

My deepest desire for everyone reading this book about my magnificent encounter with an Angel: you will believe everything is possible with **Almighty God**. The truth that brings me to my knees is **God** allowed me to see an Angel. This magnificent Angel did not appear for my benefit alone! I do not know why **God** chose me. I do not know why **God** found me worthy to receive a message from an Angel. One truth is clear **God** did allow me to see this Angel for everyone. Therefore, I can acknowledge firsthand the possibility does exist for many others to experience this heavenly gift. You must place your trust in **God**, and I can assure you something extraordinary will enter your life because you believed in the Divine Mercy of

Almighty God. Follow your heart, and you shall find peace beyond all understanding, a peace you never knew was possible.

Even when faced with the worst darkness of evil, this peace will sustain you, because God is with you always!

CHAPTER 1

I Will Begin Here

I never realized how gratifying and so spiritually uplifting it would be to write with such ease as I do now. In the past, I would write about my experiences that were important to my spiritual growth. However, for reasons that will become obvious, the holy event I personally witnessed occurred under most unusual and distinctive circumstances. There would be no comparison in my life to any of my previous experiences. Writing this now seems so natural when I tell you I received a visit from a heavenly Angel. I was in the recovery room at the hospital, and to my complete surprise, I was in the presence of an Angel. This heavenly Angel was not only gorgeous but also displayed deep compassion with her demeanor toward me. This was a fantastic and holy event directly from the will of **Almighty God**. I really thought for a brief moment the Angel was there so I would not be afraid. Was my life here at an end? If this were the case, then I was thrilled and ready to go with the Angel. However, nothing in the world could ever prepare me for what transpired. To my amazement, I began a sweet mental conversation with the Angel. The Angel said, **"I bring you a message: 'Tell them it is almost time.'"** The message conveyed to me by the Angel was beyond extraordinary. My heart told me the message came directly from **God**. I will never forget how I felt while looking so intently into the eyes of the magnificent Angel. This was a profound event I will keep in my heart for the rest of my life! Most importantly, the Angel's words are a dire message for everyone who would listen. The visit with the Angel is confirmation **God** is trying to get our attention! My mission now is to bring the words to everyone so all **God's** people will have an opportunity to discern exactly what these six words mean to them.

The humanistic side of me began to worry about the **time** it would take to complete the book. While I am typing, I still hear the Angel saying, **"It is almost time."** Previously, there were other spiritual experiences, but those definitely took place for me alone. Other private moments and what I experienced before did have their precious spiritual importance. I recognized the importance of these special gifts from **God** more as I strengthened in my spiritual life. However, this **time**, immediately what took place in the hospital was through **God's** Divine Will for the good of all **His** people. The tremendous love and merciful compassion **God** desires to bestow on all **His** children is immense if we would only accept it. I cannot count the **times God** has come to my rescue. I must repeat, **God** was always there for me even when I foolishly thought **He** was not. Amazing how human frailty causes us to think such stupid thoughts. I am sure there are **times** when other people truly believed they did not deserve **God's** love. This could not be farther from the truth. This is a ploy by the evil one to introduce this falsehood into your mind so you will not seek **God's** friendship.

I have always enjoyed writing my thoughts and feelings regarding **God's** realm. I perceive my writing as a form of prayer where I can express my feelings about **God**. There, among the pages, I see **God's** design in the sentences I write. The various aspects of what I write come directly from the very depth of my Soul where the **Holy Spirit** resides because my thoughts belong to **God.** Therefore, I will continue to write as long as the words keep coming because truly **God** wishes me to persevere in the loving task that **He** placed before me. I continue to ask **God**, "How is it possible to reach huge numbers of people with the message the Angel conveyed to me?" I pray the answers are within these many chapters. I am confident **God** will show me the way to complete what **God** began with the message brought forth from **His** heavenly angel.

Naturally, I am feeling a little anxious because I do not want to waste precious **time**. Should I try to rush as I write down the thoughts that are coming to me so naturally? Do I take everything as it comes and not worry about **time**? I never realized this word **time** would become so important for me. I have the distinct feeling after you read the book, you may discover the word **time** will be more significant to you now. Every **time** I write the word **time** or think about **time**, objectively, this word now has a more decisive meaning for me that I can no longer escape.

Now more than ever, I feel such a strong responsibility to encourage people I meet with the word of **God**. Something inside me seems to take over, and I am no longer seeking my own personal wants and needs. I have a strong urge to help people I meet in any way I can. While talking about **God**, I try to make everyone understand what should be so easy to understand. **God** expects us to put **Him** first in our daily lives. **God** is overflowing with love for all of us, and **He** only desires all of us to love **Him** in return. There is nothing complicated or complex about **God**. **God** is our **Creator**, our loving **Father**, who watches over us from Heaven. **God** should be your best friend whom you should love unconditionally always. I do not believe there are people who would disrespect or hurt their best friend intentionally. Most of us would immediately want to tell our friend we are sorry. Why then does it seem to be so easy to hurt **God**? Why do some people find it so difficult to tell **God** they are sorry for offending **Him**?

Whenever I have an opportunity to have a meaningful conversation with someone regarding the Angel, this **time** together always feels so gratifying. I sense most of the **time** this feeling is mutual. I believe most people I meet have a great need to discuss openly how they feel regarding **God** and **His** Angels. During these special moments, I sense I do reach some part of them they seldom take the **time** to visit themselves. Additionally, I also find our conversations are some**times** very emotional when discussing **God**. These conversations take place because **God** chose this precise **time** for a specific reason in order to fulfill **His** Divine Will. During this particular moment, in my heart, I sense this person needed an opportunity to have a meaningful conversation about **God**. It is amazing how **God** plans everything out so well, have you noticed? However, our plans do not always go the way we expect them too. Often, we just are not paying attention when **God**, through **His** Angels, prompts us to do something for **Him**. These opportunities presented by **God** may come to you in a form of a request for your consideration. **God** desires all **His** children to accomplish great things for the good of everyone. **God** will not force you to do anything! Sadly, this particular opportunity may be lost if you do not respond. **God** offers to you countless opportunities in your life**time**, but they may not come along again until you decide to turn your life over to **Christ.**

Multitudes of people all over the world are suffering in silence over one dilemma or another. One devastating situation such as the loss of a child is without a doubt heart-wrenching. A loss of a child is beyond what most consider deeply painful. This is a living hell for someone experiencing this awful event. I cannot imagine myself what this would be like to experience the death of my child. I have often said, "How do these parents get through it?" What came to my mind immediately is the Mother of **Jesus** who experienced the cruel death of Her own **Son Jesus Christ**. The Blessed Mother watched helplessly while her beloved **Son** was tortured so savagely at the hands of the Romans. Then the Mother of **God** watched while the Romans cruelly nailed her **Son's** bruised and battered body to a wooden Cross. It is my belief you should ask for the consolation of the Blessed Mother when meditating on the suffering of **Jesus Christ**. It is the Blessed Mother of **Jesus**, through the intersession of Her **Son**, who will console you. It is my belief we should always seek in prayer the consolation of the Blessed Mother in **times** of any suffering, especially the loss of a child. The Mother of Our sweet **Jesus** is our perfect example of the pain felt in the heart from such a personal loss. I cannot imagine what a parent must endure. The profound suffering and heartbreak, no doubt, is tremendously difficult. I truly believe, for most people, this would be nearly impossible to express in words such a great loss of a child to another person. This is why we all need to trust in **God** and be reassured that **God** definitely feels our pain. **God** does understand life is not always easy.

It is understandable why people find it very difficult to understand why certain events must take place. What is difficult for many people to understand is **God's** plan in life does not always seem fair. You must believe **God** will never abandon anyone in **times** of pain and suffering. Place your faith in **God** because **He** does hear our cries and **God** does see our tears. You must place all your trust in **Almighty God** and renew your faith in **God** during any tribulation in your life. I do know and you must believe during these **times** of suffering, you are closer to **God** than at any other **time**. At this precise moment, **God** has your undivided attention. **God** will use this troubled **time** to assure all of us of **His** unconditional love. I am sure you heard someone say, "Where does that person get their strength?" The strength to endure anything comes from the **Holy Spirit** who gives us the Grace of our Faith to persevere.

I do remain worried right now I am not reaching enough people with the message the Angel entrusted to me. I see the genuine concerns on the faces of people wherever I go. Some of the people I meet do share their concerns with me, and while discussing their concerns, it is apparent **God** is present. It seems that people are very sincere at the **time**, but the problem is their sincerity does not last long enough to make any purposeful changes in their life. Unfortunately, it is easier for a number of people to remain in the same old rut they have made for themselves. This is their comfort zone, and therefore, they continue doing everything in the same old manner because change is uncomfortable. Positive change takes a lot of effort on your part. Most people today need a spark of something drastic to happen personally before they decide to make any significant change in their life. In the future, we may all see something that will force us to seek **God's** love and mercy. When you finally have the desire to seek out **God**, He is waiting for you because scripture teaches us that **Jesus** said, **"I know My sheep and Mysheep know Me" (John 10:14)**. How much effort are you ready to grant **God** in order to prove to **Him** that you love **Him**? Christians do believe it is never too late to seek **God's** forgiveness while you are still capable. What would happen if you were unable to ask **God** for **His** forgiveness because you died before you could ask? While we cannot fully comprehend the outcome, I cannot think of a more devastating possibility. Some people have strayed so far from **God's** love, they have forgotten or may feel unworthy to ask for **God's** forgiveness. Perhaps these feel they cannot ask **God** for **His** help because they feel their sins are too great. If you are too proud to ask **God** for **His** forgiveness, then you do not know **Him** at all. We are all **God's** children; therefore, we must all pray for **God's** forgiveness, and we must all seek **God's** friendship without further delay. In the Bible, we read, **"Come now, and let us reason together, says the Lord, though your sins are like scarlet, they shall be as white as snow, though they are like crimson, they shall be like wool"** (Isaiah 1:18).

Looking back on my own life, there were many years as a young adult that I did not spend enough quality **time** contemplating **God** as I do now. While I always went to church and said my prayers, I felt there was something missing in my life. What was missing? I suppose, like other people, I felt it was my routine and my busy daily life that intruded on my quality **time** with **God**. Without a doubt, I placed the blame there. This must be the same situation for other people raising a family and establishing a career. Certainly, the hectic life I established for myself kept me from achieving where I really desired to be in my spiritual life. Looking back on this now, this was only an excuse and a choice I alone decided. After all, it is all about the choices you decide are right for yourself at the **time**. Then you may realize later, through the grace of **God**, that the choice you made was a good one. It is your actions and decisions learning how to manage your precious **time** between all the demands of your daily life that seem to be the problem. It seems reasonable; learning how to manage these demands and the stress of those demands establishes the success of how we succeed in our life. Only you can set the guideline for each priority, in order to decide the importance of the placement of these priorities, in order to accomplish anything. Knowing how you prioritize your goals seems to be the difference whether you are successful or not. Your life is like pieces of a puzzle fitting together so tightly that one missing piece can cause chaos in your life. No wonder most people find themselves stressed to the limit in their commitments. You can only hope to establish a reasonable routine that will complete the tasks you have set for yourselves. Some**times**, you place your goals too high, and then when you do not attain those goals, you are unhappy and disappointed. Where is **God** in your daily routine? The Angel appeared with a message to remind **God's** people it is **time** to place **God** first in their life. Perhaps based on your life choices, you are showing **God** you no longer need **Him**. **God** judges truth by your actions, and the lack of your response to **Him** only shows **Him** how much you need **His** love.

> The Angel who appeared to me, instructed me to
> convey to you, by way of the message, the seriousness
> of **God's** disappointment in **His** people!

Why do **God's** children refuse to remember that **He** knows your heart and your mind? I can tell you firsthand that the word *disappointed* is a vast and gross understatement! Multitudes of people have placed themselves above **God** by continually doing things they deem are more important. What could be more important than **Almighty God**? Why did so many people begin to rearrange their life in such a way that their plans never included **God** if ever? Do you remember when there was a **time** you did not need **God** as part of your daily life? If your heart tells you, you are one of these people, do you remember when this happened and what was the reason? Only if you are truthful with yourself is there any hope for you to rearrange your life now to include **God**. Perhaps the lack of interest in **God** began because our society has placed themselves under tremendous stress and confusion over the truth that is right in front of them. Frequently, people find themselves running in circles searching for **God**, when all the **time God** was right beside you waiting for you to realize **He** is there. You only need to stand still for a moment and be quiet to know **God** is there with you. Many people are struggling to have good jobs and are trying to maintain quality relationships with one another, but **God** is rarely included in their plans. It is evident why some people cannot understand why their plans and relationships are not working out. Still with all their good intentions, this still seems more difficult than ever to find quality **time** for **God**. For most busy families, **God** is rarely part of the family life. The problem is some people feel **God** will certainly understand, or will **He**, that they have so many responsibilities these days they are too tired for **Him**. However, their intentions remain high because they do intend to chat with **God** later. **God** is forever waiting patiently for you to seek **His** friendship. **God** waits for you confide in **Him** about not only your daily concerns but also your hopes and dreams for the future. You must believe **God** desires you to tell **Him** how you feel about everything! Yes, all your concerns and hopes for the future. **God** is interested in even the smallest detail of your daily life. **God** understands you and knows all of us better than we could ever know ourselves. **God** loves you so much that if you could truly grasp the enormity of **His** love for you, you would do anything to please **Him**. I have heard the following point mentioned so many **times** that people feel overwhelmed with everything going on around them. They fail to turn over their worries and troubles to **God**. You must restore your faith to be aware of the many miracles **God** grants to you every day. The truth is **God** does grant us miracles every day. Some of these miracles may seem tiny at first glance, but they are mighty rewards from **God**. Everyone needs desperately to begin looking for those tiny miracles sent to you with so much love from **Almighty God**. The reason people still fail to see the miracles in their life is because many people find themselves caught up in the noise and distractions that they have determined are more important. People are depriving themselves of what should really be most important to them. If you are not careful, you will find yourself entwined in the trappings of the trials and tribulations of your daily life.

It has become a monumental struggle between our personal, private life, as well as the overwhelming battle that society is facing over the power of evil. This aggressive evil is manipulating the population to such a degree that it is fast removing, one by one, all moral consciousness from the people regarding anything that is good and pleasing to **God**. This battle has been going on since the dawn of **time**. It is important for you to recognize and believe this war is real and this evil thinks it has already won! This is tragic that Humanity is buying into evil's scores of lies. We need to help one another overcome this attraction. This evil battle has multiplied to enormous proportions. This battle over the distraction of evil is too much to fight alone. We all need one another because collectively, we can overcome and win this battle of evil but only with the help from **Almighty God**. The Angel who appeared to me made this point incredibly clear. **God** gave us free will to say yes or no to evil. Once evil has entered your life, it is more determined than ever to hold onto you tightly. Your indecisions make this easier for the evil one. Never forget evil is a master of disguise. This evil knows your thoughts and weaknesses and uses them for his best advantage against you. Evil has plenty of **time** and knows you so well because you are too predictable from the habits you have formed. Remember evil is watching you all the **time** and waits for the right moment to destroy your Soul. Begin saying the word **No** aloud. You would be amazed how much a tiny two-letter word can annoy the evil one.

I cannot express to you enough how perfectly amazing this is to be in the presence of an Angel. When I recall that extraordinary afternoon in the recovery room, I will always remember that I am a humble servant of **God**, nothing more. The conversations between the Angel and I were not heard a loud by others in the room. The words the Angel spoke were in soft tones that the Angel placed in the recesses of my mind. Only I could understand clearly what the Angel said.

It is so apparent: what happens in the future will be the result of the decisions we all make today and tomorrow. The importance of these decisions will decide the course of history. The future of our children is weighing in the balance. The very souls of **God's** children are in danger of being lost forever. **God**, through **His** Angel, desires everyone to be responsive to the truth that Humanity is moving in the wrong direction. People are putting a vast distance between themselves and the love of **God** every minute of the day. The cause and effect of their actions are leading them farther away from **God**. All the Angels are trying to save us before it is too late. Why is it that we (the people) are not paying attention to what **God** is trying to tell us? There is no doubt that the signs are all around us. Why is it so difficult to listen to **God's** voice? Oh yes, **God** has a voice, not in the same way we converse, but you will recognize **His** voice immediately because you have heard **God's** voice before you were born. Even now, **God** is calling to everyone to remind us to trust in **His** enormous love and mercy. In the quiet of your heart, if your desire is genuine, I assure you, you will hear **God's** voice again in a way only you will understand. **God** will find a way for you to know **He** is with you.

There is no doubt we need one another more than ever in order to strengthen our commitments for the glory of **God**. Why do some people choose to forget that **God** created all of us and every living creature who resides on this beautiful planet? We strive to live together on this beautiful planet, but we are failing to remember how to live in peace together. We should all strive to live in harmony for the good and happiness of all. You need to root out the true reason you are having difficulties with your relationships. Could this be because you are only thinking of yourself and therefore are absorbed in self-interest? I assure you that you will never have harmony in your life if you are only interested in what benefits you personally. Have people in our society really become so selfish and self-centered that they cannot see the truth? Perhaps this is why some feel they no longer need **God**. Remember some people think their life is fine without **God**. This is blatantly evident; this falsehood must be true because people no longer support their local churches as they once did. As a result, our beautiful churches are now closing, and as a result, we need to consolidate the parishes that remain open. This situation began to happen recently at a very rapid rate. It is obvious why the churches are closing because people are no longer supporting them. I, along with others, did not want to face what we knew was the inevitable. Our churches continue to close, and everyone is painfully aware of the reason. Simply said, the reason is the attendance is poor! Since I am Catholic, I must ask why Catholics are leaving their faith. The poor attendance must prove Catholics do not take their faith seriously anymore. I hate to think this also means that people of the Catholic faith are not receiving the Sacraments anymore either! I am painfully aware Catholics and Christians alike are not baptizing their babies anymore! What is really going on in the minds of those that profess they are Christian?

What does it truly mean, when people say they are a Christian? In my Catholic Bible, the following is an explanation to the term: *Christian*: a name, which, according to the **(Acts of the Apostles 11:26)**, was first applied to the Disciples at Antioch in the year AD 43. Today, this term is used for all those who claim to follow **Christ** and especially for those who are members of any Christian Church and more exactly for Catholics.

In the Catholic Church, our priests are growing older, and in general, in America, we are not acquiring the young men entering the priesthood as we did in years past. In addition, our Catholic schools will soon be a memory of the past too. Who will teach our children about the wonders of **God**? Today, parents seem to think they lack the **time** to sit down quietly and talk to their children about **God.** What is still worse, too many continually push **God** out of their lives altogether? Recently, I asked a child, do you say your prayers; and the child did not know what I meant by prayers! Parents do not teach the importance of having a relationship with **Almighty God** through prayer. Therefore, parents are depriving their children of the opportunity to have a personal relationship with **Almighty God**. If you are this parent, now is the **time** to search your heart and ask yourself, "What have I done, and what can I do to change this?" Parents feel prayer is no longer important, and therefore, they do not recite prayers in the home. Children today not only have no idea of the concept of prayer, but also many children have never attended a church either. Their parents are not teaching the importance of reciting prayers as a way of communicating with **God**. At the very least, parents should teach their children to pray to **God** in a way that will be meaningful to their children. This is the only way children will learn to grow to love **God**. What really worries me is families seldom mention **God** in the home. Our society cannot lose entire generations who will never care to know **God**. Why did parents forget their children were a precious gift from **God**? No wonder respect and love for one another is becoming outdated and lost forever. We are slowly becoming a cold and callus society filled with hatred and confusion over every issue. Society cannot seem to agree over even the smallest issue. This is our responsibility collectively to preserve our religious traditions regardless of your affiliations. The truth is there is only one true **God**. I fear if we really lose generations of children who do not know **God**, what kind of world will these children inherit? Whom should we blame that our children will not know **God**? Does this present situation prove there is a definite decay in our society? Whom shall we hold responsible for our society's failures? The very fundamental foundation and the strong beliefs our previous generations held so dear are dismantling right before our eyes. I wonder in the future, will anyone ask what happened? Will history repeat itself? The Bible speaks of this truth.

Is it possible history will record that we were the generation who turned their back on Almighty God?

This possibility is very difficult to accept, but the facts speak for themselves. As **God's** children, we must all face the truth and take responsibility for what is taking place in the world. How many children today know about the existence of Angels? Is this something they might only read in fairy-tale books? Are we placing Angels in the same category as Peter Rabbit? As parents, you must ask yourself why you did not teach your children how much **God** loves them. Life in the future will be very difficult for our children without **God** in their everyday life. What is unforgivable, the children of this present generation do not know the gift of **God's** friendship. How will these children have happiness without the Grace that comes from the hand of **Almighty God**? What does **God** think about the serious dilemma we have all caused? **God** will hold us all responsible because no child should ever grow without knowledge of **God**. When I was a child, knowing **God's** friendship at the young age of six enabled me to grow stronger in the knowledge that I could accomplish anything because **God** was there with me. **God** is lovingly trying to connect with all **His** children so we will understand it is not necessary to walk through life's difficulties alone.

I SEE AN ANGEL

Dear **God**, many of **Your** people have lost their way and are struggling to find purposeful meaning in their life. Help **Your** children to find peace again in **Your** loving mercy.

God is trying to get our attention to remind us **He** loves us all dearly.

CHAPTER 2

God Is Trying to Get Our Attention

Now is the **time** to search your heart and ask yourself, is **God** included in your daily life? Where is **God** in all the confusion and downright indifference attitude people have developed toward **Him**? You should be putting forth at least the same effort toward **God** that you place on the success of your other accomplishments. Do you apply the same effort in knowing **God** as you do in the workplace and in your relationships? How do your interests stack up in proportion to the **time** you spend with **God**? This is profoundly necessary for your very Soul to desire a true and meaningful friendship with **God**. **God** knows what is truly in your heart. Only **God** sees the condition of your Soul. How often do you strive to keep **God's** Commandments? It seems to me we all expect so much from **God**, yet we give **Him** so little in return. If only everyone would tell **God** every day how much you love **Him**. This takes so little **time** to say four little words: **"Jesus, I love you."** If you do not desire **time** for **God**, what may **He** be wondering about you? Still **God** is a loving **Father** and always desires the best for **His** children even when we disappoint **Him**. Remember **God** is always waiting for us to realize **He** is always there with us. All you need to do is ask **God** for **His** help. Located in Franciscan prayers is this phrase that I love to recite: **"God, come to my assistance, Lord, make haste to help me."** This beautiful phrase always helped me, and it might be what you have been looking for because it is easy to remember.

What I have noticed is some people have lost sight of what should be relevant in their life. Many people buzz around like bees as if they have no particular place to go. In the end, you must recognize the sole purpose of your very existence and begin doing something purposeful in your life that must include **God**. Why have Christians neglected to remember the gift of Grace **God** so dearly desires to bestow upon them? The Bible mentions the term *Grace* 170 **times**. The definition of *Grace* found in my personal Bible is the following:

"Grace is **God's** unmerited favor. It is kindness
from **God** we do not deserve."
"There is nothing we have done, nor can ever do to earn this favor."

Grace is infinite mercy given to us by **God**. Grace facilitates the probability; we can live out our life in happiness. Grace is a precious gift. Therefore, people are walking as if asleep through their life without this gift of Grace. No wonder why people are unhappy. You will never be truly happy without **God's** love and forgiveness. Still **God** patiently strives to get your attention, and many people continually do not pay the smallest attention to **Him** in return. You will never hear what **God** is trying to tell you if the noise is too loud. You must turn down the volume of life and be quiet for a change. You need to take a deep breath and welcome **God** into your hearts and minds if only for a few minutes throughout the day. You will begin to see a grand change in how you feel about everything immediately. You see, you must understand the source of your unhappiness is because you do not include **God** enough in your life. When you were born, **God** was already within you and around you as a normal part of your existence. **God** created all of us because simply, **His** marvelous design for us is our happiness. **God's** expectations for all **His** children is to watch us grow in the desire to know and love **Him** throughout our life. **God** expects you and me to follow **His** commandments so we will have a happy and lead a fulfilled life. Humanity is to blame that the formula for happiness has changed and the reason is **God** is no longer the head of many households. Therefore, our culture as we know it resets itself to accept negative ideas that were never part of **God's** plan for us. There is a vast difference between the generations of the past and the generations of today. The generations of the past did not feel **God** was old-fashioned. They received the Grace from **God** wholeheartedly because what they believed by their faith in their heart was the truth. They relied unconditionally on the truth that **God** would be with them in every aspect of their daily life. It seems to me, there used to be more respect in the world for one another and more respect for **God**. At least on the surface, it seemed to me, people made a concerted effort to attain the respect for one another that any society needs to flourish. In the past, society as a whole certainly gave me the impression respect for many things then was more important and in big demand. Growing up, I definitely witnessed a greater respect for **Almighty God** throughout my school years. I witnessed a great deal more tolerance! There was more compassion in the world for one another. People feel today these old-fashioned ideals are not necessary in our present society. What type of society decides we do not need compassion or respect?

    I wonder if it might be possible, additional Angels are present with us because in the future, **God** may allow them to turn the course of our direction! If the leaders of this world are not careful, we will all face disaster on a major scale. It is my understanding that the Angels are not supposed to interfere with the course of history or our free will. How do we know what **Almighty God** will decide is best for us? Perhaps **God** will continue to test the world in severe ways in order for **God** to attain our undivided attention. Maybe there is still **time** to change what has already begun. My heart aches because the Angel who appeared to me certainly expects Humanity to consider seriously the message because it is an ominous warning from **Almighty God**. The warning contained in the message necessitates the urgency that Humanity must learn how to love one another. Humanity is creating a world that does not include **God**! We must accept the truth that the **time** for disrespect and the lack of honor for **Almighty God is over**! The Angel, by her appearance, is confirmation that someday may be nearer than we may think. What an awful thought, the occasion to turn away evil might be nearing an end. To imagine, this could be possible, the opportunities for an unbeliever to know and love **God**, as compared to a door closing, and you forgot where you put the key! What are you waiting for? When will **God** say, **"Enough?"** The Angel was adamant regarding our indiscretions toward **God's** wounded **Heart**. The Angel was very precise and to the point! **"God is trying to get our attention, and His people are not listening."** The warning signs should be evident to all of us. Who can deny the escalation of violence that filters through our cities? I have to ask myself why there is so much hatred and violence. This hatred, which is the work of the evil one, is trying to destroy love, common decency, and our way of life altogether. I can compare it to a fast-moving train, running out of control, obliterating everything in its path and there is no end in sight. We need to put an end to this pervasive and insidious evil now that is permeating through our culture.

The Angel's words were a severe warning from **God** that many people have strayed too far from the safety and love of **God**. If I am afraid of anything, I am certainly afraid of this awareness. If you search your heart, you will also agree I am right. We do not discuss our feelings openly about **God** enough with one another. Oh, sure, if you attend a church, you have an opportunity to acknowledge **God** maybe once a week. Christians feel one hour, once a week in church, will appease **God**. What does **God** think about all the people who never bother to attend a church anymore? These people are telling **God** they have no more **time** for **Him**. The truth people now feel they cannot be bothered is a terrible attitude toward **God**. People often feel they have better things to do on the weekend than go to church. There is the lawn that needs mowing and numerous other things people deem are more important than spending an hour with **God**. Humanity must accept the truth; evil has won by keeping you away from your place of worship. This one simple act is precisely one of the most important accomplishments evil has performed to date. When you think clearly about what has happened, this only proves how easy it was for evil to persuade a large portion of our society, they no longer need to gather together to honor **God**. Humanity is allowing evil to place a wedge that blocks you from the most important area of their life and that is **Almighty God**! People are turning their hearts away from **God** and never realized or cared when this took place. Consequently, this evil's accomplishment now keeps you from your devotion to **God**. Your place of worship is where **God's** people precisely gather to give thanks and praise to **Him**. Your place of worship is your safe haven where you are free to worship **God** and give thanks to **Him**. People will say they do not need to be in a particular building to honor **God**. I acknowledge here, we need to gather together as a strong force against the evil that is trying to keep you away from **God**! Only there in church do we have the rarest opportunity to honor **God** in such a special and spiritually holy way. For example, I am Catholic and it is my belief that only during the celebration of the Sacrifice of the Holy Mass, during Holy Communion, can we experience closeness to **God** that cannot be found elsewhere. **Jesus Christ** bestowed on us the precious gift of **The Last Supper**. Who would willingly refuse this uniquely holy opportunity? If you have prepared your heart, mind, and Soul properly, only then should you receive the body and blood of your **Savior Jesus Christ**. With the love from **Almighty God** and the strength from the **Holy Spirit**, we will rebuke the practices of evil. This is pure evil; pulling so many people away from their churches; and the task easily accomplished goes unnoticed. The devil's goal is to create a great divide between you and **God**. What you are not aware of is evil weakens your intellect by this one awful decision to stay away from your place of worship. By staying away, you are telling **God** loudly, you are not interested in **Him**. In addition, you are demonstrating to **God** you do not need **Him**. Without **God** in your life, you are vulnerable to the attacks of evil. It worries me when I think of the large numbers of people who have stopped attending church. I have heard some people say, they stopped going to church because they did not like what the priest or clergy said! Why have they forgotten that the people are the church and one person should never keep anyone away from **God's** house? It is only a matter of **time** before evil completes its plan because these people were not aware what they have allowed evil to do. If this is you, do you remember when your lack of interest involving **God** began? I am to blame too because

I did not pay enough attention when attendance was dropping off so severely at my own church. I presumed like other people, things would improve somehow by themselves without any additional support from me. This is so difficult for me to face the certainty in the near future; our magnificent churches will not exist. I cannot believe I have just typed this sentence! I can remember listening to the stories of how people overseas saved these gorgeous stained glass windows so that after World War II, people in the United States could enjoy them here. People died to save these magnificent windows. In addition, people who left their country of origin and migrated to this country scrimped and saved every penny they could to build our magnificent churches for the glory of **Almighty God**. What have we done? Who is responsible that our magnificent churches will not be here for future generations? I cannot believe the numbers of people who are willing to allow their churches to close without any reluctance to halt the devastation. If you had told me thirty years ago, this was a possibility; I would have said you were sadly misinformed. What will you and I say when we are asked by **God** why we allowed **God's** houses to close? In the Bible, **Jesus** said, **"For where two or three are gathered in My name there am I in the midst of them"** **(Matthew 18:20)**. Evil will only win if we allow it to win. Evil is the lack of goodness in your life. Perhaps this is a harsh test of our Faith from **God**! Have **God's** people become this complacent? What are we thinking? What are we doing? So I ask you again, who is to blame?

This is a brief explanation of the Sacrament of the Holy Eucharist:

The Sacrament and Sacrifice in which Jesus Christ, under the appearances of bread and wine, is contained, offered, and received. As a sacrifice, the Eucharist is known as the Mass; and as the Sacrament, it is known as Holy Communion.

The Sacrament of the Holy Eucharist

Before **Jesus** gave up **His** life and died for our sins, **He** lovingly bestowed a precious and most sacred gift during the evening of the "**Last Supper.**" **Jesus** miraculously changed the bread and wine into **His body** and **blood**, and **He** did this for all Humanity! **Jesus** said, "**It will be shed for you so that sins may be forgiven.**" **Jesus** also said to **His** Apostles, "**Do this in memory of Me.**" Catholics consider themselves blessed to receive this precious and powerful gift of the Holy Eucharist. There in Church, you are able to receive this powerful gift of **God's** love. The Holy Eucharist is a miraculous transformation of the most precious **body** and **blood** of Our **Savior Jesus Christ**. The precious gift of the Holy Eucharist is a powerful gift from **Jesus** and is a Divine Miracle because **Jesus Christ** is present under the appearances of bread and wine in a sacramental way. The Holy Eucharist has the power to nourish your very Soul. Why have Catholics left the church? Have they decided they no longer needed or wanted the special and holy gift that comes directly from **Jesus Christ**? This is worth repeating: as Catholics, we believe the Eucharist is a unique and holy way to become closer to **Christ** unlike at any other **time**. When you receive the Holy Eucharist, the Holy Eucharist has the power to prevent the destruction of your Soul provided you have prepared yourself through the Sacrament of Reconciliation! Do you not believe this anymore? This is so apparent to me; this is why people find themselves easily persuaded by evil to stay away from this Soul-saving gift of the Holy Eucharist. The Holy Eucharist is the power over evil! Therefore, after receiving this precious gift, we then spiritually acquire the strength and ability to triumph over every evil.

Christians desperately need this unique strength we receive from **Jesus Christ** through the Holy Eucharist in order to fight against the cunning and most aggressive evil we face every moment of the day. This horrible evil is determined to destroy the world and everything in it. I myself would no longer feel truly alive without the Eucharist, which represents the **body** and **blood** of **Jesus Christ**. Without the precious Holy Eucharist, something inside me would surely begin to die, and I would in some respects cease to exist. I believe, as a Catholic, the soul would slowly begin to die if you refused this precious gift of the Holy Eucharist. This is a spiritual death without the love, protection, and mercy of **Jesus Christ**. I truly believe the purpose of my life would be lost without the Eucharist. Multitudes of people share the same belief that they cannot thrive in happiness without the miraculous gift of the Holy Eucharist. The Holy Eucharist is the only way it is possible to encounter **Jesus** in this pure miraculous way. **Jesus** desires us all to be close to **Him** and to love **Him**. We all dearly need **God's** protection and love now more than ever before. So why are so many people saying *no* to **God**? **Jesus** also bestowed this precious gift of the Dynamite power of the **Holy Spirit** to **His** Apostles so later they would further understand the truth. Does Humanity no longer trust their faith in the **Holy Spirit**?

The Last Supper is mentioned in each of the four Gospels in the Catholic Bible (Matthew 26, Mark 14, Luke 22, John 13–17, and by Saint Paul in Corinthians 10–11).

The Holy Eucharist is the Body, Blood, Soul, and Divinity of **Jesus Christ**. This is the miracle and gift of the most Holy Eucharist from **Jesus Christ** to Humanity. The feast of **Corpus Christi** reminds us we possess an immense treasure. When a Catholic priest takes a little piece of unleavened bread and repeats the words that **Jesus** spoke at the Last Supper, **"This is My body,"** and when the priest takes a small amount of wine in a chalice and says, **"This is My blood,"** the bread is no longer bread, and the wine is no longer wine! The bread and wine become the Body and Blood of **Jesus Christ** by this miraculous transformation. This is the greatest gift **Jesus** bestowed on the church. At every Holy Sacrifice of the Mass, we participate in a marvelous miracle; this miracle, in the Latin Rite, is transubstantiation. East or West, the mystery is still the same; words cannot express it. The Eucharist is Holy Communion. **Jesus Himself**, through the Eucharist, grants to us the most powerful experience of intimacy possible within our earthly existence. As Pope Benedict explained, **"And that is what is really happening in Communion, that we allow ourselves to be drawn into Him, into His inner communion, and are thus led finally into a state of inner resemblance."**

When the Catholic priest in my church stands in front of me and says the words **"Body of Christ"** while I am receiving the Holy Eucharist, I can only imagine how many Angels are present in church. I believe the Angels are so joyous, we can almost hear them singing their praises to **God** in Heaven. Does everyone remember to recite the Act of Contrition before receiving Holy Communion? In addition, when the priest raises the precious Blessed Sacrament consecrated, it is now the body of **Jesus Christ** just as it was the night of the **Last Supper.** When you can see the Blessed Sacrament visibly, you should then respectfully say, **"My Lord and My God."** These are basic Catholic teachings taught to every Catholic, and it is most respectful for everyone to remember always to say these words silently before receiving **Jesus** in the Blessed Sacrament. May I remark further the Apostle Thomas said, "My **Lord** and my **God**" **(John 20:13)**.

These words are preceded by **"Said unto Him" and are followed by "Because thou hast seen Me, thou hast believed,"** and the words **"My Lord"** can only be referred to **Christ**. This sentence is an exclamation to **God**, addressed to **God**, and is necessary to understand this in the natural meaning of a confession by the Apostle Thomas that his **Lord** was also **God**! I pray this explanation is clear and I would encourage anyone to read the Bible in order to discover or rediscover **God's** holy words.

These magnificent encounters with the Angels and other experiences are so fascinating because this proves to us that **God** is trying to tell us through **His** Angels how much **He** loves and cares about us. This is all further proof **God** is trying to get our attention. Seeing the Angel, I realized **God** is giving us another chance to redeem ourselves before it is too late. The truth is these awesome experiences happen to people when they least expect it, and it is so wonderful and so exciting. I can now say with certainty I know the Angels enjoy these encounters with us more than we could ever realize. After seeing the Angel, I assure you the Angels are just as excited to be among us. The Angels are exceptionally close to us when we need them the most. When we are feeling sad or lonely, the Angels try desperately to let us know we are not alone. I never gave this much thought before the Angel appeared about the concept of an Angel having feelings. **God**, in **His** unfathomable love for us, did assign a Guardian Angel for specific purposes. Most people do not give it much thought regarding Angels having humanistic feelings. Angels are pure spirits whom

God created differently from us, and this is, of course, true. However, until my visit with the Angel, I never really realized to what amazing degree the Angels might actually feel tremendous sadness or joy for us. I am convinced after seeing the Angel as I did, the Angels do indeed have strong feelings for Humanity. While I was in the presence of the Angel, I observed several emotions. The Angel displayed elation, compassion, tremendous joy, and deep serious concern for **God's** people. Imagine knowing firsthand your Angel embraces genuine compassion and love for you. The Angels are with us to help guide us. Your Angels are your best friend if you would only realize it. How fantastic to have a friend who is willing to do anything for you, and in return, all you need to do is love **God**! This seems almost too easy not to take advantage of such a special friendship. An Angel is pure love who is committed to you for your entire life without any reservation or hesitation. As elated I was to see the Angel, the happiness I felt was short-lived. This encounter with this Angel, who appeared to me in the hospital, the visit proved more serious in nature than I first realized. The true mission of the Angel who appeared was soon evident to me. The Angel conveyed a message that contained a dire warning! The Angel said, **"Tell them it is almost time."** I knew the minute I heard those words the Angel spoke that the visit from the Angel demanded greater significance for all Humanity. I understand completely now the intention of the message was not only for me, but the message was for everyone who will listen. I knew immediately the seriousness of the message was for all the people of the world. The words the Angel conveyed to me contained a meaning so deep in its origin; it is monumental in its consequences. In my mind, I can still hear the Angel saying the words, **"Tell them it is almost time."** The message and the numerous meanings are constantly on my mind. Only six words yet nothing else can compare with the enormous implication found within those six words.

    I continue to ask myself every day what can I do personally to help everyone understand the enormous atrocities happening in the world; will be averted, simply by asking **God** for **His** help? Sounds so easy that I do not understand why people do not take advantage of asking for **God's** help more often. What the Angel revealed to me will happen some**time** in the future, if **God's** people do not give their heart and Soul to **Him**. This was heartbreaking for me to endure knowledge of a world in horror only existing with evil without **God**. Then I realized, tomorrow is the future. What more should I be personally doing? Will anyone really listen to me and understand what I am trying to tell them? Will knowing what the Angel said to me persuade you to change your life in a way that is pleasing to **God**? Will the visit from the Angel and the message persuade enough people to turn their hearts and minds to **Almighty God**? How can I make enough people understand and believe they must give their whole hearts to **God** and this includes everything they do in their daily life? How do I convince someone to love **God** with such intensity that every part of his or her Soul would begin to sing? I know this is a profound statement, but I find this is a huge individual dilemma for me. To think I am confronted with the very thought, I need to try to encourage more people they must embrace **God** above all else. You must love **God** in an all-consuming way. **God** must be first in every part of your life. It is disturbing to me that the very thought even exists that many people think they do not need **God**. It difficult to say this or even think there are still people who do not believe in **God**. How is this possible? I simply cannot embrace this awful thought. Feeling the way I do about **God**, I cannot understand who could not love **God**. This would be the opposite of love, and since **God** made you in **His** image, how would this be possible? You would have to hate yourself first not to believe in **God**. Sounds a little awkward; however, this is how some people turn to hate themselves and are able to do horrible acts against themselves and others. **God** is not hate. **God** is love personified! Our loving **God** continues to provide enormous opportunities to turn your attention to **Him**. Conformation of the statements made here are within the covers of your Bible. The passages, verses, and stories are documented events along with Parables **Jesus** used when preaching to the people would move your heart toward **Almighty God**. This will help you come to feel the way I do, and this will touch your Soul in the same way.

    I am determined more than ever, and I am convinced that we must all confront evil with extreme caution. However, unafraid and with the confidence **God** will protect you, everyone needs to recognize evil presents itself in unique forms. It is not easy to say *no* to what many have become so accustomed to in their daily life. Evil is a habit you must break. I am extremely aware I also have to be steadfast every minute of the day. More than ever, I am aware the snares of evil are always in front of me ready to confront me and destroy me. I witnessed an Angel, but do not think that for a moment I do not have to remain vigilant. **God** will protect me, but I have free will too. I can assure you, I still have to be on guard and be extremely cautious because evil will try to destroy me given the opportunity. The closer you become to **God**, the more aggressive evil tries to confuse anything good you do for **God**. I keep **God** on my mind and heart all day because **God** will come to my assistance if I ask **Him** too. **God** is waiting for all of us to ask **Him** for help and guidance in everything we do, especially when you are in a stressful situation. We also need the support of one another to accomplish greater things for **God**. I pray I will accomplish my mission to announce to as many people as possible the message the Angel conveyed to me. Now is the **time** for me to spread the message without further delay. This is only part of many things I must do for **God**. What I have done so far is so little in comparison to the overall responsibility granted to me by **God**. I have tried my best to speak to everyone I meet in order to convey to them what the Angel said to me. After sharing the message the Angel conveyed to me with you, together, we can discern the implications of the message. I sense some**times** whenever I am speaking to someone about the Angel, I feel as though I am reaching into the very heart of a person, especially when I speak to them, about **God**. I cannot express to you how good this feels to talk about **God** and **His** Angels. Discussing **God** and **His** Angels with your friends and people you meet will feel so gratifying, and you know, this is very pleasing to **God**. Some**times**, I sense it is not only me speaking to them because it is the **Holy Spirit** speaking through me to them. Always the right words seem to be available to me without any difficulty. In my heart, the **Holy Spirit** is directing my every word. I seem to know which people accept the message from the Angel and which people do not. Some people will think about what the Angel said, and maybe later, they will realize the words changed their life in a positive way. Perhaps these people will also share with others what they have learned about the Angel. Now that you know what the Angel said, will knowing this make a difference to you, and how you feel regarding your life and your friendship with **God**?

> I pray that when you have had an opportunity to reflect, about my encounter with the Angel; and discern the message conveyed to me for you, that this would bring you closer to **Almighty God**!

No one person should ever fear **God** so much that this will cause you to stay away from **Him**. **God** is a gentle and understanding and an all-forgiving **God** with deep compassion and mercy for everyone. **God** is reaching **His** hand to you right now and is waiting for you to place your hand in **His**. I promise you will feel **God's** awesome presence within you and **God** will change your life forever. You need only to desire to be in the presence of **God**. **God** will hear your prayers, and you will feel the awesome presence of **God** all around you. In your heart, you will be aware of **God's** awesome power and love for you. Follow your heart, and you will never want to allow **God** out of your life again. **God** will finally have your absolute attention because you will begin to see things as you never did before. Everything around you will look different somehow. For example, even the clouds will look more beautiful than you remembered. The color of the sky will recapture your attention as if you were looking at the sky for the first **time**. Even nature will arouse your interest in a most significant way. No doubt, your personal life will begin to take on a sincerely meaningful and renewed purpose. This will enhance everything you knew already, and you will finally recognize the truth in your life. Some of the world problems will cease to make you as anxious because you will remember, **God** is still in charge and **He** loves you beyond measure. You will all of a sudden realize you are happier and more content with your life. You will be better equipped to cope with daily stress because you placed **God** first in your life.

If you love **God** with your whole heart and your whole Soul, what are you going to do to help others to feel as you do? You must share with others how important this is to tell **God** that you love **Him** every day. Share your love for **God** openly with others as often as you can. Others will be watching the example you present to them without you knowing it. The example you display to others will make a difference! **God** will help you get their attention because your good example will ultimately improve their life. **God** uses **His** beloved and faithful people to spread goodness in the world for the benefit of the world. This goodness needs only to begin with one person and will multiply with the help of **God's** Grace until this love covers the entire world with **God's** love and mercy. If Humanity would allow this to happen, the people of the world would have peace in their hearts, and the world would rejoice. You must believe every person on the face of this earth is special to **God**, and like a loving **Father**, **He** desires **His** children to be happy!

I pray **God's** children will open their hearts so they can hear what **He** is trying to tell them because **He** loves all **His** children beyond measure.

> **God** is trying to get our attention because **He** loves
> all **His** people so dearly. Now is the **time** to express to
> **God** in your own way how much you love **Him**.

CHAPTER 3

What Was I Thinking the Moment I Saw the Angel?

Now when I reflect on my visit with the Angel, it is so easy for me to recall every detail of the day in the recovery room. When I first gazed upon the beautiful Angel, the amazement of the encounter took me by complete surprise. What an understatement! This was incredible to me that I was really looking at this magnificent Angel. I will never be able to express to you entirely all the thoughts and feelings I was experiencing. I was thoroughly astonished when I realized I was in the presence of an Angel. Certainly, this was an intense experience that anyone would find it a little difficult to describe. I felt the Angel drew me in somehow into another realm. I lay there on the bed, not moving a muscle, looking at the brilliant Angel, and I could feel tears welling up in my eyes for joy. I was afraid to blink my eyes for fear the Angel would disappear. I was overwhelmed with the stunning beauty of the Angel who stood within this amazing golden light. The Angel was beyond any description anyone could depict in any picture or painting. I find this terribly difficult to form the proper words to describe the true essence of the Angel. Trying to keep my emotions under control was a task in itself. I could not count the thoughts that raced through my head all at the same **time**. My mind was on overload while I tried to maintain my composure. One thing I knew for sure, no matter what happened, I was not going to take my eyes from the Angel. At first, the Angel stood there silently looking at me with an amazing smile. I felt in some way this Angel knew everything about me. What I wanted at that moment was to get off that bed and go to the Angel. The joyous excitement continued after my mind settled in to the realization what was happening was really taking place.

For centuries, people have expressed the possibility they thought an Angel helped them in one way or another. Others say they experienced some kind of spiritual encounter that they could not readily explain. Often, these experiences take place under similar circumstances such as in "near-death experience." Other people have reportedly experienced something unusual or thought what they saw could have been an Angel disguised as a Good Samaritan. These encounters always seem to take place when they needed help, and then before long, someone unexpectedly arrives just at the right **time**. Now I can say with confidence that all those people really did see an Angel sent from **God** to help them. **God** summoned the Angel to help them in their **time** of need. This is so simple to understand now. In my particular case, I was not in a near-death experience. The surgery was a success, and my life was never in any danger. I am convinced now what these other people encountered was an intervention directly from **God**. This is the one most significant moment that could ever happen to anyone in his or her life**time**. To know **God** loves us all so much, **He** will send **His** Angels on a mission; to come to our aid is confirmation how much **He** loves us. **God** cherishes us above all **His** splendid creations because **He** made us in **His** own image. I believe **God** will continue to send **His** Angels because we need their help more than ever! Now that I have looked upon the face of **God's** beautiful Angel, I realize the Angel appeared to me because **God** desires Humanity to remember we are all **His** children. Are **God's** children ready to listen to what **He** is trying to tell us? Will we continue to ignore the warning signs **God** is placing on our hearts?

All over the world, there are unsuspecting people that have already experienced something wonderful from the Grace-filled gift. This loving gift of Grace and awareness from **Almighty God** would automatically change their life in some special way. **God** touched all these people, in such a unique way, to remind them **He** is so near to them. **God**, in **His** loving compassion, is desperately trying to make us aware of **His** presence in our life. Even with all the knowledge contained in books, regarding spiritual events, this still is never enough for some people to recapture their devotion and turn to **God**. Therefore, I can only conclude, while reading about Angels or other experiences might be enjoyable, I guess the vast majority of people do not really believe these events really take place. These encounters are not fairy tales, meant to be entertaining to only children. You need to open your heart and mind to the awesome truth that all these events really do take place. This is simple to understand why these visions and magnificent encounters with Angels occur. **God** plans these magnificent events at a precise moment in our life to show us how much **He** really loves us. **God** never does anything for us without a divine purpose. This particular thought alone is so incredible. This is my personally belief: these visions and events others have experienced all happened on a spiritual level that only they would understand. **God** allowed these events to happen to them because **He** knew they needed or wanted to experience something special because of their strong faith in **Him**. Therefore, this proves to me **God** allows experiences on many spiritual levels to happen over **time** for a specific purpose known only to **Almighty God**. **God** allows these awesome experiences to take place so **He** can communicate with us in this special and uniquely holy way. I am sure you have heard someone say, "I am having a fantastic day." or, "I never felt better in my life." Well, I now believe this uplifting feeling is the truth. During this precise **time**, we are silently in total harmony with **God**. I wonder if it could be that easy. It is amazing to me how much **God** desires our happiness. It is Humanity and our societies overall that make everything so complex. Perhaps for a specific reason, on a particular day, you were able to sense your Angel or hear **God's** messages. You might say this wonderful awareness made you feel so good about everything on that day. Do you think your focus on **God** was greater on a particular day? Perhaps in the silence of your heart, you may have asked or needed something special from **God**. On that day, **God** responded to your request because **God** recognized your love for **Him** was genuine. **God** wants all of us to be happy and to love **Him** with your whole heart and soul. Therefore, for me, maybe this was precisely on one of those particularly unique occasions that I felt closest to **God** than ever before. Was my unconscious desire so great that I would receive some kind of spiritual experience from **God** in order to feel even closer to **Him**? Did my very Soul desire this so immensely, **God** said yes?

There is no doubt the experience that took place many years ago in Rome, Italy, will never compare with my visit with the Angel in the hospital. It is amazing what can take place if you are paying attention to the possibilities that can occur at any moment. It was the instant I first glimpsed the Angel in my recovery room **God** touched my soul. This **time**, I did not have to think or wonder later what took place because there in front of me stood the truth clearly. Without hesitation, there was no doubt that what I witnessed in my recovery room was divine intervention from **Almighty God**. Certainly, everything seems much clearer to me now. Previously in Italy, there were people and events that involved unique circumstances that certainly led up to something taking place unusual during that **time**. No wonder I began to be curious about a particular situation that occurred during a single afternoon there. I realize now what transpired then were like pieces of a puzzle fitting together so perfectly that what took place then was inevitable. I understood some**time** later, it was the overall event was all a beautiful plan predestined by **God**. Who but **God** would be in charge of something that nourishes the Soul?

My memory of what took place in Italy is still vivid in my mind. There is no question I followed the direction of some unseen force that was the **Holy Spirit**. What followed was the result of something wonderful because I was listening to the prompting I was receiving from **God**. I said yes to **God** because **He** knew I needed and desired something so badly to happen that particular day that concerned my Soul. **God** grants wonderful things to take place so we will remember how much **He** loves us. It is the believers Soul that knows and loves **God** immensely. The Soul necessitates every opportunity to remain in a state of Grace. Only then is the Soul offered the occasion to be in the presence of **God** ever so briefly. I wonder about the possibility of the Soul to breach some invisible boundary. For most Christians, only during the Eucharist, for a fleeting moment, is it possible for the Soul to be close to **God**. It is my belief that the Soul craves the Eucharist because in order to be close to **God**, the Soul must be in the state of Grace. It is the Soul that Christians believe is all important to **God**. Therefore, it is clear, that the circle of life revolves around the Soul in order to be in the presence of **Almighty God**!

When I first became aware of the Angel, I knew immediately something wonderful was happening, and my heart actually felt like singing. The thoughts that raced through my head were remarkable. I truly did not think it was possible for this many thoughts to process in the brain so quickly. Questions filled my mind rapidly, and some answers seem to come to me even faster. At first, these thoughts were of a personal nature. When I reflect on this moment, it was amazing to me that the Angel already knew what I wanted to ask! Then the Angel began to discuss, by way of examination, issues in a manner that is very difficult for me to describe to you. I cannot describe this in a way it would be worthy. Nevertheless, I knew and understood all the issues and concerns the Angel brought forth in her conversations with me. Most importantly, the Angel spoke of the Sin that is taking place on a monumental scale in the world. This part of my visit with the Angel was heartbreaking for me. It was very difficult to be in the presence of an Angel and face how **God** views our sinful nature. Hearing the Angel describe how severely we have all wounded the **Sacred Heart** of **Jesus** was indeed heartbreaking. I had to face the truth: our sins are so vast, our souls will smother from within as in quicksand. I realize the subject of Sin is certainly not on a list of topics many people are interested in discussing. Understandably, this is a very uncomfortable subject for most people. Yet this is one of the most important issues of our existence that we must all concern ourselves. I felt horrible to hear an Angel speak about all the Sin in the world. For a moment, my heart did sink to the brink of despair. In my heart, I could see the Angel was very sad over this truth. The Angel reminded me we must all be ready to accept difficult challenges for the love of **Almighty God**. Briefly, I felt the weight of Sin in the world weigh heavy on my own shoulders. The knowledge of these incredulous sins was heartbreaking for me to bear. Only **God** knows why so many wonderful experiences must also include a painful and stressful element. I trust in **God** because **He** is in complete charge of my life. I always knew my life would include joy as well as difficulties and hardships. Therefore, I have always accepted wholeheartedly and without hesitation whatever **God** desired of me. I know our faithful reward awaits us only in Heaven, not here on earth.

> Dear **God**, open the hearts and minds of **Your** children
> so we may see the truth that is ever before us.

God is trying to get our attention because **He** is trying to remind us **He** will always love us!

CHAPTER 4

What Took Place in the Recovery Room?

Since my visit with the Angel, I recall often while praying and meditating on my holy event, the wonder of **God's** love for **His** children is unimaginable! What I received when I first witnessed the Angel was total assurance and confirmation of my faith that I now desire with all my heart to share with you. With the appearance of the Angel, I can now assure you of the same confidence that what you believe in faith is **all true**! The message received from the Angel is a precious gift from **Almighty God** that I pray will encourage you to pray and discern the message the Angel so lovingly directed me to convey to everyone.

While I am in silent meditation, easily, I can recapture my every sensation I felt when I realized the Angel was there. I can relive the moment in my memory of the encounter with the Angel as if it was happening all over again. It was one moment to the next, and all at once, I realized the Angel was there. You might say this happened in a blink of an eye. I did not see the Angel appear because the Angel was already present and seemed to be patiently waiting for the precise moment when I would be aware of her presence. Without anything at all happening unusual prior to seeing the Angel, all of a sudden, I could see the Angel clearly standing only a few feet away. I can only conclude the Angel was obliviously waiting for me to wake up.

I remember while I was waiting for surgery, my last thought was how much I intensely loved **God**. I was never worried about

I SEE AN ANGEL

anything because I was prepared for any decision **God** would decide for me. When I awoke to this very bright golden light and opened my eyes, the Angel was standing there looking at me so intently. The Angel was standing there, as though she truly was waiting for me to acknowledge her presence. I will never forget how the Angel stood there looking at me with this amazing smile. I felt pure elation when I realized she was smiling *at me*. I cannot describe to you what I felt when the Angel's eyes looked intently into mine! For one single human moment, I felt like I was in Heaven already! As I continued to look at her sweet smile, my first thought was, **God** *had truly forgiven me*. Most Christians do believe **God** forgives and forgets their sins if you are truly contrite. However, learning how to forgive yourself is not always easy. I will admit that this particular dilemma in my life was also very difficult for me personally to overcome. I discovered the closer you are to **God**, the worse you feel about hurting **Him** when you commit Sin. I now continue to believe wholeheartedly **God**, in **His** infinite mercy, does forgive and will forget if you are sorry and intend to amend your life.

Looking at the Angel standing so close to me, everything else in the room faded away. The Angel demonstrated immense and tender love that was unlike anything I have ever experienced before. This moment was a great deal emotionally for me to absorb, especially when I realized I was staring at an Angel! The Angel's greeting left me with a profound awareness, and I will carry this moment close to my heart all the days of my life. The enormous degree of love and compassion I felt coming from the Angel was overpowering. The Angel was merely a few feet away from my bed, but I could see the Angel clearly, allowing me to see even the smallest details. I secretly wished I could hug the Angel. Initially, questions raced through my mind like the wind, but these became unimportant. These human desires faded quickly because assuredly, this was not the reason the Angel appeared. I could try to relate for you the Angel's greeting to a pale comparison of an experience where nothing but extreme happiness filled your heart. Everything that took place in the recovery room was precise right down to the tiniest of details. I stopped thinking about my own concerns and instead directed all my concentration on the Angel. Only moments passed before it became evident the Angel was there, not just for my benefit but also for the benefit of all **God's** people.

I will always maintain the opinion that the Angel was with me for a very long **time**. I surmised later realistically the **time** the Angel was there was probably brief. What took place happened in such a way I remain convinced that the Angel was there for a much longer **time**. How this was possible is unexplainable. It was not long before the Angel would tell me why she appeared to me. When I reflect on everything that took place, I am exceedingly grateful for every second **God** allowed me to be with the Angel. I am convinced while the Angel was there in the recovery room with me, **time**, as we understand it, did stand still. **Time** itself ceased, and I am so grateful it did. Even now, while I continue to discern deeply all the dramatic circumstances that took place in the recovery room, I will always remain awestruck. I will always remain humble that **God**, in **His** infinite wisdom, allowed me to see **His** precious Angel and receive the profound message that will ultimately change the lives of countless people.

> **Almighty God** sent **His** Angel, with a message, to remind all **His** children how much **He** loves them.

Later that day in my hospital room, I began to contemplate the full realization of my visit with the Angel. As I lay there, the full recognition of what transpired only a short **time** before was absolutely astonishing. Repeatedly, in my mind, I began to recapture every detail of the entire encounter with the Angel. I could not stop thinking about the Angel and her appearance to me. I was fixated on the direct message and those six words that were uniquely daunting. I also began reflecting on the dire issues discussed by the Angel to be of great importance, such as **Abortion**.

It was not until I returned home that the complete realization of the responsibility **God** had given to me became so intensely apparent. However, a quiet resolve came over me as if I already knew what I had to do. There is no doubt while I am still the same person I was before I saw the Angel, the realization of what I witnessed will forever change my life. I am becoming more aware of the importance of the crucial purpose of the Angel's visit. Personally, by the very presence of the Angel, any question I deemed important resolved quickly. This astounding visit from an Angel is not about me; it is about *all* Humanity! Now it is **time** for Humanity to ask questions and to prepare to receive the answers. The Angel came to warn **God's** children they must love **Him** above all else! Since the visit from the Angel, it has been so difficult for me to keep my mind on anything else. What is truly important is the appearance of the Angel and the message conveyed. The message is about what **God** expects from **His** children. The people of this world have a responsibility to their **Creator** to accomplish much for **Him**, and there is so little **time** left. I pray **God** will grant Humanity the discernment needed to achieve in the coming future change that will please **Almighty God**.

I have developed an obsession with every detail about the Angel because the experience brought me closer to **God**. I can close my eyes and still see the Angel standing there, her amazing compassionate smile, directed toward me. I am so grateful to **God** that **He** allowed me to see the Angel. There is not a day that goes by where I continue to miss seeing the Angel. I pray even though I cannot see the Angel now, the Angel is right beside me. I pray the Angel will continue to guide me after the book is finished. This encounter with the Angel is so miraculous knowing **God** allowed me to look upon a heavenly Angel. I continue to struggle with the proper words to express to you how I felt at the **time** to have an Angel look deeply into my heart. I was looking at an Angel of **God** who fixed those gorgeous eyes on me that seemed to pierce my very Soul. I had the distinct impression the Angel knew everything about me. An Angel standing in the golden light who appeared with enormous love and compassion, not only for me but also for all of Humanity!

It is important that I continue to concentrate on the important issues contained in the message the Angel conveyed to me. When I speak the words aloud, "An Angel appeared to me with a message," I realize the extent of the responsibility given to me. I began to understand the dire implications of the message a little at a **time**. I can only conclude, with any spiritual experience **God** allowed me to experience during my life**time**, these experiences happened because this was **God's** Divine Will. It is overwhelmingly clear **God** desires me to share this message with everyone. I must direct my attention to what the Angel requested me to do. The message is what is all important. I am merely an instrument that **God** chose to bring **His** message to all **His** people. The Angel said, **"Tell them it is almost time."** Now that you are aware of the message, what does the message mean specifically to you personally?

As I search, my own thoughts witnessing the magnificence of the Angel confirmed everything I believed, and I am bursting with gratitude. Since my visit with the Angel, my awareness of my surroundings is more acute. The **Holy Spirit**, for a brief moment, touched my very soul. A definite healing took place on that afternoon in the hospital. A healing took place for more than my surgery. Seeing the Angel reminded me of all the things that are important to me and, as a Christian, what should be important to you. This enhanced awareness has affected everything I do and say now. Do people who know me best notice anything different in my mannerism? Still I am the same person before the visit with the Angel. Evidentially, everything that makes me who I am as a person seems to be taking on a calmer resolution about life in general. Sure, I continue to be very concerned about the issues happening in the world. However, I sense a profound reassurance because **God** is always with us, waiting for us to ask for **His** help. It is **time** for all **God's** people to open their eyes to the truth. Otherwise, much evil will continue to happen. Additionally, I sense a difference concerning the way I feel about every area of life's concerns. I am greatly interested in how others feel regarding their personal love for **God**. It is so important to share how you feel about **God** with others. If you include **God** in your life, nothing is impossible to overcome. One observation that has come to my attention since I was in the presence of the Angel, my blood pressure dropped by twenty plus points and, most of the **time**, has maintained this level! Additionally, my anxiety over world affairs has improved. While I remain very concerned over the seriousness of our present challenges, **God** is still in charge! My trust in **God's** mercy is unshakeable. If more people would place their trust in **Almighty God**, what a different world this would be. Therefore, place your complete trust in **Almighty God**, and watch what will take place in your life. The love I feel for **Almighty God** will sustain me no matter what challenge confronts me. **God's** love will sustain you too no matter what challenges you may face now or in the future. You must give your heart, mind, body, and Soul completely to **God**.

When I meet someone for the first **time**, I am encouraged by the **Holy Spirit** to tell him or her, "You must not let the worries of the world cause you fear," because you must trust in **God**. **God** will give **His** children the strength to overcome adversity. I assure you **God** has already taken care of those worries if you allow **Him** into your life. Simply said, Humanity needs to love **God** and tell **Him** each day you love **Him**. The Angel expressed to me strongly **God** desires our love most of all. This is so easy to understand if you love **God** above all else, the true picture of what is so important to **Him** becomes clearer to you. If you would spend quality **time** with **God**, then you would feel more secure about what is taking place all around you. You might even discover the answers to some of the things that worry you the most if you shared your troubles with **God**. When the stresses of this world put you to the test, it is **time** to look to **God** for a solution. Never ignore the promptings from your Angel because your Angel also knows what is best for you. You need to pay closer attention because your Angels are trying to encourage you to make the right decisions. I learned so many lessons that day in the recovery room. Everything **God's** people ever needed to know in order to have a happy life is right in front of us. Gratefully, I was reassured when I witnessed the Angel that we are not alone! You must place all your trust in **God** because **He** will never leave anyone alone!

> **I must repeat once more how devastating this was for me to face the cruel truth from the Angel; that evil is on a rampage to destroy Humanity!**

It was a truth that came directly from the Angel, and she mentioned it repeatedly. This broke my heart to hear an Angel speak of the horrible offences committed toward **Almighty God**, such as **Abortion** and the murder of innocent people. The truth is no one person is without Sin. We have all greatly offended **God** and continue to offend **God** with cruel indifference and without mercy. These offences to **God's Sacred Heart** are more severe than anyone could ever imagine. **Christ** died on the Cross so Humanity would have the opportunity for their sins to be forgiven. In my opinion, we are continually putting our **Lord Jesus Christ** back on the cross because of our sins and our indifference to Sin. How did Humanity move so far away from **God**? Certainly, this is not something that has recently happened. Sin has woven itself into the fibers of society since the beginning of **time**. It is evidently clear some people are not concerned with what is going on around them if it does not directly involve them. Is it because they have lost their faith? Many people have fallen into the hands of evil to such a degree it may be very difficult for them to turn back to **God** but not impossible! To change this, it will take enormous strength and Grace only **God** can bestow on you. I am keenly aware we must use the precious **time** you and I have left for good rather than evil. We are allowing evil to transform our world right before our eyes. It is my impression when we commit a Sin, we are allowing evil to transform our beautiful world into a world soon no one would recognize. There is no doubt the world we live in is becoming a place that cannot continue to flourish without the protection and mercy of **God**. Our world is fast becoming a frightening evil place that is overflowing with murder and deceit. **God** has given us all ample **time** to redeem ourselves. No one can afford to be complacent now because **time** is a valuable commodity, we are fast using up. Humanity must turn to **God's** loving mercy before it is too late.

My heart remains very heavy with sadness because of the serious concern the Angel expressed over our indigent attitude regarding Sin. The Bible teaches us we are all sinners in the eyes of **God**. Yet many people continue to go along their merry way as before and do nothing to change what is wrong in their life. What took place that afternoon in the recovery room taught me many vital lessons. The most crucial lesson of my life is I witnessed the truth. Obviously, too many people continue to live out their life in what I call the "dead zone." Sin is the dead zone!

The Angel pointed out to me repeatedly that the consequences of turning our back onGod is the loss of our Soul! Eternal loss of your Soul is what you should be afraid!

You must believe there is no space in which to hide from **God**. **God** sees everything we do—the good, the bad, and the ugly. The Angel warned repeatedly Humanity must pray continually over the insult of **Abortion** and the atrocities that take place with **God's** children.

I believe strongly God will not be silent much longer!

I implore you, you must heed the urgent warning that the message implies. We all need to do something urgently to stop offending **God**. Not just **Abortion** but anything and everything that keeps you from the mercy of **God** must end! The people of this beautiful earth must learn how to live with one another in peace! **God's** people must turn their life over to **God** with your whole heart and your whole Soul. You cannot love **God** a little now and a little later. **God** is our **Father** in Heaven and like most parents who take delight in their children's accomplishments because **He** takes delight in our happiness. **Time** is a valuable commodity Humanity may no longer take for granted. The **Time** for us to redeem ourselves may be running out as in sand in an hourglass. An expression I read years ago, "The sands of **time**." Sands of **time** may refer to "sands of **time** (idiom), a figurative expression in the English language relating the passage of **time** to the sand in an hourglass."

It certainly is in our nature to be hopeful our problems will be resolved later, tomorrow, or some**time** in the near future. It should not be a surprise to anyone the world cannot continue on its present course. **God** is immensely sorrowful to think **His** people have given into fake ideals. Today, countless people of the world think of their future in terms of only material wealth. The term *future*, what exactly does this mean to you? Your future should be a personal aspiration of hope that includes **God**. The word *hope* is a single impressive word and, for most people, the meaning of this word holds great expectations for their future. In theory, I would hope the word *hope* would hold the same meaning of optimism for everyone. To me, the meaning of the terms *hope* and *future* are positive words of anticipation. I regard the message from the Angel while dire, but also it is a hopeful sign for all **God's** people because it proves that **God** has not given up on us yet! However, make no mistake this is an ominous warning that certainly means **God's** people have a lot of work to do. **God** is waiting patiently because **He** loves us unconditionally and because we are **His** children!

      God is watching and waiting!

Dear **God, Your** faithful children know **You** are waiting patiently for all of us to make a true effort to prove to **You** we love **You** and that we are capable of real change. I pray that the decisions Humanity makes now will have a positive effect on the future of our world. We must have peace in the world if our world is to continue. The future of the world is now completely in the hands of Humanity, and only with **You**, dear **God**, can we trust. Dear **God**, I know **You** are waiting for the world to open its eyes to the truth and turn their hearts to **You** before **You** come again to judge the world. Shower us with **Your** grace that we may love **You,** adore **You**, and praise **You** because all honor is **Yours Almighty Father** forever. Dear **God**, I pray to the very depth of my Soul that something will begin to awaken in the hearts of **Your** people.

      God is trying to get our attention!

CHAPTER 5

The Awakening

Since I witnessed seeing the Angel, I have finally begun to recognize the true significance regarding my own spiritual growth. I did not realize it at the **time**, but a special nurturing took place when I was a young child. This is when I first began to love **God** fiercely, deeply. I knew almost nothing about **God** then, but it would not be long before **He** would make **Himself** known to me. **God** announced **Himself** to me in a special way, and I responded immediately. This happened in a way only a child would understand. **God** continued to nurture my love for **Him** in countless ways through the turbulent years of my childhood. I never fully understood until later in my adult life when I began to recognize the fullness of **God's** internal love.

I first became aware of **God** when I was a child. I did not understand at the **time** that this would build the foundation for my spiritual growth. I accepted **God's** love wholeheartedly and without any reservation. This spiritual growth matured as I grew older, and I can only describe this to you as some form of awakening. I can convey to you that this as an acute awareness of the very presence of **God**. Somehow, I always knew **God** was by my side. I want to repeat, I was keenly aware of the presence of **God**, oh so well, when I was a child and this was wonderful! This was a deep trust formed between **God** and myself that was absolute love and understanding only a child knows from **God**. All **God's** children are born with **God's** unconditional love and trust. What worries me the most is how are the children of this generation going to grow to love and honor **God** if no one introduces them to the wonder of **His** friendship?

    God instilled all parents with a natural instinct that **He** knew would be necessary to raise their children to love **Him**. What happened to this natural instinct that is neglected and forgotten altogether, therefore, parents are not teaching their children the importance of having a friendship with **Almighty God**. In my particular instance, my parents were not available to teach me about **God**. As a result for a while, I did not know **God** even existed. However, **God** in **His** infinite wisdom and love for us brought about the opportunity for me to acquire the knowledge of **Him** because **He** knew the knowledge of **Him** would be necessary for me to have a happy life. I learned at an early age when to run to **God** when I was troubled because there I always found peace. During this special **time** in my life, I found **God** in the Tabernacle in my beloved Catholic Church. This wondrous **time** began in my childhood parish where I would visit daily after school. Only in the quiet of my church would I find such peace and contentment. There was no doubt I could feel **God's** love all around me in the quiet of my beloved church. I was secure in the knowledge of **God's** love for me would sustain my entire life. I will always cherish the memory of when I first obtained the knowledge of **God**. If you are a Christian, can you recall when you first received **Jesus** in your heart?

    I realize it is very difficult for some people to find the courage to awaken to the truth. **God** realizes some**times** that **His** children still get lost for a while. There were **times** later in my life when I thought I lost this special closeness with **God**. Life, with its twists and turns, often gets us going in the wrong direction. I always loved **God** dearly, but somehow, the special closeness I once felt with **God** seemed to elude me for a while. I think there are many people who have experienced this feeling of separation from **God** for a **time**. For some people, this feeling of disconnect can last longer and be very difficult to recapture again. I call this "lost in the desert," while searching for **God**, we can become lost. Oh, I hated those **times** when this would happen to me. All at once, I would think **God** was so distant from me. I could not seem to find **Him**, and I felt alone. No matter what I did, I could not feel **God's** presence. This was extremely disturbing to me; and the more I fought and struggled with this feeling, the worse this seemed to become. This is a feeling of great loss of the love and friendship that we all need so desperately from **God**. Then without any warning and without my knowledge of anything different happening, I began to realize the closeness with **God** I desired so deeply never really left me. Once I realized this truth, it was overwhelming. Then all at once, I would realize **God** had been there with me all the **time**. **God** never left me, and **He** will never leave you. This was when I knew **God's** love for me would never be lost. Only for some unknown reason, for a while, I could not feel **God's** presence in the way I thought I needed. I can only speak for myself, but I know each **time** this feeling of separation would happen, this was so painful for me. Each **time** this took place, I could feel my special relationship with **God** return stronger than ever. I could feel my personal relationship strengthened, and I felt safe again. I was so happy each **time** I recaptured my personal bond with **God**. Therefore, I can only conclude, even though the experience that takes place is painful, I definitely believe this is a form of healing. I also feel this is an important **time** for a renewal of **God's** great love for us that takes place during these **times** of loneliness. This is what I describe as "lost in the desert." While you may feel this temporary separation from **God** as unwanted, this may really be something that must take place for your spiritual growth. Each **time** you experience this distancing from **God**, the return to **Him** is even stronger and sweeter than it was before. However, remember I said **God** is always with us. Only we distance ourselves from **God**, not the other way around.

 God loves all **His** children so much that the truth of this should move even the hardest of hearts. Some people have forgotten that only with **God's** Grace are we able to accomplish the impossible. This is beyond our comprehension how much **God** really adores us. The **time** of Lent should speak volumes of how much **God** loves us. **God** so loved the world, **He** sent **His** only **Son Jesus Christ (John 3:16)**, who would willingly die a cruel death on the cross for all

Humanity. Christians believe **Jesus** was born and died on the Cross so it would be possible for **God** to forgive ours sins and overcome evil. Can you imagine what kind of world this would be if **God** did not send **His** only begotten **Son** to be crucified for us in the cruelest way possible on a wooden Cross? Why are there so many people who by their behaviors do not believe this anymore? Certainly, their actions speak volumes because they are telling **God** they no longer believe **He** died for them. The Angel expressed to me in the strongest way **God sees too many of His people have forsaken Him because they have forgotten His promises!** Try to imagine what it would be like to have an Angel face you and say these words directly to you! I can tell you it is a moment you would never forget! Hearing these words from the lips of the Angel was nearly more than I could cope with. I will never be able to erase these words from my mind. If you truly believed **God** died for you, why is it people do not live their life with this truth? Thank goodness, we do not have the Cross now as punishment in our *civilized* world; nevertheless, many people have provided themselves with personal and social crosses. Evil's deception is creating and encouraging large groups of people in order to inflict immense cruelty on the world. Our world is no longer a safe haven. The world is becoming a place that soon may not be safe for anyone.

Certainly, our society is not a safe place any longer for our children. The deliberation that continues over the unrest is spreading throughout the world with no solution in sight. People in our society continually converse over issues that really make no sense at all and solve nothing. **God's** people face a new dilemma. This new dilemma is utter confusion over truth, and it is really a form of babble, which is a tool that evil loves to use. The **time** is ripe for evil to use this tool, and so few people are paying attention. This confusion over the truth is beginning to take root. People will continue to be confused over the smallest issue. I now see confusion beginning everywhere on an immense scale. Confusion over the truth spreads easily through large populations and causes tremendous unrest. This confusion is and will never solve anything! Who do you think is ceasing the opportunity to cause this confusion? Humanity better wake up, realize we all must respect one another, and learn how to live together in peace.

This is an utter shame that society has to live in fear to the point where children are growing up in a cruel world without the knowledge of **Almighty God**. The sad thing is we all have the power to change the evil who wants to destroy anything good. We must realize this is like a disease, growing and feeding on our choices we decide, but we can all take charge of our life and stop it. **God** gave us all free will. Therefore, it is up to everyone to take charge and stop all this hatred and violence. People will ask why **God** is not putting a stop to all the violence that is happening all over the world. **God** is not responsible for all this hatred; Humanity is. We must all stand up and put an end to the hatred and violence so our children can once again live and play without fear from others. **God** can accomplish incredible miracles, but **He** needs our cooperation and our determination to bring about great change. Regardless what we do, **God** continues to wait for us to wake up and realize that we all need **Him**. **God** continues to do everything to get our attention because **He** loves us all so much. When are the people of this beautiful earth going to believe what **God** is desperately trying to tell us?

> Dear **God**, protect us from the evil that strives to destroy **Your** people until there is no more! Open the hearts of **Your** people that they will once again believe in the truth of their salvation. Open their ears that they may hear **You** calling to them. Grant **Your** children the Grace to put all hatred out of their minds, and they will learn to love one another again. In Jesus's name, I pray.

> **God** is trying to get our attention. When are **God's** children going to wake up and recognize the truth?
> **God** is patiently waiting!

CHAPTER 6

Angels Are the Guardians of the World

After what I experienced in Italy, it was only natural for me to have an increased interest in Angels. Reflecting on what I have experienced over the years, no wonder I began to have a heightened interest in Angels.

In May 2005, something unusual took place in a church in Rome, Italy. What took place there caused me to wonder immediately afterward if the people I spoke with in church were Angels. As a result, Angels were definitely on my mind more in recent years. I began to have a greater interest in knowing my personal Angel's name. A priest friend explained to me that it was possible to ask my Angel to give me his or her name. What Reverend John said to me was so intriguing. Before long, I did ask my Angel, "Please tell me your name?" To my amazement, a few months later, I discovered my Guardian Angel's name. I was in my prayer room reciting my prayers when the thought of the Angel's name entered into my mind. I felt certain the name that formed in my mind was perfectly suited to my life's accomplishments. Therefore, did I accomplish in life what **God** directed me to do? I was convinced the name was accurate in every sense of the word. The research I uncovered regarding the Angel's name was incredible! Everything I discovered later, regarding the name of my Angel, was astounding. The information I uncovered in reference to this Angel's name seemed to fit unmistakably because the name corresponded with all my personal achievements. I was confident that I truly discovered my Angel's name.

All my life, I believed my Angel would come to my aid whenever I asked for help. The Angel always seemed to find a way to let me know I was not alone. What I felt was simply a subtle awareness of the Angel's presence. This unique emotion implies no other explanation. Often, I really feel my Angel helps me remember dates or tasks I need to do. Your precious Angel is there to protect you every second of the day. However, you need to work as a team with your Angel if you desire the Angel to keep you from harm. Your free will and the decisions you make are completely up to you. **God** will not interfere because of your free will. In addition, your Angel is helpless without your cooperation because you must take charge with your life in a positive way before the Angel can assist you.

Here is an inspiring concept for you to explore as well. I would encourage anyone to ask his or her Angel for his or her name right away. Knowing your Angel's name can bring you much closer to your Angel. Thinking of your Angel by name might help you form a loving bond you desperately need. Your Angel is right now waiting for a sign from you in order to support you and help you in everything you do. Your Angel is patiently waiting and hoping you will ask for advice because your Angel is there to lead you to **God**. Next to **God**, what better council could you possibly have to guide you through your life than your Angel! Imagine your own personal Angel given to you and handpicked by **God** to direct you in all issues of your life. **God** has shown **His** immense love for everyone when **He** gave you and me an Angel to watch over us. The Angel has lovingly watched over you from the moment of conception. Even if you pay no attention to your Angel, the Angel will remain with you always. **God**, who loves you so deeply, gave you an extraordinary Angel who will remain by your side no matter what happens. We are never alone! Your Angel will continue to be with you throughout your entire life until **God** calls you home. There in the presence of **Almighty God, He** will examine every aspect of your life. **Almighty God** will evaluate the condition of your Soul. What will you tell **God** you accomplished for **Him**? **God** will decide whether you have deemed yourself to be worthy or not. **God** created you specifically for a grand purpose in life. You must try to understand **God's** design for all creation *is* grand; therefore, **God** does expect greatness from you and me. Heaven is where all creation will become conscious of this greatness because **God** created you and me perfectly in **His** image.

Actually, for the greater part of my life, I have been keenly aware of the presence of my own Guardian Angel. I always believed in an unseen guardian. I was in third grade in Catholic school when I first learned about my Guardian Angel. I used to make room at my desk chair so the Angel could sit next to me. It was a cute gesture for a young child because learning about my Angel was an important part of my Catholic education. It is unfortunate why people today feel they must grow up and put away all childish thoughts of their Angel. This was a great day for me because I felt very lonely in those early years. I was too young then to fully understand the reason I felt this way. Once I realized **God** was with me and my Angel was by my side, I would never feel alone again. I was able to face my challenges with renewed hope. No matter what transpired, I could ask **God** to help me. I feel so saddened that generations of children today will never know the happiness I felt knowing my Angel was beside me. More serious is the truth that generations of children today do not have the knowledge that **God** will be there for them when life gets complicated. What a devastating insult to **God**, and at the same **time**, a terrible injustice forced upon our precious children that these children would never know **Him**.

All my life, I have been sensitive to the truth; my life would not be complete without my Guardian Angel watching over me. There were **times** I knew my Angel was there because I noticed small things would happen. Little things I could not explain very easily. You may understand what I mean if you have ever experienced anything unusual when you needed help with a decision. Remember how good you felt when you were aware you made the right decision and quicker than you expected. Or if you completed a task without difficulty, especially if you have never encountered anything out of the ordinary you could not define, but you knew anyway something happened in an unusual way. For example, a serious problem seemed to solve itself with very little effort on your part. Some**times**, it only takes one right choice to turn a bad situation into a positive one.

I always knew in my heart that only through the Divine Will of **God** would it ever be possible to experience heavenly visions. What happens so supremely right and at the designated **time** is so amazing to me. I understand now this is purely spontaneous and **God**, with **His** mighty wisdom, grants these experiences at the precise moment to demonstrate to us how much **He** loves us. What circumstances must happen from one moment to the next? It is a miracle that **God** during these experiences alters **time** itself. Why not, after all, **God** can do anything **He** desires. During these precious moments, you are now exceptionally close to **God**. It is my belief there is an unseen plan that must be in perfect harmony in order for anyone to experience heavenly visions. Perhaps these are only human thoughts and speculations on the many things involving **God's** miracles. Of course, **God** alone would have a definite divine purpose when allowing a visit from an Angel in the first place. Christians believe there is a divine purpose for anything **God** desires for us. The unveiling of the purpose is what can be a lifelong mission for you and me to discover during our walk with **God**. Perhaps this is not important to know or even seek to understand why **God** chooses certain people to unveil these marvelous experiences. We need only to trust in our Faith that **God** knows what **His** children need or deserve.

It is amazing how often I have read where someone's car broke down and, in an instant, help arrived. Was this really just someone doing a good deed, or was it an Angel sent to help them? Was this their Guardian Angel? Imagine ordinary everyday people like you and me with no idea they are about to be in the presence of an Angel. Nothing you can recall seemed different on that particular day. Still from out of nowhere, curiously, someone just happened to be there and at precisely the right moment. I love the expression some people use, "Aren't you an Angel for helping me." Yes, a large number of people do believe an Angel appeared to them for one reason or another. Some people believe that **God** sent an Angel to help then under the appearance of an ordinary person. Then often, other people will say help arrived in an instant without a chance to say anything, the

Angel is gone. Is this some kind of test to see if we notice something unusual happened? Is **God** interested in our reaction? It is my belief this is a further test of our Faith. How do you feel the next day after something unusual happens? How quick we seem to forget! Do we really have an ungrateful nature? This is certainly evident; we all certainly have areas in our life that need improving. These unexpected opportunities exist in order to bring us closer to the light of **Christ**.

Christ is the light of all truth and understanding!

There is a great deal of documentation available that tells us about people who have experienced seeing a white light, as in near-death experiences. Now because of my own personal experience, I can say most assuredly the light I witnessed was a golden light unlike the white light other people have encountered in near-death experiences. This was an all-consuming very bright light that never disturbed my eyes. I am certain now the magnificent golden light that is normally unseen must surround each Angel. I believe this brilliant heavenly light totally envelopes an individual with the essence of **God's** love. Within this brilliant light resides harmonious awareness that captures the very essence of who you are. You become one with the light. There, in the light, you find yourself totally cradled within the love of **God**. The light softly announces and rejoices the awareness of the immense power of **Almighty God**. I felt absolute peace within the golden light. During this peaceful **time** I was conscious, I belonged only to **Almighty God**.

Why do some individuals refuse to believe in the divine power of **God**? I am shocked to the degree that people will go to discourage others from believing in **God's** holy word. It seems that these people would rather be miserable their entire life, and what is worse, they are determined to force their beliefs onto others so they can be miserable too. These unfortunate people do not realize they are refusing the unconditionalpeace that comes from the trust found only with **Almighty God**. It simply is not normal to push yourself away from **God**! I thought most everyone believed **God** created him or her in **His** image. I thought most people honored the truth: final judgment reserved only for **Almighty God**. What has changed in the minds of **God's** people? Humanity will have to account for the sins in the world. Humanity will answer to **God** on judgment day! No one has the right to judge another person for how someone may desire to believe in **God**. There certainly are enough struggles in the world; therefore, we should be using our energies to have more patience and understanding with one another.

I have to agree, who would expect to encounter an Angel? Therefore, when something out of the ordinary happens, it does take a second or two for the brain to seize the whole moment of this truth. There are people all over the world who believe they have experienced something unusual or something special took place for their spiritual benefit. These faith-filled individuals believed something out of the ordinary took place that would automatically change their life. The spiritual events that some people experience are often difficult to explain to someone else. These heavenly encounters would sincerely prompt you to pray and meditate on what took place. The experience that captured your undivided attention would cause you to search your heart in order to discern the meaning of your experience.

Are these spiritual experiences happening more often than anyone first thought were ever possible? I cannot help but wonder again, what circumstances have to take place in someone's life so perfectly that the moment is precisely perfect for **God** to allow any of these experiences to occur. To have theories about this is wonderful but to really experience a true event is quite another entirely. Although, I must say, many years ago in Italy, there were undeniable circumstances that definitely warranted my belief that I had been in the presence of Angels. However, this **time** in the hospital, there was no doubt for even a second I was in the presence of a heavenly Angel. The entire experience in the hospital was truly exceptional. I was in the presence of a magnificent Angel, and nothing in the past I may have experienced before would even come close!

Instantly and without any hesitation, I said aloud, **"I see an Angel."** I am sure my brain was working over**time** to connect with what my eyes knew was the truth. I witnessed an Angel of goodness standing within the golden light. This captivating golden light surrounded the entire Angel that proceeded to envelop the entire room. Amazing, I felt somehow, there was something vaguely familiar about this Angel, and I do not know what caused me to feel this way. I never truly experienced seeing an Angel before that was not in a dream. Is it possible I may have seen this Angel before but the Angel did not take the appearance of an Angel? I wonder now again about those people who say someone stopped to help them. No doubt, those people looked like ordinary people at the **time**. Definitely, I feel the Angel who appeared to me in the hospital was not my Guardian Angel. I realized this was an extraordinary Angel, a messenger, selected by **God** for a uniquely important purpose! This Angel was a messenger sent from the **Holy Spirit** because **God** desires Humanity to remember how much **He** loves **His** children. The Angel appeared to convey to me a precise message. This is a message of great significance that the Angel instructed me to convey to all who will listen!

I will continue to ask myself, why did the Angel show me terrible images of some future events that may occur if Humanity does not seek **God's** mercy? I continue to struggle with those images every day, and no doubt, I will the rest of my life. If you search your heart for the truth, I wonder if you study what is happening in the world, you would have to agree we are facing a global moral crisis. Observing those images forced me to face how cruel and evil the world will become without **God**. I also fully understand that the subject of evil for most people is a very uncomfortable subject for them to discuss. As a result, multitudes of people refuse to believe in Sin altogether. In addition, great numbers of people today are refusing to believe in hell! What is the basis for this belief? Do you no longer believe in the scriptures?

Jesus talked about hell more often than **He** talked about Heaven! Here are a few scripture references from the Bible noted here:

> **Matthew 3:12 and Luke 3:17—John the Baptist said the Lord will burn the chaff with unquenchable fire. This unquenchable fire is the state of eternal separation from God, that**

the Church has called "hell" for two thousand years. Some Protestant communities no longer acknowledge the reality of hell.

Matthew 25:41—Jesus says, "Depart from me, you cursed, into the eternal fire prepared for the devil and his angels."

Matthew 25:46—Jesus says, "They will go away into eternal punishment" that is in reference to this eternal fire.

Mark 9:47–48—Jesus refers to hell as where the worm does not die and the fire is not quenched. It lasts forever.

2 Thessalonians 1:6–9—The angels will come with flaming fire and the disobedient will suffer punishment of eternal destruction. It is important to note that "destruction" does not mean "annihilation," as some Protestant denominations teach. It means eternal exclusion from the presence of God.

Jude 6–7—The rebelling angels, and Sodom and Gomorrah, serves as an example by undergoing a punishment of eternal fire.

Revelation 14:11—The worshipers of the beast suffer, and the smoke of their torment goes up forever and ever.

Revelation 20:10—They're tormented in the lake of fire and brimstone day and night forever and ever.

Isaiah 33:14—"Who of us can dwell in the everlasting fire?" This is a reference to hell that is forever.

Isaiah 66:24—Their worm shall not die, and their fire shall not be quenched. We cannot fathom the pain of this eternal separation from God.

> **Jeremiah 15:14**—In my anger, a fire is kindled which shall burn forever. Hell is the proper compliment to the eternal bliss of heaven.
>
> **Judith 16:17**—In the day of judgment, the Lord will take vengeance on the wicked, and they shall weep in pain forever. Hell is a place that sinners have prepared for themselves by rejecting God, who desires all people to be saved in His Son Jesus Christ. God sends no one to hell.

These scriptures certainly spell out the truth that those who have turned their back on **God** through Sin have made their choice! They have provided themselves with their own hell, both here and after, because they will never see the face of **Christ** *if* they do not seek **His** forgiveness.

Some of these events and horrible images the Angel showed me are currently taking place in the world every day. The undeniable truth is this evil is growing and gaining strength. The Angel warned, evil is not going away any **time** soon, unless Humanity puts an end to it. I can still recall the seriousness and deep concern shown by the Angel when she talked about Sin. There is no way I could ever express to you what this feels like to be conscious all at once of massive evil on a monumental scale. It was horrible for me to stare at the face of such evil destruction. I cannot say I was surprised at what I witnessed. There is so much evil in the world already, and this evil continues relentlessly. It is very difficult for me to imagine evil could get worse, much worse. Still what are you and I going to do about the evil we are allowing to grow stronger? Yes, what is Humanity going to do? This is not an individual dilemma. What everyone needs to understand is that we all need accountability in order to abolish evil from our life. This is the **time** for everyone to decide either you are on the side of **God**, where goodness resides, or you are on the side of sinful mischief, where evil is waiting for you. It is important to seek the protection of **God** who will instruct your Guardian Angels to help you also whenever you find yourself faced with any challenge. The Angels are here with us because **God** knows Humanity needs their help. Find a quiet place and spend a few minutes getting to know your Angel. The Angels are proof of **God's** great love for us because this is why the Angels are here in the first place. The Angels are very close to you, and they strive to lead you to **God**. **God** desires to have a one-on-one relationship with you, but you must desire this relationship. This wonderful thought of friendship with **God** should make you begin to listen to your Guardian Angel. Your Guardian Angel desires to attain an important place in your life. The Divine Will of **Almighty God** sent the Angels to us so we would never be alone. All **God's** people need to honor **God's** Divine Will by allowing your Angels to guide you ultimately to the arms of **Almighty God**.

 God is trying to get your attention, have you noticed? Spend some **time** in reflection to moments in your life when you might recall where your Guardian Angel has helped you. Your perception of this special **time** may now be clearer to you, and this realization will ultimately lead you to a longing desire to become closer to **Almighty God**.

> Dear **God**, who is all good and merciful, send **Your Holy Spirit** to touch the hearts of **Your** faithful. Bestow on **Your** faithful discernment to help others to trust in **Your** infinite mercy.

CHAPTER 7

Recognizing Evil Has a Very Bad Behavior

It certainly is no secret; children are starving by the thousands every day somewhere in the world. I was appalled to learn that one in five children go hungry in America! This situation was a surprise to me personally, and is this a fact the faithful who love **God** are willing to accept? All over the world, these poor little ones are going hungry, and **God** must be wondering why we let this happen! All the while, you and I serve our families tonight with all kinds of wonderful and assorted food items. Anything we desire is waiting for us at the local supermarket minutes away from our homes. Society overall feels they are not to blame that these poor children go hungry today and tomorrow. This must face the truth because nothing significant ever seems to take place to improve this situation. I have heard people say, "These children are not our responsibility." Oh, but they are **God's** children and, therefore, our responsibility. While I type, children are crying for help, and few people are coming to their aid. **God** is crying great tears for these little ones, and not enough people seem to care anymore. Where is the love and compassion for these children? The lack of concern is overwhelming in my view. Why is our society still sitting back and waiting for someone else to help these children and their families? What is even more shameful is most people know that each year the need becomes greater. Still people continue to say, "After all, this is not my problem." This certainly is everyone's problem, and we all should be making a stronger effort to help people in need. People will say, "We have enough problems of our own." Others will insist, "We need to let someone else take care of the problem because those people are not our responsibility." Simply because these people are not next door does not mean we should not help them. People choose not to think about these issues because they silently hope the problem will just miraculously disappear. People in general do not want to get involved. Some will say, "It is too much work to get involved because people feel the supplies we send are not getting to the people who need it," and in some cases, this sadly true. I cannot understand why in our modern age governments cannot work together to feed their people. For all those cultures that deliberately refuse to feed their people, are you seriously ready to face **Almighty God** with your motives? What I hear generally is, "We can't help everybody." If we are not careful, **God's** children are going to face a humanitarian crisis on a global scale. Then Humanity will not be able to turn their hearts away because if we are not careful, the issue will be in our own homes.

In my opinion, people in general are losing sight of the purpose of their life. The evil one does not want you to recognize that you *are* important to **God**, and therefore, everyone has a significant purpose in life. Try to dwell more on your life's purpose, you would see yourself moving toward a higher objective, which is **God's** plan for you, and bad behavior is never part of this higher purpose. You need to ask yourself, what is my life's purpose? First, find the joy in your life! Look around you right now, and you will see joyfulness and a purpose in your life you may have overlooked. Your life's purpose does not always have to incorporate a professional career. It is not necessary for you to have an executive position in some big company. Primarily, the greatest purpose in your life is definitely to always first love **God** above all else and then honor **Him** by being the best person you can be! Then what **God** desires for you is that you retain your self-worth because your purpose is to love life fully, no matter what you choose to do, as long as it makes you and others around you happy. Perhaps you have an important role in someone's life, such as a live-in companion. Your purpose might be helping someone that is having a difficult **time** because they are living alone and need companionship. You may feel your life is mundane, but I assure you that if you would take a moment and think about your life, you would see how important you are to someone! Also without you realizing it, you may be fulfilling your life's purpose each day as long as what you are doing in for the greater good of others because this pleases **God**. It is amazing to me that few people ever realize that by your good example and a kind word, you might be helping a perfect stranger feel better about his or her self. If you are the mother of a sick child or your occupation is to care for the elderly in a nursing home, **God** sees your compassion displayed for someone else less fortunate. These are only a few examples, and no matter what you choose to accomplish in life, your purpose is valuable in any capacity.

If you are still looking for your purpose in life, here is a good example that I can personally suggest to you. Perhaps this may give you a starting point for you to realize just how important you are and how much **God** loves you. Did you ever think that your purpose in life is to announce to others how much **God** loves them! We are just like the first Apostils that **Jesus** chose to go and preach the "good news." **Jesus** expects us to go and do the same thing. New people are constantly entering our lives every day. There are a great many people who need to hear **God** loves them. What **God** does expect from us is to influence others with our good moral examples. Really if you think about it, many people today who travel all over the world think of the opportunities offered to those people to spread **God's** love. Some**times**, you need to say only a few words in order to get your point across. We have all lost opportunities every day to share **God's** love, and now Humanity needs to get busy and accomplish what our **Savior** expects of **His** people! We all need diligently to learn how to respect each other. We need to begin by having more patience and compassion for one another. Finally, it is essential for Humanity to remember that our life's purpose is to love one another as **Almighty God** has loved us!

God views our poor decisions and bad behavior as a simple concept that **His** children should remember we are here to help one another. **God's** children should realize that we are all brothers and sisters. We are all here on this earth to live in peace and harmony, not war and hatred. When **Jesus** walked the earth, **His** teachings were always simple concepts, such as loving and caring for one another. We need to ask ourselves, "What can I do to help someone in need?" and then ask yourself, "Did I do enough?" I personally must do more because you do not have to look far to find someone that needs something! I have to look myself in the mirror, and I do not want to see someone looking back that did not do enough to help others. No matter how small, everyone can do something! Has Humanity overall lost the will to care what happens to others? Is this how a selfish society acts when they do not include **God** in their life?

I wonder if the terrible storms we are experiencing across the country are tears from Heaven. **God** is watching us in disbelief what Humanity is doing and what we are all failing to do. **God** is trying to get our attention, and people are not listening to **Him**. While we are thinking about all of our own self-made problems, have we lost sight of what is truly important? People right in our own neighborhoods and communities are in desperate need of our help. People continue to feel this is not their concern. I hear people say they do not want to get *involved*. I realize it takes a lot of **time** and effort to get involved. The problem is we are all indirectly involved whether we like it or not. We all need to begin doing something for someone less fortunate. Then maybe next we can get involved outside of our communities. What America as a great nation can accomplish is enormous if we would only try a little harder to work together. No one in this world should ever go hungry. America was once known as, "The bread basket of the world." This is a travesty to continue allowing children to go hungry or anyone. America has the resources to feed the world! You see, no matter what you may believe, we are all going to answer to **God**. After witnessing the Angel, I can assure you of this truth. Therefore, when you are thinking of what you are going to serve for dinner tonight, perhaps you can think of someone you can begin helping. I will guarantee helping someone else will make you feel wonderful. Our **Father** who resides in Heaven is watching. **God** will never forget your kindness you demonstrate to others. I can assure you **God** does notice when you do any kind gesture for someone else. When we are good to someone, **God** is immensely pleased. **Jesus** said, **"What you do for the least of my brothers, you do for Me" (Matthew 24:40).** I guarantee a wonderful feeling of goodness will overpower you because this feeling is so gratifying you will automatically want to help others more often. **God** has placed these emotions in us from the very beginning of our life. I do not understand why some people have forgotten how good it feels to be kind to others. We need to have more consideration and patience toward others. Simply put, why do we feel at times we have no **time** to help others? What is wrong with this attitude? When will society ever learn that helping others is the basic reason we are here in the first place? Humanity is continually allowing terrible injustices to take place in the world. Perhaps I can do little by myself, but collectively, we can accomplish greatness when **God** is by our side. If enough good people, who say they really care, would get together, we could one by one change the deplorable conditions children and their parents experience every day.

We cannot continue to allow our impressionable children exposed to destructive immoral habits without dire consequences. Most of these conditions are within our control to stop. Often, people place their precious children in harm's way with improper supervision. If we would only learn to work together, we could put an end to the dangers that presently threatens the safety and well-being of our children. The situation that is accruing is becoming a ruthless problem all too often when our children cannot attend school in peace and harmony. Our society is allowing others who consumed with hatred that continue to place our children into dangerous situations. People feel helpless to stop this outrage, and I do understand why they feel this way. The problem is evident, the endless discussions and all the talk never lead to solving anything. This serious problem is despicable when our society continues to allow these atrocities to happen to their children. Unfortunately, some people in our society, for one reason or another, embrace evil and, therefore, have contempt for life. This is a simple fact; these people do not have **God** in their life, probably never did. Therefore, their hearts are black with hatred for another human being because they have overwhelmingly said yes to evil. The only answer is these people have turned their face completely away from **God**. These people have replaced goodness and love for the darkness of evil. These people are convinced that society has caused their unhappiness, and as a result, they feel they have a right somehow to make others as unhappy as they are. If God was in their life, it would be impossible for them to inflict the enormous pain and suffering on another human being. I myself am ashamed we cannot protect our children better than we do. This is an unsustainable situation, and we all have a responsibility to one another to put a stop to violence against *all* children. We must find a way to put an end to this outrage without further delay. Certainly, this is a moral issue within our society when people who are out of control commit unspeakable crimes against our children and others. It is imperative that we find solutions to these situations before more of our children become victims of the violent intentions of others!

I refuse to believe we cannot do better than we are doing. You must realize and understand our problems are not individual. Our dilemma is most of these problems belong to society in general, and therefore, we must strive to find solutions together. Certainly, the particular problem we face now regarding the safety of our children in schools is not simple to overcome. The problem is individuals who are disturbed and who cannot rationally decipher good thoughts from bad thoughts; one evil thought leads to other evil thoughts until the mind is corrupted. Now there is no room for any goodness to enter the mind because evil is in charge. We should all be working together, not arguing against one another. As I analyze this particular situation, we seem to be more interested in who has the better solution, but at the same **time**, we solve nothing. We tend to go round and round with the past, and we are not coming up with concrete solutions for the future. Is this why we never seem to agree or get anything meaningful accomplished? As a result, many problems continue to worsen until we finally have no alternative but to seek a solution. Even then, it seems to me the problem is people are in a constant dispute as to who is right and who is wrong. Does this really matter if the overall result is what is best for the good of our children? I see this as a series of missed connections. I always felt whenever I have a problem; I try to go back to the beginning of the problem and begin again in order to find a solution. This concept always seems to help me see the misconnection. The situation is we cannot solve anything when we wait for someone else to solve the problem. We need to realize our problems that exist collectively belong to everyone to insure the safety of our children.

What we need now is for everyone to be accountable and to take responsibility for the conditions and problems we are faced with and work together to find solutions. We must remind ourselves that due to our free will, only *we* hold the key to our happiness. **God** is waiting to see when **His** children intend to begin doing purposeful changes in their life, changes that are necessary to repair and improve our personal life. In addition, we face serious challenges nationally and all over the world. The people of America must unite and restore their pride and confidence in America because America is the greatest country on earth! I see a total transformation needed in order to uphold a country and a world under the direction and love of **Almighty God**.

Now might be the last opportunity for Humanity to restore peace in the world. America must show the world, by their example of goodness, under the direction of **Almighty God**, All cultures and all races must decide now how to coexist in our beautiful world.

God is trying to get our attention!

CHAPTER 8

Abortion: When Will Humanity Stop It?

One of the most prevalent crises that confront our society today is **Abortion**. The Angel referenced **this** repeatedly! This outrageous sin speaks volumes of the deliberate murder of **God's** magnificent creation. Where are the voices of those Christians who say they disapprove but then do nothing to demand it stop?

I always believed, as do many people, the creation of a new *life* is cause for great celebration. **God** saves us from ourselves! It is now more apparent than ever millions of people no longer know the difference between right and wrong. In the United States, there are approximately 3,700 babies in a single day aborted. How it is possible that so many people do not believe this atrocious event is a most grievous sin against **Almighty God**. It is simply unimaginable to me that the debate over **Abortion** goes on unresolved. I do not believe **God** will continue to observe what Humanity is allowing to happen to the precious unborn. Why are so many women finding it so easy to destroy the miracle of life? This is a travesty that their glorious bodies, created by **Almighty God**, become nothing more to them than a tool for **Abortion. "Do you not realize your body is the temple of the Holy Spirit, who is in you and who you received from God?" (Corinthians 6:19).** I will never accept the reality; the practice of **Abortion** does not seem to bother millions of people. Many of these women are so determined to honor their *right* to have an **Abortion** that they will even march in the streets to prove their point. Women will argue, "**Abortion** is their *right*." While these women believe this is their right, they have forgotten **God** gave them free will to choose right from wrong. **Abortion** is not a **God**-given right. **Abortion** is an abomination and a grievous sin against **Almighty God**. I will never understand why any women would contemplate killing their precious baby.

Yes, sadly, we do have a law that declares women have the *right* to commit murder! Reading this previous sentence again, it is unbelievable to me that this is a fact! However, this unjust law does not change the truth that **God's** sees **Abortion** as a calculated and cold-blooded murder of **His** innocent children. **God** gave every person free will in order to have the opportunity to accomplish great and wonderful things for **Him**. Why do these women choose to use their free will to destroy their precious babies? **Abortion** does not seem to bother many women in the slightest who have made this horrible decision. These women will have the opportunity someday to present their case over their *right* before **Almighty God**. **God** will sadly watch you destroy yourself, but you do not have the *right* to destroy another. I will never understand the total and callous attitude so many people profess about **Abortion**. Humanity cannot hide from the truth any longer. The truth is **Abortion** is murder, and there is no way around this truth. This is the most outrageous form of evil the world has sanctioned to date. There is no greater gift from **Almighty God** than the gift **of** a child Humanity will ever receive from their **Creator**. If this does not prove we have a sick society, I cannot think of anything else worse. The mere truth that we are allowing **Abortion** to continue shows we have no honorable intentions to the unborn. How can a loving society decide to love some children and not love all children? I will never understand how a mother could ever think of killing her child, much less complete this sinful and ugly task. To know we have a law that says this offense is perfectly acceptable is beyond my intelligent comprehension. To allow **Abortion** to become lawful in a civilized society, we are shouting loudly to **God** that the killing of **His** innocent babies is just another business day in America. Where is the justification in this evil deed? The guilt of **Abortion** has to be an enormous heavy burden for a mother after she realizes what she has done. How do women carry this guilt on their Soul? It must be hell on earth deliberately carried out with precision calculation.

Why is it always about the money? Big business and big money is what is controlling the purse strings. There are businesses getting rich off the killing of these precious babies. We are all to blame for allowing **Abortion** to continue to prosper. This proves how strong we have woven evil into the fabric of our society. The problem is there are women that believe they are justified because our laws that are in place allow them to have an **Abortion**. Well, this certainly is not **God's** justice. Have millions of people forgotten the Sixth Commandment, **"Thou shalt not kill."** It is evident that multitudes of people do not believe **Abortion** is appalling. They refuse to believe this is the most outrageous sin against **Almighty God**. Even Christian people will argue excuses that some**times Abortion** is all not right! **God** help them because they are in desperate need of **His** mercy. It is **time** for Humanity to wake up; you cannot hide from **God** forever! Evil fooled so many people into thinking they are right to think **Abortion** is a handy tool! I can only believe all those people by the choice of their decisions and the consequence of their deliberate actions against **Almighty God,** they are predestined to severe punishment from their **Creator**.

Where did the term **Abortion** originate? As near as I can determine, the word first appeared in 1540. In addition, I read that in the early 1920s, the word **Abortion** was taboo to mention aloud! I wonder do people give any thought to the fact that **Abortion** has been occurring really for centuries. How many babies can you count that have had their life destroyed because the mother changed her mind? We are also aware of the term *abort*. As found in any dictionary, the term *abort* means to terminate, cancel, or stop in midstream and to call off or end something. Condoning **Abortion,** how could this ever be a Christian concept? What are we teaching our children about the sanctity of life? We are teaching them that life no longer valuable in our society. How dare millions of people who call themselves Christians feel they are above **Almighty God**? How dare anyone end what **God** has begun? Is this why they call it pro-choice? Yes, how do they dare? Still millions of people feel comfortable with the cancelation of life known as **Abortion**. I want to warn all those people: do not dare continue to thrust this ghastly sin in **God's** face much longer. The Angel's first conversation to me was the word "**ABORTION**." The truth is we have all allowed **Abortion** to thrive is more than **God** can tolerate. Millions of our precious babies suffer this awful procedure called **Abortion**. To know we allow **Abortion** to continue without any compassion as to how the baby feels is unconscionable! This sounds similar to the practice of slaughtering pigs and cows. There is little compassion shown there either. However, we slaughter animals because this is our food sources and, therefore, this practice is acceptable.

I cannot stress enough what the Angel revealed to me is urgent. As **God's** children, we must all recognize the truth, "There is nothing left anyone could do worse too severely hurt **God** than what we have done with **Abortion**." Search your heart because the truth is waiting for you there. People will say they believe something should change, but then they do nothing on their own to support change. As Christians, we must stand together and stop **Abortion**; this is what we can all do. Please, I am begging you, we can stop **Abortion** if enough people would stop talking about it and get down to doing something to stop it. This is all about big business and big money, but we the people can change the law that allows the murder of our precious babies. We need to demand our leaders pass legislation to stop **Abortion** now before it is too late.

> Dear **God**, grant us Your grace to elect people in public office who, by their Faith in **You**, will not be afraid to do what is right. Grant us leaders with a pure heart who will not be afraid of his or her office to take a moral stance and put an end to **Abortion** forever!

Using this term **Abortion** in the same context when discussing a baby gives me a chilling feeling. This is very difficult to believe; intelligently, this term would be in the same sentence concerning the destruction of a baby. The name sounds horrible, but I think the name seems to fit the job description. Certainly, **Abortion** is nothing

I ever wanted to be involved with in any way. Yet we are all to blame because we are allowing **Abortion** to continue. What is even more shocking is everyone is very aware: **Abortion** now incorporates many shameful and shocking procedures. **God** gave us a creative mind, which evil has put to work for their evil purposes. As if **Abortion** was not gruesome enough, some have invented new ways to torture the innocent. No one can say you do not know what is going on. **God** sees what we are doing, and personally, I do not know why **He** has not punished us before now. I really do not know how much longer **God** will bear this killing of the innocent. I cannot believe there are so many companies who promote this heinous sin against **Almighty God** who is their **Creator**. Our own government condones **Abortion** and even helps promote **Abortion** with vast amounts of donated money in order to keep these death houses going. Is humanity losing their moral conscience? Yes, I feel Humanity has already lost their good conscience; otherwise, they would not be able to allow this to continue. Is it possible that this multitude of people have really lost their will to decipher the difference between right and wrong? "A woman has the *right* to choose!" Tell this to **God** if you dare! This crisis belongs to everyone.

The people of this great country should be shouting from the rooftops, "Stop this outrage." Humanity will answer to **God** for this most gravely barbaric sin. Humanity is responsible because everyone is aware what is happening and still no one is doing anything constructive to stop it. Society has a responsibility to the unborn to put this outrageous atrocity to an end. How this is possible that we, as an intelligent people, do not all believe **Abortion** is murder? Have so many people lost their capacity to see the truth? How was this so easy for evil to convince these people to destroy their Soul? The answer to this question is very clear! Countless people blinded by the truth are unaware of the fact; evil has done such a magnificent job of deceiving them. If allowed to continue, evil will manipulate everything they do in order to convince them to follow this deception. This is not difficult to understand the reality of this because far too many people are giving into this lie. Imagine how easy it is for evil to convince a woman that killing their unborn baby is an acceptable practice. Is this truly the final insult to **Almighty God**? What is even worse is that many can so easily justify the motive. What in heaven's name are we doing? Christians and believers alike believe **God** created us in **His** own image. At least I always thought Christians believed this truth. Where are these millions of voices for the unborn? Where are all the millions of Catholics who perceive they have strong morals and strong convictions? Where are all the voices of the pious Christians and **God**-fearing people who still attend their favorite place of worship? If all these people truly believed **God** created them in **His** image, then how do millions find this atrocity so easy to accept? Why are we allowing the destruction of human life that is **God's** greatest creation as unwanted garbage?

Late Term Abortion. The sound of this term makes me ill to write it. The awesome miracle of life given to us by our loving **Father Almighty God** in heaven and so many of **His** children discard this miracle with absolute distain. I cannot believe **God** has not severely punished us before now. Without knowing it, people have created for themselves their own hell right here on earth. I thought doctors signed a Hippocratic Oath to save lives whenever possible. Society is painfully aware there are professionals who have the audacity to call themselves professional doctors and nurses who with regularity carry out these **Abortions**. How can they live with themselves after killing a crying baby and then throwing the aftermath into the trash or worse? Who takes out the discarded baby parts, if not already sold for profit, to the trash? Are the cleaning people responsible to clean up the aftermath in the rooms? Are the doctors and the nurses sharing the duty in tidying up the rooms so they will be ready for the next victim? Certainly, the mother does not undertake this ugly job because her sinful deed is over.

Nothing anyone could say about the unjust law that would make it honorable. If doctors and nurses refused to do **Abortions**, then most **Abortions** would begin to cease. Yes, I know all the arguments regarding **Abortions**. People say **Abortions** would continue in the back alleys and women would be at risk. I have heard all the arguments. Therefore, the practice of killing approximately 3,700 babies a day in this country alone is to protect women from the harm of unscrupulous people? Killing a baby is murder, and as a society who professes to have honor should know better. First, whose fault is it that multitudes of women decide to do away with their baby in the first place? How easy it is to justify **Abortion** is not a sin and a severe and direct offence to **Almighty God**. It is an evil deception that **Abortion** is not wrong. Wanting to satisfy your belief that what is taken place is all right will not change the truth because it just is not a normal practice to desire the killing of your baby. **Abortion** is an abnormal condition and the gravest sin against **Almighty God**. No discussions in the world in favor of **Abortion** will ever change the truth that **Abortion** is a barbaric habit, and I know firsthand from the Angel that **God** will not continue to tolerate our sinful nature much longer. This is the ultimate truth!

By the power of the **Holy Spirit** through the Angel, I am compelled to repeat: **Abortion** is murder of the innocent and always will be unbearable for **Almighty God** to witness! There are no words to describe the pain and anguish that the **Almighty God** is suffering. Multitudes of women force **God** to witness these ghastly procedures every day. Countless people have chosen to use their wonderful creative minds for this hideous activity. Humanity is literally rubbing **Abortion** and all its evil forms into **God's** face and saying to **Him**, "**You** have given **Your** people of the world free will, and therefore, **Your** people will do as they wish." After all, **God** did give us free will to do as we please; therefore, it is a certainty, **Abortion** pleases millions greatly!

> Dear **God**, forgive the people who continue to force **You** to observe this destructive evil while they use the dear precious baby's body parts for personal monetary gain.

I must express here strongly that I do not know how it is possible for our dear **Lord** to watch what terrible sins **His** people commit and with little remorse. When individuals and even professionals cease to feel any compassion for the torture they are inflicting on an innocent baby they are aborting, they can never again call themselves civilized.

I will never, never accept why we continue to allow this practice of **Abortion** to continue and then say we care about anything! It is an absolute truth that until we put an end to **Abortion**, we as a society cannot begin to heal. We must put an end to **Abortion**; it is **God's** will. **God** will end this atrocity if we continue to do nothing. I will never forget the look of sadness by the Angel when I received confirmation from the Angel that **Abortion** must end! I am very afraid for people that remain blinded by the truth. This is the easy way out for so many women who refuse to face the responsibility of their actions. Pregnancy is not a decussating condition that you can decide to terminate at will. Therefore, society as a whole is suffering in silence because so many have turned their back on the truth. If Humanity cannot protect the unborn children, then **God's** people will never be able to protect the living children either in the future. Eventually, it only means our children will be doomed at the hands of Humanity! Our precious children are certainly doomed to a **God**less society with no remorse, a society who does not believe in **God**! Is this where we are heading?

The scenes the Angel showed me included horrible conditions that do involve the future children of the world. This horrified me very much because this was very disturbing to face the truth that could become a reality. I am beginning to understand more as certain conditions in the world transpire. It is very difficult for many people to watch all the craziness that goes on in our country as well as around the world. All of a sudden, there seems to be an acceleration of confusion over finding solutions for any issue. Society is finding it more difficult to agree on anything in order to solve even the smallest issues. It is obvious people are more comfortable these days to become judge and jury over any issue even if their information is not factual. Therefore, in the future, will it still be possible that Humanity has learned nothing? I cannot imagine how this is possible that our society and the world could get much worse. However, it is my belief we have already gone over the "moral cliff." I guess anything is possible with a society that no longer cares what happens to their children. Most people will not allow themselves drawn into the debate over **Abortion** because they feel it does not directly involve them. Sure, many good people in the world care a great deal about this moral crisis. Certainly, a great many people would help someone else in a minute.

The subject of **Abortion** does not surface often because our attention is distracted to something else the media deem more interesting and more noteworthy. **Abortion** does not give very good ratings! Thankfully, some people are relieved because they do not want the media to remind them about anything pertaining to **Abortion**. The problem is all these issues require immediate action from everyone, not from only a select few. We must put an end to these horrible and hideous conditions if we are to continue to call ourselves a normal healthy society. I repeat, **Abortion** is not a normal condition. **God's** people cannot continue to hide from the truth; **Abortion** is abnormal and immorally evil. If we all do not put an end to **Abortion**, I promise you, **Almighty God** definitely will. **God** will step in and stop the killing of **His** precious children in a way we will all understand. Do not be fooled because the mighty hand of **God** is ready to punish us. We deserve our punishment from **God** if we do not stop **Abortions. "Vengeance is Mine,** says the **Lord" (Romans 12:19).**

Why do good people continue to allow evil to enter their lives every day? Evil is simply bad behavior that enjoys watching you do evil deeds. Evil has no conscience, but you do! Evil has a definite agenda. The agenda is the ultimate destruction of Humanity. Evil will not settle for anything less than our Soul! No matter what it takes, evil will do everything and anything that is necessary to achieve this ultimate goal. Until you remember the truth, evil will continue to deceive you. These conditions are very problematic because not facing the truth will cause us to make unhealthy decisions. We alone are allowing this condition to exist. Evil finds our human weakness so easy to surpass. Together, we can crush the foot of the evil one and put an end to **Abortion**. We can accomplish anything for the love of **God**. **God** will stand with us against the worst of evil if we trust in **Him** and ask **Him** for **His** help. There is no power in hell that can defeat **God's** mighty hand. Evil has a strong foothold now, but evil is worried we might really wake up and call upon **God** for **His** help. If everyone were to call upon **God**, evil would disappear, and peace and harmony would prevail in the world. Imagine if you can, what is possible because with **Almighty God** beside us, anything and everything is possible. **"For God everything is possible" (Matthew 19:26).**

What you will read next, I felt compelled to write with the help of the Angel in order to defend the unborn with a conversation that I really feel does take place. When the Angel spoke about **Abortion**, my heart broke because I realized and I understood the awful implications. It would be in our human nature to find this difficult to read. I must admit I wrote this short piece for this exact purpose. What I wrote really cuts deep to the heart of the consequence of **Abortion. Abortion** must end.

I pray soon this nightmare will be over and we may never have to hear the word Abortion ever again!

The following is a conversation between **God**, the expectant mother, and a baby whom **God** created only 115 days before. **Almighty God**, who is our **Creator**, carefully placed this precious baby in the mother's womb because there the baby would be safe from all harm.

Here is how it began on an ordinary day.

A Guardian Angel was already with the baby in the mother's womb. However, the baby began to cry uncontrollably. The Angel called on **God** for **His** help. **God** heard the small cries coming from the very tiny voice. The baby was still so small; however, most of the main organs were already developed, and there were even fingernails evident on the tiny baby's hands. When **God** heard the tiny cries that were coming from this "oh, so small, innocent" baby, **He** was very disturbed indeed. Listening to the baby cry, **God** was very saddened beyond our comprehension. The baby would not stop crying, and this caused the baby to be in great distress. While **God** listened to the terrible cries coming from this tiny voice, **He** looked into the Soul of the mother. The mother's Soul was already showing signs; evil was consuming her Soul with darkness and ugly thoughts. **God** was inconsolable, not only for the baby but for the mother too. **God** was saddened because **He** knew why the baby crying. **God** heard the trembling soft whisper that continued to came from the womb of the mother. **God** cradled the baby and proceeded to console the baby. **God** examined the baby to make sure everything was all right and found nothing wrong with the baby's development. **God** looked at the total perfection of **His** creation, and **He** was exceedingly pleased. Every aspect of the pregnancy seemed to be right on schedule. There were no immediate dangers to the baby or the mother.

    God already knew what was going to happen, and sadly, because **He** gave the mother free will, **God** did not interfere. **God** took the baby's Soul into **His** arms far away from the evil that was about to happen. The mother's Guardian Angel tried everything previously to get the mother to listen to reason but failed. The Angel felt helpless, so **God** instructed the Angel to turn away. **God**, on the other hand, forced to watch in horror, fell to the depth of **His** sacred continence.

    Life is the greatest creation and precious gift our **Creator** will ever give to the human race. All the people in the room were prepared and could hardly wait in the anticipation of the excellence of the procedure. Everyone who was involved in this heinous procedure seemed to be exceedingly pleased with his or her accomplishment. The mother was relieved she would not have the burden of the baby. The doctors were happy to receive their money for the evil deed. No one in the room gave the baby a thought or any mercy who, by now, comingled with the garbage. The baby's body parts tossed carelessly with the other unwanted trash forgotten but not by **God**. Millions will say, "What's the problem?" I am running out of words to describe **Abortion**, and truthfully, **God** is running out of patience! Beware, **God** will not condone the killing of **His** precious babies!

The following is the disturbing details of the destruction of an unwanted baby:

GOD: "Do not cry my sweet little bundle of joy."
BABY: "Dear **God**, I am frightened. Something is wrong. I am very afraid. Is something bad going to happen to me? Please stay

with me because I see a black shadow coming toward me and I am very afraid of it now."

GOD: "Do not fear anything, my dear little one. I will never leave you. Place your hand in my hand. Do you feel my hand now? I will never leave you alone. You are my precious delight, whom I am very pleased. I am right here with you. I love you very much. You are my magnificent creation. You are so beautiful that the stars pale in comparison to you."

BABY: "I love you. I know you created me, so I would make others happy. Mommy, I sense you have been very upset over something since **God** created me for you. **God** created me because **God** was sure you needed me. What has changed? **God** created me in **His** own image. I am perfect right down to my tiny fingernails and my tiny pink toes. I will resemble you in many ways, but I cannot grow strong and healthy without your protection. I love you, and I need you, Mommy."

MOTHER: "I am afraid I made a big mistake. I do not want to ruin my figure, and I do not want to carry you for nine months in my body. There is no room for a baby in my life because I will not have **time** for you. Allowing you to grow in my body was a stupid decision, and now I must get rid of you."

BABY: "I was not a mistake! **God** does not make mistakes! **God** picked you to be my mommy, and this was no mistake. **God** hoped you would cherish every moment with me. **God** was sure you would love me. I am the greatest gift **God** could ever give you, Mommy. I am a grand miracle directly from the hand of **God**."

MOTHER: "I am confused and unhappy. Having you in my life would be too much work. I would lose my freedom caring for you. I do not know how to be a mother. I am not interested in you because you would clog up my schedule. I feel nothing for you."

BABY: "**God** told me **He** would teach you all you need to know, and **God** told me **He** would send others who will help you."

MOTHER: "I have made up my mind. I do not want you! I am not sorry. In fact, I really do not know why I am bothering with you at all because you are nothing important to me."

I SEE AN ANGEL

BABY: "Mommy, please give me a chance to live. You will be proud of me. If you let me live, there is a great chance I could make a big difference in the world. I might be a doctor and save many lives. I might be a scientist and discover an important cure that could improve the health of many people in the world. I might be a priest and save many Souls for **God**. I might even become a great leader who will stop wars. I might become a real good parent someday who will bring other children into the world to love **God**. I would be someone who you could learn to love more than yourself. One truth is for sure, I will be uniquely me who **Almighty God** created to be perfect in **His** eyes. **God** told me **He** would bless you immensely if you do not kill me. I am begging you, please give me a chance to live, Mommy. **God** said you would feel differently after I am born. I will be a good person, and I promise I will not be any burden to you."

MOTHER: "I do not want to think about you anymore. I will not listen to your voice. I am finished, and I have decided to destroy any evidence of you as soon as I can. The people who will assist me in killing you say **Abortion** is quick and easy. I will forget you and get on with the great life I have created for myself."

BABY: "Are you sure, Mommy, you will forget me? You will destroy the best part of yourself that **God** also created in **His** own image. Mommy, when you and others kill me, **will it hurt**?"

MOTHER: Silence

After the **Abortion** was finished, **God** told the innocent baby, "Do not be afraid, my child. You are safe with me now for all eternity. Those who have cast you out will answer severely to me. They will answer to me alone! Come to me, my sweet little innocent child. I love you dearly. I have prepared a special place for you. There you will be by my side and reside in my **Sacred Heart** forever."

Here are just two scriptures that I recommend you read regarding **Jesus** and the children! Please read these scriptures and include them in your prayer to **Jesus**.

Jesus said, "So it is not the will of your Father who is in Heaven that one of these little ones perish." Jesus also said, "See that you do not despise one of these little ones, for I say to you that their angels in heaven continually see the face of My Father who is in Heaven" (Matthew 18:10).

My prayer to God to end Abortion!

Merciful **God**, **You** hear the prayers of **Your** faithful. Unfortunately, many of **Your** people have lost their way and are struggling to find meaning in their life again. Dear **God**, I am sorrowfully sorry, our words and our actions do not prove to **You** we love **You**. **Your** Angel, who appeared to me, was adamantly clear when she repeatedly conveyed her serious concern over the immense Sin enveloping the world. We, **Your** people, truly do not want to be lost without **Your** love and mercy. I implore **You**, my **God**, grant **Your** people the grace to see that the severe Sin of **Abortion** must end! I promise to **You**, I personally will not rest until Humanity finally puts an end to **Abortion**. Grant us **Your** Grace to see the truth in all things. I trust in **Your** mercy and **Your** love for all the people of the world. I implore **You**, dear **Lord**, come to our assistance now in this horrifying crisis. In this I pray, Amen.

CHAPTER 9

Confusion Is Denial over Sin in the Modern World

When I am praying and meditating on the power of **Almighty God**, my prayers are a reminder to me how much **God** loves us. To realize that **God** would allow me to see **His** lovely Angel is almost more than I can contemplate fully. The immense wonder of the event is undeniably overwhelming for me to grasp. This is a true humbling experience to know **God** did choose me to receive a message from **His** heavenly Angel. **God** chose me at this precise **time** in my life because **He** knew I was prepared to undertake such a task. I always believed that **God** never does anything without **His** Divine Will. **God's** children are not supposed to question **God's** motives. **God's** intentions are always what are best for us. **God** knows why **He** chose me, and I pray that I will prove to **Him** I am worthy. The most important aspect of the entire event, of course, is the message. **God** merely chose me to convey the message to you. I am confident that my faith and trust in **God** will strengthen me with the knowledge to know what I need to do to accomplish my mission. I pray I will hear the **Holy Spirit** speaking to me so I may help others to see **God's** overwhelming love for them.

Dear **God,** I pray whatever **Your** children do, it will be in harmony with **Your** Divine Will. I personally promise **You** that I will do everything I can to help others understand the message so they will find peace in their hearts. I am content with the truth that **You** are near to everyone who loves **You**.

We are living in a world where Sin is almost nonexistent in our present society. This generation now faces a crisis of hatred, confusion, and denial over everything that is good! **God** is waiting for Humanity to ask for **His** love and friendship. **God's** children are not alone! You must place all your trust in **God** because **God** will never leave one of **His** people alone no matter what happens. You need to believe and have unwavering faith in **God's** mercy. You need to run to the safety of **God's** loving arms. **God's** children need to acknowledge to **Him** that we have severely wounded **His Sacred Heart**. Humanity needs to acknowledge to **God** that we are sorrowfully sorry for offending **Him**. It is our continued indigent attitude toward **God** that needs to cease! **God** knows we are in desperate need of peace in the world. Peace will never exist without **Almighty God**. Many people do not realize their spirit has been broken through the power of Sin. You need food to sustain your life and be healthy. You also need to feed your spirit with the Word of **God** to have a healthy mind. You need desperately to embrace often the principles found in the Bible in order to renew and mend your broken spirit. What you really need to do is go back to a church or your place of worship! It is problematic to me, people are not attending church on a regular basis; yet on Easter Sunday, people will put on their best attire and fill the churches! While **God** is pleased they are there, where are these people the rest of the year? You need to attend a church and study the Bible in order to nourish and feed your very Soul. You need to belong to a church or house of worship on a regular basis where you can gather together with your fellow Christians to honor and praise **God**!

Every **time** I reread some passage in the Bible, I rediscover something marvelous I may not have understood before. How wonderful is **God's** plan when **He** prompted the Apostles to write the Bible. Without the Bible, we would have little knowledge of what took place during the **time** of **Jesus**. The Bible is the most amazing book ever written! When I read the Bible, I feel so wonderful because the Bible does nourish my mind. If you are not accustomed to reading the Bible, you can always begin by opening the Bible to any page and read just that one page. You will be amazed how much **God's** Word will inspire you. The Psalms also contain beautiful phrases that will penetrate your very soul. I promise you reading the Bible will change your life. You will feel the power of the **Holy Spirit** teaching you what you need to know in order to have a happier life. The Bible is available to everyone as a wonderful reference point. There among those beautiful and awesome inspiring pages you can find the answers to so many truths related to **God**. The Bible is our Christian heritage and our cornerstone of the complete truth! If you desire to have a friendship with **God**, begin by reading the Bible. You will be amazed what you will encounter there. Perhaps some people are afraid to read the Bible because reading **God's** words will remind them that **He** expects them to do better. **God** knows it is not easy to face areas of your life where you should have done better. Surely, we can all agree it is never easy to face our mistakes. **God** is asking each of us to face what is wrong so we all can begin again to make all things right. While reading the Bible, you will realize that **God** is asking you to experience the power of **His** love for you. You will never experience peace of mind until you face the truth that is waiting among the pages of the Bible. Meditate on **God's** mighty words. Allow **God's** words to speak to you. These marvelous words of hope and inspiration will lead you down the path to **God**. When you find yourself stressed to the limit, with any situation, turn to the Bible and pray with all your heart. **God** does answer your prayers, even though you may not have noticed lately.

Now is a perfect opportunity to explore the Bible, to discover your "life verse."

The Bible is your guide in the everyday life of a Christian. Surprisingly enough, many Christians do not know what a life verse is. A life verse is a verse from the Bible that you choose to be your favorite verse. It is a verse you commit to memory in order to inspire others. It is a verse that most inspires you. It is important to pick a Bible verse that speaks to you directly! It also may not be easy to choose just one. Here are just a few examples:

> "And this is a promise He made to us; eternal life" (John 2:25).
>
> "Cast all your worries on Him because He cares for you" (1 Peter 5:7).
>
> "Do not be overcome by evil, but overcome evil with good" (Romans 12:21).
>
> "In his mind, a man plans his course, but the Lord directs his steps" (Proverbs 16:9).
>
> "You are the light of the world, let your light shine before men" (Matthew 5:14–16).
>
> "Be watchful, stand firm in your faith, be courageous, be strong" (1 Corinthians 16:13).

With all my faults and failures and my imperfections that I find within me, surely, I did not fit into the proper "category" of someone who I thought **God** would ever allow them to see an Angel. Amazing how **God** sees us so differently than we see ourselves. Often, we can be so tough on ourselves and then, at the same **time**, not be tough enough. I realize reaching a happy medium between the two is difficult. Therefore, I feel this word *category* is a word that some people have placed on his or himself in order to see what it is they do deserve or do not deserve. After all, most of us feel we have tried and have done our best to be good individuals. Most people do believe they are good Christians. There can be no doubt; there could always be room for improvement. We are quick to judge, and we are even quicker to ask **God** for **His** help when there is something we want or need. Our wants and needs do not always meet the expectations of what **God** desires for us.

In our present society, most people feel they do fit pretty strongly into a position that society as a whole seems to be pleased. There is a desire for a number of people to do what everyone else is doing because it just seems easier to follow the crowd. As a result, these people will remark, what is the problem? You see, today, many people have a different concept generally as to what is bad behavior. Why does it seem to me, years ago, people acted as if they had a better handle on good and evil? What has changed? Growing up, everything in the world seemed so different. I feel strongly that the past generations, in general, viewed Sin differently than people do today. Today, our society seems to view Sin as if Sin is a foreign entity. Society overall feels that most of our so-called sins are nonexistent today. It is so easy to justify the very thought of the word *sin* in today's moral compass. In addition, our modern culture chooses new contemporary names for all their faults and failures. Some of these names begin with the one letter *I*. "I deserve this, and I deserve that, and so on." Clearly, many people now have justification for all the things that once they called sins. Those were old ideas! This logic allows people to feel better about their feel-good society. Society has become so falsely proud; therefore, their conscience is clear from fault. This is a simple fact why people feel they have been so ingenious with their new fresh look at their indiscretions. This makes all the difference in the world because these people now feel more secure because they belong to this new modern society. This new and modern world measures sin in a "superior" way. Boldly, people continue to tell themselves that even **God** will understand because **His** people have moved into a new era of choice. Our current generation would prefer to call this new idea "New Age." Truly, people must believe this, or this new era of choice would not fit in with the plans this generation of people have made for themselves, would it? Society is becoming a population of selfish people who decide for themselves what is best and rarely do they worry about someone else. We are now witnessing free will of the mind that society takes to a completely new level. Is this why Humanity has decided they no longer need **God**? I am sure the people of this new age environment would say they never felt this way and what I just wrote is not true. Actions speak louder than words! These free thinkers blinded by their way of life, their souls cannot be open to love **God**. Therefore, for the present, they are refusing to allow **God** into their life, which is causing such a moral dilemma in the world. As a result, these people have determined what they contend is satisfactory or acceptable now. In reality it is a falsehood they enjoy. This new and improved way of life preferred by our society today is not working out well. **Time** ticks slowly away while you are asleep. The opportunities presented by **God** today go unused and discarded because society today does not recognize the opportunity as valuable or beneficial. These are the people that they have become superior and more capable than ever before to decide what is best for them and what is best for their families. If this is true, then why is this new era of choice not working out for them? Our chosen lifestyles are not working for our society overall because this new age of choice does not include **God**!

It is more evident than ever before our present society now truly believes they are very capable of making bolder choices and decisions and they do not need **God** to do it. The proof is this generation feels everything seems to be working out fine for them. However, is it really working out the way **God** desires your life to be? This generation is more determined with their choices that they are making regarding their moral conduct. What about some of the programs today that our society overall considers fun and entertaining? Some of the programs that parents allow their children to watch are adversely affecting their attitude, and in the future, it will directly affect their belief system about life. The worst part is what parents are teaching their children, and what they see on television is a detriment to their mental health especially in the formative years. These false narratives teach these children that they are supposed to live their own life in the same way they see on the television. Many parents are presenting to their children false idealism as to what real life is all about. Most of the programs on television that were supposed to instill good ideals in our children's minds are now a direct offence to family values and the family unity overall. We allowed our family unit to die a slow death over the years. Now I fear it is possible the wonderful family unit we all once shared will never again exist in our present society. We are continually destroying the fabric lining of the "family" that most people once cherished and respected. This generation no longer agrees their family unit is important anymore. Everyone in the family is busy doing whatever each enjoys doing, and as a result, most of the **time**, the family is separated by their particular interests. I do not see this as sharing family values. In many cases today, what children continue to view on television and the video games that they play lead them to believe hurting someone is funny. I rarely see anything anymore I can really say is comical. The awful truth, of course, most of these programs and the strong aggressive video games are affecting the impressionable minds of these young children forever. I am afraid for the future of our children because they are learning with these games to kill people and attack who they think is the enemy as fast as possible because they earn more points and, therefore, win the game. Does this sound familiar to what is going on today in our schools? These games are more aggressive all the **time** and simply form an abundance of hatred and violence in the mind of an individual, especially in someone who might already harbor these tendencies. I am not alone when I say that what these children and our young adults believe today regarding life and relationships is a twisted form of the truth. I am fearful our children will believe what they see on programs and in video games that constantly twists the truth about life. I am saddened our children no longer have the proper role models in their life that my children once enjoyed. Far too many parents are teaching their young impressionable children by their own example that anything goes and what they are allowing their children to watch is even better even if it is not true. This generation is relaxed and more content with their new rules because they have changed or modified the rules too suit themselves. Our present society believes this will make them happier and life will be easier without all those strict guidelines. We are changing the rules and moral guidelines we once honored in society right into the trash along with the unborn.

What the discipline of generations of the past once respected, especially where the church is concerned, is no longer important to a multitude of people. Some say the church is old-fashioned and needs to catch up with the modern world. What have we done that has caused multitudes of people to feel this way? Without realizing it, society has bent the rules significantly enough to suit their modern needs in the modern world. People will verbalize, "What is wrong with the way I feel or how I need to live?" Others feel they must be living their life properly because they agree and feel the same way with this analogy. They can now finally justify to themselves that the older ways do not really matter very much anymore because it only proves that the older generation was simply out of touch. **God's** children have become so used to bending the rules or stretching the truth, they have lost sight completely of what it was they used to hold so dear. What used to be so important to us in not only our personal life but also what was important to us as a nation is slowly disappearing. We have divided ourselves in so many parts, no wonder so many people are in a state of confusion. A large number of people no longer recognize the true reason for their very existence. Is it possible large portions of Humanity have lost their purpose in life altogether? Is this why people do not have the will to regain a purpose or do not have the desire to have a meaningful purpose in their life? It is my belief that the Soul is fearful it will never see the face of **God** again if we do not secure our life's purpose.

Now is the **time** to wake up for our children's sake and for the sake of the entire world. We must face the truth that our society has abandoned their youth! We are wasting precious **time** while we leave our youth to a society that is in a state of confusion over the truth and cannot seem to agree that we need solutions not more talk. When are we going to wake up and see the **time** for real change is HERE? **Time** is fast approaching the tipping point. If we are ever going to see the truth for what it really is and start doing something about protecting all the children, the **time** is NOW. We have been given the stewardship of the world by **Almighty God**, and this includes being responsible for what happens to our children that was a magnificent gift from our **Creator**.

In general, we certainly are not doing very well as a nation either because for most, greed and the influence of power is their **God**. What kind of heritage will we leave for our children? Does anyone really care anymore about the future? Even the national debt in our country does not seem to worry our present leaders anymore. I cannot believe this constant arguing and bickering that continues between our leaders seems to continue endlessly. This condition is a sad state of affairs when intellectual men and women are not getting anything constructively accomplished. I cannot understand why someone will not concede; our debates are not leading us to improving anything. The course of action for our future our society is presently taking does not look very promising to me. The Angel indicated this to me by not only her words but also her expressed concern that Humanity needs to consider very carefully. Doing nothing simply does not make any intelligent sense to the average person, yet everything continues to go on in utter confusion and nonsense. I really do not want to be pessimistic, but I really cannot see the light at the end of the tunnel right now. Good people all over the world need to continue to hope and pray that we can begin to improve the world, but we need to elect the right leaders who will really help us make a difference. I wish someone would point out to me where I am wrong. We need to say to our leaders, "Enough! Now is the **time** to stop acting like spoiled children and make this great nation of ours great again." The world is watching and waiting for America, under the direction of **Almighty God**, to lead the way to prosperity again. The world and all its struggles should be looking for a way, under the direction **God**, to have peace. When will this peace begin? Peace begins with you and me first! **God's** children must begin to be kind and patient with one another. America needs to show the world, under the direction of **Almighty God**, we will have peace. The world is looking for America to be the shining example to the rest of the world. The world is watching everything America does and so is **Almighty God**. When is Humanity going to face the truth about this terrible evil that **God's** people have allowed to strengthen by our weakness and indifference to sin? Sin is about to overflow the entire world with its hatred and wars. If you believe in **God**, then you cannot hide from the truth that **God** has already placed on your heart.

If you do not believe in God, I pray God will grant you His love and mercy to see the truth.

Let us explore further what really is meant by Sin in our modern world. What has changed that so many people feel; what they considered a Sin in years past appears to be fading away with **time** itself. It seems to be so easy now for Humanity to turn their back on the starving children of this mighty world. What must **God** be thinking about a society that does not care in the slightest over the many injustices found easily in every part of this world? What about religious freedom that many take for granted? Religious freedom is under attack all around the world. Religion is a **God**-given right that is now under tremendous scrutiny. It seems to me, and I am sure to a great many Christians will also agree, nothing good is going to survive if we do not take a stand on what is truly correct instead of what is politically correct. Humanity is being fooled into believing what is truly important now is how we judge someone by their name or how to properly name a culture so as to not offend anyone. We are spending our precious **time** on turning and twisting everything around to suit someone else while we are not spending enough **time** on what would truly make **God** happy. We are so into what might offend someone instead of caring what it is that Humanity is doing to offend **Almighty God**! We are on a path of destruction, and very little is being done to stop it. When one in five children are going hungry in this country, it is **time** to face the fact that we have a problem. No child should go hungry in this country, and personally, everyone should be ashamed to know this is true. We must stop the hunger for greed and power in this world if we intend to have a world in the future. Yes, Sin in the modern world is alive and thriving like never before, and what is truly sad is **God** has already given **His** children the power to stop what has been set in motion and we sit back and continue to do nothing!

    Here is the basic order of the life of a Sin. In order to commit a Sin, a Sin must contain three parts, and all three parts must be in place in order for anything to become a Sin. Definition of a Sin taken from my own personal Catholic Bible:

This is a free and deliberate transgression against **Almighty God**.
This is any act where our will is directly opposed to the Divine Will.

The three parts are as follows: (1) you have to know it is a Sin; (2) you have to want to Sin anyway; (3) finally, once you have committed the Sin, you then have completed all three parts.

This does not seem fair to **God** or the Angel when we force them to watch because **God** and certainly not your Angel can do nothing to stop us from committing any Sin. This is strictly your freewill decision and mine completely.

Humanity needs to face the truth that our so-called modern world is in deep trouble. Will someone please take charge and do something constructive for heaven's sake! Before we go too far, our society must collectively begin to take a stand on something, anything. It seems to me we are running in circles and accomplishing nothing that would improve our present state of affairs. We are physically moving but accomplishing absolutely very little. When are we going to accomplish something worthwhile with the decisions so many of our leaders are choosing to establish? What is wrong with this analogy? Why is it so difficult to improve society? **God** gave all **His** people free will, and **He** will not interfere with our choices and bad decisions. **God** will attempt in loving ways to let everyone know we are not on the right track. Far too many people are not listening to **God** anymore. **God** is waiting for us to ask for **His** help. Why is it people generally feel there is nothing they can do to change anything? Why do is it people continue to feel helpless? Are people feeling defeated that their opinions on important matters do not count anymore so they give up? I wonder who had a hand in that attitude! The modern indigent attitude in the world is not working for us anymore. **God** views our world so differently than we see it. **God** observes what should have been so evident to us from the very beginning. We are all still capable of greatness. There is still hope! Why is it we do not realize the effect of our decisions the same way **God** does? **God** is patiently waiting for us to wake up and see the ruin and misery we have all created for ourselves.

My direct impression, while in the presence of the Angel, there would be unequivocal consequences for our actions! In **God's time**, it is never too late to say the name of **Jesus** and sincerely mean what you are saying! Praise **God**, **He** will not forget **His** people who love

Him and who follow **His** Commandments. **God's** faithful and beloved people must continue to be steadfast in their convictions and trust in **God's** mercy. No matter what happens, you must believe **God** will be with us always.

> Dear **God,** I pray that **You** will continue to shine **Your** light on the world so **Your** people will once more begin to see the truth that is ever before them. Dear **God**, **Your** people need **You** now more than ever before. Grant **Your** children the wisdom to do only **Your** will to end **Abortion** and all things that are not pleasing to **You** so we may have hope and peace in the world.

Do you hear **God** calling you? **God** is trying to get your attention; **He** loves you dearly.

CHAPTER 10

Our Indigent Attitudes toward Almighty God

What must **God** think about all turmoil and unrest **His** people have created down here on earth? Certainly, our decisions regarding our environment are having a detrimental impact on us. Our oceans are warming, and our air quality is having negative effects on our entire world. **God's** children have managed to create many perplexing conditions throughout the world that certainly is affecting all Humanity. There is an abundance of issues, but Humanity has a tendency of avoiding the enviable until and only if forced into doing something about it.

To say that our actions in most every facet of our life have displeased **God** greatly is an understatement! **God's** people have displeased **Him** with their poor decisions that they continue to display every minute of the day. This is why Humanity finds themselves confronted daily with a very clever and determined evil. This evil is present in all aspects of our life because of our predictable behavior. People in our society today have changed their ideals of the factual truth for falsehoods of the truth. We are confused people that no longer see the difference between the truth and a non-truth. The lifestyles many people have chosen for themselves have become so gratifying to many but not to **God**. If we could only really see how much Humanity is offending **God**, deeply and in such a severe way, many people would cease to be able to speak! **God's** very tears have become like a stain over the earth. I am worried the stain of our sins against **God** have become so great, **God** will decide now is the **time** to bring **His** mighty hand down on us with a great punishment. Is it possible our sins have become so enormous that, without **God's** forgiveness, our sins will be more difficult now to wash away than when we during our baptism? Christians identify with the significance of their baptism. Have we forgotten your Baptismal promises? Do you reject Satan and all his works? We must ask **Almighty God** for forgiveness now. Only then will it ever be possible for our sins now cleansed from sin because of the blood of **Christ**. If Humanity does not show **God** we can do better, we may find ourselves swallowed up in the quagmire of our sins. **God's** people do not need a blueprint to know what clearly needs to change. We should feel the ultimate shame that so many of us have conducted ourselves so badly right in front of **God**. Where is the satisfaction in this shameful behavior? Now that I have witnessed this Angel, I want you to believe that **God** and **His** Angels are watching us and waiting to see what we are all going to do to improve our lives. How long do you expect **God** to put up with our present behavior toward **Him**? How long will **God** wait for us to wake up and remember the truth? The Angel spoke about truth as one of the most important aspects of our life. This concept of truth has left our present society. Really, how many care about the importance of truth or sin? Remember it is our example good, bad, or indifferent that people observe.

If you search your heart, most everyone will agree we have all offended **God** in countless ways. We are all sinners, no one but **Jesus** is perfect. I believed this truth all my life, but I was never face-to-face with the horrible and truthful recognition that the Angel brought forth. This was extremely difficult for me to have the truth put before me as the Angel did. In front of the Angel, I too was unable to hide from the truth that we, **God's** children, have all wounded **God** so severely and without little conscious or reservation. I felt swallowed up with the realization we have all greatly offended **God** to the point of **His** return. I had to face the truth that in so many ways, countless people have abandoned **God**! For a moment, I felt a sense of a living death. It was a sense of death without **God's** love and compassionate mercy. I could try to compare this feeling to being lost in a vast dark and desolate desert where there is no escape. I realized, in some respects, this must be what **God** is feeling; and this is complete and utter despair! This despair washed over me, and this feeling of this mountainous despair that I felt was almost more than I could endure. I began to contemplate the great sadness **Almighty God** must be feeling about **His** children. **God** must be experiencing a sense of great loss. Is **God** truly watching the beginning of an enormous loss of **His** magnificent creation? Is Humanity going to sit back and let evil win without a fight? **God** certainly knows if **His** people do not wake up in **time** to the truth, the human race will be lost to evil. After all, it is our decisions alone that have brought us to this point, not **God's**. What do we the people of the world intend to do to improve their lives in order to show **God** they will not allow evil to determine the outcome? With **Almighty God** by our side, there is always hope, but we must all stop and face the truth because the truth is staring you and me in the face now. Scripture teaches us, **"Then you will know the truth and the truth will set you free" (John 8:32).**

Having an indigent attitude toward **God** is the first reason why some people find it so difficult to think it would be possible to see Angels or any other spiritual experience. What would you rather believe when there is so much proof available for you to consider? I can tell you now because I witnessed the Angel firsthand that **God** does not leave anyone alone! **God**, with the help of **His** Angels, is looking for a chance to restore the good in us again. The wonderful truth is, Angels are here with us and intend to remain with us until and only if **God** himself calls **His** Angels home to heaven. I do not want to think what it would be like for **God** to leave us alone without the support of our Angels. I do not want to think what it might be like for **God** to close **His** eyes to the unbelievers! The Angels have always been here on earth with us in order to lead **God's** children to **Him**. The Angels walk the earth only because **God** desires the Angels to be our guide.

Our destiny and our **Creator's** original master plan for Humanity is to live our life under the direction of **Almighty God** so we will be with **Him** in Heaven for all eternity! Our Angels are taking a tally on what we do that makes us happy and what makes us sad. It was evident because I witnessed the Angel, I now am convinced that the Angels are now very worried about Humanity. In general, it is evil, not **God** or **His** Angel has their undivided attention throughout the day. It is so easy for evil to accomplish this because you did not recognize immediately that evil had such a stronghold on you. It is obvious people in our society have become accustomed to the ways of evil because evil promotes their pattern of life. For these people, evil has become their friend; whether you wish to believe this or not, this is the truth. You are deceived to the point that you do not seem to recognize the difference anymore. While evil has your undivided attention, your Angels try anything and everything to persuade you to seek their help. It is **time** to search your heart and ask yourself, what do you believe?

God, in **His** most gracious mercy, is waiting patiently for us to seek **His** forgiveness. The Angel who appeared to me told me that we must all turn to **God** for help now. **God** loves all **His** people so much that **He** will give us every opportunity to love **Him** in return. **God** is now waiting for us to discover the potential of goodness we once possessed when **God** created us. In the beginning, **God** placed this goodness within us so happiness could fill the earth. Some people, as they go through their life, decided to change their goodness to bad behavior. The problem is over **time**, this evil behavior slowly changes their moral conduct until they no longer know the difference. Then before they realize it, this moral decay has transformed them into a different person where goodness dissipates over **time** until they no longer have the desire of ridding evil from their life. Humanity must turn away quickly from everything that is keeping you from placing **God** first in your life. We all need to say to **God**, "We need **You**, and we love **You**." Here is a beautiful Psalm that countless people have read in the Bible: **"Surely goodness and mercy shall follow me all the days of my life" (Psalm 23:6)**. There is so much beauty in these words if only more people would take the **time** to discover it. If you do not read the Bible, perhaps now is the **time** to discover or rediscover what you have been missing!

Let us place a mat outside of our doors that says, "**God** dwells here." Sin will not flourish where it is not welcome! However, even in a **God**-loving atmosphere, evil will confront you in an all-out battle for your Soul. You cannot become complacent that you feel you are in good standing with **God** and, therefore, evil cannot deceive you. This could not be further from the truth. Evil will try even harder to destroy your Soul even if this takes a life**time**. Evil is anxious now because it is afraid Humanity might come to their senses and renounce evil. This is the reason everyone must be as close to **God** as possible now more than ever. **God's** children must be extremely vigilant of the dangers that are so near to us all through the day. Only if we stay true to **God** in our thoughts, our words, and our deeds will we have **God's** protection. We must ask for **God's** help! You must acknowledge to **God** you are sorry for your sins and tell **God** you intend to amend your life. Ask **God** now to bestow on you **His** Grace so you can improve your life.

I pray soon, if it is **God's** will, **He** might allow others to see an Angel or visions of **His** spiritual realm. Imagine what this would be like for you to see **God's** heavenly Angels. Angels sent to us from Heaven are absolute goodness, and they bring the light of **God's** enduring love. The Angels are longing and desperately trying to help us to make the necessary improvements in our life so we can truly be happy. The Angels cannot help us unless we desire their help. Your Angels are waiting for you to ask them for their assistance and guidance in order to show you the way to make all things right again with **God**.

The problem today is, do people have the true desire to believe in the Angels? Maybe believing in Angels would result in a completely new set of uncomfortable circumstances. This would mean you would have to examine their conscience. This deep discernment of one's self is not popular by any stretch of the imagination. In general, as part of our human condition, people are not comfortable thinking about their past and present poor decisions. The Angels are here to remind us we are not perfect. Only **Jesus** is perfect. Therefore, you need to remember what the Bible tells you: while **Jesus** was in the desert, the devil tempted **Jesus**. **Jesus** was tempted with the promise of great wealth and mighty power. In the Bible, we read about the temptation of **Christ**. It is located in the **Gospels** of **Matthew**, **Mark**, and **Luke**. Every **time** I read this, I surmise the devil thought he had a chance to persuade **Jesus** to give in to evil's lies! You see, **Jesus**, born into Humanity, possessed the same attributes and the same temptations that all Humanity faces. Evil takes advantage of your poor decisions. **God** is aware of our temptations and our daily struggles. Remember **God** became a man and entered the world so **He** would be able to relate to our struggles. **God** is aware of the choices and all the decisions we all have to make in order to do what is right. **God** gave you and me free will so we would have the capability to consider the right choices in life. The Bible tells us, in the desert, **Jesus** tempted by the devil with the promise of all the riches of the world and all **Jesus** had to do to get this mighty reward was to do homage to the devil. This is a great lesson for people of all faiths to follow. **Jesus** said to the devil, **"Do not tempt the Lord your God" (Luke 4:12)**. There is no doubt that **God** knows and understands our temptations. **God** also knows Humanity cannot thrive without **His** help. The reason the struggle against evil is greater for some people then others is simply they stopped thinking about the basic truth that they need **God** in their life. This is certainly why some people find it so difficult to attain peace and happiness in their lives. It is our failure to recognize evil is so near us that it was so easy for evil to enter into our life! We must all face the truth that Humanity is in an uphill battle with evil from the beginning of **time**. It is important to recognize the truth: evil is always looking for ways to deceive you and confuse you so you will not recognize the truth. Evil convinces good people to trust the lies they hear. Remember evil is the great pretender that constantly strives to deceive you. Understanding how evil operates will help you to recognize what you need to know to uncover the truth about this master deceiver. It is amazing to me that goodness in the world that survives even through all the madness. **God** is waiting for all of Humanity to ask for **His** help because **He** loves **His** children and desires only our happiness.

Evil has caused people to allow a terrible division between the one's we love the most. Why is it so easy to hurt the one's we love? You would have to ask yourselves, do you respect the rights of others? If not, what is it you are doing wrong? Do you feel so proud you cannot place yourselves above what it is you know is right but you continue doing the opposite due to your pride? Many people are so miserable, they are not happy until they make others around them miserable too. In doing this, they will be left to alone to their own devices.

Are people becoming so proud, they are convincing themselves they can get through life without God?

If this is not true, then why do some people find everything they do so difficult? More than a few people would say they do not enjoy talking about anything that is depressing, but we all need to admit what is wrong before we can correct it. This is why the Angel desired me to discuss these uncomfortable issues. I would encourage anyone right this very minute to search your conscience and if you are truthful with yourself, the answer will surface. Examining your life is the first step in healing. It is the first step toward happiness. We cannot change what has already taken place, but we can change everything going forward. I will warn you, this will be very disturbing and very uncomfortable but necessary to correct what needs improving in your life. If you do not do this, then the wall you have built for yourself becomes so high, it will become more difficult to scale it. Therefore, for some, it is easier to keep things the way they are and hope for the best without too much effort on their part to change anything. Still **God** struggles to get our attention because **He** loves us so much. Ask yourself this question, what do you value the most in your life? With **God's** help, you will be amazed what you might discover about yourself if you are honest with your answer. Some**times**, it is very difficult to face the truth, but you will begin to feel differently about aspects of your life in the future if you are honest with yourself.

I was puzzled with an experience that took place in 2005 in a church in Rome, Italy. Confronted with the very possibility that I observed Angels trying to assist me was an overpowering observation indeed. It was later I became curiously aware about the enhanced possibility that yes, I did indeed have an encounter with an Angel. In addition, there was a distinct possibility there were three Angels involved in what took place. These were Angels close enough for me to touch! I could see everything about them so clearly. This event certainly was an unusual circumstance that presented itself to me in such a uniquely spiritual way that left me wondering. The **Holy Spirit** allowed me to witness a glimpse into the spiritual realm. This was one of those unique circumstances where I witnessed persons, places, and things in an unusual manner; and after it was all over, the experience left me in complete awe. I will never forget this experience. For me, this was a magnificent example of the extraordinarily miracles that arise at the precise moment when **God's** Divine Will becomes fully realized. Was I spiritually in total harmony with **God** for a brief few minutes? Is this why **God** allowed me to experience then something only **God** knew I would understand? Something so astounding took place because I desired with all my heart to have an opportunity to receive the Sacrament of Reconciliation. **God** knew I needed and desired for this to take place, at that precise moment, for the sake of my Soul. **God** desires to bestow on us **His** grace so we can be aware of **God's** divine will that is constantly working in our life if we would only allow this to happen.

Years passed and my life continued as before with nothing out of the ordinary happening. How could I know, while in the hospital in 2011, that a visit with a magnificent Angel would ensue? This extraordinary event took place only with the Divine Will of **Almighty God**. On that particular day, **God** reached out through **His** Angel and touched my soul. I was embarking on a completely new understanding of the possible experiences that could take place by the will of **Almighty God**. There will always be a great many questions and so few answers. The significant lesson to this is, of course, that we should be always ready to receive a special gift from **God**. **God** allows us many opportunities in our life**time** to witness

His love in compelling ways. Most of these opportunities are lost because many people fail to see the miracle in the moment. You must believe that every day is a miracle when you are in harmony with **God**. The possibilities that await you during the dawn of a new day are endless. There are numerous possibilities overlooked because our life is so demanding, we tend to look forward only to the end of the day.

Every day is a new beginning for you and everyone you meet. Each day, **God** offers you and me an opportunity to be in **His** Graces. You must always remember the cherished love **God** has for all **His** children. You must always hold this truth close to your heart. When you arise to the new day, ask yourself, "What is the purpose of my life, and what can I do today to enrich my life?" Continuing to march through life without a purpose causes your overall life to become mundane and stagnate. With the help of **God**, you will feel reenergized with a renewed zeal for life. Everything you will accomplish today, and tomorrow will have a sense of renewed purpose. As a child of **God**, you will feel a transformation take place when you allow **God** into your life.

It is a fact; many people continue to push themselves out of bed unhappy to begin the day. Plenty of people are already miserable at the start of the new day with the prospect of facing their life and their job. The truth is they do not realize this day might be their last. What would you do differently if you knew tomorrow would never come? Countless people drag themselves off to work because they are dissatisfied with their careers and so they are unhappy. People are unhappy because they no longer feel appreciated in their workplace. Finally, many people feel they are not making enough money because they want and buy everything in sight. Society has produced material heaven because what we want is never enough. Our children feel they must have what the other kids have. So they are miserable too because they will not take no for an answer. Few family members spend quality **time** with one another anymore. In fact, many families do not even know what the other family member is doing most of the **time**. Everyone seems to have his or her own agenda. Some parents do not care what the children are doing, as long as they are not disturbed because Mom and Dad have had a difficult workday. People have lost their core values. It is my belief people are actually convinced that miserable is normal. I have noticed a large number of people who never smile very much anymore. It seems to me some people even feel that it is socially correct to act serious and be unhappy. I notice large numbers of people do not dare to speak to someone they do not know. I notice even acts of kindness seem stupid to some people because they see this as an intrusion into their private space. People continue to complain but do nothing substantial to improve any of their existing problems.

God is trying to get our attention to remind everyone we need to take a good look at our life, past and present. You need to ask yourself, what should you change in order to make your life more meaningful and pleasing to **God**? What can you do today that will please **God**? Yes, you need to ask yourself, "What should I do to please **God** every day?" You must ask yourself, "What do I intend to accomplish for **God** with the **time He** has graciously granted me here on earth?" After all, I believe strongly everyone is definitely here for a meaningful purpose. I realize that for many people, their purpose in life is uncertain. However, ask yourself this question: "Because I was here, did I touch someone's life in a positive way? Did I improve someone's life when this person needed my help?" **God** is waiting to hear your answers. It is never too late to make a positive change in your life. Even a small change in your overall attitude would make a big difference over **time**. You would be amazed to see how easy this might be if you would only try. **God** is waiting to see a positive change in all of us. **God** loves us so much that the tiniest of change would please **Him**. Humanity must take advantage of the **time** we have left. Life is marching on, and the clock is ticking. It does seem that as I get older, the days and weeks go by faster than before. **Time** is precious, and you and I must not waste the precious **time** we have left. When your life is finally finished here, what will you tell **God** when **He** asks you what you accomplished in your life**time**? Did you help someone in need? Did you learn to forgive? Have you done your part to stop the injustices in the world? What will you tell **God** when **He** asks you why you did not do something to help a child that was hungry? What did you do to stop Abortion? How will **God** respond to you when you tell **Him** you did not take the **time** to convince someone not to have an **Abortion**? The truth is no one on the face of the earth will be able to hide from **God's** justice. What will you tell **God** when **He** asks you why you did not care enough to make a difference in the world? Our merciful **God** will demand the answers to these questions and so much more. We all need to ask, "What if **God's** reply to me is not what I expect to hear?" The truth is no one person on the face of the earth will be able to hide from the justice of **Almighty God**. Now is the **time** to ask yourself, how do you think **God** will judge how you lived your life? Our loving **God** granted each one of us **His** precious gift of life in order to spread love and harmony in the world, not war and hatred. Take the opportunity to make this the first day of the rest of your life and do something good to change the world. If everyone did only one good deed for the sake of Humanity, what a different world it would become overnight. Start making serious changes in your own life that will benefit not only yourself but also others around you. Begin by showing more kindness to your fellow workers and others you meet. Small words of kindness will spread to one another, and immediate results will occur right before your eyes. Express to your family how much you love them. Most of all, tell **God** you love **Him**.

> **God** is waiting to hear your words that you love **Him** above all else! **God** is trying to get your attention!

CHAPTER 11

What Is Perfection?

How do most people understand the concept of perfection? The dictionary says the word *perfection* is "a transcendence of wholeness of something, which is fulfilled in virtue." I perceived in the past, as many people probably would, that only someone being in a state of perfection and Grace could ever see an Angel. I always believed such a level of perfection found in a particular person such as a holy Nun or a holy Priest, only with them would it ever be possible to experience seeing an Angel. However, I now understand **God** alone reserves the right to judge us for what we think about perfection. No one single person on the face of this earth is without sin. However, **God** is all merciful; therefore, it is possible for an ordinary person like me with many faults and failures to experience something astonishing. I am living proof that **God** will grant the privilege of seeing an Angel. I never thought of myself as perfect, and certainly, I am not. Only **God** can see into my heart and Soul. Having an opportunity to be in the presence of an Angel is an overwhelming and definitely a miraculous gift from **God**. A loving gift so uniquely bestowed, one cannot grasp the tremendous importance of this great gift right away. To think, to wish, and to behold such a possibility would even exist is overwhelming. To contemplate the very idea that anyone could ever experience seeing an Angel or other heavenly visions is an enormous concept for the mind to undertake. Yet with all my imperfections, **God**, in **His** infinite mercy, decided to allow me to see an Angel. **God** desired to use this opportunity to prove **His** love for all Humanity by sending **His** Angel with the message.

Why do some people feel it is all right to love **God** later when and if you ever find the **time**? You cannot love **God** only when the **time** suits you best. It is important to strive to be in perfect harmony with **God** and tell **Him** you love **Him** above all else every day. When **God** is part of your day, everything seems to work out better. Perfection and achieving perfection can be a life**time** of desire to be close to **God** in an all-consuming way. I believe there are different levels of this perfection based on your understanding and your love for **God**. This is an all-consuming love within you with the very thought of **God**. You will realize this if you have reached a point in your life where you have developed a fond need to be close to **God**. What you can count on is you will find yourself completely lost in the contemplation of **God**. You will become aware that the special closeness you desire is **God** near you. This some**times** reveals itself, as is a brief intense emotion, that takes over every thought process you possess. During this **time**, your mind refuses to think of anything except **God**. This is a deeply rooted and natural desire to be close to **God** from the day we were born. Therefore, it is a natural **God**-given desire to process thoughts of **Him** and often. There in your heart and Soul, you can find and discover **God** truly is and always was and always will be. This is an extraordinary measure of **God's** love for **His** children that **He** grants us these most precious events of heavenly encounters with the Angels. How truly enormous **God's** love is for all **His** children.

In reading about the lives of the saints, it is clear that the saints strived unceasingly to achieve perfection while in this world. All the saints were born with the same feelings and emotions we all possess. Unlike most of us, the vast difference is the saints lived out their lives in constant awareness of this perfection. Truly, it is only in Heaven where the saints would finally realize the true meaning of this perfection now in the presence of **God**. Only in Heaven does perfection truly exist in its purist spirit form in all creation residing there. Yet this is true: all the saints led holy devout lives. The saints lived out their life for the love of **God** in everything they did in their daily life. Therefore, are we to believe there exists the understanding that conceivably only certain people can identify with this perfection? I do not believe **God** would desire only the saints this tiny glimpse of Heaven. The concept of this state of perfection shares many meanings.

Even now, somewhere in the world, someone is about to experience a special gift from **God** in a uniquely holy way. Oh, not necessarily perfect people in our judgment but perhaps people who have a strong conviction or dogma regarding their love for **God**. Only **God** alone knows what we truly think and what we truly feel in our hearts. Therefore, **God** allows these special events to take place for specific purposes for our spiritual growth and for the glory of **His** kingdom. I always knew in my heart **God** indeed loved me. However, I would never fully realize how much until I was in the presence of the Angel in the hospital. Until I witnessed the Angel, I could not begin to fathom how much and how deeply **God's** love really is for all **His** children. No proper words could ever begin to describe **God's** infinite love for all Humanity.

There was a **time** in my life when I was a young adult, I was confused and felt abandoned, and I struggled to know **God** more deeply. I developed the foolish idea that this special closeness with **God** was for someone that I felt was better than I was. I perceived the notion that someone more "Holy" perhaps than I was deserved **God's** attention. Thank goodness, it was a temporarily condition that resolved quickly. In my opinion, modern Christians use this term *holy* too loosely. Little did I know that in my life**time**, I would come to grasp the true meaning of **God's** enormous love that is waiting for all those who desire **His** love! How could I know then that something so remarkably dramatic would enter my life forty-eight years later? To perhaps dream about seeing Angels would be dramatic enough but then to have this really take place before your very eyes is certainly a life-altering event. This event would forever change the interpretation of how I thought **God** identifies with the meaning of the word *perfection* and the word *love*. The path that we have chosen for ourselves will ultimately lead us to the very comprehension of the word *perfection*. **God** searches the depth of our hearts and sees various degrees of this perfection in us. Remember, **God**'s creation began with perfection. Humankind has altered this interpretation.

Who among us has the right to judge an individual for what he or she may express or how they show their love for **Almighty God**? Who among us has the right to judge when, where, and how someone chooses to pray to **God**? **God** desires us all to pray to **Him** in various ways. Certain people may find some forms of prayer odd. **God** may be asking a person to pray in a certain way to test others in their belief of **Him**. It is natural to display emotions for the love you share for **God**. I do not believe these emotions are present for a show unless this person does not display proper respect for **God**. Some people become emotional in a unique way because it is their belief the **Holy Spirit** touched them in a special way. These people believe this emotion is what draws them closer to **God**. It is during these special moments those people are not bound by earthy rules. It is very pleasing to **God** when we show our love for **Him** in any form of prayer. This is a natural and healthy way to be emotional. It is the sweetest form of love and compassion some people will ever feel. This emotion is a great deal stronger in some people than in others. Some of us have a greater desire to display this emotion, and the consent of others is never necessary. It is definitely a natural emotion for some people that may take the form of something we are not used to witnessing. These displays of emotion cause other people to feel very uncomfortable. This might be why they deem the emotion displayed is not pleasing to **God**. For some reason, some people are incapable of showing their own emotions in this way so they do not understand this emotion displayed by others. This is the reason this emotion is so misunderstood. These people simply do not have any control over their emotions when the **Holy Spirit** touches them in this special way. Some people will never understand what others may view as a conventional way to express one's love for **God**. Maybe this assumption exists because people in my generation believed prayer should be quiet and reserved. Still other people who experience a quiet meditative form of prayer become completely absorbed into their prayer. You might say they are unconscious for the moment to the rest of the world. At this moment, there is only **God**. They are simply on a different spiritual path than others if only for a brief moment. Christians may be drawn to **God** in this way, and they feel they experience the **Holy Spirit** immediately because this brings them closer to the infinite **Almighty God**. However, I can assure you, any form of love shown to **God** is pleasing to **Him**. We are not bound to the constraints of this world when we draw ourselves to **God**. I am one of those emotional people. Since my visit with the Angel, I have little control over my emotions when it involves my spiritual life. Often, these strong emotions are very difficult for me to control. I do not like to do anything that will bring attention to me especially in church. Then there are **times** I cannot control my emotions, for the love I feel for **God** merely pours out no matter where I am. In the beginning, this was my childhood impression of the church that caused me to be more reserved. However, recently, I have asked myself, is this because I was stubborn? I still try to keep some of these emotions hidden from view when possible. I would prefer to be alone during these periods of emotion for my love of **God**. I worry some**times** I am not doing the right thing. Perhaps if I were more open, this would help others. What is clear is **God** knows what is proper for me. My generation tends to be old-fashioned in many respects, and I have always followed my inner feelings when it comes to issues like this. Therefore, I can only say, I am not without fault, but I am trying to do what I feel is right for me. If **God** wishes me to display my love for **Him** more openly, **God** will find a way to let me know. Perhaps this is the **time** for me to free my emotions naturally. Others might benefit in some way if I could relax and not be concerned what others think. There will always be people who will not understand anything out of the "normal" realm because they refuse to believe these emotions are not normal and, therefore, only judge this instead. Now is the **time** for me to let **God** decide what **He** desires me to do.

During my life, it has always been very comforting to me to be able to devote **time** for **God** especially in the evenings. This is where in the still and quiet of the night the cares of the world fade away. There, in the quiet, I could be in total control and allow no distraction from my thoughts of **God**. There in the stillness you may hear only a tiny whisper while I express myself in my prayers. During this **time** when I am very quiet, is it possible to hear **God** talking to me? Oh, not in the same way we talk to one another, rather in a way only your soul could ever understand this loving communication. This prayerful communication is a spiritual union with **God** that you are expressing to **Him** so dearly. **God** accepts this expression of love in a most tender way. This may take a life**time** for some people to recognize and fully comprehend the awesome possibility that **God** is really so near to you. You must make the **time** to chat with **God** as often as possible. I like to say, you need to keep the line of communication open with **God** in order to be ready to receive **God's** unending love and guidance. **God** knows all **His** people need **His** love now more than ever. It is important that you establish your own way of communication with the **Almighty God**. There are endless ways and endless opportunities to be close to your **Creator**. **God** is waiting right this minute for you to say to **Him**, "I love you."

The Angel who appeared to me is my witness that proves to us that **God** desires us to be close to **Him**. The minute I looked into the eyes of the Angel, I realized every star in the sky was there for a purpose. I knew why no snowflake is never ever in the same size and shape as another. I realized why every creature, large and small, roams the earth. I understood instantly the purpose of your life, and my life is because **God** rejoices in our happiness. We are here to love **God** and to love one another. Why is this so difficult to understand? Most importantly, I now knew the truth regarding so many things we believed by faith alone. Everything, I mean everything, we as faithful Christians believed by our trust and faith in **God** is and always will be *all true*! These statement needs to be repeated. Everything the Bible teaches us about **God** and everything we have believed in trust and faith is and will always be the entire TRUTH! **God** touched my very Soul that afternoon in the hospital. I have witnessed the truth within the golden light that surrounded the Angel and filled everyone and everything in the room. The truth is **God** has always and will always be with **His** children. The truth is **God** has always loved us in the deepest way possible. The truth is **God** will never leave us. **Jesus** said to him, **"I am the way, the truth and the light. No one**

can come to the Father except through Me" (John 14:6). God has not changed; **His** people have changed!

Whenever I have an opportunity to talk to others, they will ask me, "What does the message mean for you personally?" Alternatively, they will ask, "What is the meaning of the message for me?" The Angel brought forth a message of truth for all **God's** children. Seeing the Angel as I did proved to me that we all have the power to recognize and overcome the evil who thinks it has already won. Evil has not won yet unless we allow it to. You must look evil right in the eye and say as **Jesus** did, **"Depart from me,"** I do not want you in my life. You should repeat the name of **Jesus** often. Write little signs around the house with the name of **Jesus** printed on the paper. A dear friend told me something recently and what she said was interesting. She said, "I heard the devil say one morning when I was getting out of bed, 'Oh no, she is awake!'" This says so much in so few words. It is so important to continue to place your trust in **God** first. **God** is waiting to see what we all intend to do to honor **God** and believe in **His** promises. Now is the **time** for the whole of Humanity to make the most important decisions of our existence.

God is waiting to help everyone who desires **His** help, but maybe you have not asked **God** in the way you should because **God** sees you are not ready to break away from your old habits. **God** is waiting to see results! We all need to show **God** we mean what we say. We need to gather together now and ask **God** to forgive all of us. We must all put aside our pride and forgive one another our differences before it is too late. **God** is trying to get our attention. The signs are all around us that **God** is greatly displeased with our horrible behavior. **God** is greatly offended! Humanity all needs to show **God** we still love **Him** and put an end to all the hatred and violence in the world. Every person that walks on **God's** beautiful world can accomplish what looks like the impossible because, **"With God, nothing is impossible" (Luke 1:37). God** is waiting for our decision. How long will **God** wait for our answer? My heart tells me we should heed the profound message the Angel conveyed to me most seriously and not test **God** further. The Angel was extremely serious when speaking of the horrendous offences to **Almighty God**. These offences are very severe and massive in **God's** eyes. Do we really need an individual written script to understand what continues to happen every day? **God** sees **His** people are in great need of **His** mercy because we continually allow hatred to grow in the world.

God is trying to get our attention!

CHAPTER 12

Dreams about Angels and Meditation on God's Magnificent Realm

Over the years, I have experienced amazing and colorful dreams regarding Angels. Most of these dreams often did seem very real at the **time**. Often, these dreams were about some fear I once harbored. For example, I sensed I was falling from a high place, and automatically, I called for an Angel to help me. Was I calling my Guardian Angel in my sleep? Then I awakened just before the Angel could reach me. Alternatively, the dream would be about something I needed to do. Clearly, there is no question I enjoyed those dramatic dreams. I was obsessed with my desire to dream about the Angels. The dreams would occur, of course, when I least expected. When I did dream about Angels, each Angel was different in their appearance. The origins of some of the dreams presented themselves to me as fantastic and dramatic journeys. Always, I would find myself floating in splendid high places. Some**times**, the height did not seem to bother me at all, while other **times**, I was not comfortable as before, and I would feel great fear. It was during those **times** I would not hesitate to ask an Angel for help. On some occasions, I seem to travel in my dreams great distances. These experiences of distance were very spiritual in their nature because Angels were always present, except once. In one dream, I traveled a long journey as if I were on mission of some kind for **God**. These are my own assumptions because no other explanation ever made sense to me at the **time**. I was often so tired the next morning. So I used to laugh and say, "Traveling was an exhausting experience even if you are asleep."

In my estimation, I do not believe the particular Angels I encountered in my dreams were necessarily my Guardian Angels. Why I feel this way, I cannot explain other than to say these Angels must be Angels sent to help me achieve my goal. I have concluded that some extraordinary experiences I have encountered while I am sleeping have an important interpretation for me alone. I am not sure I will ever fully realize why these experiences occur. I am sure many people wonder why they have amazing dreams that seem to defy the imagination. The Guardian Angels are here to support us and to teach us. However, the Angels who come to me in my dreams are altogether different each **time**. Surely, these Angels are only there to accompany me on my journey wherever I might find myself going! I have no way of knowing the difference between my Guardian Angel and the Angels in my dreams. I can only say these Angels are all different in their appearance. In so many of my dreams, everything seems so real. Over the years, I did wonder why I was dreaming about Angels. Was there a specific purpose in the appearance of these dreams? Was **God** preparing me through various dreams and experiences for what I would witness during my hospital stay in 2011? I do believe everything that happens to us has a purpose, especially when **God** is involved. As a result of these fabulous dreams, they awakened a strong urge in me to meditate on my dreams. I became so fascinated with my dreams I started writing about them. In this way, I could express myself in my own words and in my own thoughts. I wanted to find out if it was possible to know more about the purposes behind these dramatic dreams. I needed to analyze each situation so I could possibly understand what took place in my dreams. Little did I realize, this would not be long before I would experience seeing an Angel who was definitely not involved in any dream. I will never know the answers while on earth, and now I can say with complete confidence that this no longer is important because I know **God** is in charge of everything that happens in my life.

I used to have a difficult **time** falling asleep or staying asleep. For years, I, like thousands of other people, suffered from the lack of proper sleep. As usual, I always enjoyed reciting my Rosary before falling asleep. I was determined to have my last thoughts of the Blessed Mother and/or **God** before I went to sleep. It is the last prayers of the evening; I felt they were so comforting and relaxing. Then I realized that my mind was so busy with the problems of the day; this was why my mind would not allow me to relax. I concluded that if my mind wanted to be busy, why not allow my mind to be busy concentrating stronger on the Mysteries of the Rosary. This worked, and I could go to sleep without other issues on my mind. As I became older, I needed my rest and, therefore, refused to allow my mind to wander. There is no better way to fall asleep than in the middle of one's prayers. I used to feel badly that I would somehow never finish my prayers. I understand now, our life should be one continuous and complete prayer to **God**. Our prayers seem to thread together day after day, year after year, until our prayers become so much a part of us. In the end, there is only **God** and our thoughts of **Him** that should be important.

Recently, it was easier for me to go to sleep in the hope and anticipation I would dream about Angels. I would also meditate intently regarding some certain scenario in the Bible that I wished could take place in a dream. If a dream occurred, most often, these dreams were always spiritual in nature. These dreams became a very prayerful and peaceful experience for me. I treasured all these dreams, but they did not happen as often as I would have liked them to. I would also meditate about the scenes I knew so well from the Bible before going to sleep. I would think to myself, if this is on my mind before I fall asleep, then perhaps I could dream I was in this particular place. For an example, I enjoyed meditating on the many scenes in the Bible where **Jesus** was either teaching or walking with **His** Apostles. One of my favorites is the scene and there is a painting of this where the Apostles meet **Jesus** on the road to Emmaus. The painting depicts **Jesus** meeting two of **His** Apostles on the road after **He** has risen and the Apostles did not recognize **Him**. The best part of this painting is if you concentrate very diligently, you can observe the **time** of day changing to whatever **time** you want it to be. The painting can appear to be morning, afternoon, or dusk. In addition, if you concentrate very closely and meditate on the painting very intently, you can almost imaging seeing **Jesus** and **His** disciples walking along and talking together. How wondrous this must have been for all the followers of **Jesus** to be able to walk and talk with **Him**. Christians can only hope we will all someday have the opportunity to witness **Jesus** in all **His** glory. However, what **Jesus** desires you to know right now is you can talk to **Him**, as the Apostles did, any**time**. You may not see **Jesus** next to you, but I assure you **He** is there. I assure you, your Angel is beside you too. It does not matter where you are; **Jesus** is near you if you desire **His** presence always!

Some five years ago, I began to have a renewed interest to study the awesome mystery of the Holy **Trinity**. I realized one day while praying, I had the strongest desire to have a better visual understanding in my mind of **God** the **Father, God** the **Son,** and **God** the **Holy Spirit** who is **God** in three divine persons. I discovered during my meditation in front of the icon of the **Holy Trinity** a stronger desire to understand more deeply this divine mystery. This mystery is so profoundly powerful. The Holy **Trinity** is one of the most important fundamental doctrines of the Catholic Church. The icon quietly waits for anyone who desires to discover the extraordinary significance and meditate on the power found within. It is true; most people pursue vigorously what is important to them. What is also true, when most people make up their mind to do something, they strive to do their best to accomplish their endeavor well.

I want you to believe in your heart, the possibility does exist for you to sense Jesus standing right beside you.

Oh, not the way we see each other, but you will know **Jesus** is there. **Jesus** will let you know in a way you will understand that **He** is there with you if you believe nothing is impossible for **Him**. Then can we say this is also reasonable and normal to have the desire to have such dreams or desires? I have always wanted to fill my life with anything and everything that would place me nearer to **God**. I taught my children to fill their life with people, places, and things that were pleasing to **God** and then they would find true happiness.

During my teenage years, there were **times** I did not feel this close to **God**. Often, I was alone and discouraged. I understand now this condition was my fault entirely. I was in an awful struggle for a while with myself! I had allowed myself to be convinced briefly of the false idea that the very thought of an individual closeness with **God** was surely reserved for someone more worthy. Now I wonder where I got such a foolish idea when all the **time** I knew better. This was the evil one trying to convince me I would not be worthy of **God's time**. What an awful thing to happen to anyone. Yet today, people continue to allow this to take place in their life. The evil one has convinced many people that **God** has no **time** for them. **God** waits for our return to **Him** because **He** is our **Father** who is exceedingly concerned about what happens to you and me.

The problem that exists is our sins are a constant reminder to us that we have done something we may indeed often regret. Unbelievably, good-hearted people allow this condition to fester for years and even continue for the majority of their life. If this condition is left unresolved, you may feel the loss of friendship with **God** because this prevents you from being completely happy. Our conscience will not allow you to forget your failures. Therefore, you are miserable and may not realize why you are so miserable. I read somewhere, **"Confession is good for the Soul."** As Christians, we believe **God** will forgive a contrite sinner. Some**times**, the closer you become to **God**, the more difficult it might be to forgive yourself. Now I am peacefully resolved that **God** does not want anyone to feel this way. If you are truly sorry for your sins and really believe **God** will forgive you, you must draw from your faith, **God** will also forget. I am living proof of this truth.

The instant I witnessed the Angel, I knew the truth was standing there before me, and there was no doubt **God** had forgiven me! I will admit, I was deeply saddened in the past, and I silently harbored this concern for years. With the Angel's appearance, I remembered **God's** mercy, **He** opened my eyes so I would know for sure that **He** did forgive me and **He** will forgive you. I live this moment every day, and it is now very important to me too help others feel content with this solemn truth. Therefore, you must believe **God** will forgive you and **He** will forget your sins! **God** loves **His** children so dearly, and **He** understands our faults and failures. What **God** expects from us is to strive to continue to improve ourselves. All these negative thoughts placed in our minds are part of a different plan by someone other than **God**. This is an evil plan that is succeeding because there are so many people staying away from **God** and the Sacrament of Reconciliation. As a Catholic, I will never understand why anyone would choose to stay away from the precious Sacrament that is **God**'s mercy. Catholics believe after receiving this sacrament, your Soul is closer to **God** if only for a fleeting moment. I am so grateful **God** gave me the Grace to be reconciled to this truth so I may help others come to feel this peace in their hearts.

Refusing **God's** mercy is becoming a very serious dilemma for a multitude of people. Our society today is so absorbed with being the judge and jury of others that they have lost sight of their own imperfections. The most serious problem is many people are allowing their pride to get in the way. It is my belief people have forgotten that this final judgment is reserved for **God** alone. You should examine more often what you are doing and what kind of decisions you are making that is affecting your life adversely. Perhaps this is why some people "cannot seem to get it together." It is not always easy to change your accustomed course; therefore, so many people refuse to because they find some false comfort in keeping things the way they are presently. You are wasting precious **time** you should be spending with **God**. This sounds so simple because it is simple. You must have the deepest desire to give your life to **God**. Find somewhere in the part of your day where you can be exclusively be with **God**. You will soon realize this is a most profound and spiritual experience and you will soon desire these moments to be part of your everyday life. While you are quietly meditating on **God**, you will know **He** is there with you. A very dear priest I once knew, now in Heaven, used to say, **"You've tried everything else, why not try God?"** I do not think this holy priest would mind me repeating this beautiful phrase. If you were lucky enough to meet this priest, you would realize everyone was his friend, and now he is with **Almighty God**.

I have noticed within myself that my thoughts and my desire to be close to **God** have been increasing in their intensity. Even before I saw the Angel in the hospital, I was experiencing an extraordinary closeness with **God**. I could sense this closeness was more intense. This extraordinary strong feeling for the love of **God** takes over me and can happen to me at any moment no matter where I am or what I am doing. When this happens, I discover that I am completely lost in my thoughts of **God** and how much I love **Him**. When this feeling washes over me, in such a loving way, nothing else seems to matter to me when this awesome spiritual closeness to **God** occurs. This lighthearted awareness washes over me as if I were receiving some cleansing. I believe I am receiving a cleansing because the desire and the need for this cleansing is for the sake of my Soul and is more important than anything we could ever receive. I cannot continue to be the person I am and help others if I am not true to **Almighty God**. All you have to do is ask **God** and you shall receive everything you need. The overwhelming feeling I experience now is a similar emotion I experienced when I was a child. The truth is you must connect with **God** in a spiritual way that is comfortable for you. The Bible says, **"We must become like children again"** (Matthew 18:3). Now I understand this truth completely. Yes, we must become like children again, not in a childish manner but rather with a sense of confidence and innocence we all once possessed. Yes, **God's** miracle of life is innocent. What a gift to know this is possible for you to recapture your childlike confidence again. You need only to be sincere when asking **God** to be in your life, and this will happen to you in an instant. **God** will do anything to make **His** children happy. You need only to ask **God** for **His** blessing, and **He** will bless you abundantly.

Now I wonder is there a healing of some kind in all my dreams of Angels? Is there definitely a healing and a cleansing taking place at this precise **time** in my life? Does **God** begin this cleansing when we ask for **His** love? Is this healing happening now because I desire **God's** healing to be an all-consuming part of me? Have I finally reached a point in my life where I can say I am truly contrite? The appearance of this Angel in the hospital was a personal confirmation from **God** that this is true. Further, this is further confirmation of **God's** love and mercy for everyone who seeks healing from the mercy of **His Sacred Heart**. The presence of the Angel was definite proof **God** has forgiven me for my past sins. **God** knew I did so deeply desire my sins to be forgiven and forgotten. Is **God**, through **His** Angel, trying to remind the world **He** is waiting to forgive everyone? I do believe most people have a deep desire to have **God** forgive their sins because they have a deep desire to live their life as good **God**-fearing people. Everyone is in desperate need of forgiveness that is **God's** mercy. However, **God** will still let you know how much **He** loves you no matter what you do. Then why is it so difficult for people to seek out **God's** forgiveness knowing **He** has been waiting so long for us to "Get our act together?" What does **God** need to do to get your attention? Why do people continue to sit back and do nothing to improve their life? All you need to do is invite **God** into your life and with the will of your faith, marvelous things will begin to take place.

I do not believe it is prudent to wait and see what **God** decides we deserve. How far should **God's** people test **God**? Writing this part gives me shivers because after hearing the Angel's words I desire so strongly to let you know how real and serious the situation has become. It is no secret that the offences committed against the Sacred Heart of **Jesus** is frighteningly outrageous. I cannot accurately convey to you the proper words that would describe how offended **God** must be with all our deliberate and unconscionable actions. I understood precisely what the Angel who appeared to me said, **"It is almost time,"** and it broke my heart. The Angel knew I would understand the full meaning of these words in **time**. Simply, this is the **time** for Humanity to search deep into our hearts and there everyone will find the answers. **God** gave us the desire to accomplish great and wonderful things. The Angel appeared to me in order to remind everyone **God** is devastated with our overwhelming sins that continually offend **Him** because our eyes are closed and our ears no longer are able to hear the truth. Open your eyes to see the truth and open your ears so you may hear the truth.

I cannot use any words presently known to express to you how heartbreaking this was for me to hear the Angel speak about **God's** thoughts about Humanity. I must repeat, try to imagine an Angel describing to you what **God** is thinking about us! This was totally beyond any comprehension I thought I knew. I was experiencing in my heart, to a large degree, the complete and utter moral devastation of the pain **God** is experiencing! As I write this now, I do not believe I would survive this degree of sadness if I did not know **God** still loves all **His** children. Even now, I am still very sensitive to this height of emotion that came over me when the Angel expressed to me the alarming truth of **God's** sadness over our sins. If you truly believe in **God**, then you must already be consciously mindful of this recognition.

What kind of future awaits the children of the world? I assure you the world will not be a world of peace if Humanity continues to do nothing to eradicate the hatred between our cultures. Sadly, war has always been part of Humanity. **God's** people must remember we all have the power together with **Almighty God** to change our present course. There will be no future or peace in the world without the help of **Almighty God**. Now is the **time** for everyone to make some serious decisions. I assure you the world will never know peace without **God**. America must have strong **God**-fearing leaders, and together, everyone in prayer must remember to consecrate the Human Race to the wounded **Sacred Heart** of **Jesus**. Only then will this ever be possible to experience true happiness in the world. What is Humanity waiting for? The signs of **Almighty God's** vast disappointment can be seen everywhere. **God** is trying to get our attention, and unfortunately, so many people are still not listening. The Prayer of **Consecration to the Sacred Heart** is a Roman Catholic prayer composed by Pope Leo XIII. It was included in the 1899 encyclical Annum Sacrum issued by Leo XIII as he **consecrated** the entire world to the **Sacred Heart** of **Jesus**. The following is this prayer:

Consecration to the Sacred Heart of Jesus

O most sweet **Jesus**, **Redeemer** of the Human Race; behold us prostrate most humbly before **Your** altar (in **Your** presence). To **You** we belong; **Yours** we wish to be; and that we may be united to **You** more closely, we dedicate ourselves each one of us today to **Your** most **Sacred Heart**.

Many have never known **You**; many, despising **Your** commands, have rejected **You**. Have mercy on them all, most merciful **Jesus,** and draw them to **Your sacred Heart**. Be **You King**, O **Lord**, not only over the faithful who never have gone away from **You**, but also over the prodigal children who have forsaken **You**; and make them return quickly to their **Father's** house, lest they perish of misery and hunger. Be **You King**, of those who have been misled by error, or separated by schism, and call them back to the haven of truth, and the unity of faith; so that there may soon be one fold, and one **Shepherd**. Grant to **Your** Church, O **Lord,** assurance of freedom and immunity from harm; give peace and order to all nations, and grant that, over the whole earth, from pole to pole, may resound the words: Praise to the Divine **Heart**, through which was brought to us salvation; glory and honor be to It forever Amen. O **Heart** of love, I put all my trust in **You**; for I fear all things from my own weakness, but I hope for all things from **Your** goodness. Most sweet **Heart** of **Jesus**, grant that peace, the fruit of justice and charity, may reign throughout the world. **Sacred Heart** of **Jesus**, protect our families.

Please pray this prayer often!

CHAPTER 13

Angels Are Messengers Sent by the Holy Spirit

I accepted an invitation from a dear friend who was a Franciscan Nun to accompany her and her family to Rome, Italy. The reason for our trip was to attend the Beatification of Mother Marianne Cope on May 14, 2005. I will never forget this Grace-filled journey. Rome, Italy, was a trip of a life**time**, especially for an Artist! Since our visit to Rome, Mother Marianne Cope was canonized Saint Marianne Cope on October 21, 2012.

After the Canonization of Saint Marianne Cope was concluded, everyone began to leave the Basilica, and for some unknown reason, I took my **time** walking and looking at all the artwork. My feet felt like they were made of lead. My friends were already outside and probably wondered why I did not follow them out. Of course, I was enthralled with the captivating Artwork that was all around me, and so I was in no hurry to leave. However, the guards had other ideas and told me to leave immediately. Slowly, I walked toward the entrance, and all at once, I noticed I was the only one left in the Basilica. I stopped, and to this day, I have no idea why I simply stopped and stood still. I just stood there with no particular reason, and I forgot that the guards already warned me to leave. I did not mean to disobey, but it felt like I had no control over the fact that I just stood there for a moment. I

I SEE AN ANGEL

had no idea that in front of me was an elevator. To my astonishment, the elevator doors opened, and immediately, His Eminence Pope Benedict stepped through the doors. He was merely four feet away from me. I would so like to know if His Eminence Pope Benedict remembers the women wearing the red hat!

It was during this trip to Italy that something else out of the ordinary took place that caused me to wonder was it possible I was in the presence of not one Angel but three Angels. I was with my traveling companions as we had scheduled to visit numerous historic churches that day. During my visit to one of those churches, I felt overcome with the strongest desire to find a priest and go to confession. The name of the church is the Basilica Saint Paul Outside the Walls. It is customary for the churches in Italy to have many free-standing confessionals that lined both sides of the aisles. All the confessionals are marked with a sign for a different language. Somehow, in every church we visited, it seemed to be very difficult to find a confessional marked "English."

Finally, in this church, I noticed a large sign that read, "English." However, the confessional was dark, and there was no sign of a priest anywhere. I was very disappointed. I did not want to keep my friends waiting, so I began walking away. I knew there were so many other places on our schedule to visit, so I started to leave. All of a sudden, I noticed these two young boys sitting on the floor leaning against these enormous massive pillars. They said to me, "Padre will be back shortly, you wait." After waiting for a while, I started to leave a second **time**. The two boys called me back a second **time**, saying, "Padre is coming, you wait." Impatiently, I continued to wait, but still I saw no Padre in sight. Both these young men were very persistent in their urging me to continue to wait, but **time** passed and still no sign of a padre. I finally began to walk away for the third **time** when I heard one of the boys shout loudly, "Lady, lady, Padre is here." I could hear the young man's voice echo all through the vast open spaces of the church. When I turned around, to my surprise, Padre was there sitting in the center of the confessional with the curtain pulled aside and the light was on. I did not even see or hear him coming. I gestured to the boys for them to go first. After all, the boys were already there when I arrived. The boys insisted I enter the confessional first. I thought how polite these boys are. I felt an unusual calm and quiet all around me. The padre was in the center of the confessional motioning for me to come over to him. The center area was the correct location for the padre. However, Padre motioned for me to come toward him right in front of the confessional. The middle door was open, and the curtain pulled away. Ordinarily, for anyone wishing to go to confession, you would enter at one of the side entrances. The priest would remain in the center. I made my way toward the front of the confessional where Padre was sitting. I felt as if I had no recourse but to do what Padre asked me to do. There in front of him outside the confessional stood a kneeler for me to kneel on. Previously, when I was waiting, no kneeler was evident anywhere. I thought later, where was the kneeler before? Did Padre carry the kneeler with him to the confessional? Why would Padre carry a kneeler? I could not help but to wonder everything was very odd. Suddenly, the kneeler was there, and then later, when I was leaving and turned around, the kneeler was gone. Everything was the same as it was when I first entered the church. The boys were gone, Padre was gone, and the light was off as before. Strangely, it was as if this entire experience never took place, but it did! Why were the boys waiting there in the first place? Why did the boys leave the church? Where did they go so fast? What do you think?

    I was more than a little uncomfortable kneeling in front of the confessional because the door was open to the public and I felt other people passing by might hear what I was saying. Before long, my thoughts of others seem to fade from my mind. I simply felt that Padre and I were alone. Instantly, I felt enormous love and compassion coming from the padre as he spoke to me. Padre placed my hands in his and proceeded to ask me, "What is bothering you so much, my child?"

    I replied, "I do not know actually." I became very emotional because at that moment, I felt so loved. Padre did not seem to mind I was so emotional. My tears were flowing like a river. Padre continued to speak to me with his sweet gentle voice. Padre and I chatted, which seemed like a long **time**. I finished my confession and said my prayers. Then a strange feeling came over me, I did not want to leave! I did not want this beautiful experience to end. You see, at that precise moment, my Soul was pure and perfectly clean from sin because of the Sacrament of Reconciliation. My Soul felt light and happy again. I did not have a care in the world. I felt I was leaving somewhere safe because at that moment, **God** was so near to me. Who would want to leave the love and safety of **Almighty God**?

Padre told me his name and asked me not to forget him. He said to me, "I will not forget you." I told him I would never forget him, and I stood up to leave and looked around for the two young boys. The boys were nowhere in the church. It was likely these two boys were only there for a specific purpose and that was to get me to remain in the church! Where did they go? Why did they not wait? What were they doing there sitting on the floor leaning against those pillars? Right away, I felt the entire encounter was definitely more than a little out of the ordinary. Were the boys leaning against the pillars Angels? Was Padre really **Jesus**? In addition, when I looked back toward the confessional, it was completely as dark as it was before, and the kneeler, where did the kneeler go? I thought at the **time** what took place in church certainly was more than a little curious. I dismissed what I thought because from one minute to the next, there was no visible sign anyone had ever been there. I left thinking the whole experience was remarkable. Then as I approached the door to leave the church, I noticed some pamphlets in a small wicker basket. The pamphlets stated, "For today only, anyone obtaining the Sacrament of Reconciliation and receiving Holy Communion would receive a Plenary Indulgence." I became overwhelmed with excitement because I believed the encounter with Padre and the young boys implied some kind of predestiny, which took place by the Divine Will of **Holy Spirit**. The possibility never occurred to me when I entered the church I would ever have this rare opportunity or that it was even possible that particular day to receive a plenary indulgence. Here I have been a Catholic all my life, and I knew Plenary Indulgences happened only on special occasions. Plenary indulgence does not happen very often. Here is a brief explanation: Pope Boniface V111 granted Plenary Indulgence in the year 1300. Indulgence is extra

Sacramental remission of the temporal punishment due, in **God's** justice, to sin that **God** has forgiven.

Upon my arrival home, I thought a great deal about what took place in the church in Rome. Is it possible I was in the presence of heavenly Angels? The more I asked myself this question, the answer seemed to resound yes. The possible first two Angels were the two boys, which, at first glance, seemed to appear like ordinary teenage boys. I also thought Padre definitely appeared to be a traditional priest. However, I noticed one distinctive difference that stood out with both boys and Padre. It was their overall demeanor, which I noticed first. If I were to guess, I would say both boys were approximately fourteen years old. Funny why I thought these teenage boys resembled each other. I was mystified by their stunning angelic faces that seemed to glow when I looked at them; the boys appeared so distinctively beautiful. It was their faces, those beautiful sweet faces, that captured my attention immediately. Their faces appeared as though there was a light on them. I describe this light as a beautiful warm glow that was lovely to see. There was something definitely special about Padre too. Immediately, I could not help but notice that his voice was extremely gentle and kind as he spoke to me. Padre was intently interested in every word I said. Padre made me feel as if nothing in the world mattered at that precise moment but me. I could sense so much love and compassion from Padre's demeanor. Contained within the words Padre spoke to me was an overwhelming understanding of the truth.

On my arrival home, I started making inquiries about Padre. I made several long-distance phone calls to the church where I met Padre. I also tried e-mailing the church for any information I could find about him. No matter what I did, I could not get any information. I could not find out even the smallest hint that who I was trying to reach ever existed! I felt this was very odd; no one ever heard of the padre who I was trying to locate. I spoke with many different people on the phone but always with no results. I thought this was a bit unusual because Padre's name was not a common name. Therefore, if Padre was hearing confessions in the church, surely, someone would remember or knew of him. What I believed took place that day in church is simply miraculous. I will let you decide why the boys were there that day in the church. What is even more remarkable is who was Padre? Who was he and why is it no one knew him? There is no doubt I was predestined to visit this particular church in Rome. I further believe it was predestined for me to receive the Plenary Indulgence. This event will remain with me a powerful experience that I will forever hold close to my heart.

Now that I witnessed those boys and having the opportunity to talk with Padre was an amazing experience that I will always carry with me all the days of my life. I often meditate on the experience I encountered in the church in Rome. I often think about Padre because he made such a remarkable impression on me. In addition, Padre asked me not to forget him, and because of the unusual circumstances, it would be impossible to forget what took place there. Was Almighty God preparing me for what would take place six years later?

The extraordinary event that took place in the hospital in 2011 was no coincidence. There is no doubt the Angel sent by the power of the **Holy Spirit** was there to deliver the message! The Angel was beyond extraordinary in every sense of the word. I recall now, when I looked at the Angel's face, I recognized a similar glow that I witnessed on both the boys' faces in Rome. However, the gorgeous golden light that surrounded the magnificent Angel in the recovery room was, by far, significantly brighter. What I witnessed was a heavenly glow of pure magnificence that was so unmistakably beautiful. Without a doubt, the gorgeous glow of light I witnessed on the Angel's face left me with a feeling of peace. I will never forget the look on the Angel's face because I believe this was the light of **Almighty God**. Yes, I now know, this magnificent pure golden light is **God's** love. It was an honor to witness the presence of **God's** pure love that adorned the heavenly Angel's face. One of many immediate thoughts that formed in my mind was I felt the Angel's countenance had the appearance of absolute perfection!

After my encounter with the Angel in the hospital, I began to ask myself again, was it possible those two boys in Rome were Angels? Since I could not find out any information about the Padre, who was he? There was certainly the same remarkable glow of light on his face too. However, at the **time**, I did not seem to dwell on the light. Padre's eyes seemed to penetrate my very Soul. Those beautiful eyes showed tremendous compassion for me that I would never forget. Every single moment in the church was extraordinary. I was aware instantly the two boys had such a unique gentle persuasion about them. Later, everything about the boys compelled me to wonder if they were Angels. I was totally convinced of the possibility because nothing else made any sense. Since I was a mother myself, I did not think these boys acted like typical teenage boys. I was aware there was something unusually calm and reserved about them. I recognized right away it was the overall demeanor of the boys that made me want to study them more closely each **time** I began to leave. I did not want the boys to think I was staring at them. Although I did notice, they did not seem to mind me glancing at them. I understood later they were there to direct me. Nothing else seemed logical. The two boys were so adamant about me not leaving. Why were these boys so concerned I not leave? Now I understand everything. Now everything that transpired that day is so clear to me.

Thank **You**, **Jesus**, for allowing me to witness **Your** heavenly Angel. Thank **You**, my gracious **God**, for giving me the Grace to recognize **Your** marvelous and loving gifts. I pray I will spend the rest of my life proving to be worthy in the service of others. It is through my example **You** will see I am truly thankful. Amen.

The spectacular encounter with the Angel in the hospital further leads me to believe so profoundly that Angels might appear more and more to other people if it is **God's** will. I am not alone in this assumption as other Christians have told me; they believe we need a sign from Heaven in order to face the reality of our destiny. Still many people are not able to understand or recognize this pure truth yet. Angels are definitely in our midst this very minute all around us. Perhaps you too can think back at a **time** when something unusual presented itself to you. You may find yourself looking from now on at each situation differently than you ever thought possible. I promise you, I am correct. The Angels are here for us every second of the day to guide us. The Angels are waiting for us to recognize they are so close to us because **God** knows we need their help.

I can tell you definitely because of the amazing appearance of the Angel who appeared to me in October 7, 2011, yes, Angels are here with us. The Angels are waiting for the right **time** to announce to you they are here. Every day, I become more aware of the awesome possibility. I find myself paying more attention and definitely more intently than I ever did before. The Angels have intertwined themselves in every facet of our daily life. The Angels are interested in every aspect of our life. The Angels are as curious about us as we are of them. This thought is amazing! Do you think the Angels are curious to know why we do some of the things we do? Please, do not ever believe that just because you have not seen an Angel, you will never have the opportunity to experience an Angel or other spiritual events. On the other hand, it certainly is not necessary for you to experience anything extraordinary to know you love **God** and to know **He** loves you! I believe this is extremely possible someday you might encounter an Angel if this is **God's** Divine Will.

I realize the impact of the words we say to each other will have a profound effect. I have been thinking especially about the words, "**I am**." Whenever I am upset over something, I used to say, "I am so upset, or I am so tired!" Now I realize for me, these simple phrases I will not say again in the same context as to how I used to refer to them. There is an important reason why I say this to you now. The precious words "**I am**" refer to **God**. The Bible tells us that **God** told Moses to tell the people **His** name was, **"I am who I am" (Exodus 3:14).** Now I never say "**I am**" anything that is not pleasing to **God**. Therefore, without realizing this now, I may have been saying to **God**, well, I think you get the point! You see, **God's** children are all very important to **Him**, and it is what we say and how we say it that is all important. Some**times**, the smallest things we say have larger implications than we may realize. It is important to be kind to ourselves so we can be kind to others. Our words can have such a profound effect on people around us. We may never realize the words we say to others might influence someone in a negative way and cause them to make the wrong decision. Therefore, I am taking a closer look at the words I say to others and how I say them. It is so easy to hurt someone's feelings without realizing it. One word out of place can be so harmful. One improper conversation might influence someone into thinking the opposite conclusion. Is this why so many people are misunderstood? The lack of communications skills with this new age generation is only making this more difficult.

Obviously, seeing the Angel in the hospital has changed my entire life and everyone around me. Now everything I always believed about many aspects of Angels I now can say with absolute confidence is **all true**. Now when I recall my visit with the Angel in the hospital, I must conclude that Humanity must understand and finally truly believe just how enormously **God** loves us.

I find myself enjoying so much more of the day than I ever did before. Often, I have heard people say, my husband in particular, "You should enjoy every day as if this were your last." I hope and pray that now while I have seen this awesome Angel, my desire for you is that you may in some way share in this most profound experience. I pray when I tell someone I have seen the Angel, the very essence of the Angel will in some way touch these people in a special way.

Angels are everywhere. Do you think Angels are appearing more now because the world needs them more than ever before? I know the world needs **God's** love and mercy more than ever. There is always constant turmoil somewhere in the world. Our Blessed Mother said when she appeared to the children in Fatima, **"There will always be wars and rumors of wars."** It is my belief that if Humanity would place **Jesus** first in our life, we could change the heart that loves the evil of war! As **God's** children, we must place ourselves at the feet of **Jesus** and ask **Him** to direct us and help us in our daily decisions. Goodness abounds because it begins with one person and then spreads from one person to another faster than you can realize. Take the **time** to visit someone who is lonely and see what happens. It is such a gratifying feeling to know you have made someone happy. Our goodness that found in the hearts of **God's** people pleases **Him** very much. I also like to think I would rather do something good and disappear. You do not need the recognition of others because **God** always sees the good you do. The good deeds you do for others never go unnoticed by **God**.

Catholics believe Saint Michael the Archangel is weighing the good deeds and the bad deeds we all do. You need to believe this because in your heart you know this is the truth. In the Bible, we read where Saint Michael vanquished satin and his legions from Heaven and plunged them into the depths of hell. Christians all over the world all need to pray to Saint Michael daily. Ask him to defend us against the constant assaults from the devil. Saint Michael is the great defender of the church and of the faithful. The Archangel is ready to do battle for Humanity. All you have to do is implore him to help you and he will swiftly defend you.

There is overwhelming proof that **God** is trying to get Humanity's attention. Pray to **Almighty God** today, and tell **Him** you love **Him**! Ask **God** to be with you and to help you in your every need. **God** hears the prayers of the faithful, and **He** will always answer your prayers but not always in the way we expect.

> **God** knows what is truly best for **His**
> children and what we truly need.
> **God** is waiting for us to ask!

CHAPTER 14

How to Recognize the Angels Are Here with You

Have you ever wondered what it would be like to see an Angel? This is fascinating and indeed normal to have thoughts about Angels. It is not a secret, there are people all over the world who have said they have experienced some kind of vivid, unusual, and unique experience related to **God's** heavenly realm. For example, I have read where thousands of people have proclaimed they experienced a near-death experience. Some**times**, people will say they knew for sure, their experience was a vision from Heaven. In addition, people have told me directly of their many experiences they have also witnessed of a spiritual nature. These intense and often somewhat brief experiences some**times** reveal themselves similar in origin. These glorious experiences do seem to have some silent meaning for the particular individual who has experienced these truly amazing revelations. Some people who have experienced an event of profound and powerful experience feel this experience was a private and intimate moment meant for only them. Alternatively, is there a deeper meaning that we do not recognize right away? What about people like myself who have experienced a dramatic vision, encounter, or event that was a direct connection to the spiritual realm? The faithful believe there is a precise reason **God** allows these magnificent encounters to occur.

A gift from **God** so grand, you would feel embarrassed if you have not so easily accepted **God's** gifts. Miracles happen each day. Far too many people just do not see this loving jester of love from **God** because their mind is busy on what we expect is more important. We need to look for the miracles that take place every day in our life, only then will you see it for what it truly is.

God is desperately trying to get our attention before it is too late. I never thought of **God** in such deep terms of having such feelings of loss to the final depth that it may come to. The term *loss* does not express **God's** feelings enough in terms of the loss of **His** creation. You would think this word would be a more dynamic. Yet the possibility of the loss of **God's** children is mighty to **Him** in its present context. **God's** people have placed **God** in a position of enormous sadness that should make any Christian feel horrible to mention it. This monumental loss of **God's** children will ultimately lead to the destruction of our world. Yes, too many people have placed **Almighty God** in immense distress because **His** people have become despondent to **God's** invitation to receive **His** loving gifts of love and mercy. Is **God** desperate because this word proves how much **God** loves us? Yes, I believe **time** is of the essence. Oh, I never thought much about doom and gloom theories. However, I do believe Humanity has wasted precious **time** long enough, and now we need to get serious. It is possible for everyone to have a special closeness with **God** and **His** Angels. You need only to ask **God**, and you will receive **His** unending love you so desperately need every day of your life. **God** is sending **His** Angels to help the people of the world return to **His** loving arms.

There are numerous literary books regarding Angels. Over the centuries, many people have explored this subject regarding the existence of Angels. In the Bible, we read where, **"There were shepherds living out in the fields nearby, keeping watch over their flocks at night. An Angel of the Lord appeared to them and the glory of the Lord shone around them and they were terrified. But the Angel said to them, do not be afraid"** (Luke 2:8–14).

There are thousands of books published regarding Angelic experiences. Many people believe they might have encountered an Angel, and now I can tell them they did. Over the centuries, artists have painted beautiful depictions of what they believe the Angels might look like. I have often admired the numerous paintings and pictures of Angels. Yes, there is the stunning Artwork that people can view in those gorgeous stained glass church windows. In addition, there are also very many beautiful representations in the Bible regarding Angels. Centuries ago, the Bible and other books illustrated Angels in scenes with ordinary people. It seems to me in those days people talked about or knew stories about the Angels visiting with ordinary people often. For example, I love the story in the Bible about **Tobias and the Angel**.

> **Tobias and the Angel** is the title given to paintings and other artworks depicting a scene in which Tobias, son of Tobit, meets an angel without realizing he is an angel (**Book of Tobit, 5.5–6**) and is then instructed by the angel what to do with a giant fish he catches (**Book of Tobit, 6.2–9**).

There was a **time** in our history where people believed in Angels perhaps more than they do today. Was it easier to believe then because these people were more respectful of the word of **God**? Most of our great works of Art are centuries old. Strange why it is today many artists have moved away from the certainty of Angels and **God's** realm. The Angels are definitely with us, and they are closer than you think. In the Bible, with the example of Tobias, he did not realize he was in the presence of an Angel because the Angel resembled an ordinary man. An interesting lesson learned here. In my opinion, then for hundreds of years, these Angel encounters seemed to be very rare. All of a sudden in recent years, there is a renewed sense; Angels are here with us again. Most of the magnificent paintings and the pictures previous generations cherish are in the archival museums. The master painters such as Michelangelo painted Angels centuries ago because there was a greater interest and belief in the Angels and all things related to Heaven. You can visitor go online and view the Sistine Chapel to find magnificent examples. It would be rare today, and this generation would even feel it was not correct to see buildings adorned with paintings on their walls of Angels or Heaven. Why did people withdraw their interest in **God's** realm in recent centuries? Could it be that some people are even fearful of the Angels? Are they afraid to believe in **God**? Is it true that people have forgotten the true importance of their heavenly Angels? It is a simple analogy that if your hearts and minds are not centered on **God** in your daily life, then your minds will not be interested in the Angels either.

I could not begin to know what you think, but I personally always wanted to know more about those gorgeous wings. Do all Angels have those awesome huge wings? Why do they have to have any wings? The Angel who appeared to me in the hospital did not have any noticeable wings. I really looked very carefully, and I could not see any evidence of the wings. However, this does not mean the wings were not there. The possibility exists the wings were not seen because they were hidden within the golden bright light surrounding the Angel. The importance of the wings faded quickly because the Angel captured my undivided attention for a more significant reason. The Angel appeared because it was the importance of the profound message that she wanted me to share with everyone.

As rapidity as possible, my mind tried to capture every detail of the Angel, but silently, I knew the true essence of any Angel would elude me and remain a true mystery. Perhaps this is the way this should remain. Even attempting to paint what I witnessed would prove to be very challenging, if not impossible. It certainly is not easy for me to describe the Angel fully. Maybe this is the way this should be also. I find the Angel so difficult to describe because it would be like trying to describe Heaven. How do you describe the unbelievable and indescribable beauty we believe resides only in Heaven? No one artist could ever completely capture the true essence and awesome beauty of an Angel. There was a similar dilemma for Sister Faustina who was canonized Saint Maria Faustina Kowalska on April 30, 2000. Sister Faustina could never find an artist who could truly capture what she witnessed in the **Divine Mercy** Image of **Christ**. It is my beliefs all the Angels have their unique personality just as we also retain this aspect of our human nature. I believe no one Angel will ever be completely like another. The Angels created by **God** to be unique unto them because the Angels all serve **God** for uniquely specific purposes for the glory of **His** Kingdom.

- There are numerous Angels sent to us from **God** because each one is here to help us in one way or another. The Bible teaches us there are so many levels of Angels. I love to revisit this information on Angels in the Bible. I suggest you read the Bible often and you will understand better the many levels regarding Angels.
- Here is a partial list for you to research: **Seraphim, Cherubim, Thrones, Dominions or Lordships, Virtues or Strongholds, Powers or Authorities, Principalities or Rulers, Archangels Seraphim, Cherubim and, of course, Angels.**

It is my belief this opportunity to study the different level of Angels will automatically enhance your awareness of the possibility of seeing Angels or the awareness of them. It is my belief **God** sends specific Angels here specifically for each one of us for a specific need, as in the Angel that appeared to me. The **Holy Spirit** sent this Angel to convey a message for all Humanity. This is a powerful thought to know we are this important to **God**. To understand the great design of **God's** creation known as Angels, **God** created them for each of us in such a personal way.

The world is bursting with the presence of Angels, but they are powerless over worldly affair that adversely affect you and me every day. Angels can do very little without our cooperation. Therefore, is this proper to say, in every instance, the Angels need us too? The Angels must have our cooperation because we have free will. However, I now begin to wonder if **God** might give **His** Angels extended power to divert us from devastating decisions in the future. This, of course, is my own personal viewpoint because the world is in dire need of divine intervention. I do very much believe the Angels can come to our aid without our will if **God** directs them to. This is **God's** will that the Angels respond in order to protect us in **times** of danger. People who believe Angels visited them when they were in great spiritual need have documented numerous occasions of these particular experiences they encountered. Countless people do believe help arrived by way of an Angel. It is my belief that **God** allows the Angels to look deep into our heart in order to see what we believe regarding the salvation of our soul. The Angels search for a way to get our attention so they can help us. In the end, **God** alone decides what is necessary in our life. However, because we have free will, we need **God** in order to have anything benefit our life. Everyone needs to realize you are powerless to accomplish anything meaningful without **God**. **God**, in **His** infinite goodness and wisdom, provides us with everything necessary for us to be happy. However, in the end, this is still our choice to decide what happens to the Human Race in the future. Will Humanity finally learn what **God** expects from us? Alternatively, will Humanity continue on the present path with no regard to **God's** Commandments? Did Humanity forget we must be worthy to enter the Kingdom of Heaven?

Why have so many people misplaced and even destroyed their moral values? There is no doubt that this is why **God** sent **His** Angel in order to give Humanity perhaps one last opportunity to see the truth. **God** knows you and I need to be reminded and often what we should value most in our life. **God** desires us to know we are not alone. The evil one tries to convince Humanity that you and I do not need **God** anymore. It is so evident that multitudes of people by their actions are convinced of this falsehood. You must find the strength to fight the evil that has filled your heart and mind with lies and deceit. Humanity must look to **God's** holy Angels for help. I promise you a great awakening will happen in your life. This awakening will be different for everyone because each Soul is unique unto **God**. I wonder how many people think they are unique! How many people realize how special they are to **God**? Yes, you are very special to **God**. **God** loves everyone on this earth equally.

Obviously, to contemplate the possibility exists that you may have seen an Angel or experienced a heavenly vision is overwhelming. This would be unlike anything else ever possible to experience again. This experience would be one of the most thrilling experiences of a life**time**. To think those people previously were unaware something so life-changing was about to take place. To know all these wonderful and loving experiences come directly from **God** because **He** loves and adores us so much. For without the Divine Will of **God**, nothing good will happen. This truth is so fascinating to me; these visions and special encounters always take place when you are least expecting it. In the blink of an eye, you realize because of your unique experience, your life will change forever. Who does not like to be surprised? These marvelous and glorious gifts from **God** are so precious, we truly find ourselves meditating on the wonder of these gifts. This is so profoundly amazing to me to think in my life**time**, this was ever possible for me personally to see an Angel and converse with the Angel and furthermore have an Angel convey a message for all that will listen. The Angel said, **"Tell them it is almost time."** I will be forever humbled to the very core of my being to **God** because **He** bestowed such a profoundly holy gift upon me. I continue to pray to **God** that **He** will bless my decisions I will make from this day forward. I pray I will also recognize what **God** desires me to do for **Him** the rest of my life. I am nothing without **God**.

> Dear **God**, help me to make a difference in the world with my example of love for **You**. I pray that the example I demonstrate to others, this will make the most important impression that could change someone's entire life and, therefore, save their Soul.

There is no doubt that **God** is trying to warn Humanity our future might not be what we have planned and hoped. The Angel did say, **"It is almost time."** This is a severe warning from the **Holy Spirit** through the message conveyed from the Angel I pray that no one will take lightly. Seeing the Angel was a tremendously holy experience for me. However, I realized later, with the appearance of the Angel, the message contained profound and direr implications. The message is for everyone who will listen and who will heed the warning. Therefore, I must proceed with this writing because this is what the Angel instructed me to do.

God's presence is all around us every minute of the day. I see the presence of **God** in the face of an older person in the nursing home.

I sense the presence of **God** when I help someone who is lonely. I cannot express to you enough how important this is to let a lonely person know they are not alone. Tell them they will never be alone because **God** is present with them always. I see **God** in the face of someone suffering. **God** and **His** Angels are there with the homeless and anyone who is suffering. It is so difficult to understand why there are still multitudes of people in the world persecuted and even killed for their faith. I can assure you **God** is watching, and I assure you **God** and the Angels are with them. I sense the presence of **God** when I do something good for someone in need no matter how small. Most of all, I see **God** in the innocent faces of children. How can anyone know the plight of a hungry child and do nothing to help?

How sad it is that so many people do not believe **God** is with them. How sad it is that so many people no longer desire to believe this truth. **God** is always watching us, and **He** is so pleased when good people come to the aid of others. **God** patiently waits for **His** people to remember they do not walk alone. If you want to feel the presence of **God** and see Angels, you must first start feeling the pain of others in order to do something to help them. Make a positive change in one person's life, and **God** will bless you in abundance. Perhaps seeing Angels is not important to you because you are already in the presence of **God** when you do **God's** work. **God** knows how to bless each of us in a special way that only we will understand. You do not have to see an Angel to see the goodness and grace of your life that **God** has bestowed on you for the benefit of others.

> Dear **God**, allow **Your** Angels to make their presence known to all **Your** faithful people. I pray that **Your** children will see that **You** desire their happiness. I pray that **Your** children will understand now is **time** for Humanity to realize the truth before it is too late. **Your** message is clear and simple to discern. **Your** people must transform their life and dispel evil from their life and return to **Your** love and mercy! I pray that **Your** people must remember that **You** desire Humanity to love one another as **You** have loved us!

CHAPTER 15

There Is No Escape from the Images of Evil

The ominous message the Angel entrusted to me is unimaginably disturbing. I could see the seriousness in the Angel's eyes, and this saddened me greatly. Hearing the words that came directly from the Angel, **"Tell them it is all most time,"** weighed heavy on my heart. The implication of those six words became clearer to me after I witnessed the images the Angel revealed to me. There were numerous scenes of a future where because of our Sin, the world was lost without the love of **God**.

The evil images I witnessed are indescribable and terribly daunting. They are nearly impossible to describe to anyone in mere words. Rarely, I discuss these images with anyone because they are extremely disturbing. The evil images I witnessed haunt my mind and my heart. I will never be able to escape from what I was compelled to observe! These images are on my mind every day, especially when I consider what is going on in the world. How should I cope with the images the Angel showed me? What am I supposed to do now that I have seen them? This is so difficult for me to understand why this was necessary for me to witness a colossal evil yet to come! The evil behind what I witnessed was more frightening than can ever be imagined in the human mind. It is still very difficult for me to face the truth; Humanity has strayed too far from the safety of **God**! Some of the images of evil I witnessed are presently happening all over the world right now as I type. The awful truth is we are all aware of the suffering that takes place all over the world, and yet Humanity does little to stop it. I too will have to answer to **God** why I also stood silent and did nothing. I do not know why it was necessary for me to observe firsthand the evil what generations in the future allowed to take place. This was very horrifying for me personally to observe that it could ever be possible Humanity could succumb to evil on such an immense scale. There certainly is an explicit reason why I had to view this evil in such a manner. It is the unwavering Faith in my **Lord** and my **God** that compels me to love **Him** even more because **He** will never leave those who love **Him**. **God** directed **His** Angel to appear to me with a dire message for the world. Why was it necessary for me to witness firsthand the horrible evils that roam the world waiting to devour Humanity? I pray Humanity will never experience the answer!

Most people do not like to think about evil, but perhaps this is the **time** to face the truth because evil is very real. It does no one any good to pretend evil does not exist. Pretending or refusing to face the truth will not make evil disappear! People have allowed evil to expand its energy into every facet of their life. Yes, evil has gathered enormous energy, and it is drawing our energy unto itself and is growing stronger. Society is allowing evil to flourish right before their eyes because people turn their backs and pretend they do not see it. I am very disturbed because everyone has seen what evil will do if evil has a chance! What is Humanity going to do to stop it? Together with **God's** help, we can wipe evil from the face of the earth and out of our lives for good. Sounds impossible, but right now, the little secret evil does not want you to remember is evil is afraid Humanity might wake up in **time** and end the plague of evil. How do we know what **God** might decide to do if Humanity proved it was worthy? Would **God** decide to vanquish the devil for all **time**, or will the world end in total defeat without a fight and without **Almighty God**? I feel helpless to do anything about this alone. Together and with **God** by our side, we will accomplish a great change in the world. You need to begin by asking **God** what **He** desires you to do for **Him**. I assure you **God** will answer you in **His time**. Then it is up to you to take charge and allow **God** to enter your life because there miracles will begin to happen.

Why is repetitive bad behavior harmful? Continually repeating some bad behavior taking place in your life over **time** only leads to other avenues of more outrageous behavior. Soon, the habits that young people develop at an early age become acceptable as normal behavior once they reach adulthood. Evil knows if it recruits our young adults early enough, it has an increased chance of ruining a young person's life. It is so difficult to change what you have been accustomed to doing perhaps all your life. Our society is ever changing according to the mood of the opposition at the **time**. It takes great courage to stand up for what is right and to face the truth that because of your life choices, life may not be what should be a happy experience. Now is the right **time** to give your life over to **God**. Life may be difficult and your life may be hard, but **God** is waiting to take over those burdens for you. It is never too late, and I repeat it is never too late to turn your life over to **God**. **God** who loves you so much is waiting with open arms for you to recognize this truth.

In addition, rewarding bad behavior is a concept that makes absolutely no common sense. Why do we reward certain individuals, companies, and/or organizations frequently that conduct bad behavior or bad business practices? It is beyond any normal intelligence to continue this misguided practice of compensation, especially when the organization is involved in the devil's dirty work! Yet this practice goes on every day, and it is not just small business that reaps the profit. I will never understand nor accept the truth why an organization that clearly and blatantly uses taxpayers money to the tune of 1.5 billion dollars in order to inflict untold pain and suffering on the innocence of the unborn child of **God**. Christians comply only by force to follow the law, and as a result, their hard-earned money becomes part of this ugly and masterly constructed evil plot.

No wonder God sent His Angel to tell Humanity we need to reevaluate and consider carefully the decisions we are presently proposing.

It is because the Angel appeared to me and pronounced such distain for what we are doing by allowing (**Abortion**) that I have no choice but to honor **Almighty God** when I say to you that **Abortion** must end! It must be now not later on this year or when the vote comes up again for more useless debate but right now! Otherwise, we deserve what is waiting to happen because we have free will and, therefore, we will have made our choice!

Evil is not difficult to find because evil finds you first! You never have to look very far because unfortunately, evil is always near. Humanity is tempted with evil every second of the day because many people are allowing and inviting evil into their lives and into their hearts by the decisions they make. Evil is becoming stronger and more aggressive because there are people who refuse to believe evil exists; therefore, they do not see the danger. Humanity is showing their weaknesses, and therefore, evil considers us an easy target. It is evident that multitudes of people no longer believe evil will destroy their Soul! These people have already given up from the struggle and only hope that **God** might show them **His** mercy and save them. Children are suffering from shrewdness of evil, and good people stand by and do little to stop their suffering. Evil is having a field day with all of us, but I repeat, did you know evil is afraid? Yes, evil does not want you to be aware it is afraid because evil is always worried you will turn to **God** for help. Evil is a party, and we are the willing guests who have accepted the invitation. Some people even get a special invitation to attend the party and are all too willing to reply yes! Evil provides even special invitations to certain individuals, and they must choose to resist or comply. We attend and become part of the party even when we think we do not want to attend. Some**times**, you attend out of curiosity, and this is very, very dangerous. This curiosity some**times** gets more people into big trouble, and they had no idea they placed their soul in jeopardy. Oh yes, evil is very much alive and well because evil is allowed to flourish and expand its evil mischief. It is not difficult to understand why evil finds it so easy to deceive us, but goodness is more difficult to manage! We allow ourselves to be such an easy target to the thoughts and whims of evil. Many individuals simply have made the decision to love evil because it seems easier, because once you acquaint yourself with evil, there are no rules! As a result, we have a society who does not recognize right from wrong anymore. Pretending we no longer know the difference will not work for us anymore. **God** knows we do know the difference! Therefore, we all have no excuse evil is having a grand **time** with us. What Humanity is dealing with is the loss of their Souls. This is a heavy price to pay, and as a result, there will be great suffering. The loss of your Soul signifies that your life here on earth was worthless, and as a result, you forfeit eternal life. We need to be on watch now more than ever because it is not only **God** watching you! Evil will not stop until we say the word *no* and mean it. Today, the word *no* in many respects is not enough to stop evil. Evil never stops because it knows it can wear you down little by little and eventually win. We must all work together to reject evil and make a recommitment to **God** to take the necessary actions to say no as a society and as an individual. We need a demanding resolve to fight the evil who does not want to let go of us. We need to run to **God's** loving arms because only **God** will protect us. Please open your heart and hear what **God** is trying to tell you.

The Bible teaches us to: **"Pray unceasingly"** (Eph. 6; 18). Then also our **Beloved Jesus** implores **His** Disciples in the Garden of Gethsemane, **"Rise and pray, that you should not enter into temptation"** (Luke 22; 46).

Dear **God**, I pray that **Your** people will follow the true path **You** designed for each of us that will enable **Your** faithful to one day join with **You** in Heaven. Help **Your** children to follow the right path so **Your** children can promote goodness, and peace for all the people in the world. Dear **God**, I am ready to do **Your** complete Divine Will. I say a resounding, "Yes, my **Lord** and my **God**," because I truly believe I am nothing and can do nothing without **You**. I pray others will join with me in prayer and action because together we will accomplish **Your** holy Divine Will. I pray to **You**, my **God**, that **You** will reveal to **Your** faithful everything that will be necessary to complete the wonderful design **You** planned for all the people of the world. I pray **You** will bestow on all **Your** people the Grace and discernment that we will needed to improve our life in a way that is pleasing to **You**. I pray that the people of the world will turn away from the lure of temptation and turn their hearts to only **You**. In this I pray, Amen.

God is trying to get our attention!

CHAPTER 16

The Angel and Your Faith in Almighty God

I must say repeatedly how grateful I am to **God** that **He** allowed me to witness the glorious presence of a heavenly Angel. Now that I have seen the Angel, I realize people all over the world are completely unaware this astonishing possibility might exist for them too if it is the will of **Almighty God**. It is evident that people today do not take their faith seriously enough anymore. People everywhere are completely unaware an incredible spiritual experience could possibly enter into their life at any moment. To think an experience such as this and most people all over the world have no idea seeing an Angel is not only possible but also probable. I am talking about ordinary people during their routine day. Ordinary people like you and I going about our daily business that would never be aware it would be possible to have a visit from an Angel in any capacity. Start thinking more about the possibility that you too might experience one of **God's** special miracles in your life. Now look back and perhaps you can remember an opportunity you may have overlooked. Did you forget that the greatest gift of all is that **God** bestows **His** love for you every second of the day?

You never know what might take place when you least expect it. You may have missed an opportunity if you think about it. Imagine, at a precise **time** in your life, you could experience something incredible that would indeed change your life and everyone you meet. This would forever change how you would feel about everything pertaining to **God**. Nothing in your life would ever again have the same meaning. Everything you hold dear would be so much more important to you. Even issues you thought to be complicated in your life would become less stressful. Your life would change because of what you believed in faith alone, all your life, you now see is absolutely the truth. However, without question, these miraculous experiences would enhance the deeply rooted faith that was already possessed in a particular individual. You would have to say to yourself, "My **God**, everything I believed by faith alone is all true." I am speaking about everything—"everything" most people believed through their faith and the teachings of the Bible. **God** has shown me that if you trust and believe in **Him, He** will show you the plan **He** has for you. In the Bible, **Jesus** teaches us here: **"Truly I tell you, if you had Faith as small as a mustard seed, you can say to this mountain, move from here to there and it will move" (Matthew 17–20).**

Do you think these encounters with Angels could ever happen to the unbeliever? Does **God** reveal anything to the unbeliever, and if so, what? However, without faith, how could this be possible for an unbeliever to believe or understand **God's** Word? **God**, in **His** Divine Mercy, views all of us in the same manner and with the same love. **God** looks into our heart to find the truth for what we really think and what we truly believe. **God** does not judge us for what is on the surface or what we may only project to one another. **God** looks deeper into the very essence of who we are. **God** looks deeply into our Soul, and only there does **God** see, really see, who we have become and what we truly believe. **God** knows everything you believe in your heart and mind.

Is it possible to analyze why **God** allows some magnificent and often unexplained event to take place? This is amazing to me that all of a sudden, some desperately needed help appears and at the precise **time** and place. There are people who have said they were definitely convinced they felt **God** sent an Angel to help them. Some people have also experienced a word of warning that often comes in an unusual way. This could be in the form of a weird feeling of uneasiness that does not go away until you recognize this feeling is a warning. In addition, there are people who have experienced a bright light followed by feelings of inexplicable peacefulness and happiness that words cannot properly express. I have always believed **God** sends **His** Angels to us for encouragement and reassurance at a **time** when we need this assurance the most. Why do only some people believe it is possible to be in the presence of an Angel? We are in the presence of Angels every second of the day. Our Guardian Angels are with us even if we do not believe. I would think people who concede they are Christians would think it is normal to believe in their Angels. Angels are definitely not a myth, but I rarely hear anyone talk about Angels. I think belief in Angels might be only a personal interest for some people. Now I know for sure Angels are here all around us every second and every minute of the day. The Angels are a magnificent gift **God** has bestowed on us so we never have to walk through life alone. I can only imagine the immense love **God** must share for all **His** children that **He** would provide you and me a personal Guardian Angel. A uniquely personal Angel **God** provided for you and me who will stay with us our entire life. I wonder how many people really appreciate this truth anymore. Do people in our modern world even give their Guardian Angel a single thought? I know there are many people that do believe, and if this was not fantastic enough, it is my belief **God** might send additional Angels now because **He** desires to save us from the destruction of evil's plan. **God** desires the Angels to do everything possible to keep us from harm. In the Bible, we read where the Angel warned Joseph in a dream to flee to Egypt. The Angel said, "**Get up and take the child and flee to Egypt**" (**Matthew 2:13–23**).

Angels assume many different characteristics. I think each appearance is different according to our specific need at the **time**. Here is a personal example my husband's family experienced. It was a short while after I was married that my husband's parents, Daniel and Mary, told me a story regarding their strong belief that they received a visit from an Angel. It was 1938, during the depression, and my father-in-law Daniel was digging ditches to put food on the table for his family. Those depression years were very tough, and people did anything they could to make a little money for their family. It

I SEE AN ANGEL

was common in those days for lots of people to ride the trains in the back of the boxcars from town to town looking for odd jobs. Most of the townspeople were aware of the men who traveled in this manner. People called the men who rode the boxcars tramps or hoe boys. The term *hoe boys* come from the fact that many of them traveled with a shovel. During this **time**, there was a great deal of these men walking the streets looking for any job so they could eat. One afternoon, there was a knock on the door. There stood a tall stranger, it was a *hoe boy* looking for an odd job, and he was hungry too. As this man stood in the doorway, his profile resembled an exceptionally tall thin man. This man told Daniel he was very hungry and asked if they would give him something to eat. Daniel instructed his wife Mary to feed the poor hungry man. Mary was a bit surprised at the appetite this man displayed. Mary was also a little annoyed at the amount of food this person continued to devour. Mary felt a little upset because they barely had enough food in the house for their own family. When the tramp had finished his meal, he thanked them both for the food and proceeded toward the door to leave. When the stranger reached the front door, he turned to them and made the sign of the cross. Then he announced to them, "Tomorrow, someone will come to the house and offer Daniel a job that he would have as long as he wanted it." He left and nothing more was said about what the stranger had told them until the next morning. Sure enough, as the visitor had said, the next day, there was a knock on the door. It was an owner of one of the local businesses in town. He offered Daniel a job to start the next day. Daniel worked there for over forty years. Daniel did retire from the job the stranger had announced he would have as long as he wanted it. This story says volumes to us that you never know who **God** might send into your life. **God** sent an Angel to a family in need. **God** sent **His** Angel to help a family who believed **God** would help them, and **He** did.

    Seventy years have passed since the terrible hardships of the depression era. Since then, occasionally, someone in the family would chat about what happened that day. Everyone in the family is convinced this tall figure of a man who stood in the doorway asking for food was indeed an Angel. An Angel came to help a family that believed in **God**. I know how much the entire family appreciated this special offering from **God**, and they gave thanks for this gift in many ways the rest of their life. This visit from the stranger left a lasting impression for the entire family. You must understand the importance of this story is that this family recognized later the truth that stood before them in the doorway. **God** sent an Angel to them because they believed so strongly in their Faith that **God** would help them and **He** did!

There are compelling stories that these encounters with Angels are not just co instances that happen to countless people. I continue to believe the problem why some people are not open to the possibility Angels appeared in the form of an ordinary person is because they do not believe in their faith any longer. Most people do not recognize these glorious moments because when anything spiritual presents itself, they do not recognize this as a gift from **God**. The **Holy Spirit** and the Angels never give up trying to get your attention. Maybe when you have had some **time** to think about it again, you may ask yourself, what just happened? Later, when you are alone and have **time** to reflect on a specific occasion, you might be curious enough to ask, what happened might have involved an Angel? **God** is trying to get our attention by sending **His** Angels to us. Open your eyes and heart to the great possibility that something will present itself to you, and then it will be your turn to ask, "Did I see an Angel?" There is a belief among unbelievers that there is no **God** and certainly, there are no Angels to intervene on your behalf. How sad to feel this way, the world must look very small to these unbelievers. **God's** people have to be receptive to recognize these special encounters when it presents itself to you. Then you will know that the **Holy Spirit** and **His** Angels are involved and desire to be part of your life.

Most people are well aware of what is happening all around them, and there are people who are genuinely concerned. The problem is most of the **time** their concerns do not rise to the importance of their relationship with **God** and the needs of others. You need only to look in your own communities to see the desperate needs of others to know this is the truth. Then you will truly comprehend what **God** is trying to tell you.

Dear **Lord**, help **Your** children to love one another!

Yes, **God** is trying to get our attention to remind humanity **He** loves us all so dearly.

CHAPTER 17

The Message

The enormous possibility of being in the presence of an Angel are truly spectacular events no matter how, when, where, or even why **God** allows them to occur. In the Bible, we read, **"Then I looked and heard a voice of many Angels, numbering thousands upon thousands and ten thousand times ten thousand. They encircled the throne" (Revelations 5:11)**. The Angels in Heaven must number in the millions **times** millions, so why are there so many of them? It does make perfect sense to me that there would have to be millions if each one of us has a Guardian Angel. One can only speculate that these millions of Angels, sent by **God**, to assist us every day in everything we do. Individuals that have experienced something out of the ordinary can now conclude that yes, Angels often come to us in many different appearances. It is clear that the Angels do not appear as Angels rather as ordinary people because they know it is easier for us to accept. This is when the fun begins, and you may find yourself asking, is it possible; this was a visit from my Guardian Angel or another supportive Angel? After all, when anything takes place mysteriously, it is only normal to wonder what took place and the desire to know more can be captivating. What about these unique unseen occasions from designated Angels instructed by **God** to give you a specific message? It is my strong belief now that there are truly subtle ways you may receive a message from **God** but obvious enough that it does not have to be a spectacular event. How awesome **God** loves us this much; **He** will allow us to receive a message from **Him**. **God** allows everyone the opportunity to receive all kinds of messages at any **time**. To receive any message from **God**, having faith gives you the ability to be listening very carefully. In order to receive any spiritual message, you must first open your heart to the possibility. The most obvious way to receive a message from **God** is during prayer. Prayer and meditation is a simple way to hear **God** speaking to you. Obviously, not the way you would hear someone speaking to you. **God's** voice is within you because **He** is within you. Only you will hear the message and decipher the meaning. Believe me when I say, if you want to hear **God's** voice, you must be quiet and desire this with your whole heart and Soul.

Is the message I received from the Angel strictly a warning? Can we interpret any hope within the message? Yes, because the Angel appeared, it is conformation that **Almighty God** has not given up on **His** people yet! What is very important to understand is contained within these six words, **"Tell them it is almost time,"** are multiple interpretations. It is amazing how only six words would become so important and mean something differently to so many people. When I tell anyone about the message, he or she some**times** is happy to give me their explanation of what the message means to them. I feel this is encouraging to hear that these people do understand the message. There can be no doubt that these six words speak volumes of the terrible truth that we have all severely offended **God** by our sinful nature. Still faced with the truth of **God's** tremendous disappointment in **His** children, **He** would prove **His** love for us once again by sending **His** Angel to warn **His** people, we have lost our way. I always believed in my heart that **God** does send the Angels to help us when **His** people are in desperate need of **His** mercy. The Angel appeared with a message to warn **God's** children that Humanity must reach out our hearts to **God**.

How can we discern together the significance of the words contained in the message the Angel conveyed to me? **"Tell them it is almost time."** This is very evident and of the greatest importance that I help you understand the message from the Angel was for everyone to realize **God** is using the message to get our attention! I felt initially the message meant my **time** here on earth was rapidly ending. However, soon after the Angel appeared to me, what became clearer was the message was predestined for all **God's** people. The truth is we all need to declare to **God**, we still love **Him** and need **Him** in our life. **God** desires proof by that we intend to amend our life in a way that is pleasing to **Him**. The message declares Humanity has not done very well to make the world a safe place to live in, especially for our youth. The demeanor of the Angel when she spoke about the sin in the world was heartbreaking for me to witness. The overwhelming truth contained in the message is yes, **God** is extremely displeased with **His** people! Humanity must demonstrate to **God** we still care about one another. **God's** people need to prove by our actions that **His** children do care what happens to our future. There is no doubt, and this is so essential to understand, we need to prove to **God** we are accountable to what happens to our children. Most of all, we need to prove to **God** we are people capable of loving and caring what happens to the unborn child. Life is **God's** greatest gift to Humanity the world will ever know, and there are people who consider this awesome gift disposable! There are also people who throw away **God's** most wondrous and precious creation along with the other garbage they accumulate. No wonder **God** is warning us we have abandoned **Him**! If the most grievous Sin of ungodly practice of **Abortion** does not provide enough information for you to understand the message, nothing will. Until you give your entire life to **God,** you will never understand. **God** has already given Humanity repeated opportunities to amend our life, proof of **God's** tremendous love for us. Still countless people refuse to believe there is any urgency. However, we must all face the truth that people give **God** the impression with their continued bad behavior; they do not care about **Him** and all **His** Commandments! Therefore, these people are continually telling **God** by their actions that they have given up their free will that tells them everything they do is just fine. **God** never loses hope in **His** children, but the words the Angel conveyed only proves that **He** sees the tremendous failures within our societies such as the heinous Sin of **Abortion**. No wonder **God** sent **His** Angel with a profound message that Humanity must realize we are destroying **His** most sacred creation. What is important to me right now is I must convey the message to as many people as possible. I believe the **Holy Spirit** will permit me to say the right words and at the right **time**. I am deeply concerned, will people finally understand how disappointed **God** truly is with what **His** people have allowed to take place in the world? There will always be someone who may have a negative opinion about any issue. There will always be some people who will refuse to face the issues discussed throughout these chapters. Frankly, some people will not take the **time** to bother with any of this. These individuals would rather waltz around their problems rather than confront their problems head-on.

What is really happening with relationships today between two people who profess they love each other? Unfortunately, in this country, we are experiencing a high rate of divorce that has now reached 53%. The consequences of this separation are a detriment to our society in general. It is the overall attitude that a better relationship is waiting around the corner. What is worse, children of divorced parents are adversely affected. The effects on children of divorced parents can last well into adulthood for most of these children. Even though on the surface these children seem to have adjusted, often**times**, there is a more serious effect that is not apparent until the child is in his or her developmental stage. It is a proven fact that adults later in life affected by divorce when they were young are fearful of this intimacy. These children, now adults, are fearful of commitment! It is the breakdown of our moral standards pure and simple! What can we do to break the cycle that is affecting millions of people in an unsympathetic way? I fully realize that there are plenty of situations where divorce may be necessary. However, can you imagine a relationship sanctioned by **Almighty God** between a husband and wife falling apart if a few of these qualities were present in their marriage? Some of these fine qualities are kindness, patience, faithfulness, dignity, and respect. These are only some of the virtues that we receive from of the **Holy Spirit**!

Today, adults do not want to face the reality of cause and effect in order to change what is obvious because they are only concerned with their own happiness. Today, it is evident that a great deal of people are no longer interested in what makes someone else happy. It seems too easy for adults to withdraw from the problem rather than address the situation in an intelligent manner. Many have lost the will and the effort designed by **God** to manage a good relationship. This is why we have such a high rate of divorce today. People today in our modern world simply do not want to take the **time** to figure out what went wrong with their relationship. This is why they are afraid to make a commitment with one another. Our laws allow divorce to be so easy for couples to walk away when there is no true commitment. You cannot accomplish or solve anything worthwhile if you deal with your life in such callous and indifferent attitude. I never could understand one issue that is so glaring to me about marriage and this is married couples do not take their marriage vows seriously anymore. If you professed at one **time** you would love someone for the rest of your life**time**, why did your love for one another disappear so easily? Why is this so apparent, in so many relationships, love seems to die overnight? I know there are always special circumstances, but far too many people find divorce the easy way out! Divorce is not the problem; divorce is an unhealthy condition. I guess our laws make divorce too easy to switch partners because life looks better or more interesting somewhere else. **God** sees this overwhelming indecisiveness and selfishness as a total breakdown in respect for one another. The most serious problem is divorce does not only affect only the husband and wife. If children are involved, they are the ones who suffer the most, and most children spend the rest of their lives suffering from their parents' mistakes. Rarely do the split up of a family ever turn out positive for anyone. Someone always gets hurt, and the scars sometimes last a life**time**. Scripture teaches us that, **"Marriage between Christians is a Sacrament instituted by Christ" (Genesis 2:24)**. In affirming the sacramental aspect of Christian marriage, the church is officially saying that marriage among Christians is sacred! **God** views the Sacrament of Marriage as a sacred trust between a man and a woman. I see this sacred trust becoming a distant memory in our society. I love to read the story in the Bible of the marriage in Cana in Galilee. **Jesus** was an invited guest to attend the celebration.

When they ran out of wine, the Mother of **Jesus** said, **"They have no wine!" Jesus** said, **"Fill the jars with water. Now draw some out and take it to the master of the feast." Jesus** transforms the water into the finest of wine! This is the first signs **Jesus** did at Cana in Galilee, and this manifested **His** glory!

I trust in **God He** will give me the strength to convince people to open their eyes to the light and the truth of the many truths found within the message the Angel conveyed to me. The message is the light of truth **God** promises to give us if we have Faith and trust in **His** mercy. You must have Faith that **God** does not want you to be fearful because you will prevail and have happiness in your life if you would only offer up your problems to **Him** for solutions. **God** is waiting to give you the answers to all your problems if you would only listen to what **God** is trying to tell you. Generations have fallen into a sense of falsehood that today so many believe is the truth. Christians have forgotten what **Jesus** said, **"I am the light, the truth and the way. No man comes to the Father, but by Me alone" (John 14:6).**

It is easy to fall into a routine, and as a result, we continue to follow a false sense of direction. I pray that **God** will show me the way to lead others into this light so everyone will accomplish what they were born to accomplish for **Almighty God**. I continue to follow the direction from the Angel on everything I write. As my writing moves from one issue to another, I do repeat some issues. I can only say I continue to follow what the Angel is instructing me to write and certainly some issues need repeating.

Now is a very emotional **time**; nevertheless, I continue to pray more than ever because **God** never gives us more than we can handle. I have always been a very strong-willed person because my faith and my convictions are hard as a rock! No matter what I needed to face, I knew **God** was with me every step of the way. **God** was always with me in every situation no matter how challenging it seemed at the **time**. However, I realize this does not necessarily make life less difficult. Therefore, since **God** knows us better than we do, **God's** children must trust **He** knows what is best for us. I did not always see this truth as clearly or quickly as I should have. **God** understands our Humanity so well. We should never question what might happen and trust **God** instead. Under normal circumstances, worrying about something that may occur in the future is not what **God** desires from us. **God** expects you and me to do the best we can right now in order to improve our world. **God** knows what is necessary for us to do in order to improve ourselves, but **He** needs our cooperation to make this happen. How many **times** have you heard someone say, "They worried all week long about a problem, and then they realized the situation was not as serious as they first thought." or, "Everything they worried about worked out better than they could have anticipated." You must strengthen your faith that **God** does have everything under control if you would only trust in **His** mercy. We must understand this is the key to our happiness because without **God**, you and I can do nothing. This is a cooperated effort between you and **God** in order for anything to work out in a positive way.

This is a very difficult and challenging **time** for all of **God's** people. Countless people find their emotions are tremendously elevated because of all the stresses happening in the world. Some days, everything in your life seems to be more than you can handle. During this precise **time**, you need more than ever to open your heart to **God**. Open your eyes so you may see the miracles **God** sends you every day. How truly magnificent it is if you have already experienced some kind of private spiritual experience. Either recently or in the past and because of this, you now need to help others be closer to **God**. Sharing a deep and private spiritual moment you may have encountered may be too precious for you to share with others and I understand. You may choose not to share these precious experiences with anyone because telling others might be awkward. You may feel initially you would rather keep these feelings and special experiences to yourself, and maybe you should. Should you always share these experiences with others? Does **God** desire you to share your experience in order to benefit someone else spiritually? This might be **God's** Divine Will for you to share your experience with others. Only you can discern in prayer if it would be beneficial to share your experience. You need to ask yourself if this was the reason you experienced something in the first place. Clearly, it might be perfectly natural for you to keep these precious moments hidden from the scrutiny of others if you choose. The **Holy Spirit** will guide you in all things pertaining to your spiritual life.

After my visit with the Angel, I knew it was important to share with others everything related to **God** because this will strengthen your faith and together bond our convictions. After seeing the Angel, I am certain now some experiences take place for the benefit of everyone. The message the Angel conveyed to me was definitely for the benefit of everyone. The Angel said, **"Tell them."** In other words, tell everyone the message! Now finally, I have the opportunity to share the knowledge of the message I received with a multitude of individuals in order to bring them closer to **God**. The Angel said, **"Tell them it is almost time."** I pray this message will automatically bring everyone who will read this and hear the words expressed by the Angel closer to **God**. I pray that others who may have experienced a heavenly experience or event will come forward and give testimony to the truth they have also witnessed. Allowing others to be aware of the experiences are so important because these experiences are proof **God** loves us so much. Whenever you experience anything extraordinary, place yourself at the feet of **Jesus Christ**. The feelings of emotion expressed would automatically have to be part of the very essence of who we are as individuals. Please believe each of us stand before **God** at every moment, at every second. Therefore, can this also be said that during each moment, you have the opportunity to become part of an experience that is waiting for you to seize the moment? A friendship with **Almighty God** is ready and waiting for you. Your own personal friendship with **Him** is available to you whenever you desire. It is unbelievable why some people never accept these opportunities offered to them. Therefore, left unaware and never knowing, the extraordinary and dear friendship of having a personal relationship with **God** was so close. This friendship may elude you until you are willing to allow **God's** words to fill your heart at another **time**.

Here is something that people should be disturbed about. I do not understand why more people do not voice their opinions louder regarding our religious traditions that some groups are trying to dismantle. What is this religious persecution really all about? Why are so many people willing to allow unbelievers to challenge and destroy our traditions and for the sake of who? Why do you as a Christian remain silent when these unbelievers try to destroy your sacred images of your faith? The message means now is the **time** we must all be steadfast in our convictions. The message asks everyone to renew our faith in **Almighty God** because these disturbances are merely evil intentions to distract you. Why are Christians allowing others who do not believe in much of anything come between what a great many people know is the truth? You and I cannot continue to allow a select few people to destroy what **God** desires for **His** faithful people. Where is your voice because history tells me the Human Race is not shy when it comes to something they deem important? Then why is this happening? Are multitudes of people turning away from their convictions when it comes to their faith? Is it too much effort anymore to stand up for what is right? Why are multitudes of people turning their back on the church? Catholics should be going to their churches for daily Mass and definitely on Sunday in order to be close to **God** during the Sacrament of the Holy Eucharist. If you were a Christian, why would you ever turn down this opportunity to be close to **God**? Why would you not want to encourage others to attend church? Furthermore, why is it that families do not bring their children to church?

 Three of the most important **times** in the Christian calendar are Christmas, Lent, and Easter. It is during these particular **times** most Christians feel closer to **God.** Christmas is the mystery of the Incarnation. As Catholics, we believe the Virgin Mary became the Mother of **God** through the intercession of the **Holy Spirit** that was the direct intervention and Divine Will of **Almighty God.**

 Jesus becomes a man, the **Son** of **God. God's** only **Son** came into this world so Humanity may hear and know the truth. **Jesus** endured the same temptations as we are tempted today. The devil tempted **Jesus** while **He** was fasting in the desert for forty days and forty nights, a designated **time**, Christians call Lent. It is during these forty days, the faithful have an opportunity to search their mind for areas of improvement in their life. We endure the **time** of Lent for the love of **God**. This is a very important **time** for the renewal of your commitment to your faith. During this **time**, you have a special opportunity to demonstrate to **God** your love for **Him**. This is a wonderful opportunity for you to examine your conscience. How have you been doing throughout the year? Lent is especially a perfect **time** for you to refresh and renew yourself in order to improve your life. In my personal Bible, the following explanation is as follows: lent is the annual period of forty days prior to the celebration of Easter, which the church sets aside as a **time** of prayer, fasting, and penance. In this solemn and holy season, the church invites the faithful to renew their hearts and deepen their spiritual life by imitating Christ's retreat in the desert and by contemplating the events of **His** passion.

Whatever it is in your life that is keeping you from the love of God, you must remove it!

In the Bible, we read, **"For God so loved the world He gave His only Son so sins can be forgiven" (John 3:16)**. You need only to read the Passion of **Christ** to know the truth. This is a testimonial from **Almighty God** confirming **He** loves us abundantly. The Cross is **God's** answer to evil. When **Jesus** died on the Cross, **He** purchased for us everlasting eternal life in Heaven.

It is my belief that humankind is **God's** favorite creation. The Bible also teaches us in the Book of **Genesis**, **God** was very pleased with the world and everything found within this world. Certainly, this is truly the ultimate tribute when **Jesus** died on the cross for all Humanity. Still many people feel the need of further proof of the immense love that **God** gives to us so freely. If **God** would be willing to sacrifice **His** only **Son** for us, then this would make perfect sense: **God** would send **His** Angel with a message to help Humanity now.

Easter is also a very important celebration in the calendar of the Christian Faith. Easter also called Paschal (Greek, Latin) or Resurrection Sunday is a festival and holiday celebrating the Resurrection of **Jesus** from the dead described in the New Testament as having occurred on the third day of **His** burial after **His** Crucifixion by the Romans at Calvary c. AD 30. Christians celebrate the joy of

Easter because they believe **Jesus** conquered the death over the Cross and **He** is risen into Heaven so all **God's** people may live a life renewed through **Him**. This is the truth of our Faith most Christians believe because without Easter, no one would ever have the opportunity to enter the gates of Heaven. Without Easter, this possibility would not exist. Christians believe **God** sent **His** only **Son** into the world so **God's** people would have this blessed opportunity to save their Soul from Sin in order to be worthy to enter the gates of Heaven.

These celebrations are the most important and holy traditions in the calendar of the church. The faithful celebrate these important seasonal holy traditions as well as others in many churches throughout the world. I cannot understand why there are groups of people who are determined today to destroy these precious traditions and images of our faith. Why would these unbelievers go to all the trouble if they do not believe in these celebrations? Why would these unbelievers care? Deep inside of themselves, they are afraid. They have no hope in their life, so they are miserable and want to push aside anything others enjoy and believe. If they faced what bothers them so much, they would not be able to handle the truth about themselves. No one is forcing these unbelievers to believe in anything! **God** does not force anyone to believe in **Him**. Everyone is free to believe what he or she wishes. All **God's** people were born with free will to believe what they choose. However, I do not believe anyone has the right to impart his or her beliefs on anyone else. Christianity is the supreme right to believe in their **God** or images of **Him** in any capacity deemed fruitful. This is outrageous to me that decorations and symbols of a particular faith offend this misguided people. Why do they have so much distain for someone else's beliefs? What really is the problem? Do these unbelievers not believe that **Jesus** died for their sins?

God sends us messages every day, but we just do not see what is right in front of us much of the **time**. Certainly, the signs are everywhere that **God** is trying to get our attention in a way we should all understand. **God** desires all of us to know **He** loves us exceedingly. Most people believe anything good only happens because of **God's** Divine Will. We are always looking for the reason for some situation so we can better understand it. Some things need no explanation! **God** simply desires us to be happy and to love **Him**. Why is this truth not clear to everyone? Why do so many people seem to need more proof?

Why is it the Easter Bunny does not seem to offend anyone at least not yet? What is really behind all this madness? How about all the candy in the shape of the Easter Bunny should we do away with candy in the shape of the Easter Bunny? Unbelievers are free to go their merry way. **God** will not stop them. If these people are uncomfortable with symbols of Faith, this does not give them the right to impart judgment on others. **God** is looking at all these situations, and **He** is longing for **His** children to believe and have faith in **Him**. If these people could only spend their energy on something worthwhile that really needed fixing, look what they could accomplish, and the world would be farther ahead in solving some real important problems. We waste so much **time** and energy on nonsense that comes from the evil one. Every minute that goes by teaches you and me that we are wasting our **time** and energies that is a gift bestowed among **God's** people. It is important that we put our efforts to good use.

If you are still asking, what does the message mean? The message means **God's** people should understand what really is important for the salvation of their soul. Societies in general have very serious spiritual denial when it comes to the truth that confronts and involves everyone in this world. We need to begin talking about these issues more seriously. **God** has already taught everyone from the beginning of **time** what should truly be important in life. **God** sees these battles over religious representations and the hatred that comes from these concerns; and it is my belief, **He** is having great difficulty understanding why some folks have determined they are the judge over what is correct for someone else! It is what causes religious persecutions that concerns **God** greatly because it causes severe long-term effects on entire cultures. **God** is watching what is happening to **His** children, and no matter what happens, you must never lose your faith because **God** is always with you.

How do I explain the unexplainable to anyone? I do not think there are proper words that exist suitable where one can express one's thoughts completely regarding such important matters. There are no words to express properly what can seem to be so unreal, but that is very real. This does make you ask yourself, "What if I saw an Angel? What would I do, and what would I say?" You may ask yourself, "Would **God** ever bestow on me such a great gift? Would I be worthy?" More importantly, "What about the message conveyed to me from the Angel? What do the six words mean exactly? What can we discover together from all these discussions?" These are some of the first questions some people would be asking himself or herself. I always felt such experiences to be so profound and beyond our explanation and understanding to begin with. We can only imagine what it would be like to see what we could all agree is a miracle from **God**. Those who have experienced these miracles might ask, "Was the heavenly event I experienced for the benefit of everyone?" This is easy to understand now. If you open your heart to the six words of the message, the answer is waiting for you to uncover. **God** expects us to love one another. **God** expects us to help one another. Most of all, **God** expects us to love **Him** with our whole heart and soul. If Humanity truly loved **God** this much, could you imagine what this world would be like?

I have finally realized there is so much more involved in all these experiences that take place by the will of **God** than I once imagined. This knowledge does make a person stop and wonder what possibilities exist if we would only allow **God** into our life. If knowing and believing these encounters truly do happen, does this make you think of **God** and love **Him** even more? Does this honor the amazing truth **God** is allowing these wonderful experiences to happen because **He** loves us so dearly? There has to be a deep gesture of love for you and me that **God** would send **His** Angel with a message to us in such a magnificent way. **God** would most definitely have a decisive purpose to grant others these awesome heavenly occurrences. I fall these experiences, and the message I received make you pray and honor **God** more than the Angel I witnessed was from Heaven above. You will know in your heart something wonderful has happened for the benefit of everyone. If the knowledge of the Angel strengthens your faith, then this will become an exceptionally important truth for you.

This knowledge will strive to improve your faith that will ultimately lead you toward Heaven. The very need for the contemplation of Heaven and the Angels makes you naturally aware of their existence in the first place.

The message the Angel conveyed to me is clear. **God** is waiting for us to wake up and show **Him** we do love and adore **Him**. **God** is waiting for all of us to learn how to work together and love one another in order to make the world a better place. **God** desires us all to be happy and follow **His** Commandments. The message is very simple and very clear. **God** desires us to put forth a sincere effort to begin doing what we all know we need to accomplish for **Him**. **God** is waiting for our answer. What are we going to tell **Him**? What are we waiting for? The problems of the world that we all caused will not wait forever! **God** is still trying to get our attention. **God** is exceedingly disappointed, and still **His** people are not listening.

> Dear **Lord**, through the intersession of the **Holy Spirit**, **Your** Angel brought forth a message for all Humanity. Bestow on all **Your** people **Your** grace, **Your** love, and **Your** mercy to recognize that the message **Your** Angel conveyed to me translates **Your** immense love for all **Your** children.

God is trying to get our attention. How long will **God** wait for us to amend our lives?

CHAPTER 18

The Power of Prayer

The Feast of the Most Holy Rosary of the Blessed Virgin Mary, Mother of God, is celebrated on the seventh of October.

The morning of October 7, 2011, I awoke early to prepare for my trip to the hospital for my surgery. The morning was unlike any other. I was chatting with my husband about the fact that I could not have my morning tea. Upon arrival at the hospital, I did not spend much **time** thinking about the surgery because there was a lot to do with all the presurgery preparations. My husband and I were surprised when the nurses announced they were taking me up to the surgery area earlier than was originally scheduled.

As they wheeled me down the hall, I could see a rather large room near the operating theater labeled Pre-OP. Other people were already there waiting for their particular surgery to begin. The only thing that separated the beds from one another was a thin curtain. Several doctors and nurses were busy with their paperwork, and I could see many computer screens visible from my bed. It certainly was not quiet or boring waiting for surgery. Everyone there knew their place and, with the seriousness of one job or another, moved throughout the room with precision. My wonderful neurosurgeon, Dr. Eng, was there, and we talked about the procedure he would soon perform. I do not recall being nervous in the slightest. After chatting with my doctor, I lay there wondering how long it would be before they would come and retrieve me for my surgery.

Instinctively, I began to recite my Rosary that I demanded to keep at my side. I cherished the Rosary all my life; the Rosary always gave me comfort. I considered my Rosary my dearest possession. The Rosary is a complete prayer of the life of **Christ** that the devil cannot bear to hear us say! During my prayers, my mind wandered to thoughts of **God** the **Father**. My thoughts went to a more personal and deeper level that seemed to go beyond the prayers of the most holy Rosary. I forgot all the noise and the people who were all around me because the commotion did not seem to be a distraction from my thoughts or my prayers. The most important thought right then was my relationship with **Almighty God**. I wanted **God** to know how deeply I loved **Him**. As I continued to pray, I felt I was drifting away in my thoughts. I felt so light and happy, and nothing seemed to matter to me except **God**. I continued talking to **God** with what felt like a long **time**. Soon, a nurse appeared in front of me and told me they were ready for me. I gave my Rosary to the nurse and asked her to hold the Rosary for me until afterward. I knew they would not let me take my Rosary into the operating room. I was laughing and joking with the nurses about little things that were not important. One of the nurses remarked, "You sure are happy!" Something inside of me was feeling happy, and I can say I was feeling even contented. When I think about how I felt then, this does seem a little strange I was so happy prior to surgery! **God** is so good to all of us, I think we just find ourselves trapped in our daily life and forget to thank **Him** for all the blessings **He** sends our way every day.

The surgery only took a couple of hours. When the surgery was over, the nurses brought me into the recovery room. From that point, I do not know how long it took me to wake up. I felt so cozy with the nice warm blanket that one of the nurses placed on top of me. I felt wonderful, and the thought did enter my mind, this was unusual for me to feel so comfortable and contented so soon after surgery. Yes, I cannot believe how contented I felt. I prayed, "Dear **God**, allow me to enjoy this peaceful **time** for just a little while."

While waking up, I realized in my mind I was still saying the same prayers I was saying prior to the surgery. The first voice I remember hearing was Nurse M. telling me, "You can wake up now, Rose Mary." The bright light is what really caught my attention first. I remember wondering if I was still in the operating room. Goodness, I read somewhere there were some people in the past who mentioned they woke up and found they were still in the operating room! I slowly began to open my eyes to investigate the source of the light. It was a bright golden light that was awesome to look at. Even with the light shinning so bright, it did not hurt my eyes in any way. When I opened my eyes, this is when I first noticed the Angel. I could hardly believe my eyes. Without my eyeglasses, I could see the Angel very clearly standing only a few feet away from the end of my bed. I immediately remarked loudly, "**I see an Angel**."

Nurse M. said, "What did you say, honey?"

I repeated the same words again, "**I see an Angel**."

Nurse M. said, "You do, where?"

I replied to her and pointed, "Right there." I knew one thing was for sure, I was not going to take my eyes from the Angel. The golden light encapsulated the entire room and everyone who was there. It is not easy for me to interpret the incredible light and the magnificent Angel within the light that I witnessed. I believe in order to describe to you the astonishing event in the true sense of the proper words, it would be very challenging for me. I feel to appropriately and accurately describe to you what I always believed would only be seen in Heaven is nearly impossible. I can only say I will do my best soon, but nothing I could say could do justice to what I witnessed. What I felt then when I was praying to my **Lord, Jesus Christ** was a tremendously strong desire to be with **Him** in the closest way possible. In the strongest terms possible that we have available to us in the English language and with the earthly constraint of this world, my heart's desire was to become as close as possible to **God**. I can only speak for myself here, but this encounter with the Angel certainly confirmed what the power of prayer will accomplish if we would allow it to happen. **God** heard my prayers, and **He** returned **His** love by sending an Angel with a message in order to demonstrate **His** love, not only for me but also for the Human Race.

Here on earth, if you desire to be close to **God**, **He** has already provided you a way through the Sacrament of Holy Communion. Catholics and Christians alike believe receiving the Sacrament of the Holy Eucharist is the ultimate way to unite with the infinite **Christ**. The Sacrament of Holy Communion is the **Body**, **Blood**, **Soul**, and **Divinity** of **Jesus Christ**. Therefore, when receiving Holy Communion, you are in the very presence of our **Lord, Jesus Christ**!

I believe strongly, together with the power of prayer, Catholics, Christians, and all those who love **God** all over the world have the power to push back the gates of hell. It is my belief as a Catholic that the Rosary in particular is our direct defense against evil. This is our armor and shield against the worst evil can throw at us. If there is only one thing I can persuade you to incorporate into your life, please consider reciting the Rosary. The Mysteries of the Rosary have been very important to me all my life. I believe with my whole heart, there were numerous **times** in my life, life would have been more difficult for me without my Rosary to comfort me and console me. Catholics believe wholeheartedly reciting the mysteries of the most Holy Rosary of the Blessed Virgin Mary will bring you close to the Blessed Mother because it will allow her in turn intercede on your behalf to her **Son, Jesus**. Who would not accept this opportunity? This is not reserved to only Catholics. Anyone can honor **Jesus** greatly by loving **His** mother and reciting the Rosary. The Rosary brings to the mind of the one reciting the prayers the life of **Jesus**!

The Origin of the Holy Rosary

In my personal research, I read that Martin Luther, in 1517, revolted against the church by denying certain doctrines. It was Michelangelo who, in 1541, painted *The Last Judgment* on the wall just above the main altar in the Sistine Chapel. Michelangelo incorporated into the painting all doctrines that were being challenged during this **time** by the Protestant reformers. These people tried their best to deny devotion to Mary, the Mother of **God**. I could not believe how bad this was until I began to read the history myself. Michelangelo was very disturbed and languished over what to do about this serious situation. Michelangelo decided to place Mary, the Mother of **God**, in the place of honor in his painting, which is located at the right hand of her **Son, Jesus**. Today, you can view beneath the Blessed Mother, Michelangelo painted a huge Rosary that is hanging down from Heaven. On this huge Rosary, you can see two figures hanging onto the Rosary in desperation, climbing as if on a rope to Heaven. By this beautiful depiction, Michelangelo hoped to reflect his own devotion as well as the church to Mary, the Mother of **God**, and her Rosary. I was very privileged to visit Rome in 2005 and spent a great deal of **time** in the Sistine Chapel. When you look at the walls and the ceiling, you realize the immense gift **God** bestowed on this one artist. Amazing is the miracle of creativity of the mind that produced such a wonder for generations to study the marvel of Michelangelo's many masterpieces. I really must wonder after thinking about some of my experiences, did Michelangelo dream what he painted, or did he witness himself firsthand a glimpse of Heaven? We will never know; however, now that I have had the deepest privilege of seeing an Angel, I am convinced Michelangelo witnessed a spiritual event perhaps more than once. I truly believe after seeing the Sistine Chapel, **God** most definitely held the artist's hand. All of a sudden, I am seeing the Sistine Chapel in my mind in a completely different way. I think it would be beneficial and I would love to have the opportunity once more to see the Sistine Chapel again. I wholeheartedly believe any Art definitely needs viewing more than once to appreciate fully what the artist was determined to capture in his or her work.

In addition, Pope Pius V ordered a Rosary Crusade in Europe in order to help the Christians. In thanksgiving for his victory, Pope Pius V established the Feast of Our Lady of the Most Holy Rosary on October 7 during the fifteenth century. What little I have read over the years, this pope was a Dominican and was very devout.

Although there were numerous occasions where the Blessed Virgin Mary appeared with a Rosary, these few occasions all stand out as events of great importance for religious people all over the world.

However, another important occasion that I will mention here that is close to my heart is the apparition of Our Lady of Fatima that took place on October 13, 1917. Our Lady appeared as the Queen of the Holy Rosary. In one hand, the Blessed Mother held a Rosary; and in the other hand, she held a Scapular. The Scapular is a small Christian neckpiece usually made from two pieces of wool, suspended from the shoulders, usually worn underneath other clothing.

Tradition teaches us, Saint Dominic devised the Rosary (d. 1221) as it appears today. Saint Dominic said he witnessed a vision where the Blessed Mother gave him a Rosary.

The Blessed Mother Mary said to Saint Dominic, "One day through the Rosary and the Scapular, I will save the world."

Recently, I have been giving a great deal more thought to one particularly heavenly event that took place over a hundred years ago in Fatima, Portugal. I would encourage anyone to research our lady's apparitions.

Our Blessed Mother spoke the profound words that day to the three children in Fatima who witnessed the apparition of the Blessed Virgin Mary. Their names were Francisco, Jacinta Marto, and L'ucia. Her words to them were severe and clearly a stern warning! The Blessed Mother also showed the children a glimpse of hell. One of the children became a Nun, and in her Memoirs, Sister Lucy describes the vision of hell that Our Lady showed the children at Fatima. In Sister Lucy's own words, she recalls, "She opened Her hands once more, as She had done two previous months. The rays (of light) appeared to penetrate the earth, and we saw as it were a vast sea of fire. Plunged in this fire, we saw the demons and the souls (of the damned). The latter were like transparent burning embers, all blackened or burnished bronze, having human forms. They were floating about in that conflagration, now raised into the air by the flames, which issued from within themselves, together with great clouds of smoke. Now they fell back on every side like sparks in huge fires, without weight or equilibrium, amid shrieks and groans of pain and despair, which horrified us and made us tremble with fright it must have been this sight, which caused me to cry out, as people say they heard me. The demons were distinguished from the souls of the damned by their terrifying and repellent likeness to frightful and unknown animals, black and transparent like burning coals. That vision only lasted for a moment, thanks to our Heavenly Mother, Who at the first apparition had promised to take us to Heaven. Without that, I think that we would have died from terror and fear." Sister Lucy dies at the age of ninety-seven, on February 13, 2005.

On February 13, 2008 the third anniversary of her death, Pope Benedict announced that in the case of Sister Lúcia, he would waive the five-year waiting period established by ecclesiastical law before opening a cause for Beatification. This rule was also dispensed in the causes for Mother Theresa of Calcutta and Pope John Paul 11. On February 13, 2017, Sister Lucia was accorded the title Servant of **God** as the first major step toward her Canonization.

It was the Blessed Mothers call to prayer on May 7, 1917, where she called for Christians to pray for peace! At Fatima, the Blessed Virgin Mary had three requests. The first one: to consecrate Russia to Her Immaculate Heart. The second: to make sacrifices for poor sinners because "Many sinners go to hell because no one prays for them." Third: to pray the Rosary. These words now ring in my ears like a bell going off telling me. This is the **time** for everyone to heed the Blessed Mothers warnings before it is too late! I have said repeatedly, many people throughout the world are walking through life as if they were sleepwalking. Now is the precise **time** to renew in your hearts the many documented warnings from the Blessed Mother while we all still have the chance. Now is the precise **time** we need Our Lady of the Rosary to convert the hearts of the radical Islamic world from all its hatred and love of war. Devote your **time** to the Mother of **Jesus**, and while reciting Her beautiful Rosary, beseech Her to intercede for us in order to save the world! Now it is so apparent and obvious to understand the words the Angel spoke to me. **"Tell them it is almost time."**

The implication of the date the Angel appeared to me, and the significance of the message are remarkable! When I entered the hospital, it was not on my mind as to what Feast day it was. It was even more of a surprise when I remembered it was the Feast of the Holy Rosary. The full impact of the date of October 7 and the importance for me personally hit me like a thunderbolt as to the date and the timing of the appearance of the Angel. Why did the Angel appear to me on this particular date? In all the days of the year, I marvel it was the Feast of the Holy Rosary. It is my lifelong devotion to the Rosary and my love for the Blessed Mother that is important. It was certainly an extraordinary day that **God** chose because **He** desired **His** children to know how much **He** loves us. This is astounding to me; the appearance of the Angel included a message of six profound words that I must admit strangely resemble in many ways other profound messages said by our Blessed Mother during her apparitions. Should Humanity ignore these messages? I would highly encourage anyone to research the Blessed Mother's apparitions to include her messages she has left to the faithful around the world. Allow the Blessed Mother Mary, who is the Mother of **God**, to touch your heart right now.

While I am reciting the Rosary, it always helps me to identify with the life of **Jesus Christ** in a more meaningful way. Please consider this sweet form of devotion as part of your ongoing journey to **God**. You do not need to be a Catholic to recite these powerful prayers. What does this matter when surely, Christians believe in the Blessed Mother, the mother of **Jesus Christ**. The Rosary is the purest form of prayer there could ever exist. The Rosary enables us to relive the entire life of **Christ** from **His** birth to **His** death on the cross and beyond. How could you possibly refuse this opportunity afforded you with the Holy Rosary? Actually, reciting the Rosary only takes less than one half hour. If you desire to recite the entire five-fifteen decades, you will find that **time** seems to pass, and before you know it, you are finished. If your **time** is restricted, then begin by reciting only ten beads at a **time**. You can always pick up where you left off any**time** later. I can assure you, you will be surprised how happy and calm you will feel if you include the Rosary in your normal routine. My granddaughter, when she was very little, used to say to me, "Grandma, say your Rosary, you will feel better." Out of the mouth of babies comes forth the truth! **Jesus** is watching everything you and

I do every minute of the day. Imagine how pleased **He** would be if **He** witnessed you honoring **His** mother by reciting Her Rosary.

I will include here the complete fifteen promises of the Holy Rosary in case there any individuals who have forgotten these promises or most importantly for those who did not know these promises existed. Here is what the Blessed Mother Mary promises to everyone who recites Her most Holy Rosary. These promises are profound! I want to list these magnificent promises here for you so you will understand further the power of prayer and learn to love the tremendous power of the Rosary. Reciting the Rosary gives you the power to solve even the most ardent problems in your life. People all over the world will testify how the power of prayer was instrumental in overcoming some serious obstacles such as illness. When you feel so despondent, there is nothing in your life worthwhile; turn to the Rosary. Anyone who ever faithfully turned his or her heart to the power of the Rosary always found comfort in knowing the Blessed Mother would come to his or her aid.

Over the centuries, great armies followed their faith, knowing the power of prayer would allow them to win even in battle. One of the most remarkable examples was Joan of Arc who led the French Army to victory in approximately 1430 while only a teenager. Joan of Arc's faith in prayer and her cherished love for **Almighty God** proved to be her amazing strength that would defeat an army of unbelievers. Saint Joan of Arc martyred for her faith, canonized May 16, 1920. Books could fill an entire room with the awesome examples of the power of prayer. Among the various meanings in the message the Angel conveyed to me is many people are neglecting their prayers. Too many people have forgotten the astonishing power of prayer. The evil one has caused people to believe they do not have the **time** to pray, and praying is a waste of **time**, and worst of all, evil wants you to believe no one is listening! This could not be further from the truth.

The mere truth that Humanity still exists is all the proof you need to know God is listening to our prayers!

The Blessed Virgin Mary promised to Saint Dominic and to all who follow, **"Whatever you ask in the Rosary will be granted."** She, the Blessed Virgin, Mother of **God**, left for all Christians fifteen promises to those who will faithfully recite Her Holy Rosary.

Here are the fifteen promises granted to those who faithfully recite the Holy Rosary:

1. Whoever shall faithfully serve me by the recitation of the Rosary shall receive Signal Graces.
2. I promise my special protection and the greatest Graces to all those who shall recite the Rosary.
3. The Rosary shall be a powerful armor against hell; it will destroy vice, decrease sin, and defeat heresies.
4. The Rosary will cause virtue and good works to flourish. It will obtain for Souls the abundant mercy of **God**. It will withdraw the hearts of men from the love of the world and its vanities and will lift them to the desire for eternal things. Oh, those Souls would sanctify themselves by this means.
5. The Soul, which recommends itself to me by the recitation of the Rosary, shall not perish.
6. Whoever shall recite the Rosary devoutly, applying herself or himself to the consideration of its sacred mysteries, shall never be conquered by misfortune. **God** will not chastise him or her in **His** justice; he shall not perish by an unprovoked death. If he be just, he shall remain in the Grace of **God** and become worthy of eternal life.
7. Whoever shall have a true devotion for the Rosary shall not die without the Sacraments of the Church.
8. Those who are faithful to recite the Rosary shall have during their life and at their death the light of **God** and the plentitude of **His** Graces; at the moment of death, they shall participate in the merits of the Saints in paradise.
9. I shall deliver from purgatory those who have been devoted to the Rosary.

10. The faithful children of the Rosary shall merit a high degree of glory in Heaven.
11. You shall obtain all you ask of me by the recitation of the Rosary.
12. All those who propagate the Holy Rosary shall be aided by me in their necessities.
13. I have obtained from my Divine **Son** that all the advocates of the Rosary shall have for intercessors the entire celestial court during their life and at the hour of death.
14. All who recite the Rosary are my sons and daughters and brothers and sisters of my only **Son Jesus Christ**.
15. Devotion of my Rosary is a great sign of predestination.

If you would like to learn how to recite the Rosary, you can find the instructions on the Internet. There are also televised Christians broadcasts daily where you can follow along with them and learn how to recite the Rosary.

Remaining close to **God** in friendship through some form of prayer should be very important in your life. Various Graces come to you during your prayers. Some of these special Graces are Signal Graces. Signal Graces are any unexplained and extraordinary coincidences or occurrence. This occurrence is **God** trying to encourage you and/or communicate with you. Grace is the indwelling of **God** moving the soul! It is so wonderful that we can communicate with **God** and **His** Mother in this way. It amazing to know the truth, this known fact is true. Your prayer life is your lifeline to **God** and **His** mother who loves you dearly. Catholics call Mary "Mediatrix of Grace" because it comes to us through Her prayers and efforts. It is the constant teaching of the Church that Mary is the channel to us of the Grace Her **Son Jesus** won for us on the Cross.

Loving **God** should be a natural desire, not a struggle. If finding **time** to pray to **God** is felt with resistance, this is the first warning your relationship with **God** needs serious improvement. Once you can discern what this struggle represents, you can take action immediately to remove whatever is coming between you and **God**. If you allow this state of separation from **God** to continue, your soul will be in danger through sin, and this will ultimately lead you to anxiety and unhappiness. You must have a harmony within you that responds to the love of **God** instinctively. Prayer is the first step in the contemplation of **God** in your life.

All **God's** children are given a specific assignment in life from **Him**. During everyone's life**time**, we are responsible for learning various life-altering lessons. **God** works on us constantly until we get it right. Do you believe Angels are partners in this assignment? What a deeply and uniquely awesome truth that we do, in fact, all have an assignment from **God** but this always comes with great responsibility. **God** expects us to do our best in everything we do. There are many **times** in your life **God** offers you and me a chance to have a perfect allegiance with **Him**. Often**times**, **God** gives you an opportunity to do something meaningful for **Him**. Then if you are listening, **God** allows you to realize the significance of the task that **He** has chosen for you. Some**times**, the task is not about you at all. Our free will allows you to reply to **God** either positively or negatively. If you truly considered the meaning of free will, it would be easy to understand the important role this plays in your life. Even now, you may ask again, "What is the true meaning of my existence?" In addition, "What does **God** expect me to accomplish during my life**time**? What does **He** still need me to do for **Him**?" These are only a few questions you need to ask **God**, and believe me, **He** will answer you.

Receiving a very deep and profound spiritual experience could take a life**time** to contemplate it was **God's** Divine Will. You need to put into practice what you have learned through any experience. You need to place your trust in **God** that any experience involving **Him** is for your spiritual growth that will lead you ultimately to **Him**. Prayer is a wonderful and peaceful way to begin your journey to **God**. Prayer is beautiful music played from the heart for **Almighty God**. As the notes of this music rise to **God**, you are aware **He** is with you and **He** hears everything that is in your heart.

Your Soul is real and desires only to one day again be reunited with **God**. This can only take place when the Soul has been relieved of the burden of Sin. Prayer is good for the Soul, and food is good for our bodies. In the Bible, we read, **"Beloved I pray that all may go**

well with you and that you may be in good health, as it goes well with your Soul" (3 John 1:2); **"Before I formed you in the womb, I knew you" (Jeremiah 1:5)**. In the spiritual realm, the actual life of the Soul is constantly on guard. Before you were born, the Soul already knew **God** intimately. Here the truth of everything we always wanted to know begins. If you would only embrace **God's** love, you would discover so much about **Him**. In your prayers and in your deepest thoughts about **God**, you would find the truth and realize the answers are right in front of you to discern.

It is your emotions once again that play such a profound role when you are seeking **God's** friendship. This is why **God** gave us these tremendous emotions. These emotions stem from the heart of who you are as a person. Strong inner emotions that most of us poses developed solely for the very purpose of discovering what we truly believe. **God** bestowed on us these strong emotions so we would be able to express our love for **God** freely and without reservation. Most importantly, we must recognize our Soul is lonely for **God**. I doubt not many people think about the truth, the Soul is lonely for **God**! Few people rarely mention anything concerning their Soul or give the Soul much thought these days regarding the struggles the Soul must endure. Most every Christian does believe in the importance of the Soul and its connection to the **Holy Spirit**. The Soul must tolerate suffering in darkness with a mountain of sins against **God's Sacred Heart**. The Soul can do nothing but languish constantly in the darkness of Sin where you have imprisoned your Soul. The condition of your Soul is very serious due to your grievous sins, and if this condition persists, your Soul becomes totally consumed in evil darkness. Therefore, it is when we commit a Sin the Soul is unable to seek the comfort of **God** in the darkness and becomes lonely and lost. You are the only one who can save your Soul from this awful fate by loving **God** with your whole heart, mind, and body. I have discussed the importance of freeing your Soul from Sin through the Sacrament of Reconciliation. Catholics believe during this **time**, the Soul, released of the burden of Sin, is free to seek the presence of **God** if only for a fleeting moment. The Soul and your mind are then refreshed and renewed if only briefly. The corruption of the mind is a very serious condition. Corruption of the mind due to Sin and the desire for prayer are not companions. Every **time** you free your Soul from the darkness of Sin, all Heaven rejoices. The Bible we read, **"I tell you in the same way there will be more rejoicing in Heaven over one sinner that repents then over ninety-nine righteous who do not need to repent"** (Luke 15:7).

I must repeat I always found it fascinating to hear someone say he or she read about someone who said they might have experienced an Angel when they needed help. What about other people who say they experienced a vision related to Heaven? I believed **God** desired these people to know something special about them. Maybe **God** is trying to tell them everything will be all right. Is this logic as simple as it sounds? **God** has a special plan for those who love **Him**. **God** loves the world and **His** children so much **He** will send **His** Angel to warn those who honestly love and honor **Him**. This is a truth that I felt **God** placed on my heart when I witnessed the Angel. Is it possible the Human Race will experience **Jesus** coming in all **His** glory maybe sooner than we think! **God's** people must all make positive changes in their life right now. **God** is leaving this dilemma for Humanity to deicide! The truth is, before something wonderful can take place, we must first wipe evil from the face of the earth. This is a monumental task, but as difficult as this will be, we cannot accomplish this alone. Together, collectively and only with **Almighty God** by our side, will we begin to eradicate the evil who is determined to ruin the world. Nothing is impossible if you have **God** in your life. Can you imagine what could happen if everyone in the world got down on their knees all at the same **time** and asked **God** for forgiveness? If we all trust in **God's** mercy, a miracle will happen right before our eyes. This miracle can happen because **God**'s children do have the capacity for change. Right now, Christians need to pray stronger than ever before and as often as possible because Humanity needs **God's** help!

Dear **God**, come to our assistance. The world is in a state of confusion over the truth. **Your** greatest creation is in serious trouble! **Your** children are in danger of losing their Souls. Open our hearts to the truth so we may love you always with our entire self.

Who among our religious leaders will be the first to demand the change that **God** desires? Humanity simply cannot continue as if nothing is happening! Catholics are in great need of His Eminence Pope Francis and the wisdom he receives from **Almighty God** because he is **God's** representative here on earth! Pope Francis needs all Catholics to adhere to their strong religious convictions that we once held so dear to us! Together, we can accomplish greatness that will please **God**. **God** bestowed on Pope Francis an enormous responsibility. It is my belief **God** expects Pope Francis to lead by his exemplary example with the teachings of the Bible so we may honor **God** and **His** words. All Catholics and all faiths who believe in **God** need to acknowledge too many of **God's** children are completely in denial they have fallen away from **His** mercy. You do not have to look far to see the evidence of this fact because it is all around us. Great numbers of **God's** children are moving away from **Him** and not toward **Him**. The people of the world need all their leaders to be strong in their moral convictions. They must have the courage not to worry what is politically correct in order for **God's** children to follow their pious example toward the path to **Him**. It is so important to listen to the sincere efforts of our parish priests and your clergy who diligently strive to bring the Word of **God** to us. What a waste to hear the words but then go home and never put what you have heard into practice. There is no doubt these holy people ordained by **Almighty God** already are doing their best but much of Humanity remains in denial anything is wrong. What your eyes refuse to see and your ears refuse to hear is evil keeping you from **God** because only through **Him** will you see and hear the truth because **Christ** is the truth!

If you are not listening to what your leaders of the church are trying to tell you, whom are you listening too? Have you stopped listening to the truth? Without some form of prayer in your life, you do not honor the **Holy Spirit** because you continue to go your merry way without **Him**. I see this condition as a very serious problem. Perhaps our consciences are in the process of total failure. Evidently, there are people who do not to think it is important to listen to their church leaders anymore. If you are still attending a church, you might pay closer attention to what your priest or clergy teaches you through scripture before you race to the parking lot. The minute some people leave church, something strange happens to them. Some people forget everything they heard only minutes before. Do these people no longer believe what the Bible teaches them? Are you only in church because you are afraid it will be a Sin not to attend? Is prayer old-fashioned too and, therefore, you feel prayer is not worth the bother not needed or welcomed anymore? **God** expects **His** children to conduct themselves in a manner that is pleasing to **Him**. You need to begin your day in prayer to **God** and ask **Him** to be with you throughout the day. Ask **God** to bless your day and to help you succeed in your endeavors. When you are asking **God** for a favor or special need, please remember to tell **Him** thank you when **He** answers your prayers. Learn how easy it is to forgive a family member and how wonderful you will feel afterward. No one person is perfect; we all make mistakes. I assure you all your answers to everything are in prayer and meditation to **Almighty God**. I cannot stress the importance of prayer enough. Evil hates this most of all when we pray because we are calling on **God** for **His** help, pure and simple. Never stop your daily prayers especially to the Blessed Mother. Recite the Rosary and discover the promises that reciting the Rosary contain. **God** has truly blessed you with so many opportunities, so why not tell **Him** you love **Him**. Please do not let today end without telling **God** you love **Him** because **He** loves you!

Who will join me in this holy war to denounce evil? We must put an end to hatred and war among **God's** people. Right now, evil is standing in your doorway, waiting for an opportunity to deceive you. Thank goodness, there are still millions of good people in the world who love **God** very much and who recognize this truth. **God** is trying to show us the way through others with their good examples. Therefore, why do people continue to be in denial that we need desperate change? Are they afraid and is this why you are going to keep going along like business as usual? Countless people have lost their faith and trust in **God**, and they did this all by themselves with the help of evil. Are you going to wait until it is too late? Evil is putting evil thoughts in the minds of many people and enjoys attacking this generation especially right this very minute. All over the world, evil is working hard to persuade many leaders it would be fun to blow half the world to bits. Evil is moving its heavy hand all over the world, and people are marching to the drum of this evil. Evil is looking for any opening of weakness so evil can move in and destroy the world.

    Remember what took place on 9/11. Have we learned nothing since this terrible tragedy? Look what is happening right here in this country in our schools, it is a travesty. In addition, in other countries, large groups of people have radicalized their beautiful culture, which gives them a reason why they feel they are right in their justification to rule and judge the world. Scripture teaches us that **Jesus** said, **"He that is without sin among you, let him cast a stone" (John 8:1–11)**. Now **Jesus** was talking about a particular woman who the people caught in adultery. However, I feel safe we can apply this same principle of the teachings of **Christ** that **He** is the only one who will judge who is sinful! This is so evident that parts of the world, people are following a **God** I do not know. These people have forgotten the world belongs to **God** and every living creature in this glorious world of ours. Humanity is merely the stewards of this world. The world is not up for grabs where others decide they may be the judge and jury. In the Holy Bible, **God** says, **"Vengeance is Mine, saith the Lord" (Romans 12:19)**. Only **God** has the supreme right to judge what is right and just. No one has the right to feel they can take **God's** place. **God** alone will judge everyone on the face of the earth for what you have done or what you have failed to do. The problem is too many people have forgotten one truth and this is **God** made us equal. It is our attitude alone that convinces us one person is better than another one. The evil one clearly is leading people astray, and **God** is not pleased!

> Dear **God**, save **Your** children from the evil who has become their **God**. **Your** people have lost their way and simply refuse to see the seriousness of their sins they are committing that continually offend **You**. Help them to remember **Your** love and mercy.

What are your concerns during the day? Your positions in the workplace and your families are probably some of the initial thoughts. Then in my opinion, people today are concerned more and more about politics and the decisions of our government because it involves moral values. If these things were not enough, we also have so much evil destruction that continues relentlessly all over the globe. You must see, our own society is on the brink of moral collapse right here in our own country if we are not careful. The problem is society feels our issues are someone else's problem. We cannot continue to complain when we begin to lose our freedoms. Young adults today, manipulated by certain agendas, they do not realize, in so many areas, they are not being taught the truth. As a result, these young people find themselves caught in the tide of false ideals that, that our schools and universities. Our beautiful young adults must learn to be leaders not followers. How do we expect to correct anything if parents are leaving the responsibilities up to someone else all the **time**? The responsibility belongs to every one of us. We need to stop complaining, take responsibility, and take action by getting involved. Take a stronger interest and involve yourself with your church's activities. Learn what is going on in your community, and find out how you can help, there is always something you can do if you care enough. I know you can pray! I do not believe it is necessary all the **time** to follow a strict form of prayer. Talk to **God** the way you are comfortable. **God** will be very pleased with your own personal prayer. Praying to **God** should be like talking to your best friend because **Jesus** is the best friend you will ever have in this world!

    The truth is that our world is in a big mess is putting it mildly because good people do not ask **God** for help, perhaps not as much as they once did. With no fault of their own, perhaps some people where never taught how to pray. Recently, a few people have told me they do not pray to **God** at all and have not prayed in years. They say by the end of the day, they are too tired and they simply do not remember to pray. I wonder what **God** thinks about our excuses. Here are a few circumstances where you can take a minute throughout your day and pray to **God**. You can pray when you are in the car on the way to work or to school. Include prayer with your children before sporting events because remember your example will help others. Thank the good **Lord** for your food by praying before meals and especially in public. Why should you ever be embarrassed to pray anywhere? Finally, it is your responsibility to teach your children the importance of prayer before bed**time**. Your children will need **God** by their side in their adult life.

Well, it really is all about the habits formed along the way. I will bet some people do not miss a certain episode of a program they have been watching! Instead of going to **God** for help, some people really have forgotten about **God** altogether. Young people today have the impression they do not need to pray! Millions of young people today do not understand or believe in the concept of prayer. How do we ever expect to overcome the evil and the unhappiness that it brings if you simply stopped asking **God** to help you with your struggles? Evil strives to block the truth from you so you will go through your day, giving no thought to **God**. **God** is aware **His** children are feeling helpless, and **He** is aware we need **His** help, but how many people really ask for **His** help! Is this is the reason **God** is allowing more and more people to become aware now that they need not go through life feeling they are alone? Now more than ever, **God** is trying to give us additional support by allowing these wonderful visions and experiences to take place. However, you must be open to the presence of the Angels and to the truth that these experiences really do happen. Is it true that some people need to see something fabulous before they will believe in anything? In the Bible, we read where **Jesus** said, **"Blessed are they who have not seen, and yet have believed" (John 20:29)**. You must strengthen your Faith and your convictions in **Almighty God** because **He** knows what you truly need and what you deserve.

Do you begin to pray more when you read or hear someone witnessed the presence of an Angel or experienced a miracle from Heaven? Does the reality of knowing and believing Angels are here with you make you happier with your life? Does this frighten you or make you uncomfortable? As one woman told me, "Hearing about the Angel and the message gave her the willies!" She did not want to hear what the Angel said to me. She did not want to think about the words the Angel conveyed to me. I prefer to believe that most people, after hearing an Angel appeared to me, will defer to the fact that knowing will strengthen your faith and beliefs you have already accepted for the love of **God**. Grace is one of the greatest gifts **God** has bestowed on those who desire this precious gift. The mere truth you do believe in miracles is faith alone; that is also a precious gift granted to you from **God**. This Grace of faith received from **God**, in this special way, will enable you to automatically cherish what you believe. This precious Grace granted from **God**, you will cherish, and you will never want to let it go. In prayer, you should always request discernment about this gift from **God** that we all need now more than ever. **God** will surely grant **His** Grace if **He** feels you and I deserve to receive it.

    God certainly is extending extreme efforts to get our attention because **God** loves us so much. When are you ready to begin listening to **God**? Our very happiness and our very existence and the future of our children as we know it is weighing in the balance. If you are wondering what you should ask **God** first, ask **Him** to be with you and let **His** will be done. The world as we now see it may be slowly slipping away from us. In the future, I assure you, our world will not resemble the world of our yesteryears. Evil has convinced many leaders we would be better off with a "new world order." This idea of a new world order is the master plan of the evil one who wants to destroy Humanity. This new world does not include **Almighty God**. All Humanity must pray diligently day and night for our return to the safety of **God** because only there in **His** goodness and love will **He** make everything new again.

    The purpose of the message the Angel conveyed to me is clear. **God** desires you and me to remember **He** loves everyone abundantly! Now is the **time** to accept **God's** love and in return honor **Him** with your love. We all have to go through the pains of change to prove to **God** our love has returned to **Him**. The Angel who appeared to me was pure goodness sent from the **Holy Spirit** to help us understand what we must all do for **Him**. The message is clear and very simple. **God** sent **His** Angel from Heaven to remind us **God** is waiting patiently for **His** children all over the world to seek **His** help. What will our reply be to **God** when **He** asks why did we not trust in and rely on **Him** for **His** help?

Once you have given your life back to **God** will you then be ready to hear **His** plan for your future. **Time** is moving forward steadily into the future, and it is our destiny that is waiting to be the future history of the world.

>Dear **God**, please grant **Your** people the Grace
>to see the goodness in all things.

God is trying to get your attention right this very minute. I pray you are listening.

CHAPTER 19

Living a Life without God Is No Life

If all this acquired knowledge of Angels and other extraordinary experiences we have learned about brings you closer to **God**, then we must agree that in a special way, you have shared in the receiving of such a wondrous and magnificent gift. If the effect of the knowledge of all these events make you think more positively regarding **God** in your life, isn't this pure goodness? I always look for the fruits of anything when I am trying to discern the truth. Even if you never experienced something miraculous, you must place your trust in **God** that these encounters really do happen. You need only to believe in **God's** Divine Will that permit these special occasions to take place. What I want you to know now that simply having the knowledge of these experiences, **God** will strengthen your Faith in a unique way. Trust in your Faith that the events others have experienced might possibly happen to you.

A couple of years ago, I was delighted to have the opportunity to share my experience with a certain individual. To my utter horror, what followed was this man actually told me he hated **God**! When this man said this, a cold chill ran through me, and I felt sick. I was afraid at first and silently asked the **Holy Spirit** to help me. I knew at that very moment, evil announced itself to me with a challenge. I pray as a Christian, I was prepared to testify for **God**. I did impress this person with my replies and concerns for his salvation. His hatred for **God** came through loud and clear, which included a terrible attitude toward the mere mention of **God's** name. Yet at the same **time**, it was evident he was very unhappy, and I felt a deep empathy for him. What I experienced was an empty dark feeling for this man because I was fearful, I would not change his convictions. He was extremely determined to dispel everything I had to say regarding **God**. This was the first **time** in my life someone told me face-to-face they actually hated **God**. My fear for him engulfed me. I wonder silently to myself, where does this man think he is going when he dies? I am saddened for him because he may miss the promise of Heaven. Christians believe what is waiting for us all is internal life. I pray for him to this day that somehow, he will realize that living a life without **God** has hardened his heart. Certainly, eternity without the presence of **God** is a desolate isolation that is too horrible to imagine that is my image of hell. I probably will never see this person again, but one thing is for sure, he is in **God's** hands even if he does not realize this now.

Heaven is our final triumph over evil. Heaven is our reward for being faithful to **God**! This is our reward for keeping the commandments given to Moses from **Almighty God**. All the faithful should expect a fantastic journey to Heaven because after seeing the Angel, Heaven must be so incredible there would never be any description that could honor **God's** realm as it really must be. Our minds cannot contemplate the awesome journey the faithful will all be taking some day. All we can do is dream about Heaven. We should love **God** and trust in **God's** mercy that we will join **Him** in heavenly joy for all eternity. Knowing that there are people who do not believe in **God** is a devastating fearful truth. It is sad to think there are people who feel that after death, there is nothing else. Christians believe that if they have been faithful to **God**, their reward is Heaven. Catholics also believe **God** will judge us and decide if we need **time** in Purgatory to think about our sinful behavior and the effects our sins caused. Still this leaves the fate of the unbelievers. I have thought about this, and really, it is impossible to come up with a proper solution, except for the fact that **God** only holds us accountable for what we know. I can only conclude that only **God** knows what will happen to the state of the Soul of the unbeliever.

While I was witnessing the magnificence of the Angel who appeared to me, I tried to visualize if this Angel looks this amazing, what does Heaven look like? Not a day goes by that I do not have the Angel and thoughts of Heaven on my mind. The beauty of this magnificent Angel was beyond a true explanation with mere words. If this Angel were, pardon the term, a small expression of what Heaven is like, then Heaven will be astounding you for sure. It certainly would be most difficult for me and millions of others to endure another day if we thought **God** did not exist. What would be the purpose of my existence or yours? It is difficult for me to understand how an individual could ever say, "I do not believe in **God**." It is perplexing to me that there are people in the world who believe **God** does not exist. I am well aware there are millions of people who have strong beliefs in other cultures over the centuries. These beliefs seem to sustain these people, and therefore, they are free to believe what makes them happy. At the same **time**, my unwavering Faith and my belief in **Almighty God** simply will never allow me to deny **God** ever! For me personally, it would mean all the suffering and all the hardships of this world are for absolutely for nothing. Tell this to the poor and see what they have to say when you tell them their suffering is for nothing! What an ire thought, there is no purpose to anything. Another word for *nothing* is the word *blank*. I do not believe in the word *nothing*. This does not even sound right. There is "nothing" to believe in and, therefore, nothing to hope for but a "blank" nothing! I really cannot wrap my brain around the thought that someone could simply announce, "I hate **God**!" However, when something happens in your life tragically, you should be running to **God** and not away from **Him**.

With **God**, life is more meaningful, and you are never alone. This is so difficult for me to believe it could be possible for anyone to live a life without **God**. When **God** is in your life, your life becomes more fruitful and has promise; this enhances those around you and encourages them to desire that life as well. Oh, the wonders waiting for you when you leave this life will astound you. The Angel was so distressed when speaking about the endless offenses to **Almighty God** because she knows what can be lost to us. Evil is certainly winning over the hearts and minds of the unbelievers who live a life without **God**!

Take a moment and look around you right this minute, and what do you see? There is beauty all around you because **God** created all these things for your pleasure. I remarked the other day, the sky seemed to be more interesting than I had noticed before. The color of the sky was a very deep blue with fluffy white clouds that was indescribably beautiful. You may say the clouds look like this often. Still there are so many **times** that the sky amazes me as if I were seeing the sky for the first **time**. It is so easy to take for granted all the beauty **God** created. The sky was total perfection, and this made a lasting impression on me. Naturally, **God** made everything with perfection in mind for us to enjoy. If you give creation a little thought, you will realize absolutely everything in our world has a precise purpose. **God** created our planet and planned everything so perfectly for us, and with total precision, scientists today are still trying to discover the secrets of this plan. **God** created everything in the world with superior perfection because **God** is perfection! The altered perfection is leading us to our destruction.

It is unfortunate and deeply saddening that some people have chosen not to appreciate this perfection. Some days, the sky appears endless, while other **times**, it looks like someone painted the dancing clouds in the sky for our pleasure! The arrangement and predestined colors are mesmerizing. It was on this particular day, for some unknown reason, I observed the beauty of this world in an extraordinary way. **God** created all this beauty for you and me, and still some people think all this appeared only by accident. Only **Almighty God** could create this wondrous perfection. Seeing all that surrounds us in every crevice of the world makes it more difficult to believe that creation happened by accident.

We know there are people all over the world who have witnessed some kind of wonderful heavenly vision. What would be the point in any of these experiences and spiritual events that take place all over the world? Without **God**, there would be no balance of good and evil. Is this one of the situations Humanity is causing to happen with our indecisiveness over serious issues we refuse to resolve? Are we upsetting the balance of good and evil with our free will? Is the balance beginning to sway in the favor of evil? There must be a balance in all things, or this will disturb the order **God**, in **His** goodness, created for us. If the balance of goodness was ever disturbed, evil will succeed, and only darkness will prevail. There is always going to be good and evil, but goodness needs to triumph.

Praise God for all He has created.

The particular person I spoke of previously refuses to believe in the goodness of **God**, and what I said to him did not change his opinion. This person refuses to believe in the goodness of **God**. Not to mention the idea of Heaven, this definitely was out of the question entirely for him. This man's mind was convinced because the truth is he is angry with **God** over a personal matter. He lost the love and friendship of someone close to him. He gave me the impression he is very stubborn spiritually. I do fear for his Soul because right now does his Soul mean nothing to him. This brings a thought to mind. I did not think to ask him where he thought his loved one is now. He told me his wife had died, and losing her was too much for him to accept. I had to wonder if his wife believed in **God**. He said, "Science could explain all of it." This issue is very difficult to address. It is important as Christians for us to be prepared to rebuttal this line of thinking. As a Christian, prepare yourself and be confident in your Faith. **God** is always with you. The name of **Jesus** is very powerful!

The truth is we are all very special to **God** because **He** created us in **His** image. What **God** has made according to **His** wondrous design, who can believe is wonderful? Is it possible that the scientific society has missed the mark on creation? The brain is such a powerful and wondrous organ that can help us to calculate numerous ideas and theories. Of course, the theory that is closest to my heat is that **God** is our wondrous beautiful **Creator**. Through free will, the scientific society has the **God**-given right to utilize their capacities in a way they see fit. Scientists have the great minds to accomplish vast wonders in a multitude of areas in our human existence. They continue to help so much of Humanity. Let us remember that **God** has given scientists the ability to accomplish remarkable things. Without **God**, their brilliant creative minds would not be able to accomplish or design anything in the first place.

Albert Einstein once said, **"Science without religion is lame."** Thank you, Albert Einstein, this tells me you believed in **God** in some capacity. **God** desired you to have a great mind for discovery. Albert Einstein in his heart must have been a good man as well as being a genius! I have repeatedly said Christians believe **God** created us in **His** image. Then how could we ever deny what our eyes see? We have witnessed with our own eyes the marvel of **God's** creation. The complex workings of our body should answer these questions to any intelligent person. The mere fact that a woman is able to conceive further proves that **God's** creation remains a mystery to science. **God** also created millions of species for our delight: the colors, shapes, and sizes of fish, animals, and plant life that are all here for us to enjoy. This is the circle of life! Oh no, Christians believe that creation was not any mistake or something that happened by accident. This was the Divine Will and the hand of **God** who made us for the purpose of knowing and loving **Him**. Some people have blocked the plan **God** so lovingly wanted for them. **God** simply asked **His** people to follow **His** Commandments, to love **Him**, and to love one another as **God** loves us. Why does this seem to be more difficult now to learn how to love **God** and one another? During The Last Supper, **Jesus** said, **"Love one another" (John 13:30).**

God created us in **His** image, and **He** gave all of us great and wondrous opportunities to achieve great accomplishments for **Him**. **God** gave all of us endless capacities for love and friendship. Regardless, the unbeliever will have the chance repeatedly to love **God** and to know **Him**. The Bible says, **"If you hear His voice today, harden not your hearts" (Hebrews 3:15).** The unbelievers do not realize yet **God** is right now reaching out **His** hand to them. I pray that all **God's** children will realize **His** great love for them before it is too late. I pray that any unbeliever will find some peace someday in the knowledge **God** never stopped loving them. **God** never stops loving anyone and waits for everyone to acknowledge love for **Him** in return. **God** knows there will always be events in our life that will make us unhappy. When something horrific takes place, **God** knows how difficult these **times** are for us to accept. We have all said, "Why did this happen to me?" Our faith in **God** is so important during these difficult **times** because **God** grants us the consolation to overcome adversity on many levels if you would only ask **Him** to help you. **God** certainly understands how you feel because look what happened to **His Son**? You must be steadfast with your Faith in **God** in order to overcome evil in all forms. **God's** people must all stay as close as you can now to **God**. **God** will never leave us no matter what we say or do; **He** waits for us to acknowledge **Him** and repent. We are acknowledging **God** is greatly offended, and **He** desires desperately to get our attention so we will amend our lives. It appears more and more people are beginning to notice **God** is calling on them to prove; to **Him**, they still love **Him**. Does **God** feel we have forgotten **Him** because it is evident the hatred and violence that is going on in the world leads us to believe that we do not need **God** anymore. This is a shame; this idea developed by evil is now true and active in minds of **God's** people.

We no longer pass on the traditions to the next generation stories in the Bible, and if you are Catholic, we know longer talk about the lives of the Saints and the apparitions of the Blessed Mother. The power of our minds ability to meditate and focus allows us to understand and accept Angels as well as other spiritual experiences as being a natural part of our lives. Having confidence through Faith to share our experiences with others becomes the most incredible opportunity. Having a conversation with someone who has experienced a heavenly vision strengthens our Faith. It is an honor to hear firsthand someone telling you in detail what he or she witnessed and what he or she heard! It all began when I first told someone of my heavenly experience with the Angel who appeared to me in the hospital. After conveying to people on the telephone regarding the Angel and **God's** message, these people began to feel comfortable enough to tell me of their exuberant experience as well. There are people now coming forward, and they are telling me about their experiences. Once a conversation begins, it becomes easier for others to talk about what they experienced. The key is starting the conversation, and let the **Holy Spirit** do the rest. **God** and the Angels must delight when we share these holy experiences with others. Now I know I am right in my assumptions the Angels have always been here but they are becoming closer to us now because the Angels know we all need them so much. It is still difficult for people to accept these astonishing events are really happening. Some people believe this could never happen to them. After all, who in our eyes do we feel is worthy enough to experience such visions? Yet this does seem to be happening more and more no matter what people may judge. There will always be some people who would prefer to think that if a person is experiencing something unusual, then perhaps something is wrong with their mind! The truth is some people feel the need to judge everything they do not understand, and this comes from the lack of their Faith.

A dreaded conversation I have encountered with some people is they feel someone could be "too religious." How could you be too religious? If a certain person feels closer to **God** by the way they display their affection toward **Him**, who are we to condemn or judge this person for being too religious? Praise the person someone may feel is too religious, as these people have no **time** for trivial pursuits. They are spending their precious **time** on the Word of **God**. There are occasions where their experiences might be too personal to reveal to anyone. There is certainly nothing wrong with keeping a holy experience close to your heart, safely hidden in your heart and certainly hidden away from the scrutiny of others. Unless you decide, you might want to share this experience because it might benefit someone else. The purpose of Christian belief is to bring others to **God**! However, you may also feel this experience is so personal to you; therefore, you might never mention it for maybe years if ever. I am sure it is a treasured experience kept in the silence of your heart where you keep it safely tucked away. You might remain silent until some future circumstance happens and the **Holy Spirit** prompts you to speak about your experience. Nevertheless, I do believe now, with all our problems, something wonderful will take place, but **God** needs are cooperation.

The **time** is here for Humanity to realize finally we had better turn our life over to **Almighty God**. The **time** is coming when people will begin to feel more comfortable moved by the **Holy Spirit** to reveal their experiences in order to help others in their Faith. I pray that more people will come forward and tell us their experiences. Yes, we should shout to the world, "**God**, in **His** goodness, is showing us the truth and the path to Heaven." These exceptional experiences are wondrous gifts received from **Almighty God** for us because **He** desires us to know how much **He** cares about all Humanity. They are cherished moments received from **God** for the benefit of all who desire to hear about **God's** special gifts.

Now is the **time** for everyone to be bolder than ever in his or her convictions and the love they share for **God**. Christians must be extremely vigilant in all things because God is not the only one watching. The evil one is waiting and watching! **God's** people must stand up for what they know to be right in their hearts regardless what others may say or do. Christians must lead the way so others may follow. I definitely am convinced, more than ever, now is the perfect **time** for these spiritual experiences to be happening. Now is the right **time** because **God** has chosen this most special opportune **time** to make us aware again **God** is very near to everyone. We need perhaps more than ever to know the love and mercy of **God** and to believe **God** is so close, to accept the truth that **God** is still in charge and **He** will not forget the faithful in **times** of great turmoil.

With the world in all its present chaos, it is difficult to understand why more people are not including **God** in their **life**. Throughout the world, there are people with certain agendas who are continually proving to **God**, by their actions, they no longer need or want **Him** in their life while great numbers of people in other countries truly have **God** in their life such as the numerous missionaries and religious clergy strive tirelessly to bring Christianity to people all over the world.

Where is the respect for **Almighty God** who is the **Creator** of the world? Are we really to believe that our present generations do not believe in the absolute Word of **God**? Now in the parts of the world, it is all too common for multitudes of people to use the

Word of **God** to suit their own need of power and hatred. These people have appointed themselves judge and jury over the entire world. **God** did not appoint them to judge over others! **God** created all **His** people for goodness, but evil has convinced them killing others is their supreme right, and as a result, they have lost their way entirely. These people have formed their own agenda, and they are using their **Creator** for an excuse to be evil in the sight of their **God**. **God** may soon reveal to many people this grave error on Humanity's part is not **His** Divine Will. These people will be the first to see they are denying **God** altogether. **God** will judge them for not demonstrating their love and respect for **Him** with their hatred and disrespect shown to others in grievous ways. I pray people all over the world will turn their hearts to **God** and STOP the fighting and killing the murder of innocent people. **God** does not condone hatred that leads to murder and civil unrest that in the end solves nothing. Thank goodness, **God** is present and ever watching over **His** flock! Truly, what would the world be like if we did not have **Almighty God** to love us? **God's** people have strayed from the safety of **His** love and mercy, and God is waiting for their return!

> Dear **God**, I pray **Your** beautiful people will wake up from the violence and hatred that fills the hearts of the unbelievers. I pray that Humanity will learn again to love one another as you have loved them!

Empty churches prove there must be a multitude of people who feel they do not need **God** and the Sacraments of the church anymore. Our Catholic schools are closing one by one because we no longer feel it is important for us to support Catholic education. Evil is going to triumph with little effort on our part to stop it if we continue on our present course. We are walking right straight into the plan evil has devised for us due to our weakness. **God** knows **His** people need the safety of the Sanctuary where evil fears to tread. As a Catholic, I believe the more evil can keep you away from **God** and our Mother the Church, you are allowing evil to take over you and your decisions. **"Where two or more gather in my name, there am**

I" (Matthew 18:20). Will Catholics be sorry when their beautiful churches are closed? There will be few places of significance where you can find true peace. This will have been our choice when the churches are all closed! How will we explain to anyone what we have done? How will we explain to future generations we shut the door on **God**? Will they understand we did the right thing? Please pray your **time** on earth is well spent. Eternity is a very long **time** without **God**. Everyone should believe that living here on earth without **God** would only ensure a desolate existence with no hope for the future.

Why do some people feel their success is only self-made? Surely, they must feel their success happened without any help from **God**. Some people really have convinced themselves that they were so smart to accomplish great wealth without the help from **God**. Some prominent people think their success is of their own design having nothing to do with the presence of **God**. These people also feel they have found a better way and they did this all by themselves too. They have forgotten that without **God's** help, nothing good ever happens. Has a large portion of our society without knowing it made a deal with the evil one to achieve their goals here on this earth? Our society will eventually become nothing without **God**. Over **time**, we begin to experience a feeling of emptiness without **God**. Without **God**, we can become lost forever in a state of loneliness and frustration that will ultimately lead us to Sin and emptiness. Still **God's** love for us is infinite. **God** looks for you and me to remember **Him** during each day. Still all the while, **God** is trying desperately to get your center of attention, but you remain unaware **He** is calling to you. It is imperative that you discover what is blocking you from hearing **God's** voice speaking to you in the silence of your heart.

Do most people believe, even with their private fears, there will always be tomorrow? Tomorrow, I will have more **time** to change what needs to be changed. Tomorrow, I will make more **time** for my prayers. Tomorrow, I will do this; and tomorrow, I will do something different. The truth is most people, including me, feel they do intend to do many things differently; but in the end, we never seem to have the **time** to deal with everything. Suppose tomorrow never comes? No doubt, numerous opportunities have already passed you by without you realizing it. **God** gives us all these opportunities, but we some**times** remain too busy to see what we have missed. What in your life is so important you have no **time** for **God**? You think you have no **time** to thank **God** for all the goodness **He** has given you already regardless how we may decide to measure it. **God** is ready and continues to give us **His** love and goodness every day. Do you spend your prayer **time** in requests for only things you want? We should be giving thanks to **God** for **His** abundant goodness in everything **He** bestows on us. Even now, **God** continues to wait for us to prove to **Him** we love **Him** even in little ways. **God** pours out **His** love for us in such great abundance. I believe we are so used to receiving **God's** love so freely; could we be taking **God** for granted? Perhaps you feel you are unworthy of **God's** love because of something you did wrong in the past. Ask for **God's** forgiveness now because **He** never looks back at your failures. Scripture teaches us that **Jesus** said, **"Come now, let us reason together, says the LORD: though your sins are like scarlet, they shall be as white as snow; though they are red like crimson, they shall become like wool"** (Isaiah 1:18). **God** only desires you to improve yourself and love **Him** so happiness will follow automatically in your life. This is a promise **God** has given to all **His** children. It is only by **God's** Grace you will continue to grow in the love of **Him**; only then will this be possible for you to find happiness and peace within yourself. Only when you have found peace within yourself will it be possible to make others happy.

The marvelous gifts sent from **God** in any form are only the beginning of many other wonderful things that could happen if the world would only embrace it. However, something wonderful does not always take place without great change. Humanity is going to have to make some strong decisions before **God** will bless this world with peace. As I write this, I know very strongly in my heart **God** is waiting this minute for you and me to come to **Him** in a special way. As Christians, we should all need and want to lift our thoughts and minds in prayer to **God** every day. I cannot emphasize enough how much these quiet prayers and thoughts of **Him** are so pleasing to **God**. You must make **time** for **God** today right now. Even for a few moments, it will give you a sense of peace with **God** even though things may look difficult in your life right now.

In our current society, there are people who are uncomfortable with the idea of someone seeing an Angel or other heavenly visions because they refuse to understand that **God** is using these opportunities to rescue them. Perhaps this truth about Angels is not socially correct. I am getting a little disgusted with these phrases: "politically correct" and "socially correct." It has come to the point where seeing and hearing about the experiences may not be politically correct or socially correct and, certainly, to encourage openly some forms of religious expression will not be tolerated. Well, we can all remember in our history what took place when a select few thought they knew better than others about freedom of expression! In those days when this became unfashionable to speak about a certain name or event, the leaders simply removed these names or events from history so history would forget them. The Romans were famous for this practice. Is this starting to sound familiar? There are people who would love to see **God's** precious name taken off our paper money and everywhere else; these phrases with **God's** precious name adorn prominent locations. The words **"In God We Trust"** is engraved on our currency. Evidently, these words frighten a select group of people. I would seriously question what allegiance these people follow. Is this really only about someone's religious freedom? I would seriously question what is behind their fear regarding freedom. Is there a hidden agenda with a more sinister motive? Why are some people in our society so dedicated to these unmerited causes? Is this the final plan that is part of an evil scheme to ensure everyone will eventually forget **God**? Evil sure is busy, and Humanity continues to tolerate evil's lies. Well, if these people harbor so much distain for **God** or certain holiday practices, then how could they ever believe in an Angel? Why it is these people would rather look for another explanation than the truth that **God** had a hand in all that is good in their life, I will never understand. These people are hiding behind their foolishness because they are afraid to face the truth about themselves. Perhaps the reason they are not open to the very idea of heavenly visions is maybe they really do not believe in **God**, not really. If they did, then they would not have strayed so far away from **God**. They would not be wasting their precious **time** on foolishness. **God** gave them the truth in the very beginning, but they have managed to let the evil in the world twist the truth. They have forgotten all about **God's** great love for them. The Angels are here to remind you, but your eyes must be open in order to see **God's** love for all Humanity.

    I notice when I tell some folks what the Angel said, **"Tell them it is almost time**," the reply some**times** is, **"Time** for what?" When I say the Angel said, **"Tell them**," they want to know, "Who is them?" I am not judging them; this only proves that these people are not ready to realize the truth that **God** desires for all of us. Everything related to the subject of **God** and **His** Angels is still very uncomfortable for a large majority of people. Maybe they feel guilty but not guilty enough to bring about change in their life because it is not their priority. The very idea **time** might really be short is still an idea people do not want to discuss, and they definitely do not believe it. **God** knows **His** people are not ready to face **Him** because they are in total denial. When will you be ready? You have not taken the **time** to have that all-important chat with **God**. If you knew you only had twenty-four hours to get your life in order, would you go to **God** and tell **Him** you love **Him** above all else? This all has to do with what you are comfortable with no matter what you believe. Why is this true? What really causes people to be so uncomfortable? Is it the guilt that they have been harboring that is ready to swallow them up? As I continue to meet people, I am thrilled to tell them about the message and what the Angel said, **"Tell them it is almost time."** A few of them immediately say, **"Time, time** for what?" They will also add, "I do not get it." I sense a terrible sadness when they reply with those statements because I am troubled these people do not have the faintest idea what I am discussing with them. A few do not want to hear about anything the Angel said because they are frightened. Yet this is true, the majority of people are thrilled and want to know all about the Angel.

    Some people refuse to face the truth because evil tricks them into believing lies and excuses that continue to fill up their day. I never have a difficult **time** wondering what to say to people. I cannot explain it, but somehow, I seem to know what it is most people need to hear. I know this is the **Holy Spirit** working in my life at this precise **time**. However, how do I lead people to understand what I am trying to tell them? I pray that the pendulum is swinging back. Lately, more people seem to understand and really accept what I tell them about the Angel. The Angel said, **"Tell them."** I knew immediately when the Angel said, **"Tell them,"** the Angel meant for me to tell everyone! I also know that what I have said to some people might mean something different than it does to others, and this is as it should be. I know some individuals do not like the idea very much of the word **time**. People are already feeling pressured over the amount of **time** they have in a day to accomplish daily responsibilities. In this regard, I must tell them about the Angel and convey the message anyway. I can only hope later when they have a chance to think about what the Angel said, the message will motivate their thinking and bring them back to **God**. With the help of **God**, I sincerely want this message, conveyed to me by the Angel, to touch the very Soul of every person. All **God's** people need to realize the overwhelming love **God** has for them, pure and simple. The love from **God** found within the message is so great and the meaning of the message so profound that it will take **time** for you to absorb the meaning. If you study the message as I have, you will come to understand **God** does love you more than anything else **He** created in this world. Most people do understand and thoroughly enjoy hearing all about the Angel who appeared to me. While at the same **time**, a few others even cringed at the very thought of the Angel and her message.

    I recognize evil is present right in front of us at this very moment. It is easy to understand malicious evil is trying to discourage any idea of seeing an Angel because this further leads to **God**. **God** does not want to see us fail. **God** does not want to see us do harm to ourselves. We are hurting ourselves, and we have injured **God's Sacred Heart** more than you could ever comprehend. This attitude cannot continue without remorse and/or, more importantly, consequences. We must recognize the evil for the destruction evil is causing all around us. Evil strives to confuse and discourage all such thoughts of **God** and **His** Angels in your daily life. For some people, this became a normal part of their life because this in turn sets the course for what you believe or what you do not believe. It is evident, Humanity is allowing more and more evil to ruin their life because of their lifestyle choices. It is your decisions and the associations that you choose to follow that leads to Sin. This situation is not pleasing to **God**. **God** is severely offended and very disappointed in our actions that show **Him** we do not love **Him**. In addition, this problem exists even for those people who feel they are good righteous people. These good people are falling little by little into the hands of evil as well because they have let down their guard. You can never feel that you are so comfortable with your faith that you need not be concerned with any improvement. What people do not realize or refuse to face the truth, evil knows all your weaknesses and takes great pleasure in the ruin of your Soul. It is very challenging to rid yourself of evil once it has moved in, but you can eradicate evil with the mercy of **Jesus Christ**. Therefore, you must be extremely vigilant in everything you do. This is why you must keep **God** close to you every second because only **God** will protect you.

    I am on the path **God** has chosen for me. My mind dwells on what **God** expects from me, not what someone else may think. I trust in **God**, **He** alone will judge me if I have done what is right and true. **God** is with me, and I love **Him** so much. I will not fail in my mission **God** has given me. Right now, it is so important to me to reach everyone possible. No matter what the problem is, with **God** by our side, there is always an appropriate solution to every situation. **God** always makes something good out of a bad situation if you trust in **Him**. **God** is patiently waiting to help us, but you and I need to ask for **His** help. We need to tell **God** we love **Him** right this minute. **God**, at this very moment, is trying to get our attention, and still too many people are still not listening.

> Dear **God**, please show me what you desire me to do next.
> I pray that these words will touch the very Soul of the unbeliever and, in **time**, they will come to love **You** dearly.
>
> What does **God** have to do to get our attention?

CHAPTER 20

Our Faith and God's Immense Love for Everyone

Why is it people have the impression **God** is complicated or aloof? Nowhere in the Bible does it ever mention **God** is complicated or unapproachable. These thoughts only come from the root of evil that works extremely hard to keep us from **God**. The great price we are going to pay for our lack of our friendship with **God** is our Soul. The Soul, this very minute, is in horror at the dreadful possibility that if you do not amend your life, the Soul will be lost without **God**. I believe the truth our Soul could be lost forever to evil should be horrifying to anyone. This belief should be sufficient for anyone to run to **God** and beg **Him** to believe that you still love **Him**.

This certainly is a sad situation if there are truly people who have lost their faith entirely. Is it possible for someone to lose his or her faith completely? We know there are individuals that never believed in **God**. What has happened in their life to make them act in such a derogatory manner toward **God**? It also seems reasonable why these people feel so empty inside that they have lost the will to regain or discover their faith. Maybe some individuals have stayed away from **God** so long, they feel it is impossible to regain **God's** love. Maybe it is those individuals who feel their sins are so great that it has been so long since they talked to **God**, they are worried **God** will not forgive them. What you may unconsciously not realize, if you are feeling confused and lost, this is your conscience that is trying to tell you something is wrong with the way you are living your life. The great thing about your conscience is that if you are worried about being away from **God**, that is a sure sign you still want to live your life in **God's** good graces. Therefore, follow through on your feelings because it is the **Holy Spirit** calling you back.

It is never too late for you to reacquaint yourself with **God**. If you are concerned, then this can only mean one thing: you still care what **God** thinks about you! This definitely means **God** is calling you to come back into **His** presence. The Bible says, **"All of heaven rejoices when a sinner returns to God" (Luke 15:7)**. Remember **Christ** died so that sins could be forgiven. Unfortunately, over **time**, many people do not realize they have placed his or herself above **God** when they are not sorry for their sinful behavior. No one can hide from **Almighty God**. This terrible attitude may block your return to **God's** Graces. If you feel this effort is too great for you, then you might not be able to restore your faith at least for a while. Restoring your faith only happens when you decide you need **God**. **God** is always waiting for you to return to **Him**, but it remains your choice. **God** is forever giving us the chance to redeem ourselves. I do know for sure, it is never too late to restore your friendship with **God**. You must have the desire to include **God** in every facet of your life.

I have heard a few people ask, they wondered if it were possible for someone to restore his or her Faith if it has been lost for years. There are people that have stayed away from **God's** love for most of their life. You must believe **God** never gives up on you! Grace is a gift from **God**. It should be natural for you to desire this faith so badly that nothing will make you happy until you restore your Faith. Faith is something you cannot see and you cannot touch. However, you know and can sense when you have this gift of Faith. You know when you do not have Faith because situations in your life seem more difficult for you to cope with. You have to desire faith more than anything else you deem important in your life. Faith will elude you if you struggle and do not completely give yourself up to **God**. With help from the **Holy Spirit** and a deeper understanding of grace, the peace you desire with **God** will be there for you to restore at any moment. Only then is it possible to be close to **God** once more. Faith in **God** is a sense of peace, so wonderful, no one will not want to let go of this peace. Faith is a joyful peace, which embraces a lasting desire to be close to **Almighty God**. Faith is a gift from **God** that **He** bestowed on us and should remain with you for a life**time** if you so desire. Faith is surrendering to **God** your complete confidence and trust in **Him**. **God** is never done until **He** makes us into a masterpiece!

If you heard an Angel appeared to someone, how would you react? I would think that upon hearing about an Angel appearing to anyone, this would be reason enough for you to pause and think about **God** more deeply. These special **times** are Grace-filled moments cherished in faith and given to you by **Almighty God**. These special moments are truly so very precious because it forces you to realize the importance of your Faith and trust you have in **God**. The strength of your Faith tells you **God** has touched you in a special way. Your Faith encompasses the need to offer heartfelt thankfulness and joy to **God**, which reaches into the very depth of your Soul. It is impossible to define to another person the immense importance of his or her Faith. Either you possess the Grace from **God** to have Faith or you do not.

I am overjoyed to realize fully the real depth of **God's** love for all **His** people. **God's** love for us is so vast that our understanding of this great love should fill us all with much contentment, not fear. No one should fear **God's** love. Our overwhelmingly grievous sins cause **God** to be so disappointed in **His** children. The Angel showed tremendous distress with the horrendous and appalling Sin of **Abortion**. In my thoughts, the Angel made it clear, "The sins of the world have become so great; that **God** is exceptionally disappointed and gravely disheartened." Christians all over the world understand the truth that **God** will punish **His** people if they do not drastically change their lifestyles. If more people would realize the enormous love **God** embraces for everyone on earth, the world would begin to heal by loving one another. Our mere words could never fully express the complete intention of **God's** love for all **His** people. **"For God so loved the world, He gave His only Son"** (John 3:16). This verse is, without a doubt, one that we should think of often. A love so immense that **God** would give **His** life for the salvation of Humanity is beyond our conception of the term *love*.

The overwhelming proof of **God's** love that one feels when experiencing any spiritual event is indescribable. **God** loves us so deeply, **He** is doing everything in **His** Divine power to help us all have a special connection too **Him**. **God** so desires all **His** people to remember we are all truly **His** children and nothing is impossible for **Him**. **God** desires all of us to believe every single person on the face of the earth is very important to **Him**. **God** desires all of us to be aware, every second of the day, we are not alone. This is also difficult to understand how **God** can be with all of us all at the same **time**. This is a great mystery you must not question, but instead, trust in your faith, **God** loves you so unconditionally that **He** is with you. **God** will never leave anyone alone. Everyone needs to say to **God** that you love **Him** every day. The Angels are a gift from **God** because **He** loves us and knows we need their direction. **God** desires everyone to believe your Angel is constantly right there by your side. The Angels never sleep. The Angels are diligently on watch to protect you every minute of the day and through the night. **God** is trying to show all **His** children through **His** Angels the path to heaven and into **His** loving arms. I hope you believe it is never too late to seek **God's** friendship. **God** is closer to you than you could ever imagine. **God** is so near to you every minute in your heart and in your Soul. Nothing in this world will ever take **God's** presence from you. This gift of love and friendship is yours to cherish forever, but this is your choice whether or not you choose to have this relationship.

I sense strongly something might transpire in the near future that will bring Humanity to their knees. Perhaps not tomorrow or the next day, but I sense something is beginning to materialize because the intention of this evil is becoming stronger. When I was in the presence of the Angel, I realized immediately that the message is certainly a dire warning. **God** is giving Humanity an opportunity to redeem themselves, but **time** is disappearing each day that passes. Undoubtedly, there is an acute awareness by a multitude of people there are enormous problems in the world that need immediate attention. Not just the issues of world affairs but also **God's** children have strayed too far from the safety of **God** by their indifference of Sin. Perhaps you also share this acute awareness. Is **God** trying to warn **His** people we are on the brink of disaster? This probably is an awareness of truth placed on the hearts of many people by **God** so they would have an opportunity to prepare their Soul. This is certainly an uncomfortable feeling that is happening to massive populations because they realize that the unquenchable thirst for war and the seemingly unlimited hatred must end or Humanity will end! We have acquired this truth from **God**, but still Humanity refuse to deal with it, and as a result, wars rage on with seemingly no end in sight! Our society is finally awaking to this truth and awareness that it is **time** to put an end to the turmoil in the world that threatens our very existence. The path should be clear to everyone that Humanity needs great change if the world is going to survive. The entire world needs to realize that it is not wise to test **Almighty God** further!

Practicing Christians believe that **God** knows them and they know **Him**. It is by our Faith we know **God** is much closer to **His** children than we ever realized would be possible. It is my belief others will experience numerous and miraculous events because **God** is trying so desperately to get our attention. Perhaps **time** is really becoming shorter than we realized. The message from the Angel came directly from the **Holy Spirit** so we would understand that we could no longer take **time** for granted. The Angel brought forth the message, "**Tell them it is almost time**," to warn Humanity **time** is imperative now. **God** is trying to warn **His** children so they will prepare themselves to face **God** while they still have the opportunity. We all need to ask **God** to forgive us for what we have done and what we have failed to do. For many individuals, their pride is standing in the way of **God's** love and mercy. This is one reason it can be more difficult for certain people to seek **God** in a way they need to now. We must give up the pride of self and realize **God** misses our love and friendship. We will always be **God's** children. The **Father** would never deny **His** child **His** love if the child so desperately desired this love.

Those who believe in the Book of Revelation believe the gates of Heaven are going to open soon and **God's** children will see **Christ** coming for the final judgment. Christians believe in the second coming of **Christ**. Yes, **Christ** is coming again to show **His** great love and mercy to the world. Will the world be ready? Not everyone will recognize **God** when **He** returns. In the book of Revelation, we read that a multitude of people will refuse to believe what they will be seeing because the falsehood of their beliefs will blind them from the truth. The Bible teaches us, **"We know not the time, nor the hour" (Matthew 25:13)**. Our belief in **God** tells us we must be prepared to see the face of **God**. For the Bible says, **"We know not the time."** Why do some people not trust what **God** has already placed in their heart? **God's** people have an obligation to **Him** because we already know what our **Creator** expects from us. This is where your faith, once again, tells you **God** loves you, but you need to be prepared if you expect to see **God** in all **His** glory.

It certainly is not necessary to see an Angel to believe **God** loves you. I also do not feel you need to see an Angel or any vision to believe **God** will protect you. We must trust in and lean on **God** that **He** will be there with you when you need **Him** if you are faithful to **Him**. I understand there are a great many things that are so difficult to grasp all at once. In a life**time**, Humanity will never learn everything it needs to know because it is only in Heaven will we know the true meaning of **God's** love for us. We must all return to the truth that **Almighty God** is waiting for **His** children to remember **His** great love **He** shares for all **His** people. It is **Almighty God**, our **Father**, who is constantly watching over all **His** creation. Our churches and our places of worship is the main place where **God's** people gather to praise and honor **God** and to ask **Him** for **His** guidance. There together the faithful gather to renew their love and Faith for **God**. Those who believe should have peace and contentment in the knowledge that they will someday be with **God** in heaven where the troubles of this world will fade away and be no more. The Angel said, **"Tell them it is almost time."** Yes, it is **time** for Humanity to take responsibility for the conditions that we caused by our failures to respond to the truth that is ever before us. We need to raise our voices to **God** and shout loudly that we love **Him**. Until the world faces the truth, we will carry on with the present conditions with no resolution.

It is in our human nature to feel some people appear to have more hardships than do others, and so they become despondent and even angry with **God**. It does seem **God** is constantly testing our love and Faith for **Him**. It is also true **God** does appear to test everyone in some way or another until we get it right or until we, at the very least, learn something important. In addition, it does seem some people have more hardships and illness. Why do some people appear to have more than their share of problems and heartache is difficult to understand? I agree this is very difficult to grasp why **God** needs to test **His** people repeatedly and especially when we feel it is downright unfair. In the Bible, in Genesis, the story of Abraham and the story of Job are two favorites of mine. Maybe it takes a hardship for some people to be aware how much they truly love and need **God**. Maybe it takes a hardship to realize how much **God** loves them. I can only speak for myself, but when I am suffering with pain, I do think of **God** more.

We read in the Bible where, **"Peter denies Jesus three times" (Luke 22:54–62)**. This was the ultimate test of the love that Peter professed he shared for **Jesus** and a further test of disappointment for the Apostle Peter when he realized he turned his back on **Jesus**. Whom is **God** really testing? Was it only Peter who experienced the pain of his denial? Was **God** testing the people watching and doing nothing to help because they refused to see the truth about **Jesus**? **God** repeatedly searches for ways to get our attention until we do "get it right." **God**, Our **Father**, who watches us from heaven so lovingly, will never give you and me more than we can handle. I do not profess to understand why some people seem to have more unhappiness and hardships than others do. We must all rely on our faith because it is **God's** plan for each of us. During illness or other serious situations that happen in most everyone's life, it is difficult to know **God** is there. **God** knows this is not easy for us to understand why these situations have to take place. **God** does recognize our pain because remember, **God** knows how it feels to suffer. **God** must be wondering why some people do not run to **Him** in **times** of sorrow or pain in their life. Why do people run away from **Him** instead of trusting that **He** is with you always?

Through all this suffering and serious consequences that happen to all people, as a society, we cannot live in a state of compassion and forgiveness without **God** in our life. With **God** in your life, more of life's challenges would turn out positive. It is very difficult to accept failures and trials in your life. Simply, without the support and knowledge that **God** is there with you, life can be a very lonely place without **Him**. Everything you try to accomplish somehow appears to be more difficult to accomplish without **God**. **God** is the bridge you must cross in order to find true happiness and peace. With **God** near you, you can overcome any obstacle that comes your way. No matter how severe the situation, **God** is with you every step. I love the picture of the footprints in the sand. This picture depicts **God** carrying you entirely though your hardships, even when you feel **God** had abandoned you, **He** is there. **God** is there carrying you no matter how heavy the burden. We must have great Faith and trust in **God** our **Father** because **He** knows what is best for **His** children.

There are thousands of books written concerning the existence of Angels. Christians believe and trust in the knowledge; these encounters with Angels or other events only takes place through the will of **God**. However, some people convince themselves it is possible for evil to show us splendid experiences as well. I personally am convinced and strongly adhere to the truth that I would know the difference. If you search deep in your heart, anyone should be able to discern the difference. I refuse to believe **God** would ever allow such hypocrisy to happen to me or anyone else. If you believe in the power of **Almighty God**, you will understand it is only a cruel ploy from the evil to confuse you further in order to keep you away from what is pure and good. The devil NEVER does anything good! My total trust and Faith in **God** would never allow evil to come close enough to take over my entire identity as a person. How much effort does society in general give in keeping evil away from their daily life? With the help of the **Holy Spirit**, we will succeed. Keeping your mind on **God** throughout the day is a sure way to drive evil crazy. If you desire, you will have the total protection of **God** because deep inside of your Soul, you desire **His** protection. The Angel I witnessed was pure goodness who appeared through the divine power of the **Holy Spirit**. The magnificent golden light that is the love of **God** surrounded the Angel. The Angel appeared because **God** desired Humanity to hear **His** message—a message conveyed to me by the Angel for all Humanity and for the salvation of Souls. Evil's only intention is to destroy our Soul, and the result is the loss of eternal life in Heaven with **Jesus**.

To my delight, gradually, more people from all lifestyles have told me they also have experienced a spiritual gift from **God** in some form or another. These particular people did not see Angels. What they witnessed were other forms of spiritual gifts that they believe took place in order to enhance their own spiritual Faith. A few people recently shared with me they experienced something unusual they could not readily explain. People have also shared with me they knew of someone who had received a divine revelation. I have read there have been many experiences where people say their vision or unique experience took place when they needed it the most. How wonderful, **God**, in **His** infinite wisdom, **He** is always there to show us how much **He** loves us. While these experiences are spiritual in their nature, they appear to be different altogether in many cases. Did these experiences take place for only this person alone?

What I found most interesting was when these people told me of their unique experience, they accepted the event immediately as something **God** desired them to know or it was a confirmation of their Faith. Perhaps something happened to these people previously, and **God** answered their prayer in a uniquely spiritual way. I am simply overwhelmed to know there are so many other people who have been experiencing amazing events from **God**. Miracles sent from **God** in order to help others reinforce their Faith. It was not until I started talking to other people more about my own experience that these people started sharing with me their experiences. I never realized there are so many people who have been experiencing various visions and events. I would encourage these people to come forward now and share their unique experiences as often as possible. I have noticed some spiritual experiences seem to be similar in their origin.

However, what is also evident, these events include unique characteristics. This is simply fantastic, and I continue to marvel at **God's** enormous love for all of us that **He** allows these miracles to happen.

It is reassuring to know, and certainly, it should be a blessed conformation to everyone that there is so many people who have already witnessed a magnificent heavenly vision. Amazing how wonderful **God** can enter our hearts when we allow this to happen. I like to think of these awesome experiences as loving reminders sent with love to us from Heaven. These experiences are special expressions of love given to many people from **God**, our **Father**, because of your love and Faith you have shown to **Him**. However, these special occasions are some**times** for the benefit of everyone too. Now is the **time** to share these awesome experiences because these experiences have the power to strengthen our Faith among one another. Our Faith is strengthened, strong as a rock, when we talk to one another about **God**. I believe these special gifts of love come from **God** entering our life every single day in one form or another. The **time** is drawing near because **God,** who loves all **His** children immensely, will allow many believers to experience something that will enhance the life of all who will listen.

Why it is that so few people are open to the present opportunities **God** is so willingly ready to bestow on them, I do not know. In a single day, there are spiritual gifts **God** desires to give you, but maybe you are too detached to notice. The problem is some people are in a hurry and are too busy to stop for a moment and realize **God** desires your attention in one way or another.

This is a special gift from **God** when we meet people and see the good qualities they possess. **God** gives you and me the opportunity to see the special gift of other people because **God** desires us to benefit in some way by meeting them. This is an opportunity lost when you do not see the goodness of others around you. I feel that most people are very generous with their **time** if given the change. If you take the **time** to help someone in need or the elderly who may be all alone, you will understand what I am saying. Visit a shut-in or an elderly person living in a nursing home if you are looking for **God**. I can assure you, I have met some very special people in the nursing home. **God** is with them, ever watching over them in their loneliness. It is amazing to me how many of these elderly people seem to be so misunderstood! When I visit a nursing home, professional people have mentioned to me, most elderly have no idea what they are saying. While there are cases where this is true due to their illness and I find when I mention **God's** name to them, they seem to speak intelligently. What does this suggest to you? Far too many of our elderly, left alone in their room, their minds begin to wonder and ponder. They are not concerned any longer with world affairs. Certainly, they have no more of anything to prove to anyone. Now I realize that their caregivers may not be aware that some of the elderly, their mind is on **God**, whether anyone cares to notice. These frail elderly people spend their day living out their life in total trust in **God** quietly because they believe **God** loves them. They are from a generation when **God** was prevalent in their lives and the lives of those around them. They have nothing more to give to society, or do they? Some are so helpless and need to hear a kind word from someone, anyone. People walking by have forgotten these elderly people do not often have the opportunity to talk about **God** with anyone. More people need to let the elderly know they are not alone and **God** cares about them enormously. These frail individuals only wait patiently to hear **God's** voice speaking to them when their trials are finally over. I met a woman who is ninety-two years young in a nursing home while I was visiting someone else. I thought I saw something in her eyes that reminded me of the Angel that I observed in the hospital. There was something so special and innocent about this sweet woman. She made me feel so loved that I did not want to leave her side. It is amazing how some of those special **times** happen and we cannot readily explain why we feel so good. We are here each day for the benefit of one another. **God** always places people together for a reason!

    God is trying to tell us we need to come together to reinforce one another in our faith and friendship for the love we each share for **Him**! We need one another to build a healthy community where **God** is loved, wanted, and needed. In addition, we desperately need one another to instill in our youth the awareness of **God**. You must take the **time** to teach your children the love and friendship of **God**

that is waiting for them. This generation is on the threshold of losing most of their youth to false beliefs. Even now, radical agendas of huge proportions are being born in our campuses and in our universities. Evil knows our youth are vulnerable to its attack, and so evil is relentless in its pursuit of the youth. Once, universities were a place for learning the truth through great ideals. Now while I type, evil is taking a stand and is slowly destroying our impressionable youth into thinking **God** does not fit into their modern way of life. I hear intelligent people all over the world who once said they professed their faith questioning everything. Large portions of our society are now convinced **God** no longer has a place in their life because this is the old way of thinking. In our campuses, young people have been convinced they do not need **God** in their life because this means there are restrictions. They also believe it is not necessary to mention **God** in the books used for the sole purpose of expanding the intellect of their mind. Finally, what is worse, there is NO mention of prayer in any school except the Catholic schools or Christian schools that still remain open in spite of the negative attitude of others. What a shame some professors are preaching there is no **God**. Intellect in its purest form cannot survive in a state of confusion and hate and denial of **Almighty God**. A large number of students and teachers consider conscious thought and common sense dead! I have never witnessed such stubborn denial of the truth to the degree I see happening now. Evil is really having a party. It does not take a scholar to figure out who is on the guest list. Until more people begin to see the truth that comes from **God**, they will continue to babble untruth and nonsensical reason, and nothing will change!

There is the attitude among people that they feel if they are ever interested, they can find **God** in a church. Then others believe we should banish the very precious name of **God** from every public place and in our documents too. Our history is under siege, and it is perplexing to me WHY we continue to allow a few misguided people to rule the majority. If history has taught us anything, we should remember that the Romans did this when they wanted the people to forget about a king or an important person who lost favor with the elite. The freethinkers always seem to believe they know what is best for the good of the population. Our young adults today want only to have fun. There is a majority of young people today are concerned with very little and only if it does not infringe on what they deem is important to their way of life. Who is to blame that our youth attend colleges where their curriculum does not include the Word of **God**? People today act as if they do not want their conscience burdened with the idea of right or wrong because there is very little moral responsibility. Evil is very pleased with this pure fact, and as a result, the memory of what was once right fades over **time**.

Our youth today learns not to let anything stand in the way of this false happiness. Fun is where anything goes, and the very thought of **God** spoils the whole idea of this fun. What young people want now is to be free of boundaries. What they do not realize is that they have free will but have not considered the consequences of their actions. Our young adults want to be free to follow the modern new world they have created for his or her self. Here there is no room for **God's** intrusion into their lives. Oh, please, I am begging you now to believe that we have severely wounded **God's Sacred heart** with our dismissive and ugly attitude. If you could have been with me to see the Angel, when she brought forth the consequences of our misguided decisions, you would identify immediately with everything I am conveying to you. Have **God's** children forgotten that **God** so loved the world **He** sent **His** only **Son** to die for us so we would have the opportunity to be saved from eternal damnation. I hate to believe that society in general is becoming very ungrateful for all the blessings **God** has bestowed on **His** people. So why should I be surprised when someone can look me into my face and tell me he hates **God**? To think anyone would be so comfortable with those words proves my point. Why and how did it become so easy in someone's mind to say such an arrogant statement? Where have I been all my life that I never witnessed this attitude regarding **God** directly? I never realized there were people who felt this bold until recently. Have I also been oblivious to what was happening in our schools and our churches? It was finally **time** for me to wake up and face the truth no matter how much it hurts. I now see before me what has truly been a slow masterful decay in our society altogether. Perhaps the plan evil has derived for you and I will stick better if evil destroys us slowly.

At **times**, the faithful in this world feel that they cannot or should not maintain their moral convictions because of social pressures. You see the unbeliever has nothing to lose. **God's** devoted children do not want to lose **Him**. How then do we battle the intentions of evil? How do we intervene evil from continuing to steel our children and young adults? Why are people becoming so dismissive? There is a shift on how Humanity is feeling toward one another, and it is not in the line with **God's** teachings. Our society has become a society of selfish unbelievers because they have proven with their actions that they have no **time** for **God**. Why do people not make **time** for **God** anymore? Worse, they do not make quality **time** for one another either. The terrible situation is a great many people do not have **God** in their life in general; maybe they never did. Could this be why a great deal of your well-thought-out plans in your life do not always go the way you hoped? You lose your way because you are walking in the dark alone without **God**. Much of Humanity has been convinced along the way by evil they can do without **God's** help. Even those who say they do believe in **God** and entertain some ideas and foolish thoughts, they have become somehow smart enough to deal with their life without **Almighty God** beside them. Of course, never realizing their very intellectual ideas came from **God** in the first place. No matter what your affiliation, **God** must be the center of your life. If **God** is not in your life, you will have a false sense of happiness, and this will never sustain you. It is not a wonder why people do not see the special miracles **God** may send their way. Under these conditions, they will never be able to see the Angels or anything else good that comes from **God** because they are not open to the possibility.

God knows your trials can be tremendous some**times** and **He** knows you need and want the feeling everything is going to be all right. **God** knows and understands very well your difficulties you face in life. **God**, who loves you so much, is always looking for the right moment to show you **He** is there with you. **God** is trying to reach you with **His** love so **He** can secure your attention and help you. What must **God** do to get your attention? What does **God** need to do to wake you up to realize that **God** loves you and only desires your happiness? I am becoming more aware **God** might decide to do something drastic in order to get Humanity's final attention. The Angel's demeanor convinces me this is probable. **God** loves everyone the same, and I can assure you no one individual in **God's** eyes is any more special than the next. **God** looks deep into your Soul, and only there **God** determines who you are and what you believe. This is what makes us different from one another. You need now more than ever to place your trust and your total faith in **Almighty God. God** will not fail you or me, and in the end, we will have lasting peace in our hearts. **God** is trying to get the attention of all Humanity while there is still **time.**

> Please, dear **God**, help **Your** people to wake up before it is too late! Please allow **Your** Angels to help **Your** people see the truth. Save **Your** children who are in dire need of **Your** mercy. Millions of people do love **You** very much and do care immensely what happens to **Your** beautiful world. For the sake of those who love **You** and for all those who are in great need of **Your** mercy, come to their assistance swiftly.

God is trying to get our attention to remind us **He** loves us dearly!

CHAPTER 21

Gifts from God Comprise Great Responsibility

These magnificent encounters are happening all over the world because **God** desires **His** people to know how important we are to **Him**. **God's** messengers come to us in many different appearances and often under special circumstances. Some of these spiritual experiences occur only for the benefit of the one receiving such a wonderful gift. While there are other **times**, **God** allows these experiences to happen for the greater good of **His** people. The significance of my personal experience that took place in the hospital was that **God** desired an Angel to appear to me because **He** sent **His** Angel to convey a message for the benefit of Humanity. The message the Angel conveyed is a dire warning that Humanity should regard as crucial to our future existence. The implication of the message certainly implies that Humanity needs to make major decisions that are vital to the entire population of the world. **God** allowed this magnificent event to take place because **He** desires **His** people to rediscover how to love one another in peace and tranquility. No doubt, it is the intention of the Angel's appearance to remind **God's** children we have greatly offended **Him** by continually committing grievous sins against **His Sacred Heart**. It was evident to me by the Angels mannerisms that our actions and our lack of response to **God** by multitudes of **His** people because they have disappointed **Him**. Nevertheless, **God**, in **His** goodness and mercy, continues to forgive us and graciously bestows is grace on **His** children.

    God has blessed **His** people with unique experiences and spiritual visions in order to strengthen them as well as others in their faith. These faithful individuals say their life has changed because of their particular experience. Certainly, any event such as this would automatically deepen their faith. In what other ways did their experience change their life? Perhaps a profound spiritual experience persuaded them to have more patients and consideration for others. Did **God** desire these people to know they have overlooked numerous possibilities in their life? After experiencing any heavenly experience, I would expect that you should feel a sense of renewed zeal for your life. **God** now gives you the opportunity to share what you have experienced in order to strengthen others in their commitment to **Him**.

    In addition, the near-death experiences that people have encountered are fascinating. I recently spoke to a woman who says she experienced this after having a heart attack. These experiences are so uniquely amazing because the obvious reason for their occurrence is generally for the benefit of the person who is close to death. These people do not seem to have any difficulty with the appropriate words to describe clearly what they witnessed or experienced. Others appear to have a clearer understanding of the experience or event immediately while others have experienced seeing wondrous bright lights and often they see loved ones who have already passed on before them. They always express a strong feeling of warmth and love coming from an intense bright light. These people often say they experienced a sense of peace like none other they have known before. Who would not want to experience the peaceful and reassuring encounter all these people say they witnessed? So why do some people have these experiences and some do not? Only **God** can judge what is in our hearts and in our Souls. Only **God** knows for sure the purpose for any spiritual event. I do, however, believe **God** uses these occasions for **His** special intentions in order to bring others closer to **Him**. Perhaps some people have overlooked an experience because they never realized the importance of what it was that took place. It is the **Holy Spirit** that leads anyone to see what they can accomplish if they would only have faith. In the Bible, we read where **Christ said, "Verily, Verily I say unto you, he that believeth in Me, the works that I do shall he do also; and greater works than these shall he do; because I go unto my Father"** (John 14:12).

God sends **His** people important messages at precisely the **time** they need to hear from **Him**. **God** allows wondrous experiences to take place overall for the benefit of many people. It is evident the message I received from the Angel was intended for everyone who would recognize what **God** is trying to convey to them. Generally, there is a deeper meaning that accompanies with a very heavy responsibility for anyone experiencing any encounter from heaven.

Until now, only a few people knew after my visit with the Angel and having the profound knowledge of the message, I felt very lonely. I was lonesome for the presence of the Angel because I felt so safe in the Angel's presence. I felt very lonesome when I returned home because I was unsure what to do with the knowledge of the message the Angel only days before conveyed to me. The message weighed heavy on my heart. The scenes the Angel directed me to watch troubled me intensely to think about them. I needed desperately to talk with someone that could provide me with spiritual direction. I prayed diligently in the hope that **God** would place someone in my life that would provide me with some peace and guidance. I was surprised how alone I felt, and this feeling only escalated until I began actively writing the book.

There was no doubt **God** was beside me and would always be there for me. I did receive some spiritual counseling a couple of **times**, but often, I felt left alone on my "private island." I prayed to **God** that **He** would please bring someone into my life who would be my spiritual advisor. Surely, because I am human, I needed a professional that I could confide my deepest thoughts about **God**. I thought I needed help in discerning the message and I needed to discuss often the beautiful Angel. I was desperate for a while to have spiritual council because it was so important to me that everything I did forward would be proper in **God's** eyes. Over the next few months, I remained discouraged because I was still on my private island with the exception of my family and friends. Soon, I realized this human need was a further test from **Almighty God** to see what I would do with the responsibility **God** placed in my life. **God** is in charge of my life; therefore, I would rely on only **God** for my counsel unless **He** directs me differently. Every morning after my prayers, it became clearer what I needed to accomplish. Praise **God** for my family and my faith in **God** who is our Heavenly **Father**. **God** is all the comfort I ever needed.

I continue to languish quietly by myself over all the conversations between the Angel and me because I now knew the absolute truth. The words the Angel spoke regarding **Abortion** and all the other grievous offences to **Almighty God** mentioned will always remain very difficult for me to reconcile. I resigned myself from that day forward to place my heart and Soul in **God's** hands completely. My mission is clear, and by the Grace of **Almighty God**, I will not fail.

God placed a heavy responsibility on my shoulders. Witnessing the Angel and possessing the knowledge of the powerful message, I felt more than a little overwhelmed with the responsibility that would follow. The message conveyed to me by the Angel, you must agree, the entire heavenly event was intense. I do feel the weight of the enormous task that **God** placed before me. I prayed continually to **God** in order to find the appropriate way to announce the message on such a large scale. It was clear I needed to decide how to share **God's** message with not only a few but with the world!

What should be so clear for everyone to comprehend is that the great love **God** possess for all **His** children is there for the asking. Communicating the message to a few people in passing was the easy part. I feel a great responsibility for me to say the right words at the appropriate **time** that the **Holy Spirit** has provided. In the beginning, I felt reaching a large number of people might prove to be difficult. I believed then **God** would lead me in the right direction to accomplish what **He** began with the message from the Angel. It was not long before the Angel would come to my aid, and I began to write the book. I realized many of the answers would be among these pages; I was so lovingly motivated to write each day. Then I knew this would be a secure way for me to reach the world with the message. It is the message the Angel conveyed to me that is very important for Humanity to hear. I must implore everyone to realize, **God** needs to know, you still love **Him** by showing **Him** you will improve your life. **God** has waited long enough for Humanity to realize that millions of people are not contributing to a **God**-loving society. It should not be a surprise to anyone when a society is morally out of control, bad things happen. A society that blurs the lines of right from wrong will inevitably cease to exist. There is proof from our past that any society that does not place **Almighty God** first is ill and is doomed to fail. Our present society is under attack by a Machiavellian evil because **God's** people have failed to protect the unborn and children in general. Why have people forgotten how to love one another and forgotten the importance of real love? In addition, for millions of people, money has become their **God** whom they worship far more than **Almighty God**. People are turning their back on **God** because they no longer have **time** for **God**. Our present society does not want the hindrance of rules and morals. Today, people enjoy making up the rules as they go along now because this makes them feel better about their life. In a society without **God**, goodness is vulnerable. Our society has forgotten how important family unity used to mean to most everyone. **God** sent **His** Angel with a message to remind Humanity our world is in trouble because great numbers of **His** people no longer follow **His** Commandments that are the outline to a moral society.

Gradually, more people are living without **God** in their life, and so civil unrest and disorder will prevail. Hatred and violence is taking a stronghold in every facet of our society. Large numbers of people allow themselves drawn into unrest in their cities, and really few understand evil is behind this situation. The problem is people today do not seem to have the ambition to make positive changes in their life. They have forgotten **God** does not want this hate and violence to evolve in **His** world. With the power of **God**, together with the strength of the **Holy Spirit**, anyone can overcome adversity. **God** is love, and **God** sent **His** only **Son** into the world to teach us to love one another. We must for the love of **God** all learn to live together in peace before it is too late! Everyone on the face of this earth has a great responsibility to **Almighty God**. **God** gave us the greatest gift of one another, and do not forget **He** sees us as equals. Why is it we cannot see each other as **God** sees us? We are all born equal in **God's** eyes. We all have the divine right to love **God** and live together on this earth in peace and harmony. When are we going to realize finally war and hatred is not pleasing to **God** and war proves absolutely nothing! War and violence is the end, not a beginning. Those who have placed themselves above the **Almighty God** will soon know the wrath of **His** mighty justice when **His** hand comes crashing down! Evil has persuaded some leaders only they should be in charge of what happens to the world. I must remind them again **God** created the world and everything in it. **God** is giving the world another of many opportunities to show **Him** we can love and respect one another by living our life in peace and happiness. Please believe me when I tell you, if there is anything I learned from the Angel, it is that **God** will not continue to witness this hatred, violence, and needless destruction of **His** people in vain. This **time**, there will be no winner, and we will only prove to **God** again we have learned nothing! The second coming and the final judgment day may be closer than people think! Christians of all faiths believe when **Christ** comes to judge the world, some people will go to heaven, but many will not!

There is not a day that goes by that I do not realize, seeing the Angel and the responsibility bestowed on me with the message, I pray I will prove myself worthy of the magnificent Grace-filled gift that I received from **Almighty God**.

> Dear **Lord**, send Your **Holy Spirit** to dwell
> in the hearts of **Your** faithful.
>
> **God** is trying to get our attention!

CHAPTER 22

Excuses for Sin in the World Lord, Forgive Us!

We must acknowledge that all of **God's** people have committed grievous sins in one way or another. The Angel mentioned repeatedly, **God** would no longer tolerate our excuses for allowing **Abortion**! To this day, this expression of sadness that came from the Angel is very difficult for me to endure. The shameful truth is we are all allowing horrible atrocities to continue to happen to children all over the world. **God** expects us to protect both the living and the unborn children. For heaven's sake, what is Humanity doing? What is society thinking when any society continues condoning **Abortion**? When will we stop this outrageous behavior? To condone this outrage to **Almighty God**, we are proving to **Him** that we have lost all control! The Angel gently forced me to confront the truth that the Human Race is capable of terrible and horrible cruelty. Human nature, being what it is, we do not like to face reality some**times**. The Angel did not hesitate to mention first, one of the worst sins against the **Sacred Heart** of **Jesus** is yes, **Abortion**, and I am well aware I repeat this often. It is this lasting impression that the Angel imparted that I cannot seem to get past. This is very difficult for me to face the intensity of this ugly sinful deed because it is exceptionally distressful to **God**. This was very difficult for me to hear when the Angel described

God's immense pain regarding **His** darling children whom **He** created in **His** image. This was horrible to hear when the Angel spoke regarding **God's** feelings in such a personal way. I thought my heart would break because at that moment, I felt completely and utterly helpless. This is when in the recovery room, others noticed I began to get very upset. Imagine if you can, an Angel telling you firsthand of **God's** pain and suffering that we have all caused because **God** sees what we are doing to **His** precious children! How could I ever have imagined I would ever hear an Angel say how unimaginably and horrifically painful and disappointing it is for **God** to see us offend **Him** so outrageously and without any remorse or compassion for the least of **His** unborn creation. Even now, I do not know what **God** is waiting for. Why **God** does not punish us all now is remarkable? Yet the answer is clear that **God** loves us this much that **He** will give us every opportunity to redeem ourselves, but how long will **God** wait? How much evil do you think **God** is willing to see happen before **He** puts an end to it? Our free will is certainly going to have massive consequences.

This is very, very difficult for me to explain to you how so many thoughts between the Angel and I could happen in such a short **time**. There is no way to explain the **time**! I found myself feeling like a pupil and the Angel my teacher. As the Angel continued the analysis of so many issues, it was difficult for me to hear how revolting to **God** our grievous sins are to **Him**. Our **Almighty God** is the **Creator** of all the people who live on this earth. We, as a civilization, would not exist without the will of **God** in the first place. Most of us call ourselves civilized. In the dictionary, the term *civilized* means a culture, which is civil, educated, sophisticated, and humane. Instead, we have become a culture that is selfish, self-centered, and cruel, and now we are unfortunately becoming a **God**less world contaminated from within. Who is to blame?

A healthy society begins with our beloved children who know and respect the Word of **God**. The more children learn to respect and honor **God**, I would believe that this would automatically produce a **God**-loving society. As a civilized nation, we are no longer teaching our children moral boundaries because young people feel there are no boundaries. Our children are not to blame because there are parents no longer care enough to spend quality **time** with their precious children. Teaching our children about **God** is the first step to becoming good individuals, good parents, and then good citizens. Fewer parents are teaching their children to know and love **God**. This leads into the confusion and violence we see happening all around us every day. It is easier for people today to justify their evil deeds. There is no moral conclusion to any evil violence. Violence and hatred is becoming a sport in our societies. What is worse, some societies are causing massive evil destruction in the holy name of **God**. Certainly, there is no excuse for anyone hiding behind the face of evil to use the precious name of **God** as an excuse to do evil! Why this is so difficult for some cultures of people to see **God** does not give anyone the right to take another life is bewildering. In addition, our wars are in direct offence to **God** because **He** expects Humanity to live in peace with one another. Evil has persuaded some leaders throughout the world that it is all right to destroy an entire race of people to complete mass oblivion. The Sixth Commandment **God** gave to Moses was **"Thou shall not kill."** I thought people all over the world, no matter what your Faith, believed in this truth. The **God** I know is a loving gentle **God** who watches over **His** people with immense love and compassion. What **God** do you follow because I believe it is a Mortal Sin to destroy a life, pure and simple? I promise you, **God** will not tolerate this behavior much longer if we allow **Abortion** and other atrocities to continue. **God** said, **"Thou shall not kill" (Exodus 20:13)**. This is the sixth of the Ten Commandments, and the entire world is well aware of this truth. In the Bible, **God** also said, **"Justice is Mine, says the Lord" (Romans 12:19)**. How could any nation of beautiful people created in **God's** own image not remember this? If we continue allowing **Abortion** that is murder of the innocent, **God** will leave us in the darkness of our own choosing! Why is it so difficult to end the practice of **Abortion**? Why after centuries of hatred between the cultures of the world and wars that follow is it so difficult for the leaders of the world to finally accept that war solves nothing! When is Humanity going to honor the truth that no one has the right to take another life! **God** will put an end to these atrocities sooner than you think if **His** people do not!

The words the Angel conveyed to me are a direct warning from **God**. It is very bewildering to understand why I needed to see the horrible scenes that the Angel revealed to me. This is why I mention seeing the Angel was bittersweet. I pray my voice and my prayers will make a difference. Together with **God's** Grace, we will put an end to first **Abortion**. If you believe **God** sees everything, how can Christians continue in good conscience to say you love **God** and then do little to stop this outrage? If we continue these injustices toward **God's Sacred Heart**, then we deserve our punishment. If you think you will be free from **God's** judgment regarding **Abortion** and other sins, you are deceived because you refuse to see the truth. Some people will need to experience something personally to force them to rethink their opinion regarding **Abortion**. I was surprised to hear directly from an individual who considers himself a good Catholic but is convinced there are acceptable exceptions to the moral injustice and grievous sin of **Abortion**. **God** will never grant any reason for the killing of an innocent baby for our irrational excuses that some people may judge rational.

I pray people are waking up to their ungodly decisions, and until they turn to **God**, they will experience turmoil and confusion over the truth in their life. The world is experiencing what I would like to classify as a severe case of the flu. Difficult to imagine how more severe the flu can become, but indifference to sin has become an epidemic on a huge scale. We are fooling around and teasing with destiny on a massive level. The only way to turn away from our present course is to ask **God** for **His** help. **God** is looking to see if we will commit to improving the issues that will eventually cause our demise if we do nothing to change them. **God** is seeking proof from us in order to believe we are still worthy!

I have finally come to grips with the truth that multitudes of people simply do not care or they have a lack of interest about all the injustices we are now plagued with, and I am afraid it is downhill from there. Humanity is encountering a very slippery slope that will end in **time** with our destruction. I pray that I am wrong; however, why do good people accept all the craziness they see going on around them right now? Consider all the injustices that our society is allowing and our lack of response that further leads me to this conclusion. Yes, this sounds very negative, but some**times**, we must face the truth no matter how challenging. It saddens me. I wonder why people have given up on so many issues. People will say, "There is nothing I can do about it." I know people are tired of all the issues thrown at them on a daily basis. It takes a lot of effort and energy to change anything. I also have to search deep into my heart and admit I have felt discouraged and weary at **times** too, and some days, you just cannot listen anymore. Now I must also face the fact I did not do enough in the past to bring about change either. Did I turn to **God** for the answers? Maybe if I tried harder over the years myself, this might have made a difference. Sure, there are people who do care and care a lot about the serious issues facing us. Yes, millions of people love **God** immensely. Then why does the very idea regarding nativity figures bring so much distain from some people? What is really at the root of this concern? This has always puzzled me that one person could change the course of our religious freedoms in our schools. Why does prayer in school cause so much criticism? I have to ask myself, what did I do to stop this from happening? Christians of all faiths allowed prayer in public schools to end! Here is what I found. First, prayer in schools had a label called "Divisive." The explanation for the term divisive is troublesome, disruptive, and discordant! I cannot imagine why anyone would agree that prayer to **Almighty God** could be divisive. I need to ask again why prayer in schools is prohibitive. I always believed that prayer to **God** is based on Faith and, therefore, normal. If young children did have **God** in their life, they would be better equipped to function as adults. Was this the beginning of turning our life away from **God** and we used our children as the excuse? It is more than fifty years since open prayer was taken out of our public schools, and what have we learned since? It is documented that some academic leaders believe that the absence of prayer in public schools is to blame for widespread drug use among our young children. Violence and social decay is on the rise because our young children lack proper judgment and good moral habits. Sure, children may silently pray in school, but the peer pressure is so great that this is automatically discouraged. I read where the possibility of reintroducing school-sponsored prayer has weakened as the nation continues to become more diverse in general.

We must face the sad truth; there is a general feeling overall, people are afraid to challenge the opposition. It is the overall majority who feels challenging a group is too much effort. Maybe these people are right because there are those people who have strayed so far from **Him**, even a child is not worth the bother anymore. Once in a while, we view proposals on a wide spectrum of issues, but weak solutions never seem to solve anything long term. This only contributes to more unrest, frustration, and confusion. We have debated over **Abortion** and religious freedoms for too many life**times**, and still we face the same agendas. Too much **time** is lost, and nothing is ever accomplished! Why simple figures of the Blessed Mother, baby **Jesus**, Joseph, and figures of animals in a wooden stable would bring about such torment to some people, I will never understand. It is beyond my comprehension why these people do not realize what is at the root of the problem that torments these people so much. If you think this through rationally, you will see the truth that torments them is not the statues. I must conclude that these people struggle to remove anything that reminds them of **God**! This is only their misdirected will that they wish to impose on others to halt anything that reminds others of **God**. This is an abnormal attitude that commands to impose evil ideals onto our society. When we allow a select few to destroy our religious traditions, prayer in schools, bad behavior, and discipline altogether, we have lost sight of the true meaningful purpose of our existence. I can say with total conviction when a society loses its religious freedoms, we are on the road to damnation. Perhaps in some respects we have already arrived! I pray this is not true. When I am in prayer, I relive the moment the Angel became so serious because the world must first stop killing their babies! It should be so evident to everyone why the Angel was deeply devastated and even sickened over our lack of condemnation of **Abortion**. How do you think **God** feels about the injustices in the world that we continually allow?

Is this why the Angels are appearing and other events are taking place more all over the world? Are the Angels here to remind us we never should have turned our face away from **God**? I never thought I would ever live to see the day when there are women who would destroy their unborn child and not even feel remorse. There are other options to prevent pregnancy in the first place. In the early 1950s, I can remember when I was a little girl, I recall hearing conversations about a crisis happening between the mother and child during a difficult childbirth. I believe I am correct when I learned it was a common practice to save the child no matter what happened. This was a very difficult decision and, in many cases, horrible, I am sure, for the families. This proves how much people respected the significance of the gift of life. In those days, there was no question **God** was the head of the household. Any serious decision within the family always included prayer for strength and help from **Almighty God** first. Families trusted in their faith in **God** without hesitation because they believed **God** loved them beyond measure. These people believed wholeheartedly in their faith that **God** knew what was best for their family. This fine example shows the enormous faith and love between a Soul and **Almighty God** that today is being lost.

God must think Humanity has misplaced the capability to reason clearly due to evil in their life. **God's** people are surely losing their Souls. It is difficult to believe there are any mothers who would participate in the deliberate murder of their precious child. Worse, what is more than I will ever accept is the monstrous practice of **aborting** a child; even when the child has all signs of continuing life, the baby is still killed! I cannot accept there are still doctors and nurses who would be part of this horror. This is difficult for me to write these sentences repeatedly and know this truth continues with every breath I take. It does not seem real to me, and I simply will never accept it because I never did. The entire procedures are more like a terrible nightmare. It sounds so unbelievable that this really takes place on a regular basis every day. My mind does not want to believe it, yet in my heart, I know this is true. This is nothing more than mass murder of the innocent and the worst evil **God's** people could ever commit. The disgusting thing is the horror we are all allowing **Abortion** to continue and no one is stopping or trying to prevent these actions beyond a little noise or distraction from the truth. Evil is leading the way, and these people continue to follow a delusion. I refuse to stop asking, when will we put an end to **Abortion**? I can sense the Angel urging me to ask repeatedly; therefore, I must continue without apologies. More importantly, **God** is asking **His** people, when will we put an end to this atrocity, today or maybe tomorrow? If society would become disturbed enough and want to put an end to **Abortion**, it would end overnight. Now is the **time** to put an end to what millions of people feel in their hearts has gone much too far.

God's faithful people can no longer tolerate the murder of our precious children because our Lord will not tolerate it much longer!

Dear **God**, I pray **You** will send **Your** people government leaders who will honor **Your** name by respecting the unborn. My prayer is that these leaders will use their power and influence to stop **Abortion** and other atrocities. Please send **Your** people a leader who will do your will because only **You**, my **Lord** and my **God**, know what is truly best for **Your** people. Please bless all the leaders of our country so they will accomplish only **Your** will. Come **Holy Spirit** and open the eyes of the other leaders of the world so that the world will have peace. Enter their hearts of Humanity so they will feel the joy every **time** they invoke **Your** sweet name. Amen.

I have discussed the term **"Late Term Abortion"** already, and I know it seems repetitious to keep bringing it up, but I must honor the Angel, and—in turn, most importantly—I must honor **God**! We must discuss this severe problem facing us until we are tired of talking and hearing this term **Abortion**. Maybe if we get tired enough from discussing **Abortion**, we will finally demand it to stop! It makes most Christians ill every **time** they hear the words spoken; therefore, what are we waiting for? Together, please, let us do something to stop it. The Angel is further prompting me to bring this issue up repeatedly until I run out of ink! I believe we need to discuss this crisis until we can put a stop to it forever. When is enough, enough? There is no question **Abortion** is a monumental observation that is causing **God** to suffer immensely. I guarantee we will all have to face **God** regarding what we have done and what we have failed to do that causes this terrible Sin against Humanity. **God** is going to ask all of us, "What did you do to stop this most evil horror from happening to my most precious gift to you?" **God** gave us a tremendous blessing of a child and millions of people threw it away like rotting garbage. We have to stop the Sin that is causing **God** so much anguish.

How can we expect **God** to continue to forgive us if we continue to allow the children of the world to suffer without any remorse on the part of Humanity? I cringe to think Humanity forces **God** and our Angels to witness all measure of evil. Have they forgotten **God** sees all we do, both the good and the ugly? **God's** people force our loving **Creator** to watch a child die needlessly from starvation and to know we have free will to choose to help these children. Hundreds of children and their families die each day because they have nothing to eat or they do not have clean drinking water. I refuse to believe that the wealthy, and I mean wealthy nations of the world, do not have the power to stop this from happening. How is it possible that knowing these conditions persist and still very little is ever done to improve their life. When did Humanity decide that they would only help their own cultures? I do not know how **God** can cope with us anymore with so much evil in **His** sight.

We need to face the truth that societies all over the world are plagued with sins against children of all ages. The Soul of these predators' remains corrupted with evil until they ask for **God's** mercy. The degree of evil in some people is a mind-bending truth; otherwise, these people would never be capable of doing the terrible things they think up to do to others. Do these people make a deal with the devil either knowingly or unknowingly due to their life choices? How frightening this would be to believe you are alone in the madness and corruptness of you choosing. What is even worse is the truth, the prospect of living without **God** to love you and protect you, that should be a terrifying thought for anyone. You must pray to **God** right now, from the very depth of your heart, to forgive you for your sins. No Sin is so small it does not count. It is evident people have decided to justify anything wrong they do is no longer a Sin because the things they do is acceptable in today's society. Some will even say, "Everyone is doing it, so how could it be wrong?" I never hear much about the term *sin* anymore, anywhere. The concept of sin, it is as if many people have taken it out of their language altogether.

God will forgive such horrendous sins because **He** is all merciful and loving when anyone asks for **His** forgiveness. The Angel confirmed by her outward sadness, although any sin is horrendous to **Almighty God**, the outrageous sins happening to children is unbearable. However, we need to believe **God's** mercy is beyond our comprehension. After the encounter with the Angel, I fear Humanity might be reaching the limit to **God's** mercy! Most of us believe **God** is our **Father** who loves **His** children no matter what we do if we are sorry and promise **God** not to sin again. **Jesus said, "Go and sin no more" (John 8:11).** Humanity needs to remember, you must ask **God** to forgive you before it is too late. You must beg **God** to forgive you for your sins, and you need to tell **God** you intend to sin no more. We must all beg **God** to forgive us for these outrageous and unthinkable acts of destroying the unborn. We must remember this is a child of **God**, born in **His** own image, women so callously find so easy to destroy. How can we call ourselves a loving society? How could so many be so evil that they could ever not accept this awesome and precious gift from **God**? During conception that is a true miracle from **Almighty God**, **God** already knows the Soul of a child intimately. I do not really know how we can look at one another and say, "**Abortion**," is someone else's problem. I can only conclude, even the minds of good people have become so corrupt and confused over what is right. Therefore, these people put it out of their mind and remain uninterested, and evil loves them for what they have done and what they have failed to do, they should proceed to the front of the class! Yes, their minds are very corrupt because they do not feel this grave sin among others is there's. Yes, many of us say this is wrong, but what are we doing to stop **Abortion**? Under this state of illness, your mind can no longer make good decisions about other areas in your life. Even if you were not directly involved, you are still to blame by allowing **Abortion** to continue in any capacity because collectively we are accountable.

Collectively, we can accomplish a great many wonderful things in **God's** name if we believed this to be true. I believe this is why **God** is sending all **His** Angels to give us an opportunity once more to renew our love for the **Holy Spirit. God** is giving us an opportunity to renew the face of the world with love, not death. **God** has given us perhaps one last chance to become a loving society that no longer believes in allowing the destruction of **God's** precious creation. We have an opportunity to become a society who loves all creation enough to make drastic changes. NO child should go hungry tonight. How can we knowingly allow any child to be alone on the streets with nowhere to go and do nothing? NO child should ever be without someone to love and care for them! Indifference to the needs of any child of **God** is unconscionable and should never happen in a loving society in any capacity. I pray it is still possible to remove hate among the people of the world and replace it with love, understanding, and respect for all cultures, races, and all creeds. Only then will we ever be possible for Humanity to see the truth again and achieve peace in the world.

With all these overwhelming issues, it is very difficult for us to understand how our gracious **God** continues to try so desperately to find some hope in us again. What is wrong with our leaders whom we have entrusted to make our world a better place? Where is their voice, and where is their conscience? Their voices are silent because some of our leaders are no longer listening to us. Our problems did not happen overnight. Therefore, great change takes a great deal of effort for everyone. Our problems and our present challenges are collectively not individually. We are all to blame for the poor moral condition the world is in today.

Together, what are we going to do to change our present course so God will be pleased with Humanity?

The truth is, over the years, the issue of **Abortion** as well as other grave sins in general became stagnant in the minds for most people; therefore, the murder and neglect of our innocent children continues relentlessly without mercy. Too many people do not want to believe society has entered into a decay that is rapidly destroying the morals of our youth too. How can we protect our youth when we no longer care about the unborn children? I have already said our youth may never know the wonderful religious traditions I once cherished and held so dear. It was in Catholic school and while attending my Catholic church where these solid holy traditions reinforced my faith in my love for **God**. My early foundation that I was so fortunate to be a part of taught me all about the teachings of **Jesus Christ**, which prepared me to be the person I am today. I went to public school in my teenage years. However, I still never missed my religious education classes. In those days, this was the responsibility of the entire community to educate their children in the Word of **God**. What happened to this responsibility? Our Catholic schools are closing, and **God** is no longer wanted or needed in our public schools. It is obvious **God** is getting the boot in our society altogether!

The Angel who so lovingly appeared to me announced the grievous sin of **Abortion** would be central in her many conversations with me, have you noticed? These intense conversations with the Angel caused me to be exceedingly aware that **God** is extremely distressed with us altogether! Upon hearing this, I briefly experienced to the limitation of my human frailty the tremendous suffering **God** must be feeling. When I realized I must face **God's** suffering, my heart filled with deep emotion for **Him** because in my small way, I experienced the pain **He** is enduring because **He** loves **His** people. During this **time**, my own indiscretions and failures came to my mind because I am far from perfect, because I too commit sins like everyone else. You and I could never really comprehend the true degree of **God's** feelings or suffering that **His** people are all causing **Him**. If I am sincerely sorry for my sins, **God** will forgive me, and **God** will forgive anyone with a contrite heart. There are no words to express what **God** is truly feeling! However, the emotion I felt was so painful, I pray I never experience it again. However, in my deepest of prayers, I still contemplate this experience of suffering, and this is horrifying and devastating for me. I wonder if during prayer, others have felt the pain that **God** suffers every second of the day due to all the sins committed in the world. If at no other **time**, the forty days of Lent that lead to Easter, is certainly a very privileged **time** for Christians to contemplate the experience of **God's** pain. We need to remember **Christ** suffered the death on the cross for the love of all **His** people. However, in countless ways, some people must not think about **Christ** dying on the Cross, and therefore, was it not enough?

The Angel did not speak words aloud, but I understood all the issues presented to me perfectly. Therefore, I continue to ask, what are we doing about **Abortion** today and other atrocities against our children? Our present society is broken, and **God** is very, very sorrowful over our outrageous attitude. I refuse to believe our society does not want our children to know **God**. Who will these children lean on when life for them gets difficult? An architect of evil is playing with the patterns of our life, and we are buying into them fast from top to bottom. We have gone beyond reason when we continue to condone **Abortion** and other grave atrocities in the world. Yes, **God's Sacred Heart**, wounded by our sins and our comprehension of this word *wounded*, is beyond our simple understanding.

Everyone can see the destructive force dumped on us with all the electronic devices we adore. All these devices are cherished and not only by our children. While I do think technology is wonderful, there is a destructive force involved with these devices. The problem is, for many people, these devices contradict **God's** teachings. These devices are taking over the minds of our youth and young adults in such a way that nothing else is important. Our society has become more like robots. This could really happen if we are not careful and continue building a corrupt society. These individuals have attached themselves to their cell phones day and night. Most of society cannot go anywhere without their cell phones, or they would feel ill. People even say they feel lost without their phones, but do they feel the same loss without **God**? Most people dare not go anywhere without taking a cell phone wherever they go. In fact, I dare say many people would be insecure without their devices. These devices are part of the fabric of our society; they simply cannot do without them ever. There are people that even go to bed with their devices. Your mind needs a rest from the loud disturbances of your daily life. You have no **time** for **God** when you are constantly pressing buttons. You will never have

time for **God** when you are pushing your fingers on a keyboard every minute. Countless people cannot even drive their cars without these devices. This dangerous condition is killing thousands of people. Most people today feel they must have their electronics above all else. This is a terrible disturbance for the mind and a definite distraction away from anything related to **God**. Do you see the problem with this dependency?

The majority of people in our society have placed their attentions on material things that will not sustain their happiness. Has Humanity misplaced their priorities as to what should really be important in their life? Little by little, a great many people are pushing **God** out of our society and out of their life altogether. By pushing **God** out of their lives, it becomes a reflection on society. Evil in this world has the attention of multitudes of people because they have caused a division between everything that should be important, including their children. Evil sees a great weakness in our habits in our everyday life, and yet many people feel powerless to alter anything. What an awful and lonely thought that evil is gaining on us and people continue to allow this to happen without the slightest compulsion to do anything to stop it. Evil is gaining on us because most people have no inclination to change the slightest thing in their life. What even intelligent people see before their very eyes to be the truth in their life is a false narrative of the truth because evil has weaved its way so ingeniously into their life. It has been a slow and painful erosion of your values and your very spirit. The world and all its evil wants you to believe there is NO Sin and, therefore, NO hell anymore. Sin is under new management, and what many people have chosen to follow is eventual darkness, where **God** does not reside. There is no love there, only hate and intolerance. Any person with any conscience can see what is happening, for example, in our television programs. Rarely, there is any family unity left in any of the recent programs that people find entertaining. Most people would certainly never miss one episode of a sitcom that promotes bad morals. Our youth watches the bad moral behavior that has evaded our television, even during family hours, and parents do not try to stop it. Even the commercials are not appropriate for our impressionable children to watch anymore. These programs are filling your children's heads with the wrong ideals about life. However, programming is all about the ratings. Therefore, these destructive programs would not be on there in the first place if people did not watch them. Why do so many people enjoy watching programs that promote bad morals because after all, these shows are supposed to be entertaining but, instead, they are promoting bad moral behavior and that is not a joke!

Much of Humanity has lost all respect for one another and themselves too, or the interest would not be there to watch this type of programming. Have you forgotten your children are following your example? People will say, "Oh, the children will be all right!" Well, your children will not be all right. Your children are not all right now and will not be all right in the future. Your children need proper supervision and direction by the very people who profess to love them. Children today are coming home after school and are left alone to do whatever pleases them. This is the new latchkey generation! Children are alone to decide for themselves. I have said repeatedly, many people have caused their present conditions because they no longer see the presence of **God** in their lives. The problem is people are constantly telling themselves they deserve something better and they do not remember **God** is waiting to help them have something better. I pray most of us do believe that **God** alone knows what we truly deserve and what we truly need in order to be happy.

I have read many **times** where some people experience a premonition in one way or another and they felt, for example, "It's not their **time**." There must be something in their life they have left unfinished. Do we really have a job to do here? Are we really at fault for the things we have failed to accomplish? Humanity altered **God's** master plan for their happiness. When **God's** children can live their life true to **God's** teachings, only then are we capable of being the person **God** desires us to be. Only then can true happiness prevail in our life. Only if you believe in **God** are you able to spread happiness to everyone you meet. If there were room in your heart for more love and patience with one another, then your life and the world, as a whole, would immediately improve. Humanity needs to be accountable! The heavy scale that has begun to drop with the weight of all of our sins and injustices in our world is about to break from this great weight. If **God's** people are not careful, they may realize, without **God**, some of their problems might be beyond repair. Evil has crossed into a new era of your wants and needs, and this evil is not at all sympathetic with YOU. Evil has disguised itself so well, far too many people are easily satisfied and fooled. You must close this separation between **God** and yourself. Your sins have caused a wide division between you and **God**. Now is the opportunity; before it is too late, you must correct this division you caused soon because **God** is waiting for your return to **Him**. What would you do if you suddenly had the knowledge **God** was ready to turn **His** back on Humanity? Would you believe it? Would you go merrily on your way doing business as usual? What would you truly think if someone told you **God** is horrifically hurt? It is evident through sin that because of our indigent behavior to **God**, it is possible **He** will close the gates of Heaven. What Humanity must realize there is a **time** limit. What if you knew there was still some precious **time** to amend your ways? How many people would believe this and ask **God** for **His** forgiveness immediately? I pray everyone!

Imagine a world living in harmony, the way **God** desires it to be for all **His** children. Imagine, if you can, how marvelous and wonderful this would be a paradise of peace and prosperity for all. Everyone on the face of this earth is to blame the world is not this way. It remains so easy for many people to justify a reason for everything they do in their daily life, good or bad. People have managed to transform what they used to believe about Sin into a new concept of their belief. The Angels words only reinforce the truth that sin is alive and well and hell has lots of room left! The problem is too many individuals refuse to believe this evil is roaming ever nearer to them, waiting for their mistakes and misjudgments. Why is it so easy for this evil decay to enter your life? When did you allow evil to sneak in? Without **God** in your life, evil becomes relentless because its ultimate objective is your Soul. The firmer hold evil has on you, the more difficult this is to divest yourself of it. Getting rid of evil in your life might be like learning how to walk on stilts. However, if the mind is willing and the purpose great enough with **God's** mercy, you can accomplish the impossible.

I have said repeatedly, **God** loves us all dearly and to the extent that it is beyond our capacity to contemplate it. Everyone must believe this wondrous truth, but Humanity must be accountable for the sin that has wounded **God's Sacred Heart** to such a severe degree. The truth does hurt, but acknowledging this truth is the first step to avoiding the temptation of Sin. The Angel was precise in the confirmation that Humanities **time** to amend their life and turn away from Sin is ending. **God's** children must face the truth there is no more vocabulary left to describe the mountain of offences and how **God** feels about our indignant behavior. When we allow **God** to witness our evil actions, Humanity is willingly telling **God** they do not need and want **His** love anymore. If **God's** people do not put an end to their grievous Sin of **Abortion** and other indiscretions to numerous to mention, I will assure you of one important truth: **God** will.

God is trying to get our attention because **He** loves us so much! When is Humanity finally going to honor **God** by proving to **Him** we are a loving and faithful people? When is Humanity going to prove to **God** by their actions that we are a thankful people? When is Humanity going to stop the injustices in the world?

Almighty God is patiently waiting for the Human Race to demonstrate their love for **Him** first. **God** is waiting to see if Humanity will finally learn how to love one another, and only then will we have peace in the world!

CHAPTER 23

The Dawn of a New Day

Almighty God designed **His** beautiful world of ours with magnificent perfection. However, the glorious and ingenious plan of **God's** perfection can only continue to evolve through our cooperation. I like to compare the life cycle of every living creature, created by **God**, to a symphony. Each note created to form a natural rhythm and harmony. There must be a natural rhythm and harmony in all phases of human life as well as nature. Any disruption to the fragile balance of the rhythm can produce drastic events that we now see happening throughout the world. Thank goodness, **God** does bestow upon us gifts in order to enable the world to work as extraordinary as nature if humankind does not destroy these gifts.

I thoroughly enjoy the season of spring the most of all the four seasons in New York. Spring**time** brings with it the promise of renewed hope. If you live in a colder climate as I do, spring offers the assurance of the awesome natural order of regeneration of all trees and plant life. Totally, this rebirth takes place right before our eyes, and it is marvelous. What a spectacle to watch **God's** wondrous plan taking shape repeatedly each year. Even the air smells fresher with the sweet aroma of the new buds beginning to bloom. The birds do not fret but instead sing their praises to **God**. Somehow, they know instinctively **God** is watching over them and will provide them with everything they need. The Bible teaches us that **Jesus** told the people,

"Look at the birds of the air, they neither sow or reap, nor gather into barns, seek first the kingdom of God." (Matthew 6:26). All the animals rejoice because of their internal instincts; the animals instinctively know when it is **time** to repopulate their species. It is wonderful to watch nature going about doing what nature knows naturally so well. Without human assistance, some unknown force drives the rhythm of nature; and year after year, the cycle of this rebirth resumes.

The ominous message conveyed by the Angel reminds you and me that all of **God's** people have an opportunity at the dawn of each new day to renew the wonderful plan **God** created. Within the human aspect of our life, humankind also follows a harmonious rhythm unseen and often unnoticed. The awesome difference is you and I do not have to wait for a new season to begin to renew and regenerate our spirit. At the beginning of a new day, you have a perfect opportunity to sit quietly and ask **God** to help you regain zeal for your life. You need to take a few moments each day, take a deep breath, and believe you have the power to renew the freshness of your life. Each year, the seasons come and go naturally without few people giving much thought to what is really taking place. The seasons of nature teach us lessons we can learn easily by studying Mother Nature. Nature does not struggle because Mother Nature coincides in cooperation with everything it touches. Your personal environment is like nature; you need to have a natural rhythm and balance in order to achieve happiness. I pray you will believe every day is a new opportunity and a grand beginning is waiting for you. Yesterday is already history; therefore, you need to look toward tomorrow with a positive attitude of hope. I believe there is always something new waiting for you just around the corner to discover if you have faith. The best assurance you can achieve in your life is the knowledge you have done your best with **God** by your side at the end of each day.

Right this very minute is a perfect **time** for you to search your heart for the closeness of **God** you desire. Why do some people continue to search for **God's** friendship until finally one day, they realize while they were searching for **God**, they failed to notice **God** was right there beside them. Some individuals search for **God** intently and think the entire idea of **God** is so complex. **God** is there beside you all through your life. **God** is involved in everything you do and everything you hope to accomplish in your life. **God** is there patiently watching you strive to achieve your hopes and dreams that were **God's** plan for you. **God** is also there when you do not succeed but waits for you to recognize the importance of not giving up. This is so simple to understand and now so clear to me: **God** is extremely interested in every facet of our life. **God** loves everyone so much; in the beginning, **God** gave all **His** people the knowledge they would ever need to grow to know and love **Him**. It is your choice to love **God** and to know **Him**. Through the emotions of the heart and the energy and perhaps the demands of your very Soul, you will learn you can communicate with **God** easily if you desire. Free from Sin, your Soul is capable of reaching the very essence of **God**, especially during meditative prayer where you will sense the possibility you are oh so close to **God**. At this particular moment, you can imagine you are completely alone with **God**. Nothing is more important than your personal relationship with **God**. Every person has a different ability to reach this lovingly relationship with **God**. **God** desires you to know no one person is more important to **Him**. We are all special to **God**. **God** does not have favorites! In the Bible, we read where **Jesus** said, **"In my Father's house there are many mansions" (John 14:2–3)**. This beautiful phrase tells us that **God** looks deep into the purity of our soul where no one person's Soul is ever the same. This was an assurance from **Christ** to **His** disciples; they would have a place with **Him**. **Christ** also assured them **He** would never abandon them. **God's** children can only pray that we will be with **Him** in Heaven. Certainly, there are numerous levels of what we perceive Heaven to be. This is, of course, a masterful mystery known only to **Almighty God**. I assure you all you need to acquire is the sanctity of your Faith and the love and mercy of **God** that I pray you already possess in order to believe what **God** has placed in your heart.

Each day, as I recall what took place in the hospital, seeing the Angel was conformation of **God's** endless love for all **His** children. Further, to know that I, through the Grace of **God**, actually experienced this remarkable encounter with an Angel is a very humbling experience. What I experienced is so magnificent to know **God** allowed an Angel to appear to me with a message for all Humanity. When I hear myself saying the words, **"Tell them it is almost time,"** I am refreshed with the reverence I felt when I first witnessed the beautiful Angel. I myself have always believed in Angels, but I never thought I would ever visually see an Angel on earth. I am greatly humbled before **God** to know, through **His** magnificent Angel, the **Holy Spirit** entrusted me with a message that I must convey to everyone who will listen!

Throughout my life, I was aware of my special closeness with **God**. It began when I was in third grade at Saint John Evangelist Catholic School in Syracuse, New York. It was a deep love for **God** and **His** holy church that grew to mean so much to me. This was an unshakable bond that formed with **God** in those early years, and I knew then I would never live my life without **God** beside me. I knew then I would love **God** above everything else my entire life. If this were not true, it would not be possible for me to have an experience of seeing an Angel in the first place.

It is possible for the faithful who love **God** deeply to acquire a special connection with **God**, but you must have the desire. It is during these special occasions permitted by **God** that this bond seals the love between you and **Him**. This intimate and loving bond will ultimately lead you closer to **God**. First, acquiring this bond is possible with the Grace you receive from **God**. What is the difference between actual grace and sanctifying grace? Grace really enables us to act. Therefore, grace is the strength **God** gives us according to **His** will to act. Sanctifying grace is the state of grace where **God** allows us to share in **His** love and **His** life. Thus, when we speak of being in the state of grace, what we are really saying is we are in the state of sanctifying grace. This grace first comes to us in our Baptism. This is your Faith in your **Creator**, who is **God** the **Father**, **God** the **Son**, and **God** the **Holy Spirit**, who begins an amazing journey within you. You will feel **God's** presence all around you. **God** understands all your frustrations and discouragements. You must trust in **God's** love for you. You must understand and believe **God** cares deeply what happens to all **His** people. **God** desires us to accomplish wonderful things for the greater glory of **His** kingdom.

Even now, much of Humanity may harbor the thought that so much about **God** is a mystery. Why does this seem to be so challenging to some people to reach out their hearts and minds to **God**? I pray you already have a firm hold on your Faith that tells you **God** will always cherish you. If you did not believe this in the past, believe it now! Why have so many people misplaced their Faith? Perhaps this is the reason some people feel it is so difficult for them to sense **God's** presence. Nothing has ever changed in the most basic fundamental teachings of the Bible or the church. No doubt, some people are always trying to change the translation of something to fit their own immediate needs. Why was it so easy to undermine what people once believed to be the truth? Our Soul, who once knew **God** so intimately, waits for opportunities to know **God** intimately again through your friendship with **God**. Either you know and believe in **God's** love for you or you do not. Search your heart because your heart will tell you if you really believe in **God** and the teachings of the Bible.

During a life**time** of study, **God** has eluded those who call themselves religious scholars. Some of these scholars still harbor the equations of their science evaluation that convince them **God** does not exist. This is what probably cause some people to deny the idea of seeing Angels or experiencing some fantastic heavenly vision. Some people in the science field will say, "These events take place only because of the chemistry of the brain." The people who study science feel this is why people are experiencing these visions or encounters. Well, there is nothing wrong with my chemistry or my brain. Seeing the Angel as I did was not because of any medicine or something my brain thought would be delightful. I realize this is a complete truth known only between **God** and myself. Therefore, I say loudly, science is sadly mistaken. Science is leading people away from **God** with their ungodly theories. These unbelievers are putting the very reason for their existence and their Soul in serious jeopardy. Why do these scientists refuse to realize, or they do not care, that people believe what they say to be the absolute truth. To destroy the belief in **God** gives rise to the opinion there is no hope in life. However, Christians know this is the work of the evil one.

This is the supreme goal for evil, at any price, to keep us away from **God**. Evil will do anything and everything to keep you and me from loving **God**. Evil is shrewd and cunning because the supreme prize is our Soul. Evil will not stay where it is not wanted! This is the choices we make that invites evil to enter our lives. As difficult as it may be to face the awful truth, this statement is very true. It is unfortunate that there are people who tragically continue to allow evil occurrences to enter their life every day because of their life choices. Before long, the deck is stacked against them. Once evil has a firm hold on you, it is very difficult for you to get away. Evil can appear in countless disguises to mislead you. What has become commonplace and acceptable for most of your life is indeed very difficult to change. The truth is **God** is definitely not complicated! I feel you have to make a choice to either love **God** or follow evil! There is no halfway to live your life. People who say they do not believe in **God** or do not embrace the Word of **God** fully are looking to receive a strong response from evil. This truth alone should be enough proof for you to know **God** is so near to you. Amazingly, **God** is still trying to get our attention. **God** is trying desperately to help us, but because we do have free will, **God** will not interfere. **God** is sending **His** Angels to help everyone to be more aware of the love that is waiting to all who are faithful to **Him**.

Sadly, there will always be people who will perhaps never be interested in **God** or **His** Angels. These people feel it is a waste of their **time** to ponder such thoughts. They are in a hurry to get life and their daily routine behind them. How sad that some people feel this is all there is! You need to ask yourself, "Why am I in such a hurry, and what will I accomplish when I get there?" You need to ask yourself, "What is the purpose of my life?" Perhaps some**time** later, with the help of **Almighty God's** Grace, you will finally understand the importance of the answers to these questions.

If you want to be aware of the Angels near you, you must understand there is a definite partnership between you and your Angel. **God** established this partnership with you before you were born.

Once this partnership is formed, a strong union is developed with your Angel that can only be broken if you do not believe in **God** and your Angel. I have said repeatedly the Angels exist and are very close to everyone. Knowing this is the most wonderful and comforting knowledge for you to believe that you are so close to the Angels. It is your personal Guardian Angel as well as other Angels who are very close to us. Your Angel will never leave you unless **God** desires them to leave. However, it is an awful thought to realize you deliberately Sin in front of your Angel. I do not think many people think about this reality. To realize even more embarrassing is the truth that we all Sin right in front of **God**. Humanity has purchased a front-row seat for all to see. Evil loves to make a fool out of everyone and continually encourages your bad behavior. Evil convinces a large number of people that they have done well. Evil convinces you that only you are important in all things you decide to do. Therefore, evil convinces you that you should indulge yourself in anything that makes you feel good. Society as a whole has become a feel-good society who has interest in only what benefits them at the **time**. Our modern society is not interested in **God's** future design for them. Far too many people feel that what makes them happy today is the only thing important. Today might be the opportunity lost, but the dawn of a new day brings hope for change and new opportunities that await those who seek renewed faith and trust in **God**.

Your Angels are watching and waiting for the right moment for **God** to instruct them to let you know they are there to help you. What a remarkable gift to know you will never be alone. Who would ever want to be alone without **God's** love? However, are you paying attention to these unique moments when you might have an opportunity to sense an Angel is near you? Unique because I believe the Angels choose, of course, only the right moments to get your attention. Next to **God**, the Angels know you very well and know how you will react to different circumstances. This reminds me of my third thought when I first glimpsed the Angel in the hospital. After a while, I had the distinct feeling this Angel knew exactly how I was going to react to her appearance. This is marvelous to understand: the Angel knew me so perfectly.

Now is the **time**, today, to renew your love in **Almighty God** and the belief in **His** Angels. There is so much to learn about the Angels. You may sense a small polite nudge or a quick glance out of the corner of your eye that will make you aware that the Angel is there. I have read that when you smell the sweet aroma of flowers, it might be your Angel. In addition, my husband and I have experienced this strong fragrance of roses, and we contributed this to Saint Therese, the little flower. Oh my goodness, the Angels are here not only to show you the way but also to teach you everything you need to know in order to find happiness in this world. With all your imperfections, the Angels are here to prepare you for Heaven. The Angels are aware your life is not always easy. I cannot begin to know why there seems to be so many issues in life; that must be so problematic. This is why you need to pay attention to your Angels because through the power of the **Holy Spirit**, your Angel will lead you to **God**. It is my belief, it is a special feeling that comes over you to let you know, without a doubt, the feeling you are experiencing is your Angel. Everything you need to know during your life to accomplish your goals is available to you if you would pay attention to your Angel who is a ministering spirit there to carry out **God's** will. Then when your life is finished here on earth, if you have been faithful to **God**, **He** will invite you to join **Him** in all **His** glory in Heaven. Our human weakness is the reason that we fail to see that every life is precious. The very reason for your existence is only to please **God**, and therefore, your reward is Heaven. If you truly did your best to please **God**, **God** would show **His** love abundantly in return. Perhaps if you worked more diligently on what would please **God**, your life would take on a calmer resolve.

I pray that you believe the important assignment for your Angel is to lead you to **God**, I mean to bring you right to the feet of **God**. Some**times**, the Angels have to resort to all kinds of measures to get us moving in the right direction. We humans have a stubborn nature because we think we can accomplish everything alone. Motivating us is not always an easy task for our poor Angel. Struggle as they may, your Angel tries everything possible to make you aware of them. Sure, I agree, this is so difficult to know the Angels are there.

This is your faith once again that allows you to know the Angels are beside you. You see, our Angels are on a mission of great importance. The Angels' important mission is to lead you and me to **God**. Our Guardian Angels are on a mission of love. Once you learn to follow the Angel's lead, you will still make many mistakes. Getting you and me to make good choices seems to be the most difficult job for our Angels. I believe our Angels also have a sense of humor. The Angels can be childlike and have a playful spirit at **times**. Can you think of something in your life that might have happened somewhat strange but perhaps funny that you could not explain? How do you know your Angel did not play a part in this incident? Missing small items around the house I think some**times** is part of this playful **time** for the Angels. It is my belief this happens to get our attention. This certainly is one of the **times**, because I am Catholic, I remember to ask Saint Anthony for help as well. For the benefit for those who are not Catholic, Saint Anthony is the Patron Saint of finding lost items. Therefore, is it possible the Angels are not always as serious as many first thought? This playful spirit almost mirrors our own spirit, which is similar to how a child should be happy and contented, learning and growing in the word of **God**.

    I guess the dilemma remains, how do you know for sure the Angels are here? How do you learn to listen to the prompting that you feel deep within you that are your Angel? Definitely, your Angel is constantly trying to direct you to achieve goodness. In addition, your Angel is constantly trying to communicate with you to protect you from harm. Your Angel desires to protect you from extreme injury from yourself and the harm that comes from the influence of others. This internal little feeling or prompting you is from your Angel and warrants strict attention from you. Some**times**, you can recognize this special subtle prompting because you will feel very uncomfortable. This feeling is a special sensation that exists only at a particular **time**. You can easily recognize this because the feeling will continue to be annoying until you sense this feeling becoming stronger and stronger until you know you have to make a decision. What to do or what not to do, you realize immediate action is required. This is simple to recognize when you experience a very uncomfortable feeling, and this feeling will not go away until you realize you must make a decision. Some people call this sensation flight-or-fight reaction. If you have put yourself into a bad situation, you Angel is trying to warn you to leave the situation you placed yourself now. I have talked about your little inner voice you cannot hear or see, but this gentle prompting will tell you and me all we need to know if you are paying attention.

    Personally, after I witnessed the Angel in the hospital, this was definitely confirmation for me that in the past, this feeling was my Guardian Angel trying to get my attention so I would make the right decisions. Praise **God** I did listen to my Angel most of the **time**. Each of us must learn in our own way to listen to this little inner voice. In your own unique way, you will learn how to listen very intently to your Angel. When I was a young girl, at first, I did not realize this inner voice was my Angel, but when I became older, I grew in the knowledge that it was my Faith that could not be broken no matter what happened in my life. My Angel and my Faith in **God** taught me so well what I needed to know because I desired **God** would be happy with my accomplishments. Recognizing the little promptings you receive from **time** to **time** is a great way to begin to pay attention in order to know what it is your Angel is trying to tell you. Believe me, those promptings we have all experienced numerous **times** in our life is from our Guardian Angel speaking to us. Yes, some will say this feeling is only your "intuition," this perception or instinct, some also like to refer to as sixth sense. I prefer to believe it is your Guardian Angel calling you to listen and learn. These are some of the words that correspond to the word *intuition*; they are: ESP, clairvoyance, discernment, divination, feeling, foreknowledge, gut reaction, hunch, innate knowledge, inspiration, instinct, intuitiveness, nose, penetration, perception, perceptivity, premonition, presentiment, second sight, and sixth sense.

    I do not know what you may believe, but this sounds without a doubt to me that an Angel is trying to get someone's attention! The Angel is trying to express to you love and feel compassion too. The Angel is your guide to triumph over evil if you make up your mind to listen to your Angel. The evil one cringes over this idea that you may choose to listen to your Angel instead of it. Your Angel will block the way to this evil for you if you ask. You see, the Angel must have your cooperation in all matters pertaining to you. You need only to say the word *no* to evil and *yes* to your Angel. There is so much for you to learn from your Angel that it will astound you when you begin to pay attention.

What we can conclude in this chapter is everything in this world has a purpose, and there is a definite order to **God's** design for our happiness. In **God's time**, there is a reason and a season for everything within **His** world. When the goodness of this order is disturbed or altered in your life, then unhappiness and unrest begin. **God** created our world and every living creature found within for the sole purpose of our happiness. In the Bible, the **book of Genesis**, we read where **Almighty God** was pleased with **His** creation. **God** dearly loved the world and all that **He** had created was perfect. **"God saw everything He had made and behold, it was very good" (Genesis 1:31). God** expects all of us to maintain order in **His** world that **He** so lovingly created for all **His** people. If you loved **God** in the same way **He** loves you, you would finally realize how it feels to be truly happy. Try to imagine if you can what it would be like to live in a world in total harmony with our **Creator**! Nothing would be too great for **God** to bestow on **His** people, and evil would cease to exist. To some people, this sounds truly unbelievable, even impossible, but what everyone must believe is we all possess the potential to achieve the impossible. Nothing is impossible for the world to accomplish if **Almighty God** is part of this accomplishment. Nothing is impossible for **God** if the world would only ask **God** for **His** help. You must never forget we can achieve greatness but only with the help of **God**. Searching for **God** and desiring **His** friendship is there, all you have to do is ask.

With each dawning of a new day, **God** gives you the opportunity to renew again your Faith and renewed hope for the future. You must believe that **God** is right beside you at this very moment. No matter what took place the day before in your life, **God** is there waiting for you. **God** will never leave you alone, especially when you are in distress. **God** suffers along with you when you are unhappy. **God** suffers even more when you cause your own unhappiness. **God** waits patiently for you to ask **Him** for **His** help. **God** is waiting to hear from you that you love **Him** above all else. **God** will tell you how much **He** loves you if you would only pay close attention.

> Dear **God**, bestow on **Your** children **Your** grace
> that we may always do **Your** will.

God is trying so arduously to get the world's attention. Who is listening?

CHAPTER 24

Coping with Pain and Suffering

There is no doubt it was my strong trust and Faith in the love I embraced for **God** in those formative years that lead me to the pinnacle of my life. More years than I would like to believe have passed since those early years when I believed I could hear Angels singing in the church. Only in my beloved church at the tender age of seven, when I was alone, could I find such peace and contentment. At first, I did not fully understand this wonderful peacefulness. **God** unequivocally drew me near to **Him** so I could experience this inner love and peace **He** knew I so desperately needed. I learned to cherish the deep love and compassion I received from **God**. This Fatherly love was my consolation that I held very close to my heart. This profound love and friendship would sustain me through my entire life! Even when I thought **God** forgot me briefly in some later years, I realized this was a very stupid thought placed in my head by the evil one. Additionally, when I experienced some terrible illness or difficultly in my life, **God** would choose those **times** to remind me **He** was still there, and I knew **He** would never leave me. Especially when I faced a tough decision, I would remember **God** was closer to me more than ever during those difficult **times**. **God** never forgot me, and I do not know whatever made me think this would ever be possible! Moreover, when I was feeling sorry for myself and needed a friend, I always knew **God** was right beside me; therefore, I would run to **Him** with my problems. I really believe all the circumstances in my life took place so I would have a better understanding later why these difficulties needed to happen. In all the pain and suffering I have endured in my own personal life, I now understand that each **time** these health issues arose, it brought me closer to **God**. Why as humans we have to suffer tremendous challenges we will never fully understand until we reach the arms of our **Savior Jesus Christ**.

Incredibly, I understand clearly now why everything in my own life took place because the entire framework of my life was planned by **God** and for a specific purpose. Even when I strayed off the path for a **time**, I could not wait to get back into the good graces of my **Lord**. I can visualize all the events that took place in my life, and now I know why those situations happened the way they did. Each **time**, I would learn to grow deeper in my love for **God**. However, yes, some**times**, **God's** purpose for us is very difficult to understand and even harder to accept. Especially when you are in great pain or suffering some physical or mental anguish, it is more difficult to accept it as **God's** will! Few people seldom see the gift in their suffering. Yes, suffering can be a wondrous gift if you trust in **God's** enduring love for you. Your suffering is never in vain when you unite yourself with the **Lord**. In the Bible, we read, **"I consider that the suffering of this present time, are as nothing compared with the glory to be revealed to us" (Romans 8:18).**

I realized during some of my own challenging **times** of pain and sorrow, **God** had my undivided attention. It was amazing to me why I never understood this truth sooner. I never realized there was a blessing in the suffering. When you are in pain, it seems even more difficult to understand there is a blessing involved. There is so much suffering in the world, and others around you can cause your suffering as well. It is only when you can reach the feet of **Jesus** will you begin to realize your pain could never match the pain **Jesus** suffered for all of us. **Jesus** was willing to suffer unspeakable pain for the love **He** shared for the people of the world. Therefore, can you too take a little place on the Cross with **Jesus** and accept your pains with humility? You must pray diligently to align yourself with the wisdom of **God** in order to work through your suffering. In the

Bible, we read, **"Count it all joy, my brethren, when you meet various trials, for you know that the testing of your faith produces steadfastness, and let steadfastness have its full effect, that you may be perfect and complete, lacking in nothing"** (James 1:2–4).

Never think **God** does not anguish over your pain and suffering. **God** is with you and shares your pain, but some**times**, this suffering is self-inflicted. This can happen for countless reasons. Much suffering takes place because of the decisions you continue to make due to your lifestyle. Why there is so much suffering in the world, only **God** knows completely. Much of our suffering is because of our free will. **God** has nothing to do with our free will. We alone choose what takes place in our life. Some**times**, our pains are self-induced because some people decide to ingest harmful products. You must find a little place deep inside yourself where you can learn to accept, through faith and prayer, your suffering for **God**. When you finally reach a lovingly resolve that **God** is with you, only then is it possible to accept your suffering. If you can accept **God's** will for your pain and suffering, a great healing can begin to take place. Miracles happen more often than we realize. **God** is always working in our life for **His** greater glory.

I did not always accept those **times** of suffering and unhappiness. I needed to learn by trial and error just like you to accept what **God** desired of me. **God** desires all I can give to **Him** because **God** deserves all my love. I learned to accept difficult **times** as **God's** will, but this did not happen overnight. I had to trust in the will of **God** because only **God** knew what was best for me. However, I do believe it is possible to have this **time** of pain and suffering shortened if we trust in **God's** mercy. I had to lean on my own strong convictions many **times** to realize no matter what happened in my life, **God** was there with me. It was only after seeing the Angel I began to understand the entire plan **God** desired for me all along. I understand completely now why many issues needed to take place so I would learn from my mistakes. Why do we have to get older in order to get wiser? Clearly, **God's** loving hand was in everything I have ever accomplished my entire life. All the people who entered my life through the years were all there for a specific purpose. I pray I made a positive difference in the life of some of those people I met along the path of my life as well. I see **God's** plan so clearly, all my decisions over the years contributed to the person I am today. **God** placed **His** great hand on my hopes and dreams from the very beginning of my life. I am convinced now I did follow **God's** plan for me. **God** knows there were **times** I had my doubts, but now praise **God**, I understand completely.

I can remember the precise moment when I first was aware **Almighty God** was near me. I can remember exactly where I was and how I felt about **God** instantly. I knew immediately this knowledge was going to be the most important knowledge of my life. The enormous love **God** showered on me I cherished throughout my life. However, there were many **times** in my teenage years I was a prisoner of my own devices; therefore, if I had any troubles, this was my own fault. How I made it through those years is a miracle in itself. Looking back now, I can say with so much conviction, **God** never left my side. There is one thing I know for sure, no matter what happened, I was never far from the reach of **God's** mighty hand. Without my knowing it, **God** was always there to reel me in when I strayed too far from **His** protection. You see, we all need to remember how enormous **God's** love is for all **His** children. **God's** love for everyone is so immense that this deep love for **His** children will never diminish no matter what we do. **God** has an infinite capacity to forgive and to forget our sins when we are truly sorry. This loving capacity for forgiveness is **God's** greatest gift **He** could ever bestow on **His** children. With all my own faults and failures, **God**, in **His** loving mercy, did forgive me. **God** will forgive you and me our sins if we desire **His** forgiveness wholeheartedly. **God** is very aware everyone is going to make many mistakes. These mistakes some**times** cause you great pain and suffering. Unfortunately, this is the quandary of our free will, and this determines how far we are willing to stray from **God**. It is like a child testing how far to go before the parent gets upset. We all have particular boundaries we have set for ourselves. Christians certainly believe how important it is for us to stay within **God's** good graces because of the love we share for **God**. Most people believe this is the only true way to Heaven. You must understand experimenting with right and wrong has very dangerous consequences. What you must believe are most of these consequences having cause and effect can last you over a life**time**.

Why does it seem so easy to make those bad judgments that cause us so much pain when we know in our heart what we are doing is wrong? I guess Adam and Eve learned this lesson the hard way. I think in the aftermath, everyone does wish the event in the garden of Eden turned out differently. In the Bible, we read where **God** created Adam and Eve, and they disobeyed **Him** by eating the fruit of the tree of knowledge. The devil told them the fruit would make them wiser than **God**! Certainly, most people do not want to make bad choices and decisions on purpose. It sure seems to me often we become so weary, we do not show very good judgment. What about the decisions you make concerning others? Are you responsible for leading someone else in the wrong direction by your example? Have you caused others pain by your decisions? Have you cheated in business in order to benefit yourself? Perhaps these are only a few areas where you should be correcting in order to be closer to **God**. You should learn to listen to your conscience that your Angel is trying to direct you to correct your bad habits. When you are in pain and there is a crisis in your life, **God** is waiting for you to ask for **His** help. Trust in **Almighty God** and listen to your conscience because this will never tell you an untruth. It is only when you do not learn from your mistakes, **God** is very disappointed. **God** desires only our happiness and patiently waits for us to redeem ourselves. Our loving **Creator** certainly is deeply troubled with of all the suffering in the world, but because of our free will, we must persevere through our life either with **God's** help or without **His** help.

Now I can say with complete understanding that we are in a classroom all our life and **Jesus** is our teacher. I have learned it some**times** takes a life**time** for some people to have the complete knowledge and true understanding of the great gifts of forgiveness and mercy offered to us from **God**. It was not until I was with the Angel that I realized the amazing truth was standing in front of me that was confirmation **God** does have a huge capacity to forgive everyone! Some**times**, we cause pain because of misunderstandings with relationships within our own families. **Jesus** has further shown us the way to forgive others by **His** own example when **He** asked **His Father** while dying on the cross, **"Forgive them Father, for they know not what they do" (Luke 23:34)**. I am sure you realize this is a loving gift from **God** to be able to forgive others who have hurt you and caused you pain. **God** bestows on you the Grace to forgive others. This again is a most precious gift from **God** that ultimately commands a healing. This one issue took me more years than I care to count to face because I could not forgive myself for things I should not have done. This suffering is another form of self-inflicted pain that you caused from yourself from past decisions. This condition caused me pain of the heart, and I was silently unhappy for many years. This was my own selfish decisions I made throughout my life that caused me pain, and I knew better! I needed to learn how difficult this would be to forgive others and forget the past. Even when I knew **God** had forgiven me, this remained a difficult hurdle for me to forgive others as well as myself. This was a very difficult issue for me personally to overcome so I can sympathize with others who might be feeling this way. Through the Grace I received from **God**, I learned how to forgive the mistakes and cruelty of others. I needed to learn to let go of the past so the future could blossom. Most of all, I needed to learn to forgive myself. It was only when I finally could forgive others and myself that my healing began that formed my deeper feelings for **God's** mercy. The pain I caused myself for so many years began to disappear. It was not long after I accepted the truth of forgiveness that I was aware my love for **God** began to grow boundlessly.

Therefore, I ask myself again now, did I follow **God's** plan that **He** desired for me from the very beginning? Did I always accept my suffering as a gift from **Almighty God**? I fully realize that life has a way of throwing logs in the middle of our path and some**times** we follow another path. It is our true Faith in the **Lord** that gets us going again in the right direction. Search your heart, and if you can truly say you feel secure with **God's** friendship, then can you say you did follow **God's** plan for your life? This is a most profound realization and an all-important question anyone should consider carefully. In a fatherly manner, **God** looks at us so lovingly, always hopeful, because **He** desires only the best for **His** children. If you are worried you did not follow **God's** plan, then whose plan did you follow? Living with this realization is even more reason to turn to **God** for **His** direction and love. It is never too late to improve your life and live your life that is pleasing to **God**. It is never too late in your life around in order to learn the truth that **God** desires you to seek **His** love and forgiveness. If you have followed **God's** plan, then surely, happiness and contentment are within you. If you have not, it is never too late to seek **God's** unfathomable mercy; do it now!

Should you ever really feel content that you are ready to face **God**? There will always be certain strife in everyone's life. I believe it is possible for everyone to find true happiness, but this takes tremendous effort and faith on your part. Only when you can truly say to yourself that you love your **God** with your whole heart and your whole Soul will you feel secure in the friendship you have established with **God**. A friendship so powerful, you will begin to cherish this special bond formed between you and **God**. This is a bond so strong that soon you will understand this bond will never be broken if you stay true to **God**. This can be a life**time** of trust in **God's** mercy you must secure for yourself today. Along with this bond of trust and mercy, you will secure for the rest of your life the knowledge you will never walk alone. **God** does not want you to be lonely because this also causes a terrible pain of the heart. You will never be alone! Turn your life over to **God**, and you will see that **He** will take the pain of loneliness away from your heart. You must believe **God**, in **His** great goodness and **His** enduring love for all of us, is near enough to touch. Right now, if you believe this truth, it is possible for you to begin to put your life in the order that is pleasing to **Almighty God**. I pray while you read this book, you will find it in your heart to forgive someone. You will feel a great burden lifted from your heart, and you will feel happier immediately.

Jesus never promised to rid the world of suffering but, as I have pointed out previously, suffering if accepted, through your Faith and convictions, and offered back to **God** the **Father** as a kind of atonement for sins.

Dear **Jesus**, there is so much pain and suffering in the world. It is particularly difficult to understand why children have to suffer. Grant those parents who are in despair the grace to overcome this distressing **time**. Shower them, my dear sweet **Lord**, with **Your** love and deep compassion that they may always remain steadfast in their love and Faith for **You**. In the Bible, we read **Jesus** said, **"Let the little children come to me, for it is to such as these that the Kingdom of Heaven belongs"** (Matthew 19:14).

I pray that anyone who is suffering may know **Your** healing love because when there is Faith and hope, you are there with them.

What does **God** have to do to get Humanity to pay even the smallest attention?

CHAPTER 25

"I See an Angel"

What you are about to read here is a very personal and powerful spiritual event that only occurred because of the Divine Will of the **Holy Spirit**. The following is a culmination of some of my initial thoughts during my visit with the Angel, in addition, some reflections on what I witnessed when I arrived home. Throughout these chapters, I pray you will relive with me an amazing and holy experience that took place on October 7, 2011, in a hospital post-op recovery room. It was in this room where I would receive the immense honor of a visit from a magnificent and Holy Angel. The Angel was so strikingly beautiful that for an instant, my mind immediately focused from the Angel to thoughts of the Blessed Virgin Mary, the Mother of **God**. I can only presume that if my thoughts embraced the Mother of **God**, then surely, the Angel standing before me was from Heaven above.

The Angel folded her hands so sweetly in prayerful pose. This prayerful pose left me with an indelible impression. Watching the Angel's pure example further caused me to meditate even deeper thoughts regarding the Blessed Mother. I felt captivated by the manner in which the Angel folded her hands. For what seemed like a long **time**, my eyes remained on the Angel's hands, poised so respectfully at the waist area. Her hands appeared delicate, pure as a white lily. To this day, this important detail continues to cause me to contemplate thoughts of the Blessed Virgin Mary, and these thoughts are very comforting to me because they fill me with peace and contentment. Our heavenly Blessed Mother watches over everyone with so much love and compassion to even the most undeserving sinner.

While looking at the Angel, I was overwhelmed with joy because I could sense the tremendous love and deep compassion that overpowered the entire room. I could also sense the intense golden light that showered everyone and everything it touched with **God's** enduring love and mercy. I could describe the immense love that filled the room, as sweet aroma from a delicate flower. Looking at the Angel's sincere motherly smile along with her delicate hands created an indelible impact on me immediately. Briefly, I was in complete peace as I continued to gaze upon the awesome Angel that stood only a few feet away. At first, I naturally continued to assume the Angel that was so close to me was an experience meant only for me. However, soon, the primary reason would be abundantly clear to me why the Angel appeared, and the reasons are numerous. I realized immediately for me personally, I received a profound confirmation from the Angel, and I will forever hold dear this truth in my heart. It was my conformation that my dear sweet **Jesus** did forgive and forget my sins. Further, seeing the Angel standing in front of me, I knew instantly everything I ever believed in Faith alone previously was ALL TRUE! Then the Angel told me why she had appeared, and the ultimate reason for the Angel's appearance became obviously clear to me.

The Angel appeared with a dire message for all Humanity! The Angel said, "**Tell them it is almost time**." The essence of the message is the world is in trouble because Humanity is moving away from the safety of **Almighty God's** love and mercy! The world needs **Almighty God** now more than ever because much of Humanity has lost the capability to understand the truth. **God** is trying to get our attention, and **His** people are not listening! Numerous questions formed in my mind the minute I looked at the Angel. However, most of these questions may remain unanswered, and I accept this now. There is no doubt **God** desired **His** Angel to appear to me for a designated purpose. **God** sent **His** Angel on a mission to remind the world **He** loves everyone, but as the Angel indicated clearly, **He** is severely disappointed with the enormous Sin that is consuming the world. A simple word *disappointed* that I am sure does not accurately describe **God's** disappointment in **His** children. **God** sent **His** holy Angel with a simple message of love and, yes, hope; but the greater meaning of the message is a serious call to action! **God** desires a response of love from **His** people. **God** desires **His** people to follow only **His** holy Word. The message is a dire warning to the world that we have greatly offended **God** with severe offences to **His Sacred Heart**. The message is clear and precise; **God** desires serious changes from **His** children to take place in **His** world. **God** desires to see that we are willing to transform our life so we can all be happy and live in peace accordingly. **God** loves us so much that **His** people need to prove to **Him** that we indeed love **Him** by amending our life. **God** is certainly very serious; therefore, I can say with complete confidence the world needs to take this message extremely seriously! **God** does not desire us to fail because **He** loves all **His** children too much but we are causing our **Creator** great pain! **God** knows our free will most assuredly get in the way because of the choices we all make now will inevitably decide our future. It eludes me why more people do not believe we all share the same destiny. Sadly, **God** will not interfere with our decisions, and what Humanity decides to do now is crucial to our future. What will you personally decide to do with the knowledge of the message? **God** is demanding an answer from all **His** people! Humanity must decide now how our world will continue to evolve because the world cannot continue on its present path without momentous consequences.

Imagine, God loves humankind this much that He sent an Angel with a message for Humanity in order to give the world another opportunity to change what already has begun!

Knowing **God** loves us all so immensely, there would be no way to measure **His** deep love completely. Nothing you and I could understand in mere words used to express ourselves would ever be adequate! The message is the confirmation needed in the world today that **God** desires us to know, through the appearance of **His** Angel, that **He** loves everyone dearly!

Why did the Angel appear to me in the hospital? I wondered too why **God** chose me to see the Angel and why on that particular day? Most importantly, it is only normal for me to ask, why me? Then someone said to me recently, "Why not you?" Therefore, I can also say to you, the reader, why not you? Is it possible **God** will send **His** Angels with more messages? **God** knows the world is in dire need of **Him**. Christians believe that **God** sends us messages every day. We just do not always recognize the truth often enough that **God** is trying to tell us something. Everything in a single day has a meaning and a purpose, but we do not always recognize it as a message from **God**. If you have **God** in your life, you will understand that **He** is always there for you, waiting to cheer you on when you make the right life choices.

My mind was intently on **God** before the surgery. Once asleep and then waking up, I realized the strangest thing: there was no pause in my thoughts of **God**. Then all at once, the Angel was there in front of me. This is a miracle, and I am forever humbled **God** chose me to witness what my Faith believed was the truth. What happened was a perfect connection between my Soul and the Divine Will of **God**. Why **God** allowed me to experience what took place will forever remain known only to **Him**. Was it possible there is simply a right **time** and place for **God's** pure goodness to appear? I will now forever keep the appearance of the Angel close to my heart, locked away from the evils of the world. Even though I realize now the message was for everyone, the visit with the Angel will reside in my heart forever.

The Angel is now a permanent part of my daily life. In the recesses of my mind, the Angel's presence will forever be with me throughout my days and nights as long as I live. The Angel's very essence of goodness is all around me every moment. How wonderful it is that the Angel did not appear for my sake alone. The Angel's presence stirred an enormous awakening in me, and I now realize this event has the power to awaken the world as well, praise **God**!

With the visit from an Angel, I witnessed the profound love and compassion **God** possesses for everyone. The love I felt for **God** before I was in the presence of the Angel was enduring. However, there is no longer a passing reference for the phrase "For the love of **God**." Now when I think about the Angel, I relive so many emotions I felt the day in the hospital. I will forever remain humbled before **God**. With the very thought of the event, I become emotional because I know **God** is in total charge of my life. My optimism for my future rests entirely with **God** because of my unwavering Faith in **Him**. My thoughts, my dreams, and my hopes for the world rest in the mercy of our **Creator**. Silently, I am firm in my resolve that only with the help of the **Holy Spirit** I will complete my mission. I pray now to spend the rest of my life doing **God's** work wherever that may lead me. **God** should be the most important aspect in everyone's life. Nothing in your life should mean more to you other than your love for **God**. For the love of the **Holy Spirit**, I am compelled to help others in a broader way than I ever did before. My love for my family is deeper, and I understand them somehow in a different way than I did before. My sense of the world and everything around me feels differently to me in a way I cannot explain, except my eyes are wide open to the truth. Seeing the Angel has definitely deepened my resolve and my total commitment to the will of my **Lord** and my **Savior**.

Since the magnificent day in the hospital where I witnessed the golden light that surrounded the Angel, everything is becoming clearer to me. What is happening is a revelation of pure understanding what is truly important in my life. This revelation should be important in everyone's life. It is a pure truth of understanding you acquire naturally to know what should truly be important to everyone who believes in **Almighty God**. This affirmation of the truth comes directly from the **Holy Spirit** through the appearance of **His** Angel. It was when I first looked into the eyes of the Angel I felt this incredible and overwhelming love and compassion I never knew was possible. The astounding love that passed from the Angel to me has no comparison, and I cannot describe this feeling of love I felt more to you other than to say the feeling was astonishing and enduring.

The Angel's overall demeanor captured my undivided attention. I felt a definite motherly compassion come forth from the Angel that filled every part of me. Somehow, I was aware the Angel desired me to know she understood my feelings. Incredibly, I sensed the Angel opened an invisible bridge of vast space and **time** that only seconds before did not exist. The space in **time** you and I cannot visibly see opened and joined the space between the Angel and myself. It is a shame to realize we humans unknowingly form an invisible barrier between what we think we can see and what we believe we cannot see. I cannot express how important this realization has become to me now. This was the moment I realized what I always believed in faith was the ***truth***. The great truth is we all do have to become like children again, in our hearts, to be close to **God**. For an instant, I did feel like a child with the Angel so near to me. I will never forget all the emotion of love I received from the Angel, and this love will forever be within me. I will forever cherish the gift of this special awareness of love from **God** along with the gift of witnessing **His** most precious Angel.

I cannot express to you enough how overwhelmed with excitement I was to see the Angel. How do I express it further except to say the experience itself was astonishing! It is difficult to express everything, as I would really like to, because mere words seem to pale in the explanation of this experience. Try to imagine the most wonderful moment in **time** during your life that you were full of joy and happiness, a **time** of love. Then think of that feeling and multiply that feeling and add to it peace and contentment, no worries and the warmth of love that makes you feel safe and contented. Seeing the Angel was more than this much more. I wish everyone could see the Angel as I did. I know I do repeat important thoughts and explanations because I want so dearly to express the right words because I feel so strongly the urge to write everything I can so you will be able to share in my experience. The extraordinary beauty I found standing before me was so captivating I could not take my eyes off the presence of the Angel. The Angel was unlike anything I ever could imagine not even I, as an artist, could ever dare to express on canvas. The truth, the Angel was there, brought immediately to my mind what must await the faithful in heaven is so fantastic, the lifelong mission for all Humanity should be preparing for this journey. It would be impossible for our human thought to define Heaven or Angels from only our imagination. The words we try to use, I feel, are utterly useless, but we still try. Even if you were to glimpse a vision of Heaven, I feel this would be nearly impossible to describe to anyone else in a way the mind would view the unimaginable. Christians believe Heaven is a place where our Soul is in the presence of **God**. The faithful believe that in Heaven, your Soul is finally at peace. In heaven, your Soul is free from earthly cares and is protected and loved by **God** for all eternity. The Angel said, "**Tell them**," what I have said! The Angel instructed me to share the message with everyone. I try to express adequately to the best of my ability the entire encounter with the Angel, but I pray sincerely that, in some way, you will be able to share in the experience during my explanation of the event. The entire experience was exceptionally sublime, and no matter what words I use, the proper words seem to pale in the explanation of what I really witnessed, therefore, will remain inadequate!

Immediately, I did understand the importance and serious nature of the words contained in the message. It was very upsetting for me to hear those words that contained the realization of Humanity's possible final choice! After the Angel departed, I repeated the message many **times** for everyone to hear in the room. My surgeon and the nurses present said they only heard me repeating the word "**time**." This certainly was an extraordinarily holy and profound event in my life. Since I was in the presence of the Angel, I am beginning to be at peace with some issues that were burdening me previously. I am not saying you should not worry about important issues in your life, but you must constantly remember, in the end, **God** is in charge!

The most important aspect to understand perfectly is God loves you.

I continue to marvel with the beauty of this beautiful world **God** gave us to enjoy. Since I witnessed **God's** wondrous Angel, some questions I thought were important do not seem as significant as they once did. I may never receive answers to all my questions here on Earth. I am content because I witnessed the truth: **God** loves everyone so much; through our faith, **He** gives us the strength to move mountains! Here are **Jesus's** words in the Gospel of Matthew,

"Amen, I say to you, if you have faith the size of a mustard seed, you will say to this mountain, move from here to there, and it will move. Nothing is impossible for you" (Matthew 17; 20). Therefore, if you believe in the Sacred Scriptures, what mountain would you like to move first? Our merciful **God** gives **His** people the power to overcome every evil!

God's children have a curious nature, and therefore, it would be natural to contemplate the wonder of **Him** and **His** magnificent heavenly realm. All **God's** people have an obligation to trust in **His** Divine Mercy. I continue to be astonished but reverently humble that **God** would allow me to see an Angel. There remain no suitable words in our dictionary where I can properly describe how I really feel about seeing the Angel other than simply WOW. The most important aspect that I pray Humanity will recognize is the Angel appeared in order to demonstrate to Humanity **God's** unbelievable and endless love that **He** possess for all **His** children. The message is for everyone living in **His** beautiful world called Earth. Now is the **time** for Humanity to face the seriousness of the responsibility that rests with every single person. It is **time** for Humanity to focus their attention on the vital obstacles that are presently standing in the way of a viable future under the direction of **Almighty God**.

> Dear **God**, I pray that the appearance of **Your**
> Angel will open the hearts of all Humanity.

God is trying to get our attention! How long will **God** wait for Humanity to decide to love **Him** above all else?

CHAPTER 26

The Angel Said, "Tell Them It Is Almost Time"

The Angel said to me, "**Tell them**." Therefore, the Angel instructed me to share the message with everyone possible. This is a huge obligation and certainly a greater responsibility to do my very best to honor the Angel's words sent from the **Holy Spirit**. The Angel said to me, **"I bring you a message, tell them it is almost time."** Without any hesitation, I have discussed the Angel's message with everyone I meet. I am anxious to share every detail about the Angel, and more importantly, I have a sincere responsibility to do my best to convey to everyone what the Angel instructed me to say. Furthermore, to the best of my ability, I must strive to reveal the numerous implications found within the message. The seriousness of the message and the implication of the words while they are very disturbing, I do believe the words also contain a message of hope! This is true because the message is a clear warning from **Almighty God**: the **time** has come for everyone to reevaluate his or her life. No one person who says they love **God** will be surprised to hear that **God** is so disappointed in the behavior of **His** people. Now is the **time** to recognize the words demand enormous change from all Humanity. These changes must be implemented and soon because our poor decisions made today effect our future adversely. Humanity must decide and be resolved in their decisions concerning their life choices. Now that we have the knowledge of the message conveyed from the Angel, no one can hide from the truth any longer. I have discussed the message with my friends, relatives, and the people I meet; and most do seem to understand that our society in general and the world overall is in serious trouble morally. I am deeply privileged amid the responsibility given to me too honor **God's** chosen words in the message. My supreme mission now is to convey the message from the Angel to everyone possible. What is very important to me right now is that **God** will come to our assistance when needed because I know everything takes place in **God's time**, not our **time**. I have been waiting patiently and praying, wondering if I should be doing more. Should I worry about **time** that waits for no one or should I leave the worry about **time** to the wisdom of **God**? I believe strongly **God** will find a way to let me know when it is the **time** to place all the issues discussed in this book into decisive action. When that **time** arrives, I will feel a sense of urgency, and then I will know the **time** has come for me to publish this book.

I remain in awe at the varied responses I hear from people when I tell them what the Angel said. There is no doubt **God** sent **His** Angel with a dire message for everyone, and now I am merely the courier for this profound message. The message seems to suggest something different to everyone. I am beginning to understand why this is true. We are all individual people with all kinds of expectations unique unto ourselves. Therefore, what might be significant for me may not have the same meaning for someone else. A message received from an Angel may not be too interesting to an unbeliever. Perhaps later, the knowledge of the message will make a difference, and some people will have a change of heart regarding both the Angel, and the message.

I continue to be very concerned because there are still many believers and unbelievers who do not truly trust in **God's** mercy. In addition, there are people who say they think they believe in the Angels but remain reserved in their thoughts. Knowing Angels exist and trusting in **God's** mercy has everything to do with your Faith. Your strong religious belief is your Faith, and the grace received

I SEE AN ANGEL

from **Almighty God** enables you to trust and believe in **Him**. Some people are in denial about the very idea of Angels or anything they deem unexplainable. The entire idea worries some people because to believe in Angels, you would have to believe in **God** and, therefore, your mortality. This is very difficult for Humanity to understand and even more difficult to believe in what you cannot see. The Bible says, **"Then Jesus told him, because you have seen Me, you have believed; blessed are those who have not seen and yet have believed" (John 20:29).**

I will continue to share the message with everyone I meet. When I speak to others regarding the Angel, there are people who would prefer not to discuss the message at all. While at other **times**, there are people who are exceptionally pleased to hear everything regarding the Angel and, yes, the message. Some people do not want to hear the message and become even frightened. I certainly do understand the words contained in the message command deep thought, but this is proof **God** is trying to convey to us that we need to get busy and remember we are wasting precious **time**. I realize the words are not easy to grasp at first because the entire circumstances regarding the appearance of both the Angel and the message are astounding. I witnessed **God's** beautiful Angel myself, and even now, I have to take a deep breath when I relive what took place knowing what I know now. This takes **time**, no doubt, for most anyone to contemplate the exceptional and remarkable circumstances thoroughly. This is not an everyday occasion when an Angel appears. Knowing someone witnessed seeing an Angel is not something you often hear anyone say. Yes, there are people I speak with who are genuinely thrilled when I tell them I saw an Angel. In addition, most people are very interested to know, "What did the Angel look like?" Most people accept this experience and the message very seriously, and I know this is the **Holy Spirit** speaking to them. However, other people will also comment, "Really, oh dear, this does not sound too good, does it?" Later when I thought about this particular comment, I felt this person was right! She was right to feel that way because our present circumstances in our world are so challenging and definitely perplexing. People additionally will ask me again, "What did the Angel look like, and what else did the Angel say?" Often, there are people who will want to know every detail about the Angel; except in some cases, the message definitely worries some people, and really, the message should concern everyone! Maybe this is a good sign the message is worrisome because it announces you care and, therefore, proves that there is hope for the future. Then many people are overjoyed at the very mention I was in the presence of an Angel. Some people have a renewed sense of security when they hear the Angel appeared to me. I am so happy because for these people, the Angel is strong confirmation from **God** that we are not alone! This certainly is an overwhelming affirmation of our Faith. It is what Christians always believed through their Faith alone. This truth is a wonderful gift from **Almighty God** to know **He** would allow this Angel to appear with a message. I pray the appearance of the Angel will affirm your Faith and bring you closer to **God**. This should prove to everyone **God** is watching over **His** people. **God** is truly with us all the **time**. I have witnessed some people who become very emotional. This is a magnificent indication for these people because they know in their heart now what is right and true. These people do understand the meaning of the message. I have said our emotions are a very important part of who we are as individuals. You should never be afraid of shedding a few tears.

> The most difficult part of facing the true meaning of the message is the message automatically forces you to search your conscience!

It is understandable, why some people are extremely uncomfortable with the content of the message. There is no place to hide from **Almighty God**. The great importance of the six words contained in the message is there for you to determine if you search your conscience because the answers are waiting for you to discover. Then the important thing is to remember what you have discerned and put what you have learned into practice!

Considering everything that took place in my life, even through the most difficult **times**, **God** has always been very generous to me. I did not always completely appreciate the wonderful gifts I received every day from **God**. It is easy some**times** to take for granted so many blessings **God** graciously grants to us. Life has not always been easy for me personally. I, along with everyone else, must go through trials and tribulations of various kinds in order to learn from our mistakes. **God** constantly tries to teach us what we need to know in order to grow in the knowledge of **Him**. I also often**times** have asked **God**, "Why me?" However, in all these trials in my life, I still found myself praying for **God's** help because I could not get through my problems without **Him**. I could not get through life without **His** constant love and guidance. I have prayed to **God** all my life to help me and to come to my assistance. What should we all do now? **God's** children must ask **God** to come to our aid because **God's** patience is running out! Everyone must pray now even harder than ever before because **God** is searching for the goodness in the world. It is my belief that **God** is taking into account our actions and decisions in order to determine our sincerity for our future. The message is, "**Tell them it is almost time**." It is the most difficult message I have ever been asked to convey to anyone. I fully realize the magnitude of those six words are vital to what takes place in our future. It is time for the faithful to come forward. It will be difficult because of the evil one; therefore, with Faith that **God** is with us, evil will be defeated. I understood immediately what the message implied was very serious, and it caused me later to be very upset in the recovery room. The doctor and the nurses in the room heard me say one word repeatedly, and the word was **time**. Hearing the word **time** upset me greatly then because frankly, I was initially upset to hear the Angel speak those six words. Knowing the Angel was in front of me and when she conveyed the message, it was automatic that my response would be of great concern. My neurosurgeon, Dr. David Eng, told me afterward that he heard me say repeatedly something about **time**. Naturally, I was thrilled to see the Angel, yet at the same **time**, I was not prepared to hear the message and face the truth myself. If you search your heart, you will agree the words contain a most powerful message from **Almighty God**, a message everyone should discern most seriously in the quiet of your heart because the message will hold a different meaning for each person based on the gifts **God has** bestowed upon you. With prayer and sincerity, the **Holy Spirit** will guide you with what you personally should be doing to bring about change in the world. If all the faithful will do this, then a great shift from evil to goodness will occur. I must warn you, this will be difficult and even painful in some respects because often, it is the critical areas in our life that essentially are the most challenging.

My concerns now regarding the message is seriously, what are we going to do to bring about the necessary changes that will improve our world and please **Almighty God**? What is Humanity going to do, and when are we going to get started? **God** is waiting to see results from all **His** people. **God** is waiting to see what **His** people are going to decide is important for the future of the world. How long will **God** wait for our answer? **God** has patiently waited already long enough and has witnessed over eons our injustices and indignation toward **His** wounded **Sacred Heart**. Start changing your life by placing **God** the **Father** the head of your family. I fear **God** will not wait much longer for **His** children to decide to amend our lives. **God** is waiting for **His** people to prove to **Him** that we do love **Him** enough to make enormous changes in our life. **God** is waiting for **His** people to learn to live and love one another. Yes, the kindness of others is remarkable when we see and hear perfect strangers helping one another, and this is wonderful. However, too many people simply will not get involved! I can remember when I was younger hearing about a women that was being attacked on the street and over twenty people nearby would not lift a finger to come to her aid. Injustices like these continue on every day in the world. Everyone must put **God** first before all things in order to make this great change. Placing **God** first in the center of your life, you will automatically become closer to **Him**, and **He** will bestow on you **His** Grace and blessings. No one person can accomplish anything worthwhile without **God**. You will see your life has more meaning when **God** is a part of your life.

When I was very young, I was not always open to the friendship and closeness of other people. I was definitely more private regarding my thoughts in how I felt about **God** personally. My attitude toward other people who I did not know began to change some thirty years ago when I began restoring religious statues for both churches and individual people. This certainly gave me the opportunity to chat with people all across the country regarding not only the Saints but also the love we shared for **God**. I can recall the thousands of conversations I have shared with people over the years regarding **God's** love and affection for **His** children. These precious **times** were all building blocks that enhanced my spiritual life as well as those who shared **God's** enduring love with me. I feel those intense conversations over the years regarding **God** definitely reinforced a deeper sense of **God's** love and mercy.

For me personally, I began to love and know **God** in a more profound way through my personal prayer life. I realized what I really desired most was for **God** to be pleased with me. I did not always seek the support of others. I felt often**times** in the past, I was let down by others in my life. I wanted to seek out **God** instead and let **God** know I do love **Him** above all else. I agree this is very difficult to accept why circumstances in our life have to occur and often**times** in negative ways that causes us to become discouraged. Now I realize all the apprehension that more of us feel regarding our future should matter to us more now because the Angel conveyed a vital message for everyone from **Almighty God. God** sent **His** Angel to convey to **His** children that they need **Him** in their life. If Humanity achieves everything possible to bring about the great change **God** expects, then love and peace will fill the Earth. **God's** people must believe **He** will take care to protect us because our efforts will prove our love and trust for **Him**. I will never think of my future in the same way ever again, and now, and because of my experience, you may secure a new outlook on your life too. Obviously, everything I thought I understood or believed regarding **God** and **His** Angels became clearer to me when I witnessed the magnificent Angel so close. A new profound realization has taken root in my life. My relationships with my family and the people I meet have a deeper significance for me now. I am very interested in hearing how people feel about most anything that concerns them. I find myself caring and worrying about perfect strangers. I sense a powerful need to talk to people about **God**, and it is wonderful! The feeling is mutual as I rarely find someone who will not take the **time** to talk about how they feel about **God**. When most people have an opportunity to discuss **God**, afterward, they feel better about their life in many positive ways. It is important to ask the **Holy Spirit** to help you talk to people about **Him**. You need only to supply the **time**, and the **Holy Spirit** will supply the words. I am concerned with their troubles of people I meet and how people feel is very important to me. I automatically sense a strong urge to help people especially when I sense they are terribly upset. Please never feel you are alone because there is always someone willing to listen to your troubles and that special one is our merciful **God**. There are millions of good people in the world; some only need to be aware there are people who need them. It is important to have the support of others whenever a crisis occurs. In my heart, especially during this **time**, **God** desires you to ask **Him** for **His** support in every aspect of your life. You must lean on **God**, and the answers you seek or people will enter your life to help you. It is my personal observation in my own life that I can tell you with complete assurance that **God** will connect you with people of Faith in order to affirm your love for **Jesus Christ** and for the greater glory of **His Kingdom**! All you have to do is ask, and help is on the way!

Now that I have witnessed the heavenly Angel and discerned the message with you, I have discussed with you some of the intricacies of the message. It is amazing how six little words contain such a powerful meaning. The reason for this entire experience is becoming clearer to me. In my dearest of dreams, I could never have remotely imagined what it would be like to see an Angel and not be dreaming. It so difficult to express everything I witnessed. My deepest desire for everyone is that in some way, you can share my experience, through my words, that the Angel is prompting me to say and write. What I have witnessed is so out of the realm of most understanding or any expression you could ever convey to another. There is a definite reason **God** allowed me to see the Angel and receive such a profound message from **Him**. There has to be a precise reason the Angel appeared to me at this particular **time** in my life and on that particular day! It was not only the visit with the Angel but also the message the Angel brought forth, I previously wondered why now. Then I only have to be aware of the dire condition of the world to understand why now! Most of the dialog and conversations conveyed to me by the Angel I heard not in words spoken aloud but with words spoken in the quiet of my mind. It was the message the Angel spoke verbally.

I can only pray with confidence that if it is **God's** will, **He** will allow me to know what else **He** desires of me to accomplish for **Him**. Until then, I will continue to bring the message to as many people as possible in the hope this message will make a meaningful difference in their life. **God** desires you to know how much **He** truly loves you.

What Humanity needs to realize now is God's children has greatly disappointed Him.

God views all of us as sinfully reckless because we are in the process of destroying our Souls along with our beautiful world and with record-breaking speed. **God** is patiently waiting for us all to wake up to the truth that we can no longer continue our present course without severe consequences for our actions. **Time** is no longer our friend anymore. We are all wasting what precious **time** Humanity has left while **God** is still trying desperately to get our attention before it is too late!

> Dear **God**, I pray with **Your** love and support, **Your** people will abolish evil and replace it with goodness in this world. I sincerely pray that the purpose of my own life will be for the praise and glory of **Your** name, **Jesus Christ**.

God is trying to get our attention who is truly listening.

CHAPTER 27

The Angel Was Already There Waiting for Me to Wake Up

On October 7, 2011, I was a patient in Saint Joseph's Hospital here in Syracuse, New York. Nothing that morning seemed out of the ordinary except for the fact that I could not have my morning tea. I was on the schedule to arrive at the hospital early in order to prepare for a serious operation to have a cervical fusion performed. Upon settling into a room, the nurses scurried about performing a long list of routine pre-op preparations. With nothing else to do but wait, my husband and I chatted about all the things we wanted to do for the holidays that year. To my surprise, much earlier than I anticipated, a nurse appeared at the door to bring me up to the pre-op area that was located adjacent to the operating theater. Nothing to do but wait again, I began to recite my prayers. I waited for what seemed like forever, but I remember feeling so grateful to have an opportunity for some quiet prayer **time** with **God** before surgery. I wanted to examine my conscience and chat with **God** about my life. Surprisingly, I was not nervous, although the operation was serious. I was very confident with Doctor Eng; therefore, I was not concerned with the outcome of the surgery. I knew if any unforeseen problem developed, I trusted in **God** because **He** is the **"Almighty Healer**, the **Master Physician" (Ephesians 6:19)**. Therefore, why should I worry because I placed all my trust in **God's** care? I prayed for **God** to direct the doctor's hands and to bless him and everyone who would care for me. I was very calm going into the operating room and even joked with the nurses.

I always find it interesting that before surgery, it seems only a few seconds before you are asleep, and then before you know it, it is **time** to wake up. The operation went smooth, and I was in recovery beginning to be aware of my surroundings. The first sensation I noticed was the unusual fact that I was so much more comfortable than I normally would be after surgery. My goodness, how cozy and comfortable the feeling is with those warm blankets the nurses cover you with now. This was the first **time** I ever experienced such a warm and cozy feeling right after surgery, and it was wonderful! I thought, *Oh, **God**, please let me enjoy these few minutes of peace and comfort.* Usually, most people will agree that upon waking up from surgery, this can be a most unpleasant feeling. Often, it is the pain and everything else that goes along with having surgery that most people find terrible indeed. Gradually, I began to awake, and really, I must say, I did not feel rushed. The nursing staff let me wake up when I was ready! I began to listen to the different noises that I could hear all around me. Then I heard Nurse M. say, "Okay, Rose Mary, you can wake up now, the surgery is over." I could not understand when I realized that I was still saying the same prayer I was reciting before I went to sleep! This was as though my prayer to **God** continued without interruption by the surgery! I believed my prayers simply never ceased until I was fully conscience. I remember praying to **God** and telling **Him** how much I loved **Him**.

While I was waking up and with my eyes still shut, I was aware of a very bright golden light that was the first thing that caught my attention. I remember thinking, *I hope I am not still in the operating room?* I was curious to see why this light was so bright. Slowly, I opened my eyes and was surprised to see that even though the light was so bright, this light never seemed to hurt my eyes. The light was a magnificent golden light that prompted me to open my eyes wider to investigate further the source of the light. There immersed within the bright golden light stood the Angel. The Angel was located only a few feet away from the foot of my bed where I was lying. The Angel was standing there in all her glory, smiling at me. Thinking back now, I wondered at the **time** why I could see her so clearly because I was not wearing my glasses! Funny how I would think of such a trivia detail, but if you wear glasses, you would understand. With or without glasses, there was no mistaking what I was witnessing was an Angel! The Angel was silently standing in front of me; instantly, I was very emotional. Looking at the Angel, I could not control my tears of pure joy. I wanted to embrace the Angel. I wanted the Angel to come closer to me so I could hug the Angel. In my excitement, I wanted so much, and no doubt, the Angel knew what my reaction would be. The Angel remained motionless in front of me for what seemed to be a long **time**. I could hardly grasp the truth that I was staring at an Angel. I could hardly believe my eyes, but all my senses assured me what I was really witnessing was yes, an Angel. However, I think my brain needed an extra second to adjust to the very truth that the Angel was there. What I was really seeing was an Angel unlike anything else I have ever seen in a book or a picture of any kind. Truly, there could be no comparison to anything even close to what we imagined an Angel to look like.

It was my heart and everything that makes me who I am that connected with the Angel immediately in a very spiritual way. The Angel's gracious and motherly sweet smile made me quite emotional. In the next moment, **time** seemed to come to a complete halt. Everything near me just ceased to be important! I do not know why I say *her*, as in the female sense of the word. Now when I recall my **time** with the Angel, no particular gender stood out prominently except the Angel was so gorgeous! It just seems reasonable to me and more comfortable for me to say *she* or *her*. It is because the Angel appeared with such a gentle and motherly demeanor. The mere presence of the Angel seemed to envelop everything in the room. The overwhelming beauty of the Angel was so captivating; I dare not take my eyes from her. Perhaps because the Angel was so gorgeous and appeared so motherly that the notion of feminine was a natural way for me to think of the Angel.

The Angel continued looking at me with a loving smile that usually encompasses the love only a mother possesses. **Time** ceased altogether while the Angel and I continued to look at each other without anything said. The Angel remained motionless, and all at once, I had the astonishing feeling, for a brief second, I thought I was somewhere else and it was wonderful! The golden light seemed to command a definite importance. The experience was remarkable and a stunning sight to behold. I was very captivated by the golden light as I felt the light was an extraordinary element that became one with the Angel.

Every **time** I think about that particular moment, when the Angel smiling at me so tenderly, this brings tears to my eyes. What did this companionate smile mean actually? Seeing the Angel smiling at me was an intense and significant meaning for me personally. Was this loving smile an indication the Angel was pleased with me? More importantly, did the loving smile mean **God** was pleased with me? Then I began to wonder if the Angel knew I always worried about my past sins. Was this loving smile from the Angel a significant sign for me that though I made mistakes in my life, I would once and for all believe **God** did forgive me? Did the Angel bring confirmation of this great truth by her presence for me, or was this great truth for all Humanity? Did **God** desire all Humanity to remember that **He** always forgives a contrite sinner? I realized at that moment, yes, **God** knew I was still harboring anxiety over my past sins. I tried over the years to accept that **God** did forgive me. However, most of my life, I fought the memory of my past sins, and no matter how much I tried, I could not reconcile with myself. You see the closer you become to **God**, the more your sins will haunt you because you know you have hurt **God** when you commit Sin. **God** knew this worried me the most. It is harder to forgive yourself when you have offended **God** repeatedly by your Sin. Where was my trust in **His** mercy? Therefore, did **God** allow me to see the Angel so I would finally see the truth **He** did forgive me? This is unbelievable to me. While I always knew **God** loved me, I had no idea how much until that very moment!

I believed in the beginning, seeing the Angel, was a personal event for me, but here was definitely a silent message I received and understood deep in my Soul. However, soon, it was evident by the change in the Angel's serious demeanor that the major reason for the appearance of the Angel was to convey to me a message that **God** wanted everyone to hear. **God** is trying to get our attention in an astounding way by sending **His** Angel to convey a message from **Him** for all Humanity.

I relive this repeatedly in my mind, and therefore, I cannot help myself when I repeat certain areas. I could feel silently this enormous love from **God** fill the room and this love encompassed everyone who was present in the room. All those wonderful people who were standing next to my bed never realized that love descended from **God** upon everyone in the room. The golden light filled every corner of the room, even the smallest crevasse could not hide from the golden light. I felt nothing was untouched by the golden light that I believed was the pure love of **God**. This beautiful golden light filled the room with love, and nothing could escape from its grasp. I wondered afterward if the doctor and the nurses were aware something wonderful was happening. What is very significant is even though the people present could not see the Angel or the golden light, nevertheless, the light touched everyone in the room with endless love from their **Creator**. Without knowing, everyone present there became silently part of the magnificent experience right along with me. **God**, with **His** awesome goodness and enduring love for us, touched everyone in the room in a special and unique way on that particular day.

A special note to Nurse M. who held my right hand the entire time:

> I am aware that this event with the appearance of an Angel captured the total attention of one nurse in particular. Here I will identify her as Nurse M. It was you, my dear nurse, who so lovingly took wonderful care of me. I want to take this opportunity to thank you for everything you did for me while I was in your loving care. What took place in the recovery room was very emotional and certainly was an extraordinary event

for me. I was thrilled, I was able to share with you firsthand not only the details about of the Angel but also the message that the Angel conveyed to me for everyone. I want you to know I pray for you often. I know you remember the entire experience because we chatted together for a long **time** immediately afterward. I knew then what was in your heart was your love you also share for **God**. I know you did not see the Angel, but I pray the special gift of the golden light that showered you with the love of **Almighty God** will remain with you all the days of your life. Thank **God** for your faith because it is **His** grace **He** bestowed on you that allows your faith to be strong. You are very dear to me, and you are even dearer to **Almighty God**. May **God** bless you always in everything you accomplish and everything you hope to accomplish during your life**time.**

I will be asking myself for the rest of my life, how was this possible I was worthy of such a great gift? Nothing in this world will ever be the same because the Angel appeared to me with the message for all Humanity. All the details of that day etched in my mind forever, and now I must honor the **Holy Spirit** and share the words with all who will listen!

An extraordinary peace came over me as I recalled what I witnessed only a few moments before. I prayed the memory of the presence of the Angel would always remain with me. All I could think about was the Angel who was standing so close to me only minutes before. The Angel stood there continually looking at me, so intently, with that gorgeous smile I will never forget. Everything about her lovely face was so sweet and those beautiful blue/brown eyes that seemed to penetrate me in such an amazing way. I repeat I felt immediately the Angel knew everything about me. If only for a split second, I felt no longer part of this world, and I was at total peace. After my visit with the Angel, I vowed to myself that anything

I accomplished in the future, I prayed that it would be only **God's will for the glory of Jesus Christ**. In the Bible, we read, **"But for me, my prayer is to thee, O Lord. At the acceptable time, O God, in the abundance of thy steadfast love answer me with your sure salvation" (Psalm 69; 13).**

Often, I recall what I said when I first saw the Angel. I said, **"I see an Angel."** I know I repeated these six words twice to the people in the room because Nurse M. asked me, "What did you say, honey?"

This is when I repeated again, **"I see an Angel."**

My sweet Nurse M. said, "You do? Where?"

I answered, "Right there," and I pointed in the direction where the Angel was standing. I was answering the questions without hesitation. I was not thinking or caring about anything or anyone else near me but instinctively answered her. In the next moment, I was only aware of the Angel. I thought at the **time** certainly everyone else could see her too because I could see the Angel's appearance, she appeared so natural. This never occurred to me that I was the only one who could see the Angel! I am sure I was making a real fuss in the recovery room, but I could not help myself. I was so excited I never gave a thought to the fact only minutes before I was in the operating room. I remember trying to get off the bed in order to be closer to the Angel. A part of me definitely wanted to go with the Angel. At that moment, earthly cares disappeared, and I focused on the Angel. I prayed my **time** with this awesome Angel would never end. Afterward, the nurses told me there were other people in the room around my bed, including my doctor, but I never noticed them or were aware they were present until afterward. I was aware of only the Angel and the golden light that poured out abundantly **God's** immense love too everyone in the room.

When I realized I could no longer see the Angel and others left my side, only one nurse remained by my side, my dear Nurse M. She stayed to watch over me and continued to hold my hand so gently. This loving nurse was to the right side of me the entire **time**. She was very sweet to me and seemed genuinely interested in what I previously witnessed. We talked for what seemed like a very long **time**. We chatted all about the Angel and what the Angel said to me.

I SEE AN ANGEL

I felt the conversation between the nurse and I was very important to her as well as myself. No matter how tired I became, I felt it was important to convey to this nurse everything because the Angel said, "**Tell them**." I was anxious to tell this nurse everything about the Angel, and primarily, I wanted to tell her what the Angel said to me, "**I bring you a message. Tell them it is almost time**."

    I only recently learned the nurse's name, and I pray, in some special way, what has taken place will forever affect this nurse in a most positive manner. The nurse continued to talk to me while holding my right hand. She asked me different questions regarding the Angel. I must admit I really enjoyed talking to Nurse M. very much, as I must repeat she was very motherly toward me. This nurse, in some ways, felt like an extension of the Angel because she was so gentle and caring. I wonder if she was ever aware that I thought of her in this way. I remember telling her, "Everyone is special in **God's** eyes!" If she ever reads my book, I know she will recall this special **time** we spent together with the Angel.

    I was exhausted after seeing the Angel. I thought a great deal about the responsibility that would follow. After I shared everything with Nurse M., I passed out from sheer exhaustion because I do not remember going to my room. When I awoke, I was in my private room where my son and husband were waiting for me. I was so tired, but I wanted them to know I had witnessed an Angel in the recovery room upstairs. I was anxious to tell them all about the Angel and the message. When I told them an Angel appeared to me, at first, they did not know what to say. No doubt, hearing this would be a surprise for anyone to know that someone saw an Angel, notwithstanding the fact that it was your wife and your son's mother that witnessed an Angel! I remember being so exhausted after the encounter with the Angel. My stay in the hospital was short; therefore, I did not get a chance to discuss seeing the Angel further with anyone else until after I arrived home.

    It was a month later during my follow-up appointment with my surgeon, Doctor Eng, that I knew this would be a perfect opportunity for me to discuss with him actually what he thought took place in the recovery room. It was then that Doctor Eng told me he was standing right there, to the left of me, in the recovery room, the entire **time**. Doctor Eng mentioned that I kept saying something about **time**. Until then, I was unsure how many people stood near my bed. Doctor Eng did not realize I was talking to an Angel but said I kept repeating the word **time**. Amazing, I was never aware my surgeon was standing next to me during the **time** the Angel was visible to me until after, I briefly noticed Doctor Eng. Strange how I was never aware my doctor or the other nurses were there when the Angel was visible to me! My doctor's surgical nurse was there next to him along with other nurses who were present probably because I was becoming excited and upset all at the same **time**. Some may have heard me say there was an Angel standing in front of me. They really had no idea how close the Angel was to all them. The Angel was only standing a few feet away. I will never believe there was any medication my doctor may have prescribed for me before, during, or after the surgery that would ever cause me to see or hear anything unusual. Over the course of my life, my surgeries total more than a dozen. Therefore, during all those surgeries, I needed sedation, and I never experienced anything unusual before, during, or after all these procedures. Further, in all these years, I have never experienced any adverse reactions to any of the drugs that the doctors administer before, during surgery, or afterward. I am sure some of the people near me felt they thought something was taking place. I was pleased my doctor did share with me during a post-op office visit that he said I kept repeating something about **time** and this is all he heard me say. Who would ever realize the word **time** would come to mean so much too millions of people? Only afterward did I confirm with the others that no one in the room with me witnessed the Angel or heard anything the Angel said to me!

All the conversations that took place between the doctor and the other nurses seemed to be off in a distance or the conversations were in another room. I could hear them talking, but it sounded like background noise. I simply tuned out all the background sounds so I could concentrate more intently on the Angel. My eyes and my mind remained focused solely on the Angel. I remember feeling irritated when anyone in the room tried to disturb me. I knew my doctor, and the nurses were thinking only what was best for me, but nothing in this world mattered to me other than the Angel. I wish I had a better sense of the **time**, but I do not. I have tried, but it remains impossible to judge entirely how long the Angel was with me. I have thought about this issue so many **times**, and I must conclude, **time**, as we understand **time**, ceased and it did not start again until the encounter with the Angel was over. There is no simple explanation for the **time** it took, for the intricate and numerous conversations between the Angel and me.

For a brief moment when I first looked at the Angel, the reason for my entire existence flashed before me. I understood everything immediately without even asking a question. I do not know how I understood, but I can say I did. Again, when I first glimpsed the Angel, I had the strongest urge to go with her and asked her if she was going to take me. I was not thinking about my family or anything else, only the Angel. None of my own thoughts and questions to the Angel were heard aloud where others could hear. Therefore, others in the room did not hear any of the verbal conversations between the Angel and me except for the word **time**. Most all the conversations between the Angel and myself formed in my mind, and I understood everything completely. Only twice did I verbally hear the Angel say something aloud. The first **time** was when she said to me gently in a soft voice, **"You cannot go with me now!"** The second **time** was when the Angel said, **"I bring you a message. Tell them it is almost time."** The reason the Angel appeared was not for my benefit alone! It seemed like a natural observation at the **time**, but I soon learned that it was for the benefit of all **God's** children. Then it also became apparent, the Angel was there for a specific purpose! Otherwise, I would have gone with her right away without any hesitation.

While the Angel was so close to me, I tried anxiously to capture every detail about the Angel. I wanted to make sure I could forever preserve the vision of the Angel in my mind. I kept repeatedly saying in my mind every detail. I did not want the Angel to go, but I knew the Angel would only be there oh so briefly. I was completely overwhelmed because I struggled with many emotions. I struggled to keep control of my emotions so I could concentrate on the Angel's words. I knew the Angel would not be with me long and I would have to return to reality. I tried not to think about the Angel leaving. I struggled to hold back the tears and hang on to every second the Angel was with me. The nurses told me afterward, they were concerned to see me so upset and excited so soon after undergoing major surgery. They really struggled to calm me down, especially Nurse M., who was holding so tightly onto my right hand the entire **time**. Naturally, I was uncontrollably excited when I first saw the Angel. However, afterward, I became more upset when I thought about the implications of the Angel's words that were contained in the message she conveyed to me. I heard someone say that I believed I was communicating with someone! I also heard someone mention something was taking place but that it was unclear what exactly was going on! I knew silently in my heart that it was a matter of fact to everyone in the room, that certainly I felt something spiritually was definitely taking place after I told them what the Angel said to me. One of the nurses told me afterward, when I first told her I saw an Angel, everyone remained quiet for a while. I have tried repeatedly, but it remains a mystery the length of **time** the Angel was there in front of me. The **time** seemed limitless, but in fact, the **time** was probably brief. Time is the indefinite continued progress of events that occur in irreversible succession from the past through the present.

Astounded by the Angel's awesome presence, I dare not take my eyes away from the Angel. Suddenly, the Angel's expression became different, and the change made me feel slightly uncomfortable. It was only seconds before the Angel displayed this amazing smile for me. Now the Angel displayed a seriousness that concerned me. Nevertheless, the Angel continued to look toward me with immense compassion. In my heart, I sensed something was drastically wrong. The Angel continued to look at me so seriously, and without hesitation, she said, **"I bring you a message. Tell them it is almost time."** The words **"almost time"** rang in my ears repeatedly. Then I started saying the words several **times** aloud, **"Time, almost time."** I repeat, my surgeon told me afterward that Doctor Eng heard me repeating something about **time** and, of course, he did not understand why I was saying this word. While I was talking to Nurse M.

regarding what just took place only seconds before, the enormous consequences of those six words made me gravely concerned. I was immediately aware that the message seriously conveyed to me by the Angel would be profoundly significant to everyone!

While gazing at the Angel, I could feel myself becoming increasingly concerned as if I knew there was going to be something more. I could not imagine what more there could be. Instantly, there was something important the Angel wanted me to see. It would turn out to be something I never could have expected. The Angel moved her eyes slightly to the right not moving her head. Her hands still folded in prayer never moved the entire **time**. Instinctively, I followed where the Angel directed me to look. I looked to the left with my eyes as to follow her lead. I looked but, at first, saw nothing. It was then the Angel instructed me to watch. As I looked at what the Angel wanted me to see, it was horrible! What I witnessed was devastating. What I was witnessing was almost too much for me emotionally. For a second, I was in a state of astonishment and shock. Then I realized that what I was witnessing was what could happen if we do not turn our life over to **God**.

To my amazement, for some reason afterward, I was resigned to the truth and calmed down fairly soon. Somehow, I knew that much of what I witnessed was already happening in the world. Certainly, everyone should be aware of such grave sins being committed against our precious little children. I was already painfully aware of what would happen in the future if we did not return to the safety of **God's** arms. It certainly should not be any surprise to anyone what the consequence of evil will do. Would it really be any surprise to anyone if **God's** people continue on their present path so many have chosen for himself or herself that it will lead us to eventual ruin? Humanity is nearing the total failure of our present moral society. Countless people do not care anymore about their Souls because there are people who no longer want to believe they are doing anything wrong. If **God's** children do not bring about moral change in their life, the building blocks of life we have all built for ourselves will soon come crashing down on our heads. We all need to ask **God** for forgiveness now because there is no **time** to waste.

The Angel continued to show me what I did not want to see. What the Angel asked me to look at made me very sad. I did not want the Angel to remind me of the awful sins filling up in the world. Certainly, Christians and anyone who believes in **God** feels helpless at **times**, and they feel all they can do is pray endlessly to **God** for **His** help. Continually, pray to **Almighty God** because **He** is listening to your prayers. Pray diligently that what the Angel showed me will never take place in the world. I observed a glimpse into the reality of evil so unspeakable and so horrible; looking at the consequence of evil almost broke my heart. I pray to **Almighty God** that our love and prayers to **Him** will stop the indescribable evil I witnessed before it is too late. I was seeing the devastation caused by evil that Humanity continues to allow in a way I never knew could exist. **God** will protect **His** children and watch over us when we invite **Him** into our life. The Angel said, **"Tell them."** The Angel did not say I should not speak about the images. I try not to think about the scenes and seldom speak about them to anyone. Some**times**, when I am talking to someone about the Angel and the message, no words become available in my mind to describe the devastating scenes.

When I began writing, I have said I was very anxious because I did not want to waste precious **time**. In addition, compiling all the pertinent information for the book seemed to be taking me much longer than I anticipated. I realized to complete the book as the Angel requested this would take even longer because this book has to be perfect! I needed **time** to discern all the issues that the Angel revealed to me. While I continued to type, it was reassuring to know the Angel was always there encouraging me. This book will be finished when **God** desires it to be finished. Everything we do in life is determined in **God's time**, not ours. Writing about my glorious experience, the message and seeing the Angel, was only the beginning. I pray when the **time** is right to publish the book, I will know what **God** desires me to do next. I am prepared to accept that it is **God's** will and, therefore, I will persevere as long as it takes to accomplish everything because the Angel said, **"Tell them."**

However, as I continued typing, always the words seem to be there as easily as before. The words are available to me because the

Angel is by my side to make sure I do not forget any issues that the Angel deemed pertinent. However, the evil one is doing everything possible to stop me from writing this book. Oh yes, I have watched the computer screen perform unusual performances all meant to disturb me. I cannot always say evil did not succeed in their mission to annoy me. There were numerous **times**, while typing, I thought I would not be able to tolerate much more nonsense. It was awful what took place on a daily basis until I finished the book. Even though I recognized right away what was happening, the matter remained very precarious. However, my strong will that is a gift from **God** provided me with the strength to overcome the nonsense that was occurring. There is no doubt in my mind the evil one will do anything to stop this book and evil will do anything to stop Humanity from reaching out to **God** for **His** help. Moving forward with my ferocious will power intact, I could always draw on the strength **God** has given me to tolerate this condition until it would give up and leave me alone. I watched the computer do things I did not know the computer was capable of doing. There were **times** my husband and I would laugh at the antics that would play out over the computer screen. Other **times**, we would watch the font go from very large to tiny without me touching any keys. At **times**, whole paragraphs would disappear, and I would find them in another chapter. In addition, the worst challenge and the most difficult to overcome was when I was proofreading the chapters, I would find the stupidest sentences twisted all around that made no sense, and it continues even now, and I certainly did not type this nonsense. Today, as I continue, I can tell you this nonsense continues because I still find all kinds of outrageous mistakes that I have already corrected many, many **times** before. In the end, **God** will help me succeed because **He** desired **His** children to know the message that good will prevail over evil. I am anxious to share everything I experienced because it is **God's** divine will that the Angel appeared.

As I sit here typing, I can hardly believe how much **time** has passed since I witnessed the presence of the gorgeous Angel. All the issues the Angel prompts me to type are complex and take **time** for me to structure them properly. When I meditate about the issues while praying, I sense an assurance from **God** that there is a purpose for the delay in finishing the book known only to **Him**. Throughout my writing, the Angel provides me with the main content of the issues, but I must put the words together, and the words must contain clarity and conviction! The Angel in the hospital mentioned these issues, but she is still by my side to remind me if I forget anything. Some of the topics are extremely difficult for me to discuss because I must search my own conscience and it is not pleasant task. I am confident the completion of the book will happen in **God's time**, not in my **time**. **God** sent the Angel, **His** messenger, to remind Humanity that we must stop offending **His Sacred Heart** with our sinful behavior. This book is not about me and never will be about me as far as I am concerned. I do not want people to dwell on me because I am merely the instrument that **God** chose in order to accomplish a vital mission for **Him**. It is the Angel and the message that must be in the forefront in the mind of the person who wishes to contemplate this wondrous event.

How does **God** view religious communities today? Are some religious communities truly becoming too worldly? Religious life today in some communities, **time** spent contemplating the wonder and the Word of **God** is dwindling. Some religious communities have replaced this precious **time** with **God** with an agenda filled with other cares and concerns. In the past, the most important objective was **Almighty God**. The only objective was pleasing **God** and serving the needs of others. What was happening went unnoticed for decades, but slowly, an erosion of the pure contemplative life began to disappear in many religious communities, destroying their beautiful way of life. It is evident that Catholic religious nuns who live in a community and wear the habit are thriving in **God's** love. The habit the nuns choose to wear is a reflection of **God's** love, and it represents the giving of vows for a life**time** to **Almighty God**. I have heard it said many **times** that people find it difficult to distinguish between a nun and a layperson because nuns today dress like everyone else!

The Angel was very meticulous in her observation that many of **God's** people are moving farther and farther away from **Him**. Please pray to **God** that if this is **His** divine will, more men and women will seek vocations to the religious life. Catholics must pray to the Blessed

Mother that She will invite more men to the priesthood because Catholics believe that our heavenly Mother chooses Her sons to the Sacrament of Holy Orders. The beginning of the love for religious life begins in the home! If parents do not teach their children about **God** or if they do not teach them how important it is to have a friendship with **God**, how will this end? We need our clergy to instill in us the Word of **God** and to provide us with the opportunity of receive the Sacraments.

Please pray for vocations to the religious life.

Is it possible Humanity will have only a short **time** left to experience a deep love for their **Creator**? Even now as **time** passes, I am very reluctant to discuss some areas I witnessed with anyone. I may not be able to share everything ever. It is difficult to describe the evil that wants to destroy humankind! Is what I witnessed the true destiny of **God's** people if they refuse to obey **God** and **His** Commandments? What I witnessed is a front row seat into the decisions of world leaders and the severe effects of those decisions. It is imperative now to understand the consequences and how it will affect Humanity in the future! However, what the Angel presented to me resembles in many ways what is already happening in the world today right now. Only briefly, what I witnessed consisted of worldly affairs and the devastating cause and effects of decisions made by world leaders. **God's** people need to decide what could have a devastating effect on the future of the world. What I witnessed overall is what will happen in the future if society does not change their present course of action. What will happen to our beautiful world if we cannot change our indecisiveness? It is the decisions Humanity will make now for the future that will determine the outcome. What everyone should realize is all **God's** people share the same destiny. **God** has given all **His** people the power to alter our present course, but we have diverted from God's original plan, and it is not working out well for our nation or the world. Why are we hesitating when **God** so desires to help us? It is **time** for the faithful to stand up and take back what our **Creator** has given to all **His** people.

What I viewed is a vision of a world in chaos without the love of **God**. It is sad to face the truth that it is possible the world and the mountain of sins that continue against **Almighty God** will destroy our way of life. Yet where there is life, there is hope! There is the hope that **God** is waiting for us to ask him for **His** help. There are certainly a great deal people who are feeling helpless about events they see happening all around them. I have no power to stop evil's intentions alone. I have no power alone to stop what has already begun. We all need to work together in order to stop the level of Sin that is out of control now. We are all on a train speeding headlong into oblivion with no particular direction and with no conductor, and the destination is total destruction of our world!

Evil is on a rampage, and this evil is determined to win over the total destruction of our soul unless we all change our present path. However, before we are destroyed, evil is going to have its way with total enjoyment first. It is evident that great numbers of Humanity are refusing to face what is happening. Most of the evil is right in front of your face. You cannot say you do not realize what is going on. I knew before the Angel appeared to me we all live in a world full of hate, unrest, and unhappiness. I am not the only one who feels this way. People are becoming more and more frustrated with the present direction the world is heading, but like other people, we must continue to trust in and rely on **God's** love for us. Humanity must understand finally that the answers rest with **Almighty God**. **God** is our rod and our staff, and **He** will be our protection against all evil if we ask for **His** help. **God** will do the battle for us if **His** people would only ask for **His** help. In the Bible, **God** tells us **He** will prevail **(Revelation 17:14)**. The greatest question is, who will join **God** in eternal happiness?

Do we remember to ask God to come to our assistance?
Do we remember to say thank you when He does?

It is my belief that too many people just do not understand our problems in the world belong to everyone and, therefore, everyone should be involved in generating solutions. What is generally said is,

"Let someone else do it, or I'm too busy because really this does not affect me!" The problem is many people in our society are feeling overwhelmed; therefore, it seems easier to do nothing in the hope the situation will resolve itself. I realize people have grown weary of it all. I see this weariness as a warning that our society is ill and in real trouble. Certainly, there are people who do understand what needs to change, more people still sit back and wait for **God** to step in and stop the madness! Yes, **God** allows miracles to happen every day, but **God** needs us to believe miracles will happen but only when we deserve it. This is where the danger is greater from evil because society is becoming complacent. People do not realize that evil is causing their casual and indecisive attitude. People are allowing this to happen right before their eyes, and yet they continue to do nothing while **God** watches us and waits for **His** people to wake up. **God** is waiting to see if you will use your free will to make the choice to follow **Him** and invite **Him** into your life.

God loves us all so much that it is difficult to face how much we hurt **Him** with our actions. We continually offend **God** outrageously when we do such stupid and hurtful things, not only to one another but also to ourselves. Why is it so difficult for people to love one another? Why is it that the very love we once professed for someone ceases so abruptly? Love should be a natural emotion but seems to be more difficult to attain and keep today. There are people who seem to enjoy being miserable. People are miserable in the workplace, and they are miserable in their relationships. Even parents are miserable because they feel their children drive them crazy. Seems to me, now is **time** to stop being miserable and begin to do something that will allow you to be happy again. It is my belief that you cannot live in harmony and true happiness without **God** in his or her life. You must include **God** as part of your daily life. America and the people of this great nation will once again become a great people and a great nation only if we include our **Creator** in our decisions because our country is founded as one nation under **God**! Only with the protection and direction of **Almighty God** can we win the battle over evil. Without **God**, the world is doomed to failure. **God** is trying to get our attention because **He** loves us dearly.

I pray to **God** what took place in the recovery room with a message from an Angel will make a positive difference to everyone. Furthermore, I pray to **God** the appearance of the Angel will touch the hearts of everyone in a special way to all who believe in **God's** unfathomable mercy. With **Almighty God's** love, I pray this message will spread from one person to another until love replaces hate in the world. **God** surely knows who loves **Him**, and **He** expects those of us who do to continue to do our part by our example of goodness we show to others. The world is waiting for people who love **God** and who are like-minded in their Faith to stand up for what is right and true. **God** has waited long enough to see how many of **His** people are willing to take a stand and to put an end to, for example, **Abortion**.

I pray no one will ever see what I witnessed and how horrible the world will become without the love and mercy of **God**. The thought of those scenes I observed make me feel sick inside. It is a feeling of dread that I pray no one experiences! How do I live with the scenes I witnessed is the greatest challenge for me because what happens in the future I can do nothing alone to stop. If I did not have **Almighty God** near me, I would wither away from unhappiness. Unless **God's** people face the truth or if Humanity continues on its present course, nothing will change, and we will solve nothing! Humanity must face the truth that our only hope is with **Almighty God**!

> Dear **God**, I pray for all those who have forgotten **Your** promises that they will hear **Your** voice and believe in the truth of **Your** infinite mercy. I pray **Your** people will always be thankful for the enormous love that awaits all those who come to **You** with a contrite heart. It is **You**, my **God**, who is all deserving of all our love. Bestow on **Your** children **Your** grace that we may always see and hear the truth.

God is trying to get our attention. God knows we need **His** guidance.

CHAPTER 28

There Is No Future without the Protection of Almighty God

My generation believed wholeheartedly in the mercy of **God**! There are people today that are completely unaware of the plans evil masterfully placed within the fabric of our society. **God's** faithful people need to pray diligently that under the direction of **God,** we will be able to overcome this malicious evil. Otherwise, evil will continue its slow decay into our life while good people stand by and do nothing to improve anything. To think this is even possible for people who profess to be a Christian yet sit by and allow evil to take over their entire life. If you think this is not true, think again! I pray to **God** we will all recognize what is happening before it is too late. We must put an end to everything not pleasing to **God**. The Angel, even now, would stop me if what I was writing were not the truth! Certainly, your conscience will always allow you to know what would not be pleasing to **Almighty God**. If you would be ashamed to do anything in front of **God**, then obviously, you might be committing a Sin. If you feel you do not care what **God** thinks about you, then you are in great need of **God's** love and mercy. This can lead you down the path toward evil where evil is waiting to deceive you again. If you can, in good conscience, feel that you are happy with your accomplishments in the sight of **God**, only then are you safely in the mercy of **God**. Are you comfortable enough with your Faith that you can say truthfully you have invited **Jesus** into your heart? The wonderful thing about your conscience is your conscience cannot lie to you. You know when you have done something that does not make you feel happy with your decisions. If you do not recognize the strong feeling, that is a warning, you are in great need of **God's** forgiveness.

The scenes the Angel showed me seemed to go on and on but appeared as one concise event in a world that I did not recognize. The scenes were a pattern of places and events in the future that are destined to take place only if Humanity does not change our present course. No wonder **God** is so disappointed! There are people who are stumbling through their life without **Him**. I cannot emphasize enough now that **God** must be the center of your life and the head of your families! There will be terrible awakenings of horror in the world if the Human Race does not turn their hearts to **God**. The people of the world are opening new doors to evil every day. Right now, as I type, I feel a great deal of dread, but in my heart, I have to ask myself, why am I surprised? This should not be any big surprise to anyone that there is more hatred in the world every day. This ruthless hatred and misunderstanding between the cultures of the world must stop! This hatred is nothing more than evil stirring up dissolution between the cultures and races of the world. Hatred and violence is pure evil that is trying to permeate every part of **God's** world, and this hate is about to cause a major situation for all the people of the world if Humanity does not ask **Almighty God** for **His** help!

It should be obvious to everyone why the Angel appeared!

Why is it that young people today find it difficult to maintain a lasting relationship? A common saying today is, "Anything goes." Today, some parents do not protect their children from the destructive forces that plague our lifestyles. **God** is grieving for the safety of **His** young children. The greed and the high cost of striving for money and power are about to destroy everything we hold dear to us. Some say they love **God** but refuse to believe in even the most basic principles because they are convinced their life is just fine! What about the people who have stopped going to church because they are in desperate need of the Word of **God** found in the Gospels? Maybe some people if they faced the truth, the truth is they are unhappy inside because they know they are wrong, so they try to justify their lives. The one true aspect of our nature is we cannot lie to ourselves! Actually, if you think about it, this wonderful gift of our conscience is an automatic protection, and there are people today who no longer believe in the importance of their conscience.

Other individuals refuse to see the truth because they have lost their Faith to believe in their **Creator**. To realize anyone person or any one group would find it so significant or even their duty to remove any representation of **God** from our society is mind boggling to me. These people are on a misguided mission to remove everything that reinforces Faith in **God**, and I will never understand why these actions take place. Sure, freedom of speech is great, and I am all for it, but when it crosses the line and begins to dictate policy, what other people may believe is right, this is wrong! What direction is this taking our society? These performances use so much wasted energy. **God** is not the only one watching these foolhardy displays. **God** is not pleased with these performances. This sickness has spread so deep within our society that there are really people who believe openly praising **God** is not fashionable, especially praying openly, for example at a football game. To think today, people find it so distasteful to watch someone openly praying to **God**, this only proves to me that there are people in our society who have succeeded in unraveling the truth of their very existence. No doubt, where all this is coming from is simple to understand, but it is still very disconcerting to see people openly acting in such a shameful manner.

Why did this become an embarrassment for thousands of people to watch someone openly asking **God** to help him or her? What in the world are these people thinking? Have they really distanced themselves so far from **God**, they no longer care about anything pertaining to **God**? Are people in our society becoming only concerned with themselves sand what they think is correct? Are there people becoming so judgmental, they believe they have the power over others? I hope you realize what you may say and what you may do wrong is a direct offense to **God**. These people should be ashamed with their horrible attitude but not for the person who is praying but for themselves. Yes, they should be ashamed because they have allowed evil to convince them in believing in such nonsense in the first place. You see, we all place ourselves in harm's way when we conduct ourselves in such a despicable manner. I will never understand why people have allowed so much evil to come into their homes and their businesses. **God** knows it is very difficult for **His** people to dispel the desired habits they have become accustomed to. The world is surely in deep trouble and not only in the area of world affairs. People in general are losing the capability to care about others, and in turn, they are losing respect for themselves.

God's people must realize are souls are in extreme danger. Far too many souls are shaking in fear that the Soul will never again see the face of **God**! I repeat: everyone, with no exception, needs to ask **God** for **His** forgiveness now and for **His** protection before it is too late! We all need to ask **God** for **His** help and really stand up for what you believe. If Christians will stand together, we can reverse what evil has tried to destroy. How much evil is **God** going to tolerate is the big question? We are traveling headlong into a collision with evil at such a colossal proportion that you and I may not be able to stop this evil in **time**. The world is so filled with hatred, the world is about to turn its ugly head toward even the righteous. Dispelling evil from our lives is going to be very difficult even for the person who thinks he or she walks in the shadow of **God**. I am very worried, but I have an unwavering attitude toward evil because I have witnessed the truth. Now I pray you will feel the same way. I myself must be on guard more than ever before. I have seen the worst of evil; therefore, I am not so naive to think that evil, if given an opportunity, would do anything to destroy me! This is why I will continue to bring the issue of evil up repeatedly until there are no more words left. There is no one person in the world that may have the luxury of thinking he or she is ready to see the face of **God**. We become unready the minute we wake up in the morning and begin our day. **God** grants a new day so we may constantly have the opportunity to turn our back on Sin and love **God** instead.

I SEE AN ANGEL

Dear **God**, we love **You** and we need **You**. Grant **Your** children the grace to help others to believe and trust in **Your** love and mercy. Together, with **Almighty God** by our side, Humanity will succeed against the most challenging **times** ahead.

The memory of the afternoon in the hospital and seeing the Angel is so vivid in my mind. I cannot escape from the truth that **God's** children need to do better; this fact continues to be very troubling for me. Without **God** by our side and the Angel prompting me, we would be alone indeed. I cannot hide from the seriousness of the issues facing the Human Race. In my prayers and meditation with **Almighty God**, a sense of calm comes over me, even though somewhere in the world there is turmoil. The message is our affirmation that **God** desires the world to know **His** love is enduring, but we are offending **Him** greatly! I must face these issues head-on and come to terms with the ugly truth that Humanity is on the verge of moral collapse. No one has the luxury of hiding from the truth any longer. I never paid much attention to people who say they could predict the future. I never gave the idea of predictions much thought before I witnessed the Angel. I always silently relied on **God** for all those answers. Only **God** knows for sure what will happen to **His** beautiful world and **His** beloved people. **God's** people have the power to make the world a loving place. The **Holy Spirit** is patiently waiting for us to ask for **His** guidance. We know there were a few people centuries ago in our history that did seem to have insight into the future. What did these people really see? Who showed them the future, and why? What has Humanity learned along the way from these predictions? Now I wonder if it was an Angel who appeared to them with a message to warn them of some future event yet to come. Was it an Angel with a message from **God**?

I welcome each day with renewed confidence because I know **God** is watching over us. I truly believe that my mission now is to accomplish **God's** plan **He** designed for my life. I still wake up some days, like other people, with a heavy heart for this beautiful world we all share. I am worried, not so much for myself, but for those who will never really have trust and real Faith in **God**. There are

times when it is as if I can feel the sins of the world devouring everything in its path. I see this mound of Sin as thick mud pilling up so high that the souls of multitudes will fall within the quicksand. How many people will heed the message and hear **God's** voice in the words from the Angel? Christians believe we will soon all face the final test from **God**. Will Humanity be ready when **Christ** appears? The Bible teaches us what we should do. **"Therefore keep watch, because you do not know the day nor hour" (Matthew 25:13).** Keeping watch means that **God's** people must be prepared when **Christ** comes again!

When you and I least expect it, we will all be confronted with a malignant evil that, if given the opportunity, will spread and confuse even the most pious of us all. Countless people have already given evil authority over them due to their everyday lifestyles. This evil has been patiently waiting to crush everything in its path, and what we presently hold dear will vanish. Humanity needs to wake up and turn your eyes and hearts to **God**. You must see you need to give yourself up totally to the mercy of **God**. What is very difficult for most people to do is to humble themselves before **Almighty God** and ask for **His** forgiveness. It is evident with our churches closing that people now are too proud to ask. Are they afraid that **God** will say no? They are afraid they will have to give up their lifestyles in order for **God** to be pleased with them. **God** loves you so much that it would be impossible for **Him** to refuse your request. Who should ever pass up an opportunity to tell **God** you love **Him** by proving to **Him** that you intend to emend your life? **God** is waiting for **His** children to show **Him** we desperately need **Him** at the head of our families. We need desperately to ask **God** for **His** direction and guidance. **God** will never abandon **His** people. **God** is looking for Humanity to prove to **Him** that **His** children still love **Him**.

It is easy to deceive others and perhaps convince ourselves, but we can never fool God!

It is true, most people look forward to a brighter tomorrow because they are confident the sun will rise in the sky just as it did the day before. What if today would be your last day and there was no tomorrow? Your tomorrow brings forth with the dawning of a new glorious day, the opportunity to trust in **God's** love and mercy. Each tomorrow is a wonderful gift from **God**, a Grace-filled gift so many people take for granted. With the dawning of each new day, **God** bestows on us all a new opportunity for a new beginning. **God** is watching and waiting for our answer! There is no doubt because the signs are all around us that **God** is trying to get our attention. How much longer will **God** wait for us to wake up and face the truth? Please pray for **God's** protection. Pray to **God** right now and tell **Him** you love **Him**. When you arrive home today from work, tell your husband you love him. Today, when you see your children after they arrive home from school, tell your children you love them. Teach your children to love and know **God**. Help someone in need today. Attend church and bring **God** back into your entire life. Renew your Faith and trust in **Almighty God** now! You will be amazed how wonderful you will feel, and **God** will be so pleased. This is a beginning of your conversion when you can get beyond yourself and put someone else first in your life. I read a fabulous phrase a long **time** ago that if you spend **time** in the interpretation of this phrase, the meaning is clear. The phrase is, remember to look up at the stars and not down at your feet! Begin your day with **God**, and I promise you **God** will open the door to your happiness. I pray to **Almighty God** Humanity will win this evil battle. I am ready to do my best, but as I have said, I cannot do this alone. Together, we will transform our world, and we will have peace! Give up your pride, get on your knees, and pray to **Almighty God** for **His** direction and **His** mercy right now.

God is waiting for you to put **Him** first in your life.
God is trying to get our attention!

CHAPTER 29

Jesus Is the Light of the World!

Again, Jesus spoke to them saying, "I am the light of the world: he who follows Me will not walk in darkness, but will have the Light of life" (John 8:12). With the memory of what took place, I can still recall the gorgeous light that surrounded the Angel and filled the entire room. There is no doubt that the golden light I witnessed in the recovery room was the immense love and light that encompasses **Jesus Christ**. Yes, the powerful light touched everyone that was present in the room, and briefly, I was at peace. I decided to write here what my own personal Bible says on the subject of "Light." I could not think of a better way to express this then what the Bible already says beautifully concerning the Light. I was pleasantly surprised when I realized this directly speaks of much that I have discussed in the book. I know you will enjoy discerning the following:

Figuratively, Light symbolizes truth and holiness. St. John, throughout his Gospel and Epistles, uses this word to characterize **Christ** the supernatural Light of the World. "**He enlightens every man**" **(John 1:19).** "Those who love truth come to Him" (John 3:21). "Darkness, the symbol of the powers of evil, is dispelled by the Light" (John 12:26). Those who do not walk in Christ, the Light, stumble and fall, and lose their way" (John 11:10; 12:35). "Christ the Light; is received wholeheartedly by some, and rejected by others. To all who receive Him He gives new life, divine life" (John 1:13). "They became the sons of Light" (John 12:26, 46). "They have fellowship with God, who is Light" (1 John 1:7). "As children of Light, they have the obligation of walking in the divine truth, of avoiding sin, and of loving their fellowman" (1 John 2:2–11; Eph. 5:9; 1 Thess. 5:5).

I would also like to include here a brief synopsis on the holy names of **Jesus Christ**.

Jesus is the Latin form of a Greek word, which in turn comes from the Hebrew. It means **Savior** or "**Yahweh** is salvation." Our **Lord** received this name by **God's** express direction. "**And you shall call His name Jesus**" (Matthew 1:21; Luke 1:31) in order to indicate the mission for which **He** was sent into the world by **His Heavenly Father**: "**For He shall save His people from their sins**" (Matthew 1:21).

Christ is taken from the Greek and means "The **Anointed One**."

Our Lord is a name or title of **Jesus**. It indicated that **He** is truly **Master** of life and death, that **He** is our **God** and has divine claims and absolute dominion over the Human Race.

Savior is a title that designates the work **Christ** came to accomplish according to the words of **Matthew 1:21**. It is another form of the name **Jesus**.

Messiah or Messias is a Hebrew word also for "The **Anointed One**." For many years before **His** birth, **Christ's** coming had been foretold in the Old Testament prophecies. **He** was to be the anointed of the **Lord**, the great deliverer, the great **King**, **Teacher**, and **High Priest** in a far deeper sense than the kings, priests, and prophets or teachers of the Old Law.

Son of God is a name indicating that **Jesus** is truly the Second **Divine Persons** of the **Blessed Trinity**, as we profess in the Nicene Creed. "The only begotten **Son** of **God**, born of the **Father** of all ages: **God** of **God**, Light of Light, true **God** of true **God**; begotten, not made, consubstantial with the **Father**, by whom all things were made."

Son of Man is the title often used by **Christ Himself** in **His** own regard and indicates that **He** is truly **Man**!

Jesus, when talking to **His** Apostils, said to them, "**You are the Light of the world. A city on a hill; cannot be hidden! Neither do**

people, light a lamp and put it under a bowl. Instead, they put it on its stand, and it gives light to everyone in the house. In the same way, let your light shine before men, that they may see your good deeds and praise your Father in Heaven" (Matthew 5:13–16).**

You cannot make yourself the Light of the world! **Jesus** says, "**You are the Light of the world,**" because of your relationship with **Him**. **Jesus** also said, **"Out of the darkness the Light shall shine, is the same God who made His Light shine in the hearts, to bring us the knowledge of God's glory shining in the face of Christ"** (2 Corinthians 4:6). In addition, **Jesus** also said, **"His followers are in Him and He is in them!"** (John 14; 20).

In my heart and in my Soul, the Light I witnessed in the recovery room is the Light of **Jesus Christ** that does dwell within me, Praise **Jesus**! It is my belief that the Light of **Jesus** dwells in every person, who is faithful to **Him**. Our sweet **Jesus** suffered and died for all Humanity in order for us to have the opportunity to receive eternal life with **Him**. **Jesus** is love personified! Yes, **Christ** is the shining Light that will save all those who are faithful to **Him**. In the Bible, we read, **"Let your light shine before men, that they may see your good works and glorify your Father in Heaven"** (Matthew 5:16).

I am compelled to discuss the Light I witnessed in the recovery room repeatedly because the Light I experienced is the Light of **Christ** who is the **Redeemer** of the world! Now I can say with complete confidence that what other people have said they experienced, as in near-death experiences, is an extraordinary loving gift because *it is* the Light of **Christ**! People who have experienced this glorious heavenly Light always say that they could feel a peacefulness take over them unlike at any other **time.** In addition, other people say, they felt loved beyond anything else they have ever experienced before. The beautiful golden light that I witnessed surrounded the Angel and everything the light touched. There is no doubt that this *Light* was the *Light* of the love sent by our **Savior Jesus Christ**. This soft golden light filled the room with **God's** eternal love and touched everyone who was present in the recovery room. The Angel's face glowed bright like the sun from the intense golden light that encircled all around the Angel. Although, nothing impaired my view of the smallest details of the Angel's face. I thought, I am looking straight into the face of an Angel who has looked upon **Almighty God**. This single thought was overwhelming for my humanistic mind, and I still go weak at the very thought of this truth! It was evident, everything about the Angel commanded reverence because the Angel was sent by the **Holy Spirit**.

It is extremely important to me that I help everyone realize that you must protect your Faith no matter what is happening in your life; you must love **God** with all your might and put all your trust in **Him** who loves you dearly. **God**, in **His** wisdom and mercy, has a tremendous love for all **His** children, and **He** will never leave the faithful alone! **God's** love for us is so infinite; we will never fully appreciate the conception of **His** enormous love waiting for you and me. This is why we all have a responsibility to **God** to prove to **Him** that we will honor this love in return!

The Bible says, **"Surely goodness and mercy shall follow me all the days of my life, and I shall dwell in the house of the LORD forever" (Psalm 26)**. I sincerely pray that it is the ultimate goal for every Christian that when our **time** comes and our life here on earth ends, **God** will say, **"Well done, good and faithful servant" (Matthew 25:23)**.

I am totally committed in my mission that began with the message from an Angel. I rely on the wisdom of the **Holy Spirit** who is the Light within all who love **Him**. There is not a day that goes by I do not think about the Angel wrapped in the glorious golden light. It is truly wonderful that other people have witnessed a bright light and always they say that this light caused them to feel safe and loved. Perhaps their experiences took place under different circumstances, but regardless of the occasion, the appearances of the light these people describe does sound very similar in its origin to my experience. After intense thought regarding this heavenly golden light I witnessed, there is no doubt this light represents the love of **Almighty God**. **God's** love is so precious and pure that **He** has revealed this Light to people of all faiths because **He** desires them to know how much **He** loves them. Now is the **time** for all **God's** people to believe in the power of the Light of **Christ** because **He** is trying to get our attention. The knowledge of the Light and listening to other people firsthand tell me what they have witnessed will forever be an important aspect in our journey together to **Almighty God**.

> Dear **Lord**, receive the prayers of **Your** faithful. Shine the Light of **Your** love on all **Your** faithful that we may do only **Your** will. Dear **Lord**, my **God**, "Use me until there is no more, and I am dust for love of **Thee**."

God is trying to convey to us how much **He** loves all **His** children!

Take the **time** to chat with **Jesus** today in your own words and in your own way. Tell **Jesus** you intend to improve your life. Tell **Jesus** that You love **Him** and ask **Him** to help you. Most importantly, remember to tell **Jesus** that you are thankful for all **His** blessings that **He** has bestowed on you. Welcome **His** grace unto your heart because our loving and merciful **God** loves you exceedingly!

CHAPTER 30

I Will Endeavor to Describe to You the Glorious Angel in Detail

Naturally, it is not easy for me to describe the Angel to you in a manner where the words would truly encompass the magnificence I witnessed. I feel that in our vocabulary of words available, in order to describe this event with the Angel to you, the words simply do not exist! There are no accurate words to describe beauty only found in Heaven. How do I describe what is the indescribable? How do I describe what I thought would only be seen in heaven? However, I will do my best here to help you visualize in detail the Angel's glorious appearance to me. I will also do my best to convey to you again when I first realized the Angel was there. It is important to acknowledge often that the Angel appeared because **God** desired Humanity to know how precious we all are to **Him**. The major reason **God** chose this particular **time** for the Angel to appear is because **God** knows the world is in dire need of **His** love and mercy.

I will attempt to describe to you in detail what I observed when I looked at the Angel for the first **time**. When I first saw the Angel, I felt as if I was already on my way to Heaven. Uncontrolled emotions of joy rushed through my body and my mind. For a few seconds, I could not control my emotions. The enormous excitement I displayed when I first realized the Angel was there, I thought, surely others in the room could see the Angel. After my initial excitement, I could feel a great peace come over me as I continued to gaze at the astounding miracle of the Angel who stood only a few feet from my bed.

Upon waking up, I first noticed an awesome golden light that I have repeatedly mentioned previously, but no doubt, this is worth mentioning again. The first words I said were, **"I see an Angel."** I could not see those magnificent wings we always picture in our mind. It would have been obvious for me to see the Angel's wings, but the wings were not noticeable. I wondered afterward if this glorious light was what we would consider *wings*. There is a great possibility this could be the answer. Most people expect those gorgeous wings because they believe Angels must have wings in order to appear, and I agree the wings look marvelous. Since I was in the presence of the Angel, I have changed my opinion on this theory that Angels need wings in order to appear. While I have to admit the Angel wings we see in pictures are magnificent, I can say with confidence now the wings are not necessary for Angels to journey from one place to another. Angels abound within our space and in other dimensions that we cannot see because this is the Divine Will of **Almighty God**. Space technology is now revealing the possibility that the Universe might be endless. Therefore, Heaven must be endless too!

As I continued to gaze at the Angel's exquisite face, what I noticed first was the Angel appeared youthful and full of joy. The Angel's face appeared small and more round than oval. When I studied her gorgeous face, what came to my mind was her features resembled the texture of porcelain because the Angel's face was complete and utter perfection. The heavenly Angel's face I witnessed before me glowed as bright as the sun, yet the light that filtered through the room touched the Angel's face softly as if to embrace the Angel. Her most loving, compassionate, and sweet face combined with this magnificent golden light was breathtaking beyond what I could ever describe in mere words. The Angel's face was pure magnificence that is impossible for me to draw a distinction to express to anyone the glorious vision of beauty! It would be impossible to distinguish the entire event to anything! The Angel's overall features were exquisite where as nothing in this world could ever compare! Anything I could ever imagine I have ever seen before would surely pale in the thought of what I witnessed in the recovery room. The Angel continued to look at me with those gorgeous eyes that at first glance looked brown. Then I realized the Angel's mesmerizing eyes were a shade of brown unlike any brown color I myself as an artist could recognize. Yet looking deeper into the Angel's eyes, her eyes looked bluer unlike any blue I have ever seen, with a slight color of brown filtering through. The centers of her eyes were spectacular and really captured my attention. The Angel's eyes were like stars twinkling in the night. I remember wondering, what have those eyes witnessed? I realized those gorgeous eyes have looked upon the face of **Almighty God**, and now, praise **God**, those eyes are looking at me! The moment was very intense, and thoughts began to enter my mind while I continued to gaze at the beautiful Angel.

The Angel's head was leaning slightly to the left as if to say to me, "Surprise, here I am." The color of the Angel's hair was a very soft golden brown that flowed down gently to her shoulders. The Angel's hair shimmered from the glow of the golden light that softly touched her hair. The golden glow enveloped everything around the Angel and beyond. What I noticed immediately was that the Angel's sweetest features were very petite. I remembered thinking, as I looked at her, how tiny her rosy lips were and how perfect the rest of her features were in every way possible.

The Angel continued to express herself with a warm motherly smile to me that captured my attention and my heart instantly. Her tiny sweet lips would make the perfect red-rose blush in comparison. The Angel was not very tall. I would say approximately five feet two or perhaps slightly taller. It is very difficult to judge exactly how tall the Angel was from the distance of my bed. I mention again, I repeat, I did not see any wings visible because, believe me, I definitely looked intently for those wings. However, the area around the Angel and directly behind her seemed to be moving in a slight back-and-forth motion, but I still could not see any wings, but this does not mean they were not there. I need to consider again, was this slight dancing of light behind the Angel in correlation to the wings? The Angel stood perfectly still and never changed her position. The dazzling golden light did not seem to affect the Angel in any way. As bright as the golden light was, it never mirrored more attention than the Angel did.

The beautiful garment that adorned the Angel, for lack of a more deserving word, I will use the term *gown*. The term *gown* seems to be so unworthy of what the Angel was wearing. At first glance, against the golden light, the gown appeared to be gold, but again, the gown mirrored its own prominence. Within the soft golden color of the gown, I could see hues of violet and blue that were exquisite. I really have difficulty explaining how these three colors meet in total and glorious perfection. Again, this color appeared to look very, very soft and was not like any color that is familiar to me. I have never observed this particular golden-violet color before. The exquisit e material the Angel was wearing looked unusually heavy in its first appearance because it draped downward to cover the Angel completely. The magnificent gown looked as if it were made of very thick silk or satin. This gorgeous gown was extremely elaborate as I could see very fine details all over this magnificent garment. The embellishment resembled some kind of very small petite flowers. I must say, the tiny flower designs appeared to be white rose buds that looked real as if they were alive! Imagine real flowers happily adorning the Angel's gown! This gorgeous satin gown also flowed all the way up and rested under the Angel's chin. The same beautiful material covered the entire arm area down to the Angel's wrist. I could not help but notice how intricate the entire garment was, and with only her hands and face showing, the Angel was stunning! The vision of her loveliness would bring you to tears, and right this minute, that is exactly what is happening to me. I could see the Angel's exquisite slender hands intertwined at the waist in solemn prayer. Her adorable hands appeared to be in perpetual prayer that perhaps would never cease! This most spiritual gesture of the Angel's hands commanded a deep and personal meaning for me. The entire **time**, the Angel folded her hands in a formal pose. The Angel's hands never moved from this position ever!

I could not help but notice the way the Angel folded her hands in prayer because it reminded me how Catholics all used to hold their hands in prayer. This one specific expression of reverence made a huge impression on me because this reminded me how I held my hands for my first Holy Communion. It was during this extraordinary **time** in my life that I learned how important it is to fold my hands in prayer reverently. It makes me wonder now why many Catholics do not fold their hands this way anymore. Is it possible that along the way, for some reason, we decided this was too formal? Are we worried someone is watching? **God** is watching, and perhaps even the Angels are wondering why many people today no longer fold their hands reverently while in prayer. When I received my first Holy Communion, I learned that pointing my fingers properly in prayer toward Heaven displayed respect and reverence for **God**. Did the Angel intend for me to notice how she had her hands folded so I would once again follow her example? Was the Angel trying to teach me a lesson? This certainly made me think why I myself stopped holding my hands this way in prayer a few years ago. Did I just forget, or was I just lazy? This definitely seems to be a more respectful way to position our hands while praying to **Almighty God**. Some people would say this is such a little thing. **God** sees the importance of these little gestures we do for **Him**. Please believe you can never out do **God's** goodness because **He** loves us dearly!

The Angel allowed me to gaze at her for what seemed a long **time**. I felt the Angel wanted me to remember even the smallest detail so I could share the details with you. I wanted to make sure I would remember the tiniest of details no matter how small. Every detail of that afternoon in the recovery room is forever in my heart and in my mind, and nothing will ever remove the memory. Amazing how the Angel did not seem to be in any hurry. **Time** did stand still for me. It is my profound prayer for you, as you continue to read, you may share in the delight of what I witnessed. The appearance of the Angel was not only for me, but also it was for everyone who will listen to the message and listen to **God's** holy Word.

The Angel was not of this world, as we understand this term. I was in the presence of a messenger sent by the **Holy Spirit**. What is certain is the Angel appeared to me for a specific reason for all **God's** people. This magnificent event remains with me every second of the day. This experience does not come without great responsibility. I am also aware of this profound realization every day. I am further reminded constantly how much we all need divine intervention in our life. **God** will definitely walk among **His** people again. **God** will bring **His** Angels when **He** presents to the world what the world has forgotten. The world has forgotten the truth. In the Bible, **Jesus** answered, **"I am the way and the truth and the life. No one comes to the Father except through Me" (John 14:6). "Surely, goodness and mercy shall follow me all the days of my life and I shall dwell in the house of the LORD forever" (Psalm 23).** **God** also said, **"I have told you these things, so in me, you shall have peace" (John 16:33).**

God is trying to get the world's attention! The Angel appeared with a dire message for you and me because the world is facing chaos on an immense scale and we need to recognize the truth and ask **Almighty God** for **His** help and **His** loving mercy. The message conveys the truth; we all need to love one another. In addition, the message conveys the truth we all need to help one another because we are all a gift to one another. The message is an ominous call to action, but at the same **time**, the message does contain hope.

Humanity must face the ultimate truth that **God** will not tolerate the repulsive Sin against **His** precious children much longer! The action we take now or the lack of action will determine what will happen to the future of the world. The choices we make and the decisions we all decide now will determine the destiny of this beautiful world.

> Dear **God**, thank you for permitting **Your** Angel to appear to me so I can share with others **Your** infinite love.

> **God** is waiting for us to realize that we are only here for a short while. What is Humanity going to do collectivity to improve our world?

CHAPTER 31

I Miss Seeing the Angel, but I Sense Her Presence

I will forever remain humble before **God** that **He** allowed me to see **His** magnificent Angel. My thoughts remain filled with love for **Almighty God** because in my heart, I know I cannot accomplish anything fruitful without **God's** blessing. The book the Angel so lovingly compelled me to write is nearly completed. Writing this book is the most important endeavor of my life. I poured my heart and Soul into this book for the love of **God** and for all Humanity. The purpose for my life has come full circle, and I am content with this truth! There is so much more work to do for **Almighty God**. I do not feel **God** is through using me for the greater good of **His** glory. I will always remain **God's** tiny worker, ready and willing to do only **His** will to accomplish goodness for **Him**.

I am deeply concerned regarding the issues contained in the chapters of the book. We all need to get busy and ask ourselves, "What are we going to accomplish for **God**?" After the book is finished, there is plenty of **God's** work waiting for someone to take up the next challenge. In some aspects, something is already taking place in my life right this minute. This book began with the message from the Angel, **"Tell them it is almost time."** With the completion of the book, I have accomplished what **God** desired of me for now. I have accomplished to the best of my ability what the Angel asked me to convey to you. I have conveyed to you everything the Angel desired me to discuss. With every word I have written, the Angel's presence is constantly by my side. There is so much joy in my heart to know I received a visit from a dear sweet Angel. I pray with all my heart **God**'s Divine Will shall be done. I pray that when you read this book, the truth will touch his or her heart. I have the prayerful feeling there has been something already placed in motion with the contents of this book. I pray to **God His** children will remember love has the power to destroy all evil.

> Dear **Lord**, all the words contained within these pages I have written with so much love for **You. Your** Angel urged me to write about the awful anguish that we, **Your** people, have caused **You** from all the Sin committed in the world. I am sorrowfully sorry we have all caused **You** so much pain and disappointment. Please help the people of the world to dispel hatred from their hearts. Please save us from the evil that roams the earth, looking for the destruction of souls. Help us to love one another so we can have peace in the world. In this, I pray.

I must admit, writing about some areas in this book was devastating for me to write because I too needed to face the truth and then write the words repeatedly. I can only pray the words that the Angel prompted me to write will encourage more people to invoke the name of **Jesus Christ** all over the world. My **God** is the **God** of all the people of the world! Humanity cannot continue to wound the **Sacred Heart** of **Jesus** any further. We all need to ask for **His** forgiveness if we expect **Him** to come to our aid.

Now that the book is almost completed, I am again very concerned for our children because of all the craziness that continues to take place both here and abroad. I must persist in other ways to announce the message **God** has entrusted to me. It should be evident by now to everyone that we must all turn our attention to **God** right this minute!

I SEE AN ANGEL

God is trying to get our attention, and **He** is waiting for Humanity to respond to **Him**.

Please confide in **God** today because **He** loves you and **He** is deeply concerned about your happiness. Tell **God** in your own way how you love **Him**. Talk to **God** every day, and **God** will let you know **He** does hear your prayers, and **He** does care what happens in your life. The Angels are also trying to lead the way for us, but we must pay closer attention to them now. Everyone needs to find quality **time** during the day, even for a few minutes, in quiet contemplation of the nearness of **God** in your life. **God** is there with you even if you may not recognize this truth right now. Do not give up on **God** because **He** never gives up on you! Never stop believing in **God's** mercy because **He** loves you dearly.

If you desire, gradually, **God** will reveal **Himself** to you. The presence of **God** will begin with a subtle awareness, and you will sense something is changing within you. Your senses will become so acutely keen during this special **time**. If you would only pay closer attention to this truth, you would realize **God** is right beside you. **God** loves you so immensely, **He** will respond to you in a way only you will recognize. This will be in a very personal way only you will understand. **God's** love for you is personal because **God** knows your hopes and your dreams and everything about you. **God** is aware how you truly feel about everything in your life. Please, today, show **God** you trust in **His** mercy with your whole heart and your whole Soul. The world and everyone in this world needs **God** close especially now.

When I arrived home from the hospital, something began to happen, especially in the evening. I have become very aware of the presence of an Angel more at bed**time**. I seem to be able to know if the Angel is there or not. I do not know if this Angel is my Guardian Angel or the Messenger Angel who conveyed the message to me. I need only to silently begin to recite the **Lord's** Prayer and the Act of Contrition when I notice the golden light begins to appear softly. The Act of Contrition is a beautiful prayer; when recited, it conveys to **God** you are sorry for your sins. Even with my eyes closed, I can see a golden light that seems to have a slight pulse. Is this light I see now the same golden light I witnessed surrounding the Angel in the hospital? The only difference is the light I see now is very subtle. Seeing this light tells me the Angel is very close to me. What a blessing and a comfort to me to know the Angel is there beside me. What a comfort to my husband as he also has seen an unusual light near our bedroom once. I cannot see the Angel, but the light is a pure sign to me that she is definitely there. This light always appears on the left side of my bed. Was the Angel always there before but I neglected to be aware of the Angel? Do you believe that your Angel is next to you as well? The Angel knows I am aware of her presence. I am confident the Angel is there with me every night while I recite my prayers. I am content to recite my prayers and then peacefully go to sleep. I do not worry about tomorrow because I pray I have accomplished everything I could during this day and now this is the **time** for me to rest. I am acutely aware that I cannot continue to do **God's** work if I do not get my proper rest. I try not to allow anything else to interfere with my thoughts and prayers to **Almighty God**. I cannot tell **God** enough how much I love **Him**. You cannot outdo **God's** immense love for you. I love **God** so much that surely, someday, I will burst for love of **Him**. What I feel for **God** is waiting for everyone to discover, all you have to do is ask!

    I have a designated prayer room in my home. I would strongly encourage you to prepare a small place in your home where you can quietly pray without being disturbed. Some people turn a large closet or attic area into a prayer space. You should only use this designated area for the sole purpose of a prayer space. I prepared my own prayer space twenty years ago after completing an Hermitage experience. This special prayer room is a place where I can be quiet and peaceful. Here is a brief explanation of a hermitage experience.

    In the spirit of Franciscan hospitality, the resident hermits, who are Francium nuns and who prefer to live at **times** in silence, offer opportunities for people seeking a deeper prayer in solitude to enter Hermitage life. This **time** is usually for a weekend, but some people may choose to stay longer. I had no idea what I was missing until I met the Sisters of Saint Francis. I will forever be grateful for their friendship.

After I have gone to bed, during my prayers, the subtle light is a constant reminder to me I am not alone. **God's** children are never alone because it is **His** promise to **His** people **He** will never leave anyone alone! **God** will never leave anyone alone if you believe in **His** mercy. You distance yourself through your own fault when you deliberately Sin. Then **God** patiently waits for your return to **Him**, and all heaven rejoices!

Your Angels are constantly on guard and watching over you. The Angels are a constant part of your day and night. Angels proclaim the greatness of **God**, echoing the good news of salvation in the heavens and throughout the earth. I am fearful many people have forgotten this amazing truth. Why do some people feel it is childish to believe in Angels? You alone know if you believe this truth. I am comforted, though I cannot see my Guardian Angel or the Angel who appeared to me in the hospital now. Nevertheless, I pray **God's** children will have a renewed sense of peace knowing the Angels really do exist. The subtle golden light remains until I am finished with my prayers. My Guardian Angel is always with me during the day and near me while I sleep. Your Guardian Angel never leaves your side not even for a second. When the Angel needs to let you know she or he is there, you may sense their presence even stronger. I have thought about my dearest Guardian Angel often who has been with me from the day I was born. I thank **God** with all my heart that **He** has given me an Angel who is always with me guiding me to be ever closer to **Him**. I sense the presence of my Guardian Angel much more now than I ever did before with the growth of my Faith. I may never see the Angel who appeared to me in the hospital again in my life**time**, but what I witnessed will remain with me always. This event took place with the will of **Almighty God** for all **His** children.

Since my encounter with the Angel in the hospital, I have a great longing to be with the Angel. During my prayers when I see the light, this does remind me how I felt, looking at the Angel in all her magnificence. The light reminds me that **God** is our **Father** and **He** loves us all so much. This knowledge of **God's** immense love for all **His** people is growing stronger within me every day. I know I cannot live one second without **God** in my life. Perhaps my longing for the Angel is because my own **time** here on earth might be at an end soon. I do not worry about this aspect of dying. I hope you do not concern yourself with worry over dying either. If you do, then this is a sign that you need to adjust something in your life that is keeping you from the mercy of **God**. I sincerely pray, in some small measure, you can now be more aware of the truth in your life. There is so much for you to discover about yourself, in prayer, to **God**. A dark thought about dying is the evil one trying to disillusion you from believing in **God**. The truth is I am excited about the journey you and I must take someday. I sense a spirit of resolve with my life, and I continue to pray I have prepared myself properly to see the face of **Almighty God**. When **God** decides I have fulfilled the purpose of my life, I pray my Soul will be ready to be with **Almighty God** for all eternity. I pray diligently I will be able to help others strengthen their lasting closeness to **God**. The most important question you need to ask yourself is: what is it I need to accomplish in order to prepare myself to face **God**? **God** is trying to get your attention because **He** loves everyone so very, very much! You must believe always that the Human Race is the most important creation of **Almighty God**. Every individual on the face of this earth is immensely important to **God**. You must never allow anything or anyone to interfere with this all-important truth of **God's** love for you.

> Dear **God**, please come to the aid of **Your** people. Please, **Lord**, make haste to grant them your unfathomable mercy. I pray for all those people that do not know **God** or say that they do not want to know **Him** because to know **Him** is to Love **Him**!

> **God** is trying to get your attention because each person is tremendously special to **Him**!

CHAPTER 32

What Is Truth?

Jesus before Pilate

> Therefore, Pilate said to Him, "So You are a king?" Jesus answered, "You say correctly that I am a king. For this I have been born, and for this I have come into the world, to testify to the truth. Everyone who is of the truth hears My voice." Pilate said to Him, "What is *truth*?" And when he had said this, he went out again to the Jews and said to them, "I find no guilt in Him." (John 13:37–38)

Yes, what is truth in the world today? I have mentioned the word *truth* numerous **times** throughout this book. The word *truth* is one of the single most important words in the English language. Truth has always been a significant part of our society. I remember how important it was to tell the truth when I was a child. Are parents today teaching their children the importance of telling the truth? How many children know the difference between telling the truth and stretching the truth? How do you teach a child to always tell the truth when they listen to the adults in their life tell untruths every day? There are people who are convinced that speaking an untruth really does not incorporate an entire lie. It is also now a common belief that a lie is only "a little lie." Alternatively, another common belief is "partly truthful." We have been brainwashed by evil into believing these untruths. Today, people have accepted and justified much of these untruths in their life. It is only a matter of **time** before these untruths become even reasonable in their mind. Now all you need is to expand on the lie, change a few things, and now this creates a completely new set of untruths. Some**times**, the truth is difficult to figure out after it has undergone major changes because evil hides the truth among the untruth. The lie builds and builds until now it is difficult to understand where the beginning of the truth started. Evil twists and turns the truth on you so often that you really have to be on guard to be able to recognize the truth and determine what has happened.

A large number of people in our society now have become so complacent in important areas of their life; they are now convinced most everything in their life "is as good as it gets." Most people in today's world consider their highest priority is the fact they need to make more money. People in our society today find themselves in an extraordinary complex and confusing environment. We are all responsible for the multifaceted conditions that exist in the world today. Like it or not, the world has reached a pinnacle where as we must find solutions or risk additional unrest and hardships. Hatred and violence is center stage. **God** is waiting to see what Humanity is going to do to restore peace and happiness in the world!

Where does God fit into Humanity's future?

The truth is, our world as we now see it is in serious trouble! The truth is the world is becoming an ungodly place to live. The Angel was very clear; without **God** intertwined in our lives, the result will be a slow death of dissolution and hostility! The truth is there are people who no longer believe in the truth; we can improve our societies and live in peace. Who is giving us this false idea? The truth is Humanity is certainly capable of ending **Abortion** and other atrocities in this world. The truth is, we were all born with a **God** given right to be happy! At the same **time**, there are millions of very good and very smart people in our world, so why must it be a battle all the **time** in order to accomplish anything worthwhile? Too many individuals are acting as if Humanity has all the **time** in the world to make serious changes. The dilemma confronting all of us now is Humanity does not have all the **time** in the world! We are at a crossroads in not only our country but also the entire world. If we do not make the right decisions now, there will be no turning back without **God**. The awful truth is there are people who can no longer see the truth or hear the truth because the devil has blinded them. In the Bible, we read, **"In their case the god of this world has blinded the minds of the unbelievers, to keep them from seeing the light of the Gospel of the glory of Christ, who is the image of God!" (2 Corinthians 4:4)**.

The problem remains because the truth is difficult for us to cope with and, therefore, we continue to be in a conundrum of huge proportions. The worst part is there are people who actually believe if what they are saying even if it is not the truth. They have justified the truth because they refuse to believe only what suits them at the **time**. Therefore, we must go back to the beginning of what I said regarding truth and untruths. Dismantling the truth is very easy for evil because we follow its command all the **time** from our habits. Humanity tends to take the easy road, but we are fast running out of road!

Humanity is in a terrible struggle with evil, and when I say we need to pray, I mean people of all faiths. No matter what your affiliation or religion, you had better pray your heart out! If you did not realize the importance of prayer before, now you do! **God** is waiting to see just how far we are willing to gamble with our souls. When I pray, I become afraid when I think the possibility exists that **God** might not come to our assistance because we are not asking **Him** too. Do not forget everything you say and do involves your free will. You must trust in **God** with all your heart because I know there are millions of people who love **God** and have total Faith in **Him**. Then there are others who have pushed **God** to the limit! I am very concerned now that I have witnessed the Angel, I have to ask, how much more will

God endure? The Angel demonstrated extreme disapproval over our indifference to ending **Abortion**, which by now should be evident to you. The Angel was precise that if we do not stop **Abortion**, **God** would. Please pray for all the people who refuse to see the truth that **Abortion** is evil in all its most hideous forms. Everything involved with **Abortion** is an atrocity and an abomination that we force **God** to endure that society should no longer condone for ANY reason. I pray that while I am writing this book, Humanity may begin to wake up and see this truth.

Recently, I sense the tide might be turning against the barbaric practices of **Abortion**. The power of prayer is a beautiful truth. I feel if enough good people in the world would beg **God** for help, because **God** does hear our prayers, the practice of **Abortion** would end. **God** is listening to the prayers of all the faithful. However, are all these good people, myself included, doing enough? Where is the outcry to end **Abortion** by the good Christians in our country? Where is the outcry from our leaders? I cannot believe the silence! Is the silence a sign that evil has run amuck in the minds of good Christians as well as our leaders deeper than I original thought? I certainly pray this is not the case, but what is the reason for the silence? No matter how horrible the situation persists, too many voices still remain silent! The truth is shameful; **Abortion** is a big moneymaker, and the goal for big business is to make money. In addition, this big money continues to fill the pockets of people in immoral and unethical ways using **God's** precious children to do it. Prominent people donate money to keep these organizations going. It is inevitable; evil has convinced the minds of good people as well because they are silent! It is a circus of evil that goes round and round. What is wrong with this scenario? In the end, **God** will prevail. I pray all **God's** children will see the truth. Evil took over a great deal of our society, and like little children, society in general is supposed to believe the lies dished out to them every day because people have been conditioned over **time** to believe untruths. I am confident that soon, the majority of the people in our country will begin to demand change. I pray that there are millions of people who might be beginning to wake up to the truth because we can all agree, our serious state of affairs we are all confronted with is not going to be easy to change what has been allowed to take place over decades.

> **The Angel was clear and precise, and I am confident we can agree; without Almighty God, our life, as we know it, will become like scorched earth!**

I sincerely pray all who read this book would heed the warning contained in the message brought forth by the Angel through the power of the **Holy Spirit**. The Angel said, "**Tell them it is almost time.**" I truly believe, **God** has granted us perhaps one last chance to prove to **Him** we mean what we say when we pray to **Him**. **God** is waiting to see the truth in our actions. Humanity cannot keep telling **God** we care, then sit back and do nothing to change the injustices in the world.

I myself must take a stand and do something more than I have done in the past. I simply cannot wait any longer for someone else to do what the Christians in this country must continue to persevere and protect the truth. No matter how small my effort may be, I have to do something more. I am begging everyone to reach into the very depth of your heart and stand together with courage for the love you share for **Christ**. Everyone must take a firm position on some issue and allow your convictions heard. You already know what is right, and you already know the truth. Please, I am begging you to take a stand with me because together and with **Almighty God** by our side, we will stop **Abortion**, hatred, and all the violence that is presently plaguing the world. I pray that through our prayers and our efforts, together, we will stop **Abortion** and other sins against our precious children. These sins against our children have to stop not only in America but also in the entire world! If not, I promise you Humanity will all hear **God's** voice loudly in one form or another because **God** will not be silent forever and **He** will not allow these sins to continue against **His** children. Please help me get this accomplished. Together with a strong heart, love, and Faith in **God**, **He** will grant us the Grace and the strength to accomplish the destruction of this horrendous evil that wants to destroy all Humanity. In only **God**, we trust!

The following information from my personal Catholic Bible on *Truth*:

> Truth is correspondence with reality. The primary meaning of the Hebrew word *emeth*, translated "truth," is that of stability or firmness; but from this, it easily passes to something like our notion of the word. Thus, it frequently stands for constancy, fidelity, peace, and truth **(Genesis 24:27, 47:29; Book of Joshua 2:14; 2 Kings 2:6, 15:20, 4; Kings 20:19; Isa. 39:8; etc.). Christ, who is full of Grace and truth (John 1:14), in whom are all the treasures of wisdom and knowledge, says of Himself that He is the way, the truth, and the life (John 14:6). God is in Himself essential and sovereign truth, first truth and cause of all truths. For the sacred realities that Christians believe by faith, they have the authority of God, "who can neither deceive nor be deceived." Truth in word and action is veracity, the expression of our thoughts, as they really are and ourselves.**

I pray that with this understanding of the truth, you will now identify with what **God** is trying to tell **His** children, loud and clear! The marvelous truth is **God** is trying to get our attention because **He** loves all **His** children dearly. **Almighty God's** love is absolute and infinite, and **He** desires our happiness!

CHAPTER 33

Come, Holy Spirit, Enter My Life That I May Do Only Your Will Now and Always

It is incredible how the years of my life seem to disappear faster as I get older! **Time** is so precious to me since the appearance of the Angel. It is true everything we accomplish takes place in **God's time**, not ours. As I mentioned, I used to be very anxious over finishing the book because the Angel said, "**It is almost time**." Then thank you, **Jesus**, I felt a peaceful reassurance to remain steadfast in my mission and not concern myself with **time**.

I look for the Angel, wondering often if I glance in a certain direction the Angel might be there. I miss the Angel enormously because during those moments when I could see her physically, **God** was also closer within the golden light of **His** love. This extraordinary Angel appeared to me for a very significant and solemn purpose to announce to Humanity we are offending **God**! When the book is finished, no doubt, for the Angel, this mission will be complete too.

It is important to give thanks to **God** before you start your busy day. **God** and **His** Angels are there to help you through life's daily struggles. The **Holy Spirit** is there, waiting for you to seek **His** council. This truth should be a great comfort for you to personally be aware of just how much we all need **Almighty God** by our side. How wonderful it is to know the Angels are so near us because the Angels are so close to **God**. I pray now that you will realize or reconsider the profound truth that we all have a Guardian Angel to watch over us! I pray now you will now think about your own Guardian Angel and the important role this Angel will become in your life. You must embrace the love your Angel has for you. Treasure the **time** you have with your Guardian Angel, but remember, there is only one area in our life that should be of the upmost importance to everyone; this is your personal relationship with **God**! You should be focused on **Almighty God** and living out your life in a way that is pleasing to **Him**. This is the true recipe for a happy and contented life when you will finally realize you do not walk alone! It seems so simple that all you have to do is love **God**! If you would only realize that by doing this one loving gesture for your **Creator**, your entire life would become one complete blessing.

Now that I witnessed this glorious Angel, I can tell you undeniably, the **Holy Spirit** is waiting patiently for you to acknowledge **Him** because only when you invite **Jesus** to walk with you through your life is **He** able to inspire you to improve yourself in a way that is pleasing to **Him**. I pray with all my heart that you will find comfort in knowing that **God** is sending **His** holy Angels to help Humanity; this truth should bring about a renewed sense of their awareness in your own life. **God** has placed **His** Angels near to us in order to watch over us day and night. In the very beginning of your tiny life in your mother's womb, your Angel was with you. This truth is a most dear and loving gift from our Heavenly **Father** because **He** loves us dearly! There is no doubt now the Angels are here watching over us because **God** will never leave anyone alone who has Faith and trust in **His** mercy. The truth is this knowledge is a genuine promise from **Almighty God**. In the Bible, we read, **"Fear not, for I am with you. Be not dismayed, for I am your God. I will strengthen you, yes, I will help you, I will uphold you with My righteous right hand, and I will not leave you helpless nor forsake nor let you down or relax My hold on you! Assuredly not!"** (Hebrews 13:35; Isaiah 41:10).

The days go by so quickly, but before me always is the responsibility placed with me by **God** through **His** loving Angel. We know the word **time** means the length of action needed to accomplish anything. Humanity must, without further delay, accomplish a great deal, and **time** is ticking away. Certainly, unexpected and all-consuming problems seem to take **God's** people to the limits of their capacity. However, there is a strong belief, **God** never gives us more than we can handle. This is very difficult to accept for many people and often misunderstood. Nevertheless, we should be aware **God** is always there with us during our personal struggles. **God** has already granted **His** children the Grace needed in order to accomplish our tasks. Our strength is with **Almighty God** because **He** has bestowed on you **His** Grace and, therefore, **He** has provided you with the strength to get through the demands placed on you. No matter what is happening in your life, most issues do work out in the end because of your faith in **God**. Some**times**, the result is not always completely to your satisfaction, but knowing **God** is in charge, it seems easier for you to accept the truth that **God** knows what is best for all **His** children. It is important that **God's** children express their love to **God** often. Allow **God** to know how much you love **Him** and how much you need **Him**. Give thanks to **God** every day for the blessings **He** has bestowed on you throughout your entire life. **God** showers us with **His** blessing every minute of the day, but there are people who still refuse to be aware **He** is always working in our life. These blessings are too numerous to count, but here are only a few. The first one is the gift of your Faith that will lead you through the worst **times** in your life. The second one is the gift of trust because you believe **God** will never abandon you if you remain faithful to **Him**. The third one and the most important one is the knowledge that **God** loves you. Loves you, and I pray you will repeat this often, **"God loves me and He is with me always!"** Finally, the fourth one is the gift of the message from the Angel. The words conveyed in the message should be affirmation to Humanity that **God** loves **His** children beyond anything we could ever imagine. **God** sent **His** magnificent Angel to remind Humanity **God** loves all **His** people, *but* we must transform our life that it is pleasing to **God**. This next statement is the most significant point I need to place in the hearts of everyone I meet. Please, **"Just tell God you love Him."** **God** is waiting for you to tell

Him in your own special way you love **Him** and need **Him** in your life! There are people who still find it so difficult to share with **God** their deepest thoughts. **God** already knows what we all need and what we all deserve! All of **God's** people are equal in **God's** eyes. We are unique unto ourselves because **God** created us this way. In this special way, no one person could ever be the same in mind, body, and spirit. **God** shares **His** love for every single person equally. **God** made us so marvelous and uniquely individual, have you noticed? **God** does not love one person more than **He** loves another. **God** seeks the goodness found in each person. To **God**, *every* Soul is special! Most importantly, our Soul that once knew **God** on the day **He** created us, and out of respect for our Soul, we should strive to be better individuals. I have always believed that the Soul struggles with a great desire throughout our life to return to the presence of **God** once again. In the Bible, we read **God** said, "**Before I formed you in the womb I knew you**" (**Jeremiah 1**). This beautiful scripture is the circle of truth. The divine power of the **Holy Spirit** is already within us to acquire and preserve if we so desire. The **Holy Spirit** dwells within us and is the Light we cannot see that is as bright as the sun! This Light shines through us and is all around us and has the power to change the hearts of even the most stubborn individual.

This book began with a message from an Angel. The Angel said, "**Tell them it is almost time.**" I cannot explain this further, but there is no doubt, often, I receive strong promptings from the **Holy Spirit** to follow my heart when discussing any issue. Some**times**, the words stop coming to me for a while because I need to rest. Did I need to rest my mind from the dreadful evil Humanity must confront? Surely, this cannot be difficult for anyone to understand; it was not easy for me to mention repeatedly the countless dilemmas facing this world today. Can we agree we all know the problems of the world are not going away any**time** soon if we sit back and do nothing? It is evident **God** desires **His** children to improve their life in a way that will be pleasing to **Him**. For example, what are we all going to do to stop **Abortion**? Humanity has the power over evil, but millions of **God's** children are deceived into thinking it is an impossible task to dispel evil from our lives. It is true, we have all allowed evil in some form to intertwine itself with unfettered deception within the societies of the world and ridding it from our lives must be our decision. There are a great many people who do not want to face the truth that unfortunately, it is in our nature to Sin! Humanity needs to remember that evil is very real and represents a colossal danger to all Humanity. The devil is a fallen Angel who is cunning and smart and will do anything to claim your Soul! Yes, it is **time** to face the truth that what we are dealing with is a serious entity that harbors colossal hatred for all Humanity. You must start by saying the word NO to its deceitful lies. Great numbers of people feel they do recognize evil as a nuisance in their life, but for some unknown reason, evil's persistence continues benefited by millions. It seems that Humanity has always included evil as a part of their life, and therefore, even though it is an annoyance, evil remains tolerated by millions of people. **God** is waiting for Humanity to recognize the truth; we need to ask the **Holy Spirit** for **His** help because without **God** in your heart and in your life, this will not be resolved any **time** soon.

I really had no idea when I began writing this book, the complexity of the issues and through the intersession of the **Holy Spirit**, the Angel would continue to prompt me to persist in my writing. I was not prepared for all the issues that I discuss throughout the book, and certainly, I did not know it would become so intense. No matter what I write regarding a few of my personal life experiences, etc., the book is not and never will be about me! This book is devoted in truth to the praise and glory of **Almighty God**! This book only originated because the **Holy Spirit** sent and Angel with a message for all Humanity. Only six words, "**Tell them it is almost time**," and together, we will discern not only the seriousness of the message but also the hope contained within as well. I realized too all the Angels are faithfully committed to witnessing Humanity prevail over evil! Certainly, the Angel is confirmation that **God** is severely distressed over the truth that **His** children have forgotten how to love one another! The Angel indicated to me how much we have all offended **Almighty God**. This statement brings me to my knees to comprehend firsthand from the Angel that **God** loves **His** children this much, **He** would send an Angel to reveal a forewarning that

Humanity must turn their life over to **Him**! The Angel appeared to announce the truth many people have forgotten! It is the truth **God's** children need to hear in order to have a chance to discover or rediscover **God's** love in a deeper and more meaningful way. Over the years, it was difficult not to interject a few of my own thoughts, but always, I felt it was with the permission of the **Holy Spirit** because this book was entirely inspired by **Him** who loves us dearly!

I only accomplished this part of my mission with the help of the Angel through the intersession of the **Holy Spirit**. There is no question I could not have written this book alone. Therefore, who really was the author of this book? Certainly, the Angel deserves to be acknowledged here because it was the Angel that conveyed the message. Most importantly, it is imperative that I acknowledge the book began with a message of deep compassion from **Almighty God** for **His** people because **He** desires them to remember **His** infinite love and mercy that await all those who seek **His** forgiveness. It is also **time** for **God's** children to count their blessings and give thanks to **Almighty God**. Now is the **time** to convince **God** we are serious with our love for **Him** by being accountable for our actions and by taking responsibility to amend our lives.

God desires Humanity to remember that nothing is impossible for Him!

Often, in the middle of the night, I felt the Angel would wake me with a subtle nudge to begin typing again. Approximately three **times**, I thought the book was almost finished! Yet I knew I needed to continue faithfully what the Angel requested because of the profound importance of the message and the dire implications to follow. I learned that when I relaxed and did not worry about **time**, I advanced further into the book. Most importantly, the Angel was continually encouraging me to write and, yes, repeat issues in numerous areas. I realized right away that this needed to happen in accordance with the seriousness of the particular issues.

In **God's time** and with **His** help, **His** children will accomplish what **He** expects from us in order to find complete happiness. The

Angel directly supported and inspired me in every syllable I typed. All the issues and concerns were direct comments and/or serious concerns noted from the Angel when I was in the recovery room. Now when I pray deeply regarding this moment, it was **Almighty God** who sent the Angel to convey to us what Humanity needs to hear. I do believe, in my heart, all these issues discussed in this book define the truth that you and I repeatedly need to hear. The truth is that the world needs drastic change! **God** has given **His** people an opportunity to begin to take the necessary steps to improve **His** beautiful world that **He** created for all **His** children. When are we going to begin to take the necessary steps needed for this change? What could Humanity possibly be waiting for?

I am very saddened, I may not see the Angel again in my life**time**, but I understand and I want you to believe no one's life ends here on earth. Life truly begins when you reach **Almighty God** in Heaven. Heaven is the true beginning of your life eternal! The appearance of the Angel was all the confirmation I needed to see clearly what awaits the faithful. I sincerely pray that I have provided you with the knowledge of the Angel and the message, and I pray you will feel resolved in **God's** love for you. When I am in deep thought about the magnificent Angel, thinking of her always brings tears to my eyes because now I am witness to the truth.

I have thought so much about what I will do next for **God**. I have a great need to convey to all people **God's** immense love and mercy await all those who seek **His** mercy. I want to help others to strengthen their Faith to know the power of the golden light that I witnessed in my recovery room that it is **God's** immense love for all **His** children. I have a great desire to let everyone know how deeply **God** loves you. I can only do my best to provide all who read this book with the knowledge, and then the **Holy Spirit** will work miracles in your life. Repeat these words when you have a minute: "Come, **Holy Spirit**, and enter my life, that I may know **You** and love **You**, with my complete self." Recite this powerful prayer to the **Holy Spirit** often because the **Holy Spirit** will sustain you in your **time** of hardship and suffering.

Act of Consecration to the Holy Spirit

On my knees before the great multitude of heavenly witnesses, I offer myself, soul, and body to You, Eternal Spirit of God. I adore the brightness of Your purity the unerring keenness of Your justice and the might of Your love. You are the Strength and the Light of my Soul. In You I live and move and am. I desire never to grieve You by my unfaithfulness, and I pray with all my heart to be kept from the smallest Sin against You. Mercifully, guard my every thought and grant that I may always watch for Your light and listen to Your voice and follow Your gracious inspirations. I cling to you and give myself to You and ask You, by Your compassion, to watch over me in my weakness. Holding the pierced feet of Jesus and looking at His Five Wounds and trusting in His precious Blood, I implore You, Holy Spirit, Helper of my infirmity to keep me in Your Grace that I may never Sin against you. Give me Grace, O Holy Spirit, Spirit of the Father and the Son, to say to You always and everywhere, "Speak Lord for Your servant listens." Amen.

My Soul is the temple of the **Holy Spirit**. Graciously, hear me,
O **Holy Spirit**, enter my life and strengthen me in my weakness.
Place the light of **Your** love in my heart, my Soul, and my
mind that I may only do **Your** will all the days of my life.

I do believe my Guardian Angel will also let me know when my **time** in this world will no longer be significant for me. However, I am so grateful to **God, He** allowed me to be in the presence of an Angel during my life**time**. This visit with the Angel is a very deep resolve for me. I pray you will feel the same way now that you have the knowledge of the Angel and knowledge of the message. You must have Faith and trust in **God's** mercy. All our Angels will be with us to take you and me home to **God** when our **time** here on Earth is finished. **God** will never leave **His** children alone in the last minute of our life. At this moment, you will finally realize the full measure of **God's** love for you. At that moment, you will finally be at peace with your **Creator**.

I need to chat briefly again about death. Just the other day, a woman I know told me she was very afraid of death. This subject regarding death is a deep concern to a great many people. Death used to be a little uneasy subject for me also before the Angel appeared to me. I feel that this is only natural to be fearful of the unknown. I pray now I can assure you since I witnessed this heavenly Angel, you must never be concerned about your death. Death is nothing more than a transition into a spectacular spiritual realm where the faithful will be in the loving arms of their **Creator**. This truth is a promise from **God**: if you have lived your life faithfully, **His** children will be in absolute peace with **Almighty God** for all eternity. You must believe in this solemn truth from **Almighty God** and cherish this truth in your heart! In the Bible, we read where **Jesus** said, **"This is the bread that came down from Heaven. Unlike your fathers, who ate the manna and died, the one who eats this bread will live forever" (John 8:51). "Whoever lives by believing in Me will never die" (John 11:26)**. AMEN.

I am sincerely content to know firsthand and then to be able to tell you that Angels are so close to all of us. This wonderful thought should bring pause to everyone now. Our **time** is not the same as **God's time**. I pray you will believe what the Bible teaches you: **"But as for the day nor the hour no one knows" (Matthew 36)**. You must turn your hearts to **God** for **His** help without further delay and renew your trust in **God's** mercy. You must return to your church or your house of worship where you will once more be refreshed and renewed in the **Holy Spirit**.

The meaning of the words contained within the message the Angel brought forth should be clearer to you now. The Angel instructed me to convey to all of **God's** people; Humanity should prepare their Souls to see the face of **God**! There is nothing in the world that should be more important to anyone than his or her Soul. At some point, if we have been faithful, our souls will return to **God**. Humanity needs to prepare now for a spiritual journey we were all born to take. It will be a fantastic journey where **God's** children will finally see **God** and remain in **His** loving arms for all eternity. Our minds have no proper concept now what this journey will be like. If you search your heart, you will find the courage and the conviction you need to accomplish this journey to **God**. With peace in your heart and a pure Soul, you will return to **God**. The closeness and friendship you seek with **God** is already within the grasp of each person who desires this special closeness. Do not be afraid because **God** is very close to you already. **God** loves you very much. **God's** promise is **He** will be with you until the end of **time**! Do you believe this truth? If you do not believe this, you need to ask yourself, why not?

The Angel said to me, **"I bring you a message, tell them it is almost time."** With this book, I have accomplished, to the best of my ability, this part of my responsibility, here among the pages of this book. I must continue to spread the message to anyone who will listen to me. I am consoled, and I continue to pray with confidence that **God** is pleased with this book. I pray that all the people who will read this book that they will also receive the same consolation from **Almighty God**.

The Angels are here to remind us of the many things Humanity may have forgotten along the road through life. **Jesus Christ** taught **His** Apostles a very special prayer. I believe this is the ultimate guide for all people, no matter what your culture or religious affiliation. These beautiful words are not difficult to understand. Even a child would understand the meaning of the words. The message behind the precious prayer **Jesus** desired us to recite is clear! This prayer contains a great lesson for all **God's** people of the world. The following is a most precious prayer that takes only a minute to recite. This is a very powerful prayer, the precious words said by our sweet **Jesus**, with the intention for all cultures and all races. **Jesus** desired this loving prayer recited by everyone! If you profess the desire to have **God** in your heart, then how would be impossible to have hatred and misunderstanding in your heart at the same **time**. Recite this prayer as often as you can. This prayer will give you peace! You will never be truly happy in this life if you walk through life alone without **God** beside you.

I SEE AN ANGEL

The Lord's Prayer

Our **Father** who art in heaven
hallowed be thy name.
Thy kingdom come,
Thy will be done on earth as it is in heaven.
Give us this day our daily bread,
and forgive us our trespasses,
as we forgive those who trespass against us,
and lead us not into temptation,
but deliver us from evil.
For thine is the kingdom, and the power
and the glory, forever and ever.
Amen.

Summary

"I am the Alpha and the Omega,' says the Lord God, who is, who was, and who is to come, the Almighty."
—Revelation 1:8

This book began with a visit from a heavenly Angel who, by the power of the **Holy Spirit**, communicated **God's** infinite love for all **His** children. The Angel said to me, **"I bring you a message, tell them it is almost time."** It is evident by the appearance of the Angel that **God** desires **His** children's undivided attention! The Angel was exceedingly firm regarding **God's** disappointment with our sinful failures and grievous offences to **His Sacred Heart**. Therefore, I must honor the Angel who is the representative of the **Holy Spirit** and place before you the most important question Humanity has ever had to contemplate! What is Humanity going to do to prove to **God** that **His** children's intentions are morally honorable? **God** is conveying to us in so many other ways, we must be prepared! Throughout the Bible, scripture teaches us that we need to focus on the spiritual preparation for the coming of our **Lord, Jesus Christ**! Now that I witnessed **God's** magnificent heavenly Angel, I must beg you to consider the truth that **Almighty God** has already placed on your heart when you read this book.

The implication of the message is overwhelmingly significant and vital to the perpetuation of the future of the world! **God**, in **His** infinite mercy, is conveying to all Humanity through **His** heavenly Angel that due to the offense of Sin, we have seriously compromised our Soul, and consequently, our eternal salvation is in serious jeopardy. It is imperative now for all **God's** children to believe that our loving **Father** in Heaven, who loved us into existence, is waiting for us to seek **His** council in order to ensure our happiness, but **He** needs our cooperation in order to fulfill **His** divine plan **He** began for all of us in the beginning. In the Bible, we read, **"No one has ever seen God; if we love one another, God abides in us and His love is perfected in us"** (John 4:12). **God** does not desire **His** children to look back on our failures because *if* we have a contrite heart, **God** has already forgiven those failures. The message is clear that we must begin again our journey together toward our loving arms of our **Creator** with love in our hearts and absolute trust in the mercy of **Almighty God!**

With absolute confidence, we can derive from the message that **God** is also conveying to Humanity: we must remain steadfast in our Faith, Hope, Charity, and Love. The people of the world, especially now, must be diligent in their *faith* in **Almighty God** and trust in **His** *love* for the Human Race because **He** loves **His** children dearly! We must stop the hatred and violence that has permeated throughout the world and learn how to work together and love one another as **God** loves us. We must stop the insidious ridicule and judgment of others. **God** reaches out always to **His** children in *love*, but now we must learn how to reach out to others with this same *love*! Our dear **Lord** taught us that only those who are without Sin are worthy to throw the first stone! In the **Lord's** Prayer, we read, **"Forgive us our trespasses as we forgive those who trespass against us"** (Matthew 6:12). Humanity must never forget that our *hopes* and our dreams for the future of the world rest entirely with **Almighty God** who is constantly watching over us!

The Bible teaches us, "*Hope* is a theological virtue by, which we desire **God** as our highest good and by, which we expect with a firm confidence, that **He**, because of **His** infinite goodness and power, will bring Humanity to eternal happiness and in this life, give Humanity all the grace necessary to reach this happiness! This as a supernatural virtue, *hope* far surpasses the sensitive impulse or passion of *hope* (the natural sentiment of *hope*). It has **God** as its primary and essential object—**God** who **Himself** constitutes our eternal happiness. This supernatural *hope*, like *faith* and *charity*, cannot be acquired by man's own efforts. It is given to Humanity by **God**; along with sanctifying grace in Baptism. Therefore, the term *hope* implies a *love* and desire for **God**, for we do not *hope* for that, which we in no way desire! It also includes reliance on, and expectation of the all-powerful grace of **God**, without whom we can do nothing; and so by the motive, of our *hope* is not found in ourselves, in other words, (our own goodness, or power, or deservingness)." Still this virtue does imply that we make earnest efforts to corporate with **God's** grace, namely, with all the means **He** gives us to reach Heaven!

What about charity? Do you have charity in your heart? Are you ready to help someone less fortunate that yourself? The Bible teaches us also, "*Charity* is the virtue, which inclines us to *love* **God** above all things for **His** own sake, our neighbor for the *love* of **Almighty God**! What is clear is *charity*, or *love* is the most excellent of the three theological virtues." To have *charity* is to *love* **God** above all things and to be ready to renounce all created things rather than offend **Him** by serious Sin! The most famous biblical passage on *charity* is as follows: "If I speak in tongues of men and Angels, but do not have *love*, I am only a resounding gong or clanging cymbal. If I have the gift of prophecy and can fathom all mysteries and all knowledge, and if I have *faith*, that can move mountains, but do not have *love*, I am nothing! If I give all I possess to the poor and give over my body to hardship, that I may boast, but do not have *love*, I gain nothing. Love is patient and *love* is kind. It does not envy, and it does not boast, and it is not proud. Love does not dishonor others. Love is not self-seeking, and it is not easily angered; it keeps no record of wrongs. Love does not delight in evil, but rejoices with the truth! It always protects, always trusts, and always hopes and always preserves" **(1 Corinthians 13:1–7)**.

Humanity has been given the stewardship of this beautiful planet we call Earth from **Almighty God. God**, who so loved the world and all **He** created, created man and women in **His** image and bestowed on Humanity the grace needed to love one another in order to procure our happiness! **God** is waiting for Humanity to seek **His** forgiveness and **His** everlasting and loving friendship. **God** is giving us an opportunity to redeem ourselves. I pray that we will finally respect the truth that only with **God's** love will we begin to heal our inclined selfishness, our foolish prejudices, and our interior and exterior divisions that we have allowed between cultures and races of the people of the world! The truth is humanity cannot count on anyone individual because it is only **Almighty God** and **His** promises to US that we can count on! The destiny of our future is also waiting for our decision. Until Humanity can truthfully say with your whole heart and in your mind and in your heart that **God** dwells in your house, Humanity will never have peace or happiness, and the world will continue in turmoil, and to what end? I pray that all who truly loves **Almighty God** will take this journey of transformation. **God** has bestowed on us a great sign of **His** infinite love. I pray that the world will embrace **God's** call to action that began with a message from a heavenly Angel.

Only recently, I had a dream that I should include here regarding a rare phenomenon we call a Rainbow. This gorgeous phenomenon appears in the sky opposite the sun when refraction and reflection of the sun's rays forms in drops of rain or mist that form a circular arc of bands of light. When this magnificent display of **God's** infinite love takes place, it exhibits the colors of the spectrum. The Israelites recognized this phenomenon as a wonderful work of the **Creator**! This glorious manifestation almost seems to appear as to unite Heaven and Earth in an enormous bridge, and it symbolizes the peace between **God** and man after the great flood **(Genesis 9:12–13)**. In the Bible, we also read where Ezekiel also considered the Rainbow a symbol of grace and peace **(Ezekiel 1:28)**. How will you feel the next **time** you see a Rainbow? Give thanks to your **Creator** for all **His** blessings because it is our love and our happiness that **God** desires!

I will end the book here, but it is up to Humanity how this book will really end! We must unite in love under the direction of **Almighty God** if we are to have lasting peace in the world.

Almighty God is waiting!

The Greatest Commandment

"Matthew asked, 'teacher, which is the greatest commandment of the law?' **Jesus** replied, '**Love the Lord your God with all your heart and with all your Soul and all your mind**'" **(Matthew 22:36–40)**. This is the first and greatest commandment, and the second is, **"Love your neighbor as yourself."**

Jesus gave us the greatest commandment of all. Everyone must love **God** primarily because this love encompasses all your mind, your Soul, and your heart. This means your devotion toward **God** must be first **(Matthew 6:33)**. This love involves all we think about in our mind. It also is all we think about of our Soul, which encompasses everything we do. In addition, this includes all your heart, which is what we desire the most to accomplish. **Jesus** also teaches us in the Bible to, "**Love our neighbors as ourselves**" **(Mark 12:31)**. Loving others means you should take care of them as you take care of your own mind, body, and Soul.

Jesus's new commandment:

Jesus said, "**A new commandment I give you. Love one another, as I have loved you, so you must love one another. By this everyone will know you are my Disciples, if you love one another**" **(John 13:34–35)**.

Trust in the mercy of **Almighty God** because **He** will forgive us when we can show **Him** we can live in peace and love with our neighbors. Now is the **time** to wake up with renewed conviction for the truth in order to change the face of the world with love and respect for one another. Only then will Humanity ever hope to have peace in the world.

Millions of people believe **God** so loved the earth and every creature within this world that when **He** created the world, **He** was very pleased! **God's** children must fill their hearts with joy and happiness again. The people of the world all need to put aside their differences, live in peace, and love one another for the benefit of all the people of the earth. Ask **Almighty God** to help you discover the true meaning of your life. Please, I am begging you, everyone must put aside all the intolerance and misunderstanding that evil is pervading in the societies of the world. I refuse to believe the people of the world cannot do better to have more patience and understanding with one another because **God** created us all in **His** image equally. **God's** children are born with a **God**-given right to live in a peaceful world. Please, Humanity needs to prove to **God** we do love **Him** by finally achieving lasting peace in the world under the direction of our **Creator**!

All praise and honor is yours, Almighty Father, forever and ever.

It is **time** for me to end the book here. **God** has placed on my heart that now is the **time** to release this book! It is my intention to use this opportunity to give honor and praise to **Almighty God**, and I pray that this book will touch your heart and give you peace in the knowledge that **God** is always with you until the end of **time**! What happens in the future is for Humanity to decide now how the book will really end. Will the people of the world attain peace together with the help of **Almighty God**? Will we decide to use our free will to blow the world to bits? Alternatively, will the people of the world decide to reach out to **God** and really mean it? Finally, will Humanity wait until the last minute to ask **God** to save us? **God** will never turn **His** back on us, but we must ask **Him** for **His** forgiveness. **God** is trying to get our attention, and still **His** people are not listening. I pray this book will open the hearts and minds of **God's** people everywhere in order to see and hear the truth. **God** has bestowed **His** grace to all Humanity. Now it is up to all of us to prove to **Almighty God** how we will use this precious gift in **His** honor. I am begging everyone who profess to love **God**, to get down on your knees, and to ask **God** to forgive us all. What would happen if the people of this beautiful country all knelt in prayer and thanksgiving to **Almighty God** all at the same **time**, for example on National Prayer day? Seems to me we could utilize this day of national prayer in May to give praise and honor to **God**! Perhaps our church leaders could designate a particular day at another **time**. **We must accomplish this together**

and soon! What would **Almighty God** do if the entire world knelt down to honor **Him** on a certain day and begged **Him** for forgiveness? I refuse to believe **God** would never resist such a marvelous gesture of love from **His** people. Right this minute, you need to tell **God** you love **Him** above all else. Approximately eighty percent of people in America believe in **God**. If this figure is true, where are the voices of Christianity in this country? When are we going to put an end to all the hatred and violence taking place over religious freedoms and horrific atrocities that continue to happen all over the world. We must stand together for what is truly right and just. Only then will it ever be possible to restore peace and happiness in the world. There is no doubt **God** is trying to get our attention! I pray to **Almighty God** Humanity is listening to **His** loving voice. Please, I pray the people of America, the beautiful land of the free, will show the rest of the world their gracious example of love and compassion for all people and all cultures of the world under the direction of **Almighty God**.

Peace begins with you and me first! America must lead the way if we are to have lasting peace in the world!

Noteworthy Observations

I also wanted to share with you something else I observed while writing this book. It was amazing to me one day, while I was proofreading the various chapters and watching the pages scroll down, something extraordinary caught my eye. The word **God** or any word expressing thereof the names referencing **God's** holy name seemed to jump off the page. There are twenty-nine loving and expressionistic terms used throughout this book to express the holy name of **God** the **Father, God** the **Son,** and the **Holy Spirit**. The holy names were so prominent among the thousands of words contained in this book. It was amazing to me how easy it was to spot the word **God** in the middle of thousand of words. Therefore, in my book, I decided to exercise my personal option to have any word that directly describes the names that reference **God** outlined in bold letters. I felt it would be interesting to see the total amount of **times** I used the word **God** or any references to **Almighty God** in my book. After all, without the love and will of **Almighty God**, this book would not exist in the first place.

I was astonished when I tallied the amount of **times** I referenced **God's** holy name. I was amazed and pleased when I realized the large numbers of **times** these words and others appeared in the book. I pray and do believe **God** is also pleased. With all my heart, these bold letters give honor and praise to the glory to our heavenly **Father** and **Creator**. In addition, I also decided to count the number of **times** I used the word **time** because this word **time** is one of the six words in the message the Angel conveyed to me. Finally, I took a count of how many **times** I used the word ***Abortion***. All three of these words, especially references to **God**, strongly placed an important role in the content of the book.

> This tiny gesture of the descriptions of **God's** holy names in bold print gives honor and praise to **Almighty God** who has bestowed on me so many blessings my entire life. All praise and all glory is yours, **Almighty Father**, forever and ever!

> The words of **God's** holy name was mentioned in this book 12,365 **times**.
> The word **Abortion** I mentioned in this book 147 **times**.
> The word **time** I mentioned in this book 715 **times**.
> Total words are 140,749.

In addition, while reading my Bible, I realized something wonderful that over the years I overlooked. I happen to be looking through the index located in the back of the Bible, and there among the pages were detailed explanations available for analysis, which is found in any index, for the reader for a particular area of interest. I was chatting with a dear friend last night, and I was telling her of my observation that in the past I never spent much **time** looking through the index. My friend agreed that certainly from now on, we were going to look through the index starting from the beginning. Here is just one example of what I read and, as a Catholic, did not realize was possible before!

The following is what I am pleased to share with you. **Indulgence for reading the Bible**: "The special indulgence granted by Pope Leo X11 and increased by Pope Pius X11 for reading the Sacred Scriptures. To the faithful who shall read for at least a quarter of an hour the books of the Sacred Scripture; with the veneration due to the Word of **God**, and in the manner of spiritual reading, an indulgence of three years is given."

Footnote

When I began writing this book, I noticed some strange things starting to take place that affected the computer and changing computers did not change what was happening! At first, I ignored the subtle annoyances as usual computer glitches. I was typing in chapter 8 when the computer seemed to take on a mind of its own. Small problems started to happen, such as the font moving from the tiniest of letters to the largest of letters without me doing anything to change them. I tried to overlook the font changes, but from that moment, something was set in motion that would be a real evil nuisance all throughout the book. The font changes that took place on a daily basis were only the beginning. While typing, the paragraphs would change their margin sizes. Then I would have an awful **time** resetting those paragraphs to line up again with the rest of the page. The computer would shut off without any notice. I learned quickly to save my work after typing only a few sentences. This, of course, took more **time**, but it became necessary in order for me not to lose my work. Beginning a new day, I would notice a paragraph I typed the night before missing, only to find either whole or parts of the paragraph in another chapter! I learned to print chapters at the end of each day. I saved my work on many other computers and thumb drives only to have two of the thumb drives not open. The most unnerving alteration that both my husband and I witnessed once was when the entire page turned upside down and then sideways. This is when I truly realized what I was dealing with was an all-out battle with the devil because it was obvious, (it) did not want this book written and certainly (it) did not want the book printed! Looking back on all this now, all the frustration with these "Glitches" was the most difficult challenge I have ever experienced in my life. How I overcame such adversity is a true testament of my Faith in **Almighty God**. In the end, I always knew, with the Angel by my side and my unwavering love and trust for the **Lord**, I would complete what the **Holy Spirit** desired me to accomplish for **Him**. In the end, **God** always triumphs!

Here Are a Few Suggestions for Further Research

Below are a few suggestions you may want to further research either from the Internet or from the source of your personal Bible. All these suggestions correspond to the related topics in my book. What does the Bible say regarding "**Abortion**?" In addition, there is so much information available in numerous books and on the Internet. However, as always in any research, it is better to have the correct information in order to discern anything properly.

In addition, a more complete explanation for the meaning of the term "Indulgences" you can research easily. You can discover the entire history of Indulgences. I think you will find researching this as well as the other suggestions I have listed below, which are very interesting too.

- I found forty-nine biblical verses concerning the word "**time**."
- I found forty-five biblical verses regarding "love one another."
- Grace is mentioned in the Bible 170 **times**.
- Plenary Indulgences, what does this term mean?
- Angels
- How many types of Grace are there?
- The Sacraments of the Catholic Church
- Lives of the saints can be a very prayerful part of your daily life. Pick any Saint and learn about the life of this particular Saint.

- Read the Bible from cover to cover and discover or rediscover what you have been missing!

There are quality sources of information that can easily be located on Christian sites on the Internet. However, I always recommend strongly that your best source of information is your Bible. Begin reading the Bible. If you have in the past already read the Bible, open the Bible to any page and begin again. You will be surprised reading the Bible will change your life. There is always something new you can discover or rediscover when reading any book more than once. Personally, I enjoy reading the Bible and particularly love to read the book of Psalms. However, I would strongly recommend opening the Bible anywhere and begin reading. The **Holy Spirit** will do the rest!

What Does the Bible Say about Abortion?

This is a brief explanation of the term **Abortion** taken from my own personal Catholic Bible. This explanation cannot stray from the truth.

> **Abortion** is, "The international expulsion of a fetus from the womb if that fetus is unable to live outside the mother's body. If the expulsion is accidental and unintended, this is usually called a miscarriage. The international expulsion of a fetus that cannot live outside the uterus, no matter what the reason may be, is a serious Sin of murder since the fetus is a human being. All who have a part in procuring an **Abortion** are automatically excommunicated from the Church."
>
> Update: In 2016, Pope Francis has extended indefinitely the power of Catholic priests to forgive that said, the Catholic Church's stance on **Abortion** has not changed! However, the church now makes it easier for women who have had an **Abortion** to be absolved from this grievous Sin if they are remorseful!

While the Bible does not specifically mention the word **Abortion**, it mentions a number of things about unborn children. These biblical statements indicate that the unborn are persons; therefore, "**Abortion** is wrong since it is killing a human being."

The following are simple to understand:

1. It is wrong to murder a person.
2. The unborn is a person.

In any intelligent mind, it is morally wrong to murder the unborn child. This is a most grievous Sin against **Almighty God**. While most Christians believe in their faith that **Almighty God** is a forgiving and merciful **God**, we must acknowledge the Sin and then ask **God** for forgiveness!

Notes

About the Author

Rose Mary Luke resides in East Syracuse, New York, with her husband John. They celebrated their Golden Jubilee in 2015. Together, they have three children, five grandchildren, and four great-grandchildren. Rose Mary is an associate with the Sisters of Saint Francis and is a member of Saint Matthews Catholic Church. She also is a member of the League of National American Pen Women. She attended Onondaga Community College. In addition to Rose Mary's many accomplishments are real estate broker and restaurant owner, and most notably, she is an international liturgical artist and restorer of religious statuary for the past thirty-five years. Her exemplarly skills are recognized in churches and private homes throughout the United States. Her handpainted artwork now resides in the Central Pacific Islands of Samoa and Apia. Rose Mary was instrumental in the coordination and the shipping of numerous crates of church goods to these islands.

Rose Mary personally witnessed a magnificent Angel who appeared to her in the hospital on October 7, 2011. The Angel revealed to Rose Mary a profound message. The Angel requested Rose Mary to convey this message to everyone. The Angel said, **"I bring you a message. Tell them it is almost time."** The Angel inspired Rose Mary, through the intersession of the **Holy Spirit**, to write this book.

Rose Mary is a woman of great faith and strives to promote the truth that Humanity must love one another as **God** has loved us!

CPSIA information can be obtained
at www.ICGtesting.com
Printed in the USA
FSHW010430270619
59421FS